Blog Design Solutions

Andy Budd, Simon Collison,
Chris J. Davis, Michael Heilemann,
John Oxton, David Powers, Richard Rutter, Phil Sherry

DESIGNER TO DESIGNER™

an Apress® company

TS5337
006.7

Blog Design Solutions

ISBN-13 (pbk): 978-1-59059-581-7
ISBN-10 (pbk): 1-59059-581-5

Printed and bound in the United States of America 9 8 7 6 5 4 3 2

Distributed to the book trade worldwide by Springer-Verlag New York, Inc., 233 Spring Street, 6th Floor,
New York, NY 10013. Phone 1-800-SPRINGER, fax 201-348-4505, e-mail orders-ny@springer-sbm.com,
or visit www.springeronline.com.

For information on translations, please contact Apress directly at 2560 Ninth Street, Suite 219, Berkeley, CA 94710.
Phone 510-549-5930, fax 510-549-5939, e-mail info@apress.com, or visit www.apress.com.

The source code for this book is freely available to readers at www.friendsofed.com in the Downloads section.

Credits

Lead Editor	**Copy Editor**
Chris Mills	Nancy Sixsmith
Technical Reviewer	**Assistant Production Director**
Jake Smith	Kari Brooks-Copony
Editorial Board	**Production Editor**
Steve Anglin	Ellie Fountain
Dan Appleman	
Ewan Buckingham	**Compositor and Artist**
Gary Cornell	Diana Van Winkle
Jason Gilmore	
Jonathan Hassell	**Proofreader**
James Huddleston	Nancy Riddiough
Chris Mills	
Matthew Moodie	**Indexer**
Dominic Shakeshaft	Julie Grady
Jim Sumser	
Matt Wade	**Interior and Cover Designer**
	Kurt Krames
Project Manager	
Kylie Johnston	**Manufacturing Director**
	Tom Debolski
Copy Edit Manager	
Nicole LeClerc	

To my wife Heather and my son Jakob,
my reasons for being
—Chris J. Davis

To the Missus and my children, for whom this
chapter will mean absolutely nothing
—John Oxton

I would like to thank Wendy for bearing with me
and doing more than her fair share of washing up
—Richard Rutter

For my brother, Simon Sherry
October 24, 1965–April 6, 2005
—Phil Sherry

CONTENTS AT A GLANCE

CONTENTS

CONTENTS

ABOUT THE AUTHORS

 **Andy Budd** is a user experience designer and web standards developer living and working in Brighton, England. As the creative director of web design consultancy Clearleft (www.clearleft.com), Andy enjoys building attractive, accessible, and standards-compliant websites. His online home can be found at www.andybudd.com, in which he writes about modern web design practices.

Andy is a regular speaker at international design conferences, workshops, and training events, as well as organizing the UK's first web 2.0 conference (www.dconstruct.org). Passionate about the quality of education in the industry, Andy runs SkillSwap (www.skillswap.org), a free community training and networking project. Andy also helped set up the Web Standards Awards (www.webstandardsawards.com), a project that aims to recognize websites for their use of web standards.

When he's not building websites, Andy is a keen travel photographer. Never happier than when he's diving some remote tropical atoll, Andy is also a qualified PADI dive instructor and retired shark wrangler.

 **Simon Collison** is Lead Web Developer at Agenzia (www.agenzia. co.uk), and has worked on numerous web projects for record labels, high-profile recording artists, and leading visual artists and illustrators, including The Libertines, Black Convoy, and Project Facade. Simon also oversees a production line of business, community, and voluntary sector websites, and passionately ensures that everything he builds is accessible, usable, and complies with current web standards. Simon regularly reviews CSS-based websites for Stylegala and does his best to keep his highly popular blog (www.collylogic.com) updated with noise about web standards, music, film, travels, and more web standards.

On those rare occasions away from the computer, Simon can be found in the pub or trying to con free gig tickets out of his clients. A little too obsessed with music, he is very likely to bore you with his latest musical Top 100 or give you a potted history of the UK indie/ alternative scene from 1979 to the present day.

Simon used to be a successful visual artist, with a number of solo exhibitions to his name. In 1999 he founded You Are Here Visual Arts, an artist-support organization that spawned two city-wide festivals. He resigned from You Are Here in 2004 to concentrate on web design, taking his artistic inspiration instead from music, film, and design. Simon has lived in many cities, including London and Reykjavik, but now lives happily in Nottingham with Emma and a cat called Ziggy.

Chris J. Davis has been a blogging enthusiast and software developer since 1999, with most of his time spent hacking on b2 and later its successor, WordPress. He is also an international speaker on Technology and Social Software, traveling to places as far-flung as Stuttgart, Germany or as close as San Diego.

You can read more about Chris and check for his upcoming speaking dates by surfing to www.chrisjdavis.org.

Michael Heilemann is a bipedal omnivore, living on a small speck of land just next to the word "Denmark" in your atlas. Once a mighty Norse power, filled with bloodthirsty Vikings who would go pillage and whatnot in other countries, Denmark's position as a country is now being doubted by many. This has come about mainly due to its lack of a nuclear arsenal and Starbucks, obviously the benchmarks of any respectable country. Though none of this pertains as such to the person of Michael Heilemann, it is a good deal more interesting than his actual bio.

John Oxton has been developing websites since 1999. He quite literally stumbled upon CSS and all that standards stuff while looking for a way to make hyperlinks pink on rollover and he hasn't slept a great deal since.

When John isn't building sites for clients or posting to his own site, http://johnoxton.co.uk, he can generally be found leaving inane comments on other people's blogs, claiming to be too busy to talk right now or watching *Futurama* with his son for the 100th time.

David Powers is a professional writer who has been involved in electronic media for more than 30 years, first with BBC radio and television, and more recently with the Internet. He's written or coauthored five books on PHP, including the highly successful *Foundation PHP 5 for Flash* (friends of ED, ISBN 1-59059-466-5) and *Foundation PHP for Dreamweaver 8* (friends of ED, ISBN 1-59059-569-6). David's other main area of expertise is Japan. He was a BBC correspondent in Tokyo during the late 1980s and early 1990s, and later was Editor at BBC Japanese TV. He has also translated several plays from Japanese to English.

Richard Rutter lives and works in Brighton, UK. He is Production Director for the web consultancy Clearleft (www.clearleft.com). Richard has been designing and developing websites for nigh on ten years. Early in 2003, he built his first blogging engine, which still powers his weblog Clagnut (www.clagnut.com), in which he harps on about accessibility, web standards, and mountain biking.

Phil Sherry has previously worked on several friends of ED books as author and technical reviewer, as well as being an official beta tester for Adobe and Apple.

He currently lives in Stockholm and likes his Bombay Sapphire served with tonic, ice, and a slice of lime, preferably in India. Check out www.freakindesign.com.

ABOUT THE TECHNICAL REVIEWER

Jake Smith's first homepage was made on a Mac with Photoshop 2.5 and SimpleText in about 1994. Since then he's been full circle through GoLive and Dreamweaver back around to hand coding CSS and XHTML.

Jake is currently creative director with JP74, a UK-based digital agency. His everyday knowledge of online development ensures that the reviews are grounded in the real world and accessible to as many people as possible. Jake also lectures on the BA (Hons) Multimedia course at the local college, so can see firsthand how people come to grips with evolving web technologies.

Besides spending late nights reviewing and working on personal projects, Jake now stays up watching kung-fu movies with his newborn son, Eloy.

ACKNOWLEDGMENTS

I would like to thank Rick Ellis, Paul Burdick, and Chris Curtis from the Expression Engine team for allowing EE to be covered in this book, and for all their hard work building and updating the system itself. Thanks also to those that tech edited this chapter for me and helped me iron out the creases. A life debt is owed to Chris Mills for helping me understand the whole publishing process and for being such an ally. Largest thanks are reserved for the Agenzia boys and their tolerance of all my personal projects, and last but not least the incredibly supportive Emma.

—Simon Collison

Thank you: my family; Paul Baines, Laura Ward-Swietlinska, Caroline Wänström, and Rickard Persson for always being able to say the right things at the worst times; Melissa Auf der Maur, just for rocking; all the people who bought my last book; Jake Smith, I said; my fellow designers for believing in my idea to write this book; Chris Mills and everyone at Apress, without whom I'd be nothing.

I love yiz all!

—Phil Sherry

INTRODUCTION

Greetings and welcome to *Blog Design Solutions*. Given that you're thumbing through this book, it's probably fair to guess that either you want to set up a blog of your very own, or you already have one and want to make it stand out and look a bit, well, less boring.

Let's face it: Unless you code your own blog from scratch (which, incidentally, is exactly what Chapter 7 of this book shows you how to do), you will have used a third-party blog engine of some kind to whip up your blog site. This has major advantages in that you don't have to be a web-development expert to get a blog running, and it is a huge timesaver, but this is a double-edged sword: thousands of other people will have done exactly the same thing as you, so your blog will be far from individual in appearance, even if your postings have Oscar Wilde proportions of literary excellence.

But there's a man who can help you. Eight men, in fact. And they wrote this book with one overriding goal in mind: to help you produce a blog that will stand out above the rest and attract more visitors to it, giving your hard-wrought prose the exposure it deserves. It doesn't matter what level of technical know-how you have achieved; you'll find something in here to improve your blog—whether it's setting one up in the first place and giving it a bit of added sparkle, or taking your current blog and giving it an overhaul with some advanced CSS and template magic.

So how do we do it?

We start off our teachings slowly. In Chapter 1, Phil Sherry gives you a introduction to blogs and how they fit into today's web community—how things work, what's hot, and what's not. In Chapter 2, we start to get a bit more technical, but don't panic! A little thought now will save a lot of frustration later. Here, David Powers takes you gently through setting up your local machine to develop and test your blog and your remote server to host your final creation. Whether you are using Windows or Mac, you're in good hands.

Chapters 3 to 6 explore four of today's most popular blogging engines: Andy Budd looks at Movable Type in Chapter 3; Simon Collison looks at ExpressionEngine in Chapter 4; Chris J. Davis and Michael Heilemann look at WordPress in Chapter 5; and John Oxton looks at Textpattern in Chapter 6. In each chapter, the authors take you through installing the default blog on your system, and how to configure and customize it in a basic fashion. Then they run riot, showing you how to turn the default design into a mind-blowing custom blog by using a variety of CSS, Photoshop, templating, and other techniques!

But the ride isn't over yet. As a special bonus, we commissioned Rich Rutter to write a chapter (Chapter 7) on building your own blog from scratch, using PHP and MySQL, for the ultimate level of customization.

What do you need?

As hinted earlier, this book is written to be fully compatible with both Windows PCs and Macs. Because all the blog engines discussed are built with PHP/Perl and MySQL (open-source software, which runs on basically any platform), you should also be able to get most of the examples to run on Linux/Unix-based systems if so inclined (although we don't specifically cover these systems).

Everything you need to use this book can be downloaded from the Web; the locations of all software you need to set up your development environment are listed in Chapter 2, and the locations of the blog engines themselves are detailed in Chapters 3–6 in the relevant places. Finally, all the source files for the custom sites developed by the authors throughout the course of Chapters 3–7 are available from the friends of ED website, www.friendsofed.com. Just search for the book using the books option on the main navigation menu, and all will become clear.

Layout conventions

To keep this book as clear and easy to follow as possible, the following text conventions are used throughout.

Important words or concepts are normally highlighted on the first appearance in **bold type**.

Code is presented in fixed-width font.

New or changed code is normally presented in **bold fixed-width font**.

Pseudo-code and variable input are written in *italic fixed-width font*.

Menu commands are written in the form Menu ➤ Submenu ➤ Submenu.

Where I want to draw your attention to something, I've highlighted it like this:

> *Ahem, don't say I didn't warn you.*

Sometimes code won't fit on a single line in a book. Where this happens, I use an arrow like this: ➡.

```
This is a very, very long section of code that should be written all ➡
on the same line without a break.
```

1 THE "WEB LOG"

by Phil Sherry

What this chapter covers:

- Background on blogging
- Blogging options
- Technologies involved
- Really Simple Syndication (RSS)

The "web log"

Computers. They pretty much dictate our daily lives by now. The book you're holding was written on one. The plans of the store you bought it in were most likely drafted on one. The very subject of this book means that you're probably a computer junkie, and you're looking for a way to make your next fix more interesting. You're reading this book because you feel the need to enhance your life on the Internet. You probably spend over half of your day online . . . and you love it.

The Internet is slowly taking over your life, whether you like it or not. These days, it even dictates how people speak. Need an example? I hear people actually say "LOL!" (Internet-speak for "laugh out loud!") when someone says something funny to them. A more applicable example is when my dad recently asked me if I knew what a "blog" was after he'd heard the word mentioned a few times at work. Rather than fumble around for an explanation, I directed him straight to the good old online dictionary (via an instant message, of course). Here's what the dictionary has to say on the matter:

Main Entry: weblog

Function: noun

Definition: a personal Web site that provides updated headlines and news articles of other sites that are of interest to the user; also may include journal entries, commentaries and recommendations compiled by the user; also written web log, Weblog; also called blog

Usage: computing

Source: `http://dictionary.reference.com/search?q=blog`

Mac OS X Tiger's Dictionary application has a slightly different take on things, though, as you can see in Figure 1-1. Now, as a 30-something Englishman who lives in Sweden, I have to find fault with that description. Maybe I'll bring it up during my next visit to Apple head-quarters, in Cupertino, California.

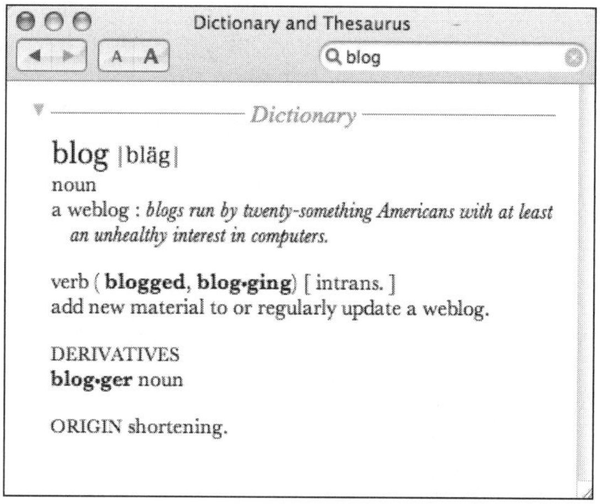

Figure 1-1. Mac OS X Tiger's Dictionary definition of "blog"

Blogging

Previously the realm of angst-ridden teens spilling their guts about how nobody under-stands them (back in my day, it was just "That is SO unfair! I HATE you! **SLAM**" and stomp up the stairs to the bedroom to sulk), the blog has quickly become big business. Everyone is doing it, from Joe Public in the high street, to politicians, to Microsoft in Redmond.

Blogging, ladies and gentlemen, isn't just for the kids any more.

For some people, it's a release. They might keep a daily diary of how they're coping with cancer, so they don't have to constantly tell friends and family the same news over and over, but also so they can say the things that they find too hard to discuss face to face with people.

Others blog because they're isolated from the world—whether physically or mentally. Maybe they live in the middle of war-torn Iraq, like Salam Pax, the "Baghdad Blogger" (dear_raed.blogspot.com). Writing their thoughts as a web page helps these people feel like part of something and gives them hope. The Internet, after all, is just a big network.

Some use the blog purely as a publicity tool. **"I AM ON THE INTERNET!"** is the cry you can hear from around the globe. This blogging can be anything from a school kid making his first trip onto the big ol' Information Superhighway to a politician trying to take over the world (John Kerry's blog at www.johnkerry.com was actually in the top five search results for "blog" on Google when I wrote this). Even high-profile rock stars are blogging these days. The UK band *Doves* uses Moveable Type (doves.musicblog.co.uk) to get their point across, while foxy Canadian rock chick Melissa Auf der Maur favors Blogger (lightningismygirl.blogspot.com) to update people on what's happening in her world. (See Figure 1-2.)

Figure 1-2. Rock stars, rockin' the blog (Pictures ©2005 Paul Baines and Laura Ward-Swietlinska)

Most of the blogs I read, however, are by web designers and self-confessed geeks. People such as Andy Budd (www.andybudd.com), Simon Collison (www.collylogic.com), Chris J. Davis (www.chrisjdavis.org), Michael Heilemann (www.binarybonsai.com), John Oxton (www.joshuaink.com), Richard Rutter (www.clagnut.com), and David Powers (http://foundationphp.com/blog) are all daily reads for me. You can learn more from reading their sites daily than you can by reading the average book. That's why this is no average book—I assembled them to write the ultimate guide to aid you, the user, in your quest for standing out with your blog.

Okay, class. Let's have a bit of a look at this thing called blog.

2004: Year of the blog

Blogging kicked off big style in 2004. It was around for quite a few years before that, but not really mainstream. The word "blog" certainly couldn't be found in the pages of a dictionary, and was only really used in conversations online, by those who were "in the know." These days, you hear it everywhere.

Blogging options were fairly limited back then, but as they became more flexible it became easier to blog on your own terms. Didn't like the way LiveJournal looked? Change the look of it. Didn't like LiveJournal? Learn some basics about File Transfer Protocol (FTP) and install your own scripts—easily downloaded for free from any number of web resources (such as cgi.resourceindex.com or php.resourceindex.com).

Up until the last few years, Perl was widely regarded as "the duct tape that holds the Internet together" and was the principal language in the majority of early blogging scripts. These days, PHP is taking over as the scripting language of choice, which makes things more accessible to the beginner because the learning curve is nowhere near as steep.

At the time of writing, there are more options for the blogger than ever, and those options will only increase and get easier with time. So, let's have a look at some of those options now.

Blogging options

Whether you have any knowledge of scripting languages isn't even a factor because there is now a wide range of blogging solutions to choose from; whether it be paying for a ready-made blog site, such as www.typepad.com; using a free ready-made system, such as Blogger (www.blogger.com) or LiveJournal (www.livejournal.com); downloading some free scripts, such as Movable Type, Textpattern, or WordPress; right down to getting your hands dirty and coding your own by using a book such as this one.

Blogging has become easier to do, so more people have started doing it. And, as with pretty much any Internet trend, word spreads quickly. But what's the appeal of doing all the hard work yourself if you can get a ready-made package?

The book you're holding is—hopefully—about to unlock some secrets for you. Whether you know nothing about blogging at all or you just want to change the look of your existing blog installation, *Blog Design Solutions* is your invaluable guide to deciding which blogging option is right for you and how to get the most out of your blog.

Ready made

Some people simply have no desire to sit and play around with coding languages or databases. Like, dude, that's for geeks, isn't it? The average person in the street—let's call him "my dad" for now—just wants to be able to arrive at a site, fill in a few details, and then start typing. None of that "upload this file to the cgi-bin in ascii, these to htdocs in binary, and then chmod these files to 666" stuff. That's just plain Greek to those people.

Maybe you don't even have any server space to host your blog on. In either case, you need a ready-made solution. TypePad (www.typepad.com) is owned by Six Apart (www.sixapart.com), which is currently one of the biggest names in the blogging industry (see Figure 1-3). Six Apart is also responsible for Movable Type and LiveJournal (which it acquired in 2005).

Blogger (www.blogger.com) offers a whole host of templates for its blogging service. These templates were designed by such Internet gurus as Jeffery Zeldman (www.zeldman.com), Douglas Bowman (www.stopdesign.com), Dan Cederholm (www.simplebits.com), and Dave Shea (www.mezzoblue.com), among others. The service is extremely easy to get up and running, and looking good.

Figure 1-3. TypePad, which is part of the Six Apart group

Install your own

Maybe you have a load of web space to use or you want a bit more control than the ready-made scripts offer. In this case, you have some seriously powerful scripts at your disposal, and (mostly) all are free. For awhile, Movable Type (www.sixapart.com/movabletype) was the first port of call for many people venturing into the world of self-installed blogging scripts. This was written in Perl, though, which is notoriously awkward for the layperson to learn, meaning that it was tough to tweak the code for your own gains. Add some licensing changes (as detailed in Chapter 3), and you end up with a lot of people jumping ship to WordPress.

WordPress (www.wordpress.org) is written in PHP and uses MySQL to store data. More and more people are using the combination of PHP and MySQL, which are both open source and free. This makes for a far more appealing setup. Other choices using this tag team are Textpattern (www.textpattern.com), and Expression Engine (www.pmachine.com/ee); both of which are covered in this book. Expression Engine is the only one that could have you exchanging any money if you decide to use it after the 14-day trial version, but I'll leave the reasons why you might want to do that to Simon Collison in Chapter 4.

This book will take you through the installation of four of these blogging solutions, and show you how to make them look good. Briefly, here's how we'll tackle this:

- Chapter 3: Movable Type, with Andy Budd
- Chapter 4: Expression Engine, with Simon Collison
- Chapter 5: WordPress, with Michael Heilemann and Chris J Davis
- Chapter 6: Textpattern, with John Oxton

Code your own

What with all the free options available, why the hell would you want to code your own blog? Well, some people just prefer to code their own stuff. I've done it before, and it's certainly satisfying to see the end result after all that hard work. It also allows you to add only the features you want and, therefore, none of the ones you don't.

Should you fancy a bit of DIY action, you should like what Richard Rutter has in store for you in the final chapter. For those who want to take things a bit further after that, I heartily recommend the following as further reading:

- *Beginning PHP and MySQL 5: From Novice to Professional, Second Edition*, by W. J. Gilmore (Apress, 2006)
- *The Definitive Guide to MySQL 5, Third Edition*, by Michael Kofler (Apress, 2005)
- *Beginning MySQL Database Design and Optimization: From Novice to Professional*, by Chad Russell and Jon Stephens (Apress, 2004)

I've mentioned a few technologies up to now, so let's take a closer look.

Technologies

To create a blogging system, you need three essential items: a web server application to serve the pages, a scripting language to code the pages with, and a database to store all your information. They are all easily available, whether you're running Mac OS X, Linux, or Windows.

No longer is learning Perl necessary to get powerful results, which certainly causes fewer headaches in my house. And with point-and-click installers—on both Mac OS X and Windows—just about anyone can now set up a home computer as a test web server (see Chapter 2!). This gives you a lot more freedom to install whatever you need on the server, and it doesn't matter as much as if you break the database while you're learning, because you can just reinstall MySQL.

The continual development of Apache (httpd.apache.org), the world's most popular web server (news.netcraft.com/archives/web_server_survey.html), and the rapid development of languages such as PHP (PHP: Hypertext Preprocessor—www.php.net), combined with a free open-source database such as MySQL (www.mysql.com), means that it is far easier for the average web developer to come to grips with this new school of coding.

The Apache Server (named "a patchy server" after being cobbled together from the remnants of another server application by a few nerds—www.apache.org) comes as standard with Mac OS X, and is as easy to turn on and off as clicking a button in System Preferences, as you can see in Figure 1-4. Windows comes with its own web server, in the form of Internet Information Services (IIS), but for the sake of sanity and security, a lot of people prefer to use Apache on Windows.

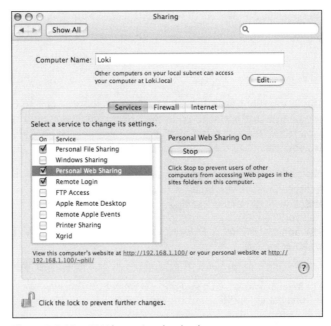

Figure 1-4. Mac OS X keeps Apache simple.

If you're handy with HTML, learning some quick-and-easy PHP won't give you many gray hairs. You can pretty much code your page in HTML and then insert PHP tags where you want the action to happen. Of course, it gets much more involved than that when you have a serious application to write, but that's about the size of it for the beginner.

When it comes to storing your data, MySQL, which is "the world's most popular open-source database," is free and also easy to install. People are often put off by the phrase "relational database" because it just sounds a bit scary if you're new to this whole technology shebang. There's really nothing to it, though, and there's a whole host of graphical user interface (GUI) tools to administer your database these days, so you don't have to use a geeky command-line application such as Mac OS X's Terminal.app (unless you prefer to do so). In any case, never fear, as installing all the technologies you'll need for this book is covered in considerable detail by David Powers in Chapter 2, who not only makes it look easy, but also teaches you that it actually is.

How does it work?

The blog process is fairly easy to understand. A user will call up the blog page in the browser. The page is made up of some code that has placeholders for the data. The code calls in the actual blog data from the database and spits it back out into the placeholders on the page.

Adding to a blog is similarly easy. A blogger posts an entry in his or her blog online by filling in a subject line and a body of text (pretty much like when writing an e-mail). This entry is typically anything from "I just fed my cat, Ekko. Ekko rocks!" to a 1000+ word rant about how Microsoft is the very devil itself. There's no set format, topic, or word count to reach (unlike writing a book, for instance). Depending on the user, there is usually a comments function, which is where anyone can give comment on the blogger's posting. And that, folks, is blogging in a nutshell.

Typically, people check a number of blogs on a daily or even hourly basis. You can do this in any standard web browser because blogs are just regular web pages. However, using something called RSS makes things even easier. So, what's RSS?

Really Simple Syndication (RSS)

The clue is in the name, really. RSS is a way to publish—or syndicate—your site, and these days . . . it's really simple! Most blogs offer this service as standard. How does it work?

When a new blog entry is made, the content is fed into a database of some kind (typically MySQL, Access, or a flat text file). The script takes that data and inserts it into an eXtensible Markup Language (XML) file that is linked on the site, along with the freshly published blog. Anyone can then use an RSS reader (or **aggregator**) to fetch this information automatically and display it in a simple-to-read format. Easy!

RSS readers are small applications whose sole purpose in life is to fetch updated information. The user can specify how often this is done, although some servers will ban you if you grab more quickly than every 30 minutes (Hello, Slashdot). As with most software, aggregators come in two flavors: free and shareware.

If you're using Mac OS X Tiger, you have this feature built into Safari already, as you can see in Figure 1-5. Firefox users should also be familiar with their browser's RSS capabilities.

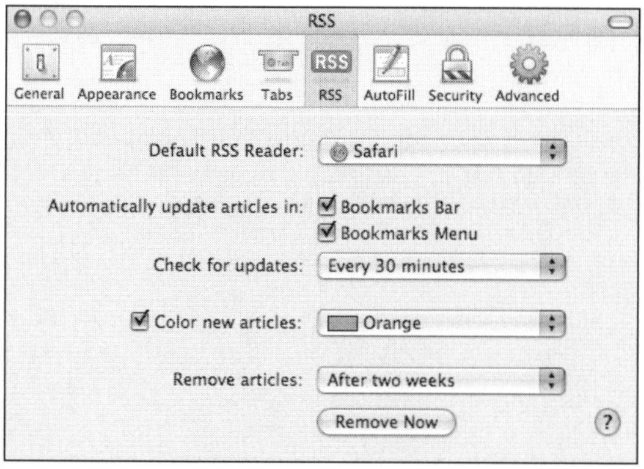

Figure 1-5. Configuring MacOS X Tiger's Safari 2.0 RSS capabilities

If you want a dedicated RSS reader, you have a number of options, which we'll take a quick look at now.

Mac OS X

NetNewsWire (www.ranchero.com/netnewswire) offers a shareware Pro version, and a free Lite version. It's one of the most popular with Mac users and one of the oldest. Freshly Squeezed Software's **PulpFiction** (www.freshlysqueezedsoftware.com/products/pulpfiction) is also available in a Lite version for those who don't need all the features of the full version (or those too tight to pay a few bucks for some shareware). **NewsFire** (www.newsfirerss.com) is shareware, but has some nice Mac OS X-style eye candy (see Figure 1-6).

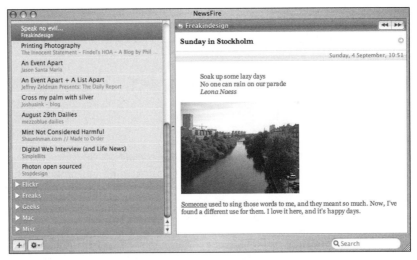

Figure 1-6. NewsFire has some really nice visual touches.

Windows

FeedDemon (www.bradsoft.com/feeddemon) is one of the most popular RSS readers for Windows (see Figure 1-7). It is shareware, but you get a 20-day trial period. Some other popular readers for Windows are **Tristana** (www.charlwood.com/tristana/reader) and **ActiveRefresh** (www.activerefresh.com).

A lot of these RSS readers have a podcasting browser, but this isn't a book about podcasting, so if you're interested in finding out more, I suggest that you pick up a copy of *Podcast Solutions: The Complete Guide to Podcasting*, by Michael Geoghegan and Dan Klass (friends of ED, 2005).

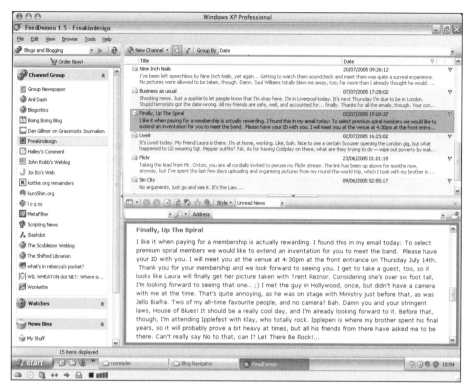

Figure 1-7. FeedDemon is one of the most popular RSS readers for Windows

Technorati

With all these blogs online, it would be pretty cool if you could search through them. The thing is, Google's spiders take days to index a site and add it to their search engine. Luckily, Technorati is at hand. Technorati (`www.technorati.com`) tracks blogs in real time, meaning that as soon as you blog, your data is instantly searchable via its search engine. It's as easy as signing up and adding some code to your blog page. At the time of writing, Technorati is tracking 16.9 million sites and 1.5 billion links in real time. That's a lot of data!

One of the chief geeks behind this service is Tantek Çelik, author of the infamous Box Model Hack and chief developer of the standards-compliant Tasman rendering engine that drove Mac IE 5 (`www.tantek.com/CSS/Examples/boxmodelhack.html`) among other things. I met Tantek in the Technorati offices about a year ago, and he was simultaneously typing on a PowerBook with one hand and an iBook with the other while talking to me. Look up the word "nerd" in the dictionary, and there should be a picture of that guy. And that's a compliment!

Tags

The way Technorati can search these blogs so easily is by bloggers using tags. **Tags** are just words used as easy search references. You can see some of the most popular tags at www.technorati.com/tag, as shown in Figure 1-8.

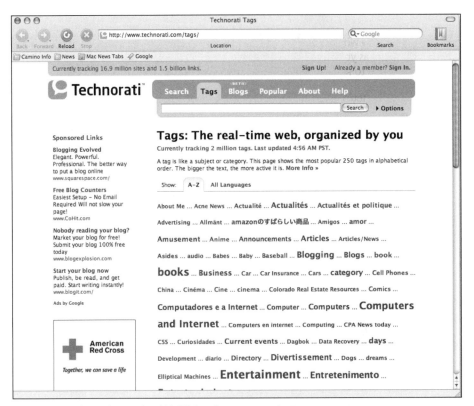

Figure 1-8. Technorati's tag cloud highlights the most popular tags.

To use a tag, just include rel="tag" in your linked text, like so:

```
<a href="http://technorati.com/tag/[tagname]" rel="tag">[tagname]</a>
```

So, if you wanted to add a tag for the 80's Saturday morning UK TV show, *TISWAS*, you'd simply add the following code to your blog:

```
<a href="http://tv.cream.org/lookin/tiswas" rel="tag">TISWAS</a>
```

All you have to do then is ping the Technorati server and let it know that your blog is there. Oh, wait . . . ping?

> Ping: Packet INternet Gopher. A utility used to query another computer on a TCP/IP network in order to determine whether there is a connection to it.

Okay, now you know what pinging is about, and some blogging scripts (such as Movable Type) ping automatically as you submit your new blog. For those that don't, you can manually ping the server by going to www.technorati.com/ping and submitting the new blog's URL.

Another new Internet service that uses tags is the awesome Flickr.

Flickr

At first glance, Flickr is just some web space to upload your photos to, but it goes much further than that. It's a big community, which pretty much doubles as a huge, searchable image bank. Users add tags to their pictures, which allow anyone to search for those terms (as shown circled in Figure 1-9).

Figure 1-9. Flickr users add tags to allow for easy searching.

Placing pictures into photo sets makes things kinda neat and tidy. Search for "Sherry Farewell" and you'll find some sets of pictures of this author and the book's technical reviewer, taken a few days before I moved from Liverpool to Stockholm, as you can see in Figure 1-10. If a few friends all have a set of similar pictures, you can create a group. Groups are either public, or private; it's up to the group's administrator. It's a fun way of seeing great pictures and meeting some cool people.

Figure 1-10. Flickr rocks, and it's really easy to add your images to your blog.

You can add your pictures to your blog easily enough, thanks to a simple piece of JavaScript that is generated for you. Flickr is nice enough to do this in several ways because it offers code for the following:

- Single pictures in different sizes
- A bunch of pictures from a specific photo set
- A bunch of pictures from all your photos
- The whole enchilada option, which grabs pictures from the whole community

You can have static images or utilize the groovy zeitgeist (www.flickr.com/fun/zeitgeist), which is a small Flash application, as shown in Figure 1-11.

Get your Daily Zeitgeist here!

flickr daily zeitgeist

All you need to do to get your own Daily Zeitgeist up and running is tell us which Flickr photos you'd like to include. Doing that will customize the script you see in the text area below, and then you simply copy and paste that code into your web page.

Which photos would you like to display?

○ Everyone's photos
○ Your photos
○ Your contacts' photos
● You and your contacts' photos

GET YOUR OWN

The Daily Zeitgeist is a little bit of fun that you can add to your website. It is built in Flash, and displays recent photos from Flickr.

This is just an initial version. We'll be playing around with it and adding more features. We'll let you know when new versions are available.

Copy and paste the code below into your own web page:

```
<script type="text/javascript">
var zg_person_scope = 2;
var zg_scope_nsid = '16959230@N00';
</script>
<script src="http://www.flickr.com/fun/zeitgeist/badge.js.gne"
type="text/javascript"></script>
```

Figure 1-11. The Flickr zeitgeist

Summary

By this point in the book, you should know more than enough about blogging to decide which solution to investigate. Obviously, if you bought this book, you've decided that you're ready to enter what some see as a world of pain and get your hands dirty with some code.

The next step is deciding which of the current blog engines you're going to fire up. Over the course of this book, you'll learn about Movable Type, Expression Engine, WordPress, and Textpattern. In the final chapter, Richard Rutter will take the more adventurous of you through coding your own blogging system.

Through the use of tags, you know how to get your blog noticed, and by embedding your Flickr images in your blog, you'll have even more people flocking to your new blog.

Before you even touch any code, though, it makes sense to get yourself a testing server that we'll use to run all the examples in this book. So, without further ado, it's over to David Powers, who will guide you through how to set your machine up for that very job.

2 CREATING A LOCAL TEST ENVIRONMENT FOR YOUR BLOG

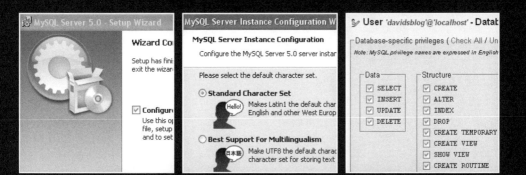

What this chapter covers:

- Setting up Apache and PHP on Windows and Mac OS X
- Configuring PHP to suit your requirements
- Configuring Apache to run CGI scripts
- Installing MySQL on Windows and Mac OS X
- Securing your MySQL installation
- Installing and using the phpMyAdmin user interface for MySQL
- Creating MySQL user accounts
- Backing up and transferring your blog to another server

So you've finally decided to share your innermost thoughts and brilliant insights with the rest of the world. The first requirement is a website, but not any website will do. Blogs store your masterful prose in a database, so you need a website with access to a database. All the blogging software in this book uses MySQL, the world's most popular open-source database, which is powerful, easy to use, and—best of all—free for most people. The way your website communicates with the database is through a scripting language. The one most frequently found in combination with MySQL is PHP, another open-source project that's also powerful, easy to use—and free.

With the exception of Movable Type (covered in Chapter 3), the PHP/MySQL combination is all you need for the blogging solutions covered in the rest of this book. Although Movable Type can be enhanced with PHP, what actually drives it is Perl, the main language behind Common Gateway Interface (CGI) scripting. If all this sounds like alphabet soup, don't worry. PHP, MySQL, and CGI are standard options with many hosting companies. To give you an indication of just how widespread PHP is, as of late 2005, it was in use on more than 22 million domains; and MySQL is estimated to be in use in more than 6 million installations. Also, with most blogging solutions, the complicated scripting has already been done for you. All you need is to set up a few configuration options, and you can blog away to your heart's content.

Although you can go straight ahead and install your blog on a live website, it's often a good idea to set up a local test environment on your own computer to get everything working the way you want. That way, you can stun the rest of the world with your brilliance rather than embarrassing mistakes.

Taking a quick look under the hood

The term **blog** first made an appearance in 1999 (and achieved an official seal of approval by being listed in the Oxford English Dictionary four years later), but the underlying technology has been around for much longer. Basically, a blog is a series of records held in a database, which are normally presented in reverse order—most recent first, but which can be easily searched or resorted by subject.

The way everything fits together relies on a combination of three technologies:

- A web server, such as Apache. The term **web server** is used here in the sense of a piece of software that "serves up" web pages in response to requests from other computers.

- A database system, such as MySQL.

- A scripting language that acts as an intermediary between the web server and the database. The language used by most blogs, PHP, is normally embedded in the (X)HTML of web pages. CGI scripts are located separately. Unless you intend to get involved in creating your own scripts, the blogging software handles everything for you, and the scripts work seamlessly in the background.

Like all database-driven websites, blogs have a front-end—the pretty face that you present to the rest of the world—and a back-end, which is where you do all the administrative work. Figure 2-1 shows what happens when you click the Save button after writing a blog entry in the administrative back-end. The contents of the form are sent by the Apache web server to either a PHP or a CGI script, which opens a connection to your MySQL database, in which everything is stored in readiness for visitors to your blog.

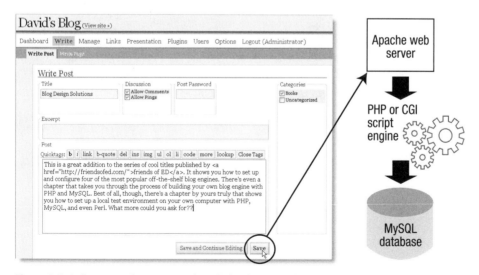

Figure 2-1. A diagrammatic representation of what happens when you store a blog entry

What happens when visitors come to your site is a little more complicated, but it all happens so smoothly in the background that it looks just like an ordinary web page. Figure 2-2 shows the process in simplified terms.

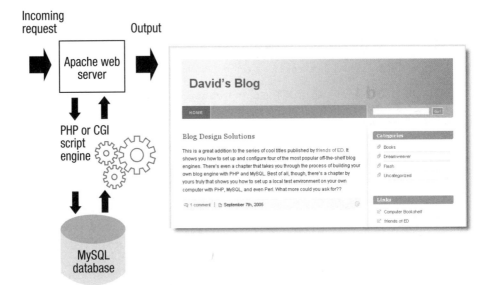

Figure 2-2. A simplified view of what happens when a blog page is requested

This is what happens when somebody visits your blog:

1. The request for the page is received by the Apache web server.
2. Apache summons the PHP or CGI script. Most times this will trigger a call to the database, but sometimes the script can send the necessary XHTML output straight back to the web server, bypassing the remaining stages.
3. The script usually needs to fetch your blog entries from the database, so it sends a username and password to MySQL, along with instructions of what to retrieve.
4. MySQL sends the information back to the script, which generates the necessary XHTML to display the particular view of the blog requested by the visitor.
5. The script sends the finished page to Apache, which serves up all the XHTML, Cascading Style Sheets (CSS), and images just like an ordinary web page.

Although it sounds complicated, it all takes place in microseconds unless the server is unusually busy. The biggest delay occurs in transmitting the data back over the Internet.

2

> *Although many web designers still use Hypertext Markup Language (HTML), the standard recommended by the World Wide Web Consortium (W3C) is eXtensible HyperText Markup Language (XHTML). It's basically the same as HTML, but written according to stricter standards. To learn more about the differences, and why the change is being made, see the W3C XHTML FAQ at www.w3.org/MarkUp/2004/xhtml-faq.*

What you need to build a local test environment

If you plan to test your blog locally, and particularly if you want to build your own blog engine as described in Chapter 7, you need to reproduce on your own computer the setup shown in Figures 2-1 and 2-2. For this process, you need the following:

- A web server—Apache 2.0 (on Mac OS X, use Apache 1.3, which is already installed)
- PHP
- MySQL
- Perl (required only if you want to test Movable Type locally)

In addition to these, you also need to download phpMyAdmin, a PHP-based graphical front-end to MySQL. Most hosting companies provide phpMyAdmin as the default method of working with MySQL. It's easy to set up, and makes working with MySQL straightforward and intuitive.

How much does it all cost?

Nothing. All the software listed previously is free. The only cost to you is the time it takes to download the necessary files from the Internet, plus, of course, the time to install and configure everything. Depending on the speed of your Internet connection and how comfortable you feel changing a few configuration files, you could be up and running in little more than an hour. However, I urge you not to rush things. All the configuration files are written in plain text, but a comma or semicolon out of place could bring everything to a screeching halt.

Windows users need to download all the files listed previously. If you're using Mac OS X, Apache and Perl are already installed on your computer. Mac OS X also comes with PHP preinstalled, but it's not activated and should be upgraded to a more fully featured version.

Why not use an all-in-one package?

Some people are so terrified of installing programs not originally designed for Windows or Mac OS X that they desperately seek a precompiled package that bundles Apache, PHP, and MySQL together. One that has become very popular recently is XAMMP (www.apachefriends.org/en), which is available for both Windows and Mac OS X. XAMMP has a good reputation, but I still recommend installing each program separately. The problem with an all-in-one package is that it frequently robs you of a great amount of control, and you might not get the most up-to-date version of each program.

For a long time, phpdev423 was one of the most popular all-in-one packages for Windows, but many people have reported problems with uninstalling it. The main problem occurs if you uninstall phpdev423 before removing Apache as a Windows service. If you need to uninstall phpdev423, close down Apache and run C:\phpdev\uninstall_apache_service.bat before proceeding with the rest of the process.

Perhaps the biggest danger with precompiled packages is that they are often created by individuals or small groups of enthusiasts. There is no guarantee that they will still be around to support you when you need them. PHP, Apache, and MySQL all have the backing of large development teams and an even larger user base. Help is always much more likely to be at hand—and if you run into difficulty with the instructions in this book, I'll be happy to help you out in the Back End Blight section of the friends of ED forum at www.friendsofed.com/forums.

The installation instructions for Windows and Mac OS X are completely different, so make sure you read the correct part of the chapter. Of course, if you already have a working PHP/MySQL test environment, you can skip the large parts. Check the section for your operating system on enabling support for CGI scripts; and also read the section at the end of the chapter on MySQL user accounts to make sure that you have an account with the necessary permissions for working with a blogging package.

> *New versions of open-source software are released much more frequently than commercial programs. I recommend that you check this book's errata page at www.friendsofed.com before starting installation. Any important changes to the installation process will be detailed there*

Setting up on Windows

These instructions assume that you are using Windows 2000 or later. Make sure that you're logged on as an Administrator.

Getting Windows to display filename extensions

By default, most Windows computers hide the three- or four-letter filename extension, such as .doc or .html, so all you see in dialog boxes and Windows Explorer is thisfile instead of thisfile.doc or thisfile.html. The ability to see these filename extensions is essential for working with PHP.

If you haven't already enabled the display of filename extensions on your computer, open My Computer (it's a desktop icon on Windows 2000, but on the Start menu on more recent versions of Windows). Then from the menu at the top of the window, choose Tools ➤ Folder Options ➤ View. Uncheck the box marked Hide extensions for known file types, as shown in the screenshot alongside. Click OK.

I recommend that you leave your computer permanently at this setting because it is more secure—you can tell if a virus writer has attached an EXE or SCR executable file to an innocent-looking document.

Installing Apache on Windows

As explained earlier, Apache is a web server. It normally runs in the background, taking up very few resources, waiting for requests. By default, Apache listens for these requests on port 80. Although you can run several different web servers on the same computer, each one must use a different port.

> Apache 2.2 was released in December 2005, but as of this writing is not available for Windows, so it wasn't possible to test it for this book. Therefore, I recommend that you install the latest version of Apache 2.0, even when a Windows version of Apache 2.2 becomes available. The new features in Apache 2.2 are not required for local development and testing of PHP pages. Moreover, the Apache development team continues to upgrade and support existing versions for several years after the release of a new series, so Apache 2.0 will fulfill all your needs more than adequately.

Deciding which port to run Apache on

If you have never developed dynamic websites using PHP, ASP, or ASP.NET, you can be fairly confident that you don't already have an active web server on your computer. However, to make sure, open a browser and type the following URL in the address bar:

```
http://localhost/
```

This is the URL that every computer uses to refer to websites running on a locally installed web server.

- If you get a message that the server cannot be found or that the connection was refused, that means you don't have a web server. You can safely install Apache to run on the default port 80.

- If you see a web page, or if you know already that you have another web server such as IIS or PWS installed, you need to run Apache on a different port—8080 is the most common choice. The only difference is that you need to use localhost:8080 instead of localhost in the URLs for your test pages.

- ColdFusion runs by default on port 8500, so you can run Apache on the default port 80 without worrying about any conflicts.

- If you already have Apache 1.3 installed and you want to upgrade to Apache 2.0, follow the instructions in the next section.

Removing an existing installation of Apache 1.3

Apache 2.0 is installed as a completely separate program, not as an upgrade to an existing one, so you must begin by removing Apache as a Windows service. Do this by opening a Windows Command Prompt window, and typing NET STOP APACHE. When Apache has stopped, type the following commands, both followed by Enter:

```
cd c:\program files\apache group\apache
apache -u -n 'Apache'
```

You can then uninstall Apache 1.3 through Control Panel ➤ Add or Remove Programs. Although your original Apache configuration file, httpd.conf, will remain intact, do not attempt to use it for Apache 2.0 because many of the configuration commands are different. Delete the original Apache folder and all its contents before installing Apache 2.0.

Downloading and installing Apache 2.0

1. Go to http://httpd.apache.org/download.cgi. Scroll down to the section for Apache 2.0.*xx*, and select the file marked Win32 Binary (MSI Installer), as shown in the screenshot. The xx in the number represents the most recent version of the 2.0 series (at the time of this writing, it was 2.0.55). The download is approximately 4.6MB. Save the file to a temporary folder on your hard disk.

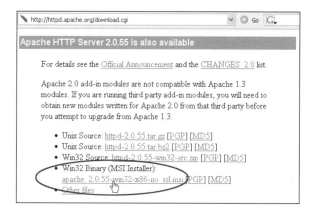

2. Apache comes in a Windows installer package and is installed like any other software. Close all open programs and temporarily disable virus-scanning software. Double-click the Apache installer package icon.

3. A wizard will take you through the installation process. Click Next to start. The first thing to appear is the Apache License agreement. Read the conditions and terms of use, select the Accept terms radio button, and click Next.

4. The next screen contains information about Apache. Read it and click Next.

5. The Server Information screen follows (shown in the next screenshot), in which you enter the default settings for your web server. In the Network Domain and Server Name fields, enter localhost; in the last field, enter an e-mail address. The localhost address tells Apache you will be using it on your own computer. The e-mail address does not need to be a genuine one; it has no bearing on the way the program runs and is normally of relevance only on a live production server.

25

6. Select the option labeled for All Users, on Port 80, as a Service. Apache will run in the background, and you don't need to worry about starting it. Click Next.

> *If you already have a web server, such as IIS or PWS running on port 80, you must select the option labeled* only for the Current User, on Port 8080, when started Manually. *You can change the option to start Apache automatically later.*

7. The next dialog box asks you to select the setup type. Select the Typical option, and click Next to continue.

8. You are then given an opportunity to change where Apache will be installed. The default location, C:\Program Files\Apache Group, is fine. Click Next. The final dialog box gives you an opportunity to go back and change any of your options. Assuming that you're happy, click Install to finish the Apache installation.

9. The process is quite quick, but don't be alarmed if you see a Command Prompt window open and close several times while the program is being installed. This is perfectly normal. If a software firewall is installed, such as Norton Internet Security (NIS), you will probably see a warning message like the one shown here.

Although NIS recommends blocking all connections, accepting this recommendation will prevent Apache from working correctly. Select the option to allow all connections, or—if you're feeling particularly cautious—create your own security rules manually. Manual settings will depend on your individual setup.

10. If you're running a local network, Windows might also attempt to block Apache. If you see a dialog box similar to the one shown here, choose the Unblock option.

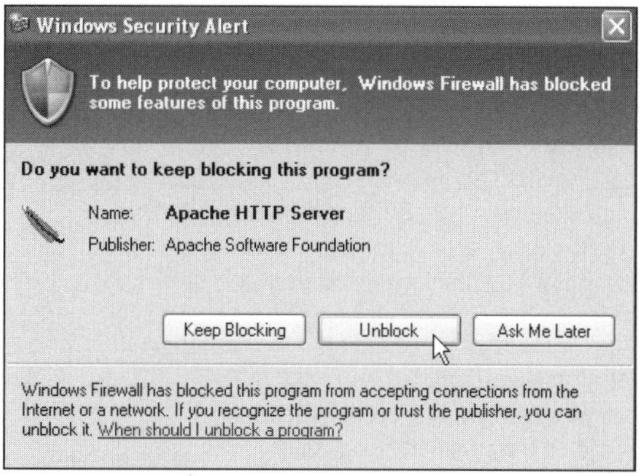

11. Unless you chose the option in step 6 to run Apache on port 8080, open a browser and type http://localhost/ into the address bar. If all has gone well, you should see the test page shown in Figure 2-3.

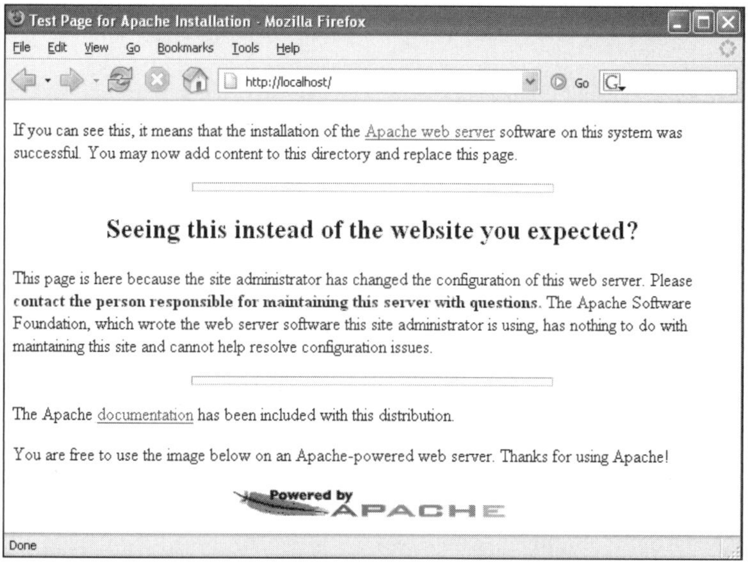

Figure 2-3. Confirmation that Apache is running successfully on Windows

If you chose the option to start Apache 2 on port 8080, you need to start Apache first, as described in the next section, and then use the address http://localhost:8080/.

12. If you get an error message, it probably means that the Apache server is not running. Start up the server, as described in the next section, and try again. If you still get problems, check C:\Program Files\Apache Group\Apache2\logs\error.log.

Starting and stopping Apache on Windows

Apache 2.0 places a tiny icon (it looks like a red feather with a white circle) in the tray (or notification area) at the right end of the Windows taskbar. This is the Apache Service Monitor, which shows you at a glance whether Apache is running. If it's running, there is a green, right-facing arrow in the white circle. When Apache has stopped, the arrow turns to a red dot (see screenshots alongside).

Click once on the icon, and you will be presented with a context menu, as shown in the screenshot. This menu provides a quick way of starting, stopping, and restarting Apache.

Changing startup preferences or disabling Apache

It's very easy to change the way Apache starts. If you want to switch between automatic and manual startup, or if you want to disable Apache temporarily, use the following instructions:

1. Open the Windows Services panel by selecting Start ➤ Control Panel ➤ Administrative Tools ➤ Services.

2. When the Windows Services panel opens, highlight Apache2, right-click, and select Properties.

3. From the Startup type drop-down menu (see the screenshot alongside), select Automatic, Manual, or Disabled. If you want to start or stop Apache at the same time, click the appropriate Service status button before clicking OK.

The Apache Services Monitor will display in the taskbar tray every time your computer starts, even if you switch to manual operation or disable Apache.

Setting up PHP on Windows

These instructions are for a completely new installation of PHP. If PHP has never been installed on your computer, simply follow the instructions.

However, if you have an old installation of PHP, you must first remove any PHP-related files from your main Windows folder (C:\WINDOWS or C:\WINNT, depending on your system) and the system32 subfolder. Changing the contents of the Windows system folders is not to be undertaken lightly, so I suggest that you cut and paste them to a temporary folder, instead of just deleting them,. Then, if anything goes wrong, you can easily restore them.

The PHP files you need to remove are php.ini (in the main Windows folder), and php4ts.dll or php5ts.dll in the system32 subfolder. You should also remove any other PHP-related DLL files from the system32 subfolder. They are easy to recognize because they all begin with php. If there's a copy of libmysql.dll in your Windows system folder, remove that, too.

> *These instructions are based on PHP 5.1.1, which is the stable version at the time of this writing. The release of PHP 5.1 in late November 2005 introduced PHP Data Objects (PDO), which greatly simplify communication with databases. That's the good news. The bad news is that hosting companies are notoriously slow to upgrade to major new versions of PHP. Until there is sufficiently wide-spread support for PDO, the blogging solutions presented in this book will continue to rely on MySQL-specific database functions. Consequently, there will be no further discussion of PDO in this book.*

Downloading and installing the PHP files

1. Go to www.php.net/downloads.php and select the Windows binaries ZIP file for the latest stable version of PHP 5. Even if your hosting company is still running PHP 4, download the version marked PHP 5.*x.x* zip package. It's about 8.6MB. I suggest downloading the latest version of PHP because you're likely to run into problems if you try to use MySQL 4.1 or later with PHP 4. The blogging packages should all run without problems on the latest versions of PHP and MySQL. If for any reason they don't, you should be wary about using them because they're likely to break whenever your hosting company eventually upgrades.

   As you can see from the screenshot of the PHP download page, a Windows installer is also available for PHP. I'm sure many of you will be tempted to use it. *Resist the temptation.* The PHP Windows installer runs PHP in a very restricted way and is likely to cause you considerable problems. The method I am about to show you makes no changes to either your operating system or web server, so in the unlikely event that anything goes wrong, it can be removed completely safely.

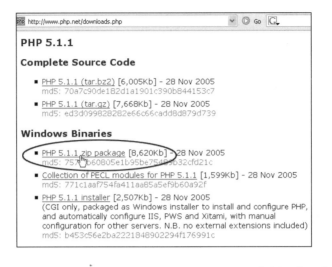

When you click the download link, you will be presented with a list of mirror sites. Choose the one closest to your location and download the ZIP file to a temporary folder on your hard disk.

2. Unzip the contents of the ZIP file to a new folder called C:\php5. Check that the new folder contains about 30 files and several folders at the top level, as shown here. The path to php5apache2.dll should be C:\php5\php5apache2.dll.

If you choose a location different from C:\php5, *you need to substitute the name of your new folder in all later steps. You should avoid locating the PHP files in a folder that contains spaces in either its name or pathname because it can create problems with the Apache configuration.*

3. In the php5 folder, locate the file called php.ini-dist, make a copy of it, and rename the copy php.ini. As soon as you rename the file, its associated icon in Windows Explorer will change, as shown alongside, indicating that it's an INI file that Windows will use to configure PHP each time you start up your web server.

php.ini

4. Open php.ini in any text editor. Notepad will do, but it's better to use a dedicated script editor—such as TextPad (www.textpad.com) or a program such as Dreamweaver that displays line numbers—because finding the relevant sections will be a lot easier.

> *Lines that begin with a semicolon (;) are treated as comments in* php.ini, *so make sure any changes you make in the following steps are to configuration settings and not to comments.*

5. Scroll down (or use a search facility—Ctrl+F in Notepad and Dreamweaver or F5 in TextPad) until you find the following line in the Paths and Directories section (around line 461):

extension_dir = "./"

Change it to

extension_dir = "C:\php5\ext\"

This is the name of the folder in which PHP will look for any extensions. This assumes you extracted the PHP files to the recommended location. If you chose a different location, change the path accordingly.

6. Scroll further down until you come to Dynamic Extensions. You will see a long list titled Windows Extensions (around line 563), all of them commented out. These extensions add extra features to the core functionality of PHP. You can enable any of them at any time simply by removing the semicolon from the beginning of the line for the extension you want, saving php.ini, and restarting Apache.

Locate the following line (around line 569):

;extension=php_mbstring.dll

Enable it by removing the semicolon from the beginning of the line like this:

extension=php_mbstring.dll

This enables support for Unicode. Even if you never plan to use anything other than English, it's required to work with MySQL 4.1 and above.

7. About 24 lines further down, locate the line containing php_mysql.dll. Copy and paste it on the line immediately below. Remove the semicolon from the beginning of both lines and amend the second line so they look like this:

extension=php_mysql.dll
extension=php_mysqli.dll

This enables support for the MySQL-specific functions that will be used by your blog.

8. Save php.ini, and close it. Leave it inside the C:\php5 folder.

31

2

Adding PHP to your Windows startup procedure

The installation of PHP is complete, but it still needs to be added to your Windows startup procedure.

1. Open the Windows Control Panel (Start ➤ Settings ➤ Control Panel or Start ➤ Control Panel). Double-click the System icon. Select the Advanced tab and click Environment Variables, as shown alongside.

2. In the System variables pane at the bottom of the dialog box that opens, highlight Path as shown and click Edit.

3. A smaller dialog box opens. Click inside the Variable value field and move your cursor to the end of the existing value. Type a semicolon followed by the name of the PHP folder you created in step 2 of the previous section (C:\php5). As shown in the screenshot, there should be no spaces between the existing value or in the new pathname.

4. Click OK. With the Environment Variables dialog box still open, click New in the System variables pane. Another small dialog box opens, in which you enter the details of the new system variable. In the Variable name field, type PHPRC. In the Variable value field, enter the path of the PHP folder (C:\php5).

5. Click OK to close all the dialog boxes. The next time you restart your computer, Windows will now know where to find all the necessary files to run PHP. You still need to make some changes to the Apache configuration file, so continue with the next section before restarting your computer.

Configuring Apache to work with PHP

Now that all the configuration settings have been made for PHP, you need to make some adjustments to the main configuration file for Apache.

> Note that all the pathnames in the Apache configuration file use forward slashes instead of the Windows convention of backward slashes. So, c:\php5 becomes c:/php5. Any path- or filenames that contain spaces must be enclosed in quotes.

1. The Apache configuration file httpd.conf is located in C:\Program Files\Apache Group\Apache2\conf. You can either use Windows Explorer to locate the file directly and open it in a script editor or select Start ➤ Programs ➤ Apache HTTP Server ➤ Configure Apache Server ➤ Edit the Apache httpd.conf Configuration File. Like php.ini, httpd.conf is a very long file composed mainly of comments, which in this case can be distinguished by a pound or hash sign (#) at the beginning of the line.

2. Scroll down until you find a long list of items that begin with LoadModule (many of them will be commented out). At the end of the list, add the following on a new line, as shown:

LoadModule php5_module c:/php5/php5apache2.dll

```
164  #LoadModule rewrite_module modules/mod_rewrite.so
165  LoadModule setenvif_module modules/mod_setenvif.so
166  #LoadModule speling_module modules/mod_speling.so
167  #LoadModule status_module modules/mod_status.so
168  #LoadModule unique_id_module modules/mod_unique_id
169  LoadModule userdir_module modules/mod_userdir.so
170  #LoadModule usertrack_module modules/mod_usertrack
171  #LoadModule vhost_alias_module modules/mod_vhost_a
172  #LoadModule ssl_module modules/mod_ssl.so
173
174 ▶LoadModule php5_module c:/php5/php5apache2.dll
175
```

The pathname assumes that you installed PHP in c:\php5. Change it accordingly if you used a different installation folder, and don't forget to use forward slashes in the pathname. Enclose the path in quotes if there are spaces in any of the folder names.

3. Scroll down again until you find the section shown in the following screenshot.

```
226  # DocumentRoot: The directory out of which you will serve your
227  # documents. By default, all requests are taken from this directory, but
228  # symbolic links and aliases may be used to point to other locations.
229  #
230 ▶DocumentRoot "C:/Program Files/Apache Group/Apache2/htdocs"
231
232  #
233  # Each directory to which Apache has access can be configured with respect
234  # to which services and features are allowed and/or disabled in that
235  # directory (and its subdirectories).
236  #
237  # First, we configure the "default" to be a very restrictive set of
238  # features.
239  #
240  <Directory />
241      Options FollowSymLinks
242      AllowOverride None
243  </Directory>
244
245  #
246  # Note that from this point forward you must specifically allow
247  # particular features to be enabled - so if something's not working as
248  # you might expect, make sure that you have specifically enabled it
249  # below.
250  #
251
252  #
253  # This should be changed to whatever you set DocumentRoot to.
254  #
255 ▶<Directory "C:/Program Files/Apache Group/Apache2/htdocs">
256
```

When working with PHP and/or CGI scripts, Apache automatically looks for all web pages in the **server root** (or DocumentRoot as Apache calls it). This is so it can process (or **parse**) the scripts and send the right information to both the database and the browser. The two lines indicated by an arrow (lines 230 and 255 in the screenshot) are where you specify the location of the server root. In a browser this becomes the equivalent of http://localhost/.

Because this folder is where all your web files will be stored, it's not a good idea to keep them in the same place as your vital program files. So whenever I set up a new computer, I always create a dedicated folder called htdocs at the top level of my C drive, and I put all my websites in subfolders of htdocs. I chose that name because it's the traditional name used by Apache for the server root folder. You can use whatever name you like, but I suggest you do the same. Change both lines to indicate the same location, like this:

```
DocumentRoot "C:/htdocs"
#
# Omitted section
#
<Directory "C:/htdocs">
```

4. Scroll down a bit further until you come to the following command (around line 323):

```
DirectoryIndex index.html index.html.var
```

This setting tells web servers what to display by default if a URL doesn't end with a filename, but contains only a folder name or the domain name (for instance, www.friendsofed.com). Apache will choose the first available page from a space-separated list. The whole purpose of this book is to work with PHP, so you need to add index.php.

```
DirectoryIndex index.html index.html.var index.php
```

> The rather strange-looking index.html.var is used in a specialized feature known as content negotiation, which can automatically serve up different language versions of the same page by detecting the default language of the computer's operating system. I don't recommend its use, but if you're curious, see http://httpd.apache.org/docs-2.0/content-negotiation.html.

5. Close to the end of httpd.conf, you'll find a section that includes several commands that begin with AddType. Add the following line in that section on a line of its own, as shown:

```
AddType application/x-httpd-php .php
```

```
756  AddType application/x-compress .Z
757  AddType application/x-gzip .gz .tgz
758
759 ▶AddType application/x-httpd-php .php
760
```

6. Save and close httpd.conf.

7. You now need to create a test file in the folder you designated as server root in step 3. Open Notepad and enter the following line of code:

```
<?php phpinfo(); ?>
```

8. Save the file as `index.php` in the server root (if you decided to follow my setup, you will need to create a new `htdocs` folder).

9. You now need to restart your computer so that the changes made to the Windows path and startup procedure can take effect. Apache should start automatically unless you opted to control it manually.

10. If there are any mistakes in `httpd.conf`, Apache will refuse to start. Depending on the version you have installed, you might get a helpful message in a Command Prompt window that tells you what the problem is and which line of `httpd.conf` it occurred on. Reopen `httpd.conf`

and correct the error (probably a typo). On the other hand, Windows might display the very unhelpful message shown alongside.

Check the Apache error log for clues about what went wrong. Alternatively, open a Command Prompt window (select Start ➤ Run, enter cmd in the Open field, and click OK). Inside the Command Prompt window, change to the appropriate Apache folder by typing the following command and pressing Enter:

```
cd c:\program files\apache group\apache2\bin
```

Then type this (followed by Enter):

```
apache
```

The reason for the failure should appear onscreen, usually with a line number pinpointing the problem in `httpd.conf`. The following screenshot shows what happened when I mistyped the location of `php5apache2.dll`.

After you correct any problems in `httpd.conf`, resave the file and restart Apache using the Apache Service Monitor or choose Control Apache Server from the Apache listing on the Start menu.

> *If you type* apache *in the Command Prompt window and nothing appears to happen, it doesn't mean that Apache has hung. It indicates that Apache has started normally. However, while Apache is running, it doesn't return you to the command line; and if you close the window, Apache will crash. To close Apache gracefully, open another Command Prompt window, change the directory to the* apache2\bin *folder, and type the following command:*
>
> ```
> apache -k shutdown
> ```
>
> *You can then restart Apache using the Apache Service Monitor.*
>
> *There is also a* Test Configuration *option on the Apache menu that can be accessed from the Start button. It displays the same information as in the method just described. On some systems, however, it snaps closed after 30 seconds. Opening a Command Prompt window involves more typing, but gives you the chance to read the results at leisure—something that's often very important if you're unfamiliar with Apache.*

11. After Apache has restarted, open your browser and type `http://localhost/` into the address bar (or `http://localhost:8080/` if you chose the option to start Apache manually on port 8080). You should see a page similar to the one shown in Figure 2-4. Welcome to the world of PHP!

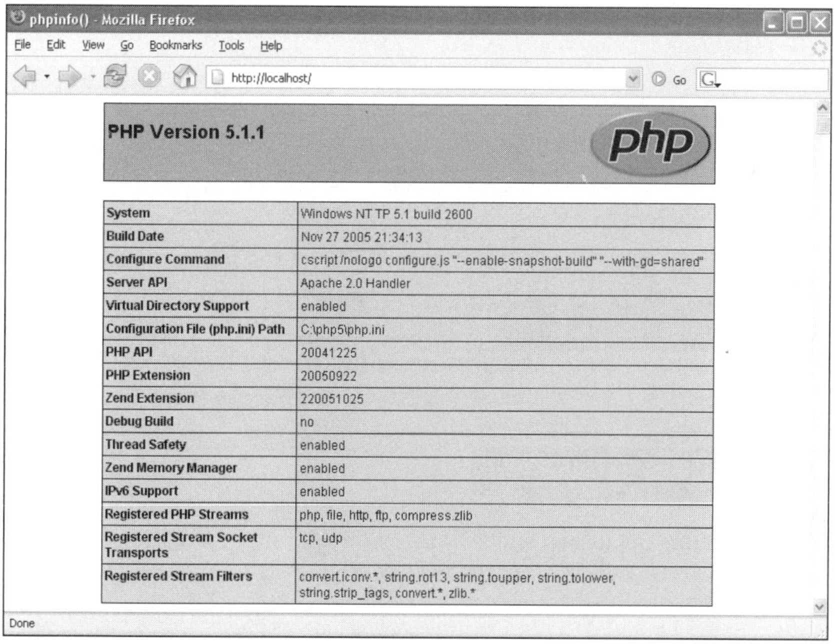

Figure 2-4. The `phpinfo()` command displays copious data showing your PHP configuration.

12. In the unfortunate event that anything goes wrong, check the next section. If that's not the answer, retrace your steps, and make sure that you have followed the instructions precisely. Check the short piece of code in step 7 and make sure that there is no gap in the opening <?php tag. Try an ordinary HTML page in the same folder (remember that it must be the folder you designated as the server root in step 3). If the ordinary HTML page displays correctly, there's something wrong with the PHP part of your installation. If it doesn't display, the problem lies in the way you configured Apache.

13. Assuming that everything is running smoothly, skip ahead to the section titled "Enabling support for CGI scripting on Windows."

"Cannot load mysqli extension"

This error message is one of the most common that display after installing PHP 5. It occurs because the web server can't find the correct code library for the PHP MySQL Improved extension (mysqli). It's located in libmysql.dll, which should be in C:\php5. However, some third-party programs install libmysql.dll directly into the Windows\system32 folder.

The problem arises if the version used by the third-party program is older than the one in C:\php5. Wherever possible, you should avoid littering the system32 folder with DLL files, so remove libmysql.dll from system32. However, if this causes problems with the third-party program, you have little alternative but to copy the more recent version from the php5 folder to system32.

Enabling support for CGI scripting on Windows

This section is required only if you plan to test Movable Type on your local computer. Installation is very easy, and can be done at any time as long as you have a working installation of Apache. It involves three stages:

- Downloading and installing the Windows version of Perl, the most commonly used language for CGI scripts
- Creating a folder outside the Apache server root to store any CGI scripts
- Making a couple of small changes to the Apache configuration file

Although Perl itself has a reputation for being difficult to learn, you don't need any specialist knowledge to configure your computer to support CGI.

Downloading and installing Perl

1. To get Perl, go to www.activestate.com/Products/ ActivePerl, and click the Free Download link. This will take you to a registration page, which is entirely optional. If you decide to register, ActiveState will keep you informed of any updates, but if you prefer not to register, clicking Next will take you directly to the download page. Choose the latest version of Perl (currently 5.8.7.815), scroll down to the Windows section, and select the MSI link, as shown alongside.

Windows	
AS package	12.9MB
MSI	12.7MB

2. When you have downloaded the MSI installer, close all other programs, and double-click the Windows Installer icon, as shown alongside.

3. This launches the setup wizard, which is just like any other Windows program. Click Next to start the installation process.

4. Accept the license when prompted. You then see a screen that invites you to choose which features to be installed. The default options are fine, so just click Next.

5. You are asked to choose a number of setup options. Some of them are grayed-out if they aren't applicable to your system, but the others are selected by default. You should accept the options to add Perl to the PATH environment variable and to create a Perl file extension association. This ensures that Windows knows where to find Perl and recognizes Perl scripts correctly. Then click Next.

6. The rest of the installation is automatic, but it might take a few minutes because it generates HTML documentation. If you have a software firewall installed, you might be warned to block the program; if you do, however, the CGI scripts will fail to work.

Configuring Apache to use CGI scripts

1. Although all web files connected with a PHP site must be kept in the Apache server root, all CGI files must be kept in a special folder *outside* the server root. It's not important where the folder is located or what it's called, but the conventional name for it is cgi-bin. I suggest that you create a folder called cgi-bin at the top level of your C drive.

2. Open the Apache configuration file, httpd.conf in Notepad or a text editor, and locate the section of code shown in the following screenshot.

```
518  #
519 ▶ScriptAlias /cgi-bin/ "C:/Program Files/Apache Group/Apache2/cgi-bin/"
520
521  #
522  # "C:/Program Files/Apache Group/Apache2/cgi-bin" should be changed to
523  # CGI directory exists, if you have that configured.
524  #
525 ▶<Directory "C:/Program Files/Apache Group/Apache2/cgi-bin">
526      AllowOverride None
527      Options None
528      Order allow,deny
529      Allow from all
530  </Directory>
```

3. Change the pathname in both lines indicated by an arrow to the name of the folder you created in step 1. If you followed my suggestion, the lines look like this:

```
ScriptAlias /cgi-bin/ "C:/cgi-bin/"
<Directory "C:/cgi-bin">
```

4. Save httpd.conf and restart Apache.

5. Open Notepad and enter the following script (it's also available as script_test.cgi in the download files for this chapter):

```
#! c:\perl\bin\perl.exe

print "Content-type:text/html\n\n";
print "Yes, it really works!\n";
```

6. Save the file as windows_test.cgi in the C:\cgi-bin folder.

7. Type the following URL in your browser address bar and press Enter:

```
http://localhost/cgi-bin/windows_test.cgi
```

8. You should see "Yes, it really works!" in your browser window, confirming that CGI is up and running.

Installing MySQL on Windows

MySQL comes in a range of versions, but the one you should choose is **Windows Essentials**. It contains all the important stuff, and certainly everything you need for this book. These instructions assume that you have never installed MySQL on your computer before. If you have a version older than MySQL 4.1.5, you *must* uninstall the old version first.

The instructions are based on the 5.0 series of MySQL, which is installed in C:\Program Files\MySQL\MySQL Server 5.0. This location is different from the default location for the Windows Essentials version of MySQL 4.1, and Windows treats the two series as completely different programs. If you upgrade from MySQL 4.1 to MySQL 5.0, any existing databases need to be transferred to the new version as if it were a different server (see the section titled "Backing up and transferring your blog to another server" at the end of this chapter).

Installing the Windows Essentials version of MySQL

1. Go to the MySQL downloads page at http://dev.mysql.com/downloads. Select the link for the Generally Available (recommended) release of MySQL database server & standard clients.

2. In the page that opens, scroll down to find the section marked Windows downloads. Choose Windows Essentials (x86), and click the download link.

3. Download the MySQL file to your hard disk. It will have a name like mysql-essential-x.x.x-win32.msi, where x.x.x represents the version number.

4. Exit all other Windows programs, and double-click the icon of the file you have just downloaded, as shown alongside. This is a self-extracting Windows Installer package.

5. Windows Installer will begin the installation process and open a welcome dialog box. If you are upgrading an existing version of the *same series* of Windows Essentials to a more recent one, the dialog box will inform you that it has detected your current installation and will remove it before installing the new one. However, all your databases will remain intact. Click Next to continue.

6. The next dialog box gives you the opportunity to change the installation destination. Accept the default and click Next.

7. In the next dialog box, accept the default setup (Typical) and click Next.

8. If you're happy to go ahead with installation, click Install in the next dialog box. Otherwise, click Back and make any necessary changes.

9. Before launching into the actual installation, MySQL invites you to sign up for a free MySQL.com account. I suggest that you select Skip Sign-Up (see screenshot) and click Next. After you finish setting everything up, visit www.mysql.com/register.php to see if you're interested in the benefits offered. The main advantage is that you get automatic e-mails advising about new versions and links to helpful background articles about new features of MySQL. Signing up is quick and hassle-free.

10. The actual installation now takes place and is normally very quick. When every-thing's finished, you're presented with a final dialog box, as shown.

The Configure the MySQL Server now check box is selected by default.

- If this is a new installation or if you are upgrading from one series to another, leave the check box selected. Click Finish, and then move on to the next section.

- If you are simply upgrading to a later version of the same series (such as from 5.0.10 to 5.0.16), deselect the check box before clicking Finish. Your version of MySQL should be ready to use, but will need to be restarted manually (see "Starting and stopping MySQL manually on Windows" later in the chapter). If you have a software firewall, such as Norton Internet Security, you might also be prompted to allow connections to and from MySQL.

Configuring MySQL Windows Essentials

There are quite a lot of dialog boxes to go through, although all you usually need to do is accept the default setting. These instructions are based on version 1.0.8 of the Configuration Wizard.

1. The Configuration Wizard opens with a welcome screen. Click Next to proceed.

2. The first dialog box asks whether you want a detailed or standard configuration. Choose the default Detailed Configuration option and click Next.

3. The three options on the next screen affect the amount of computer resources devoted to MySQL. Accept the default Developer Machine and click Next. If you choose either of the other options, be prepared for all your other programs to slow down to a crawl.

4. The next dialog box asks you to select from the following three types of database, as shown in the screenshot:

- Multifunctional Database: Allows you to use both InnoDB and MyISAM tables.

- Transactional Database Only: InnoDB tables only. MyISAM is disabled.

- Non-Transactional Database Only: MyISAM tables only. InnoDB is disabled.

Most hosting companies support only MyISAM tables, so choose the final option: Non-Transactional Database Only. Unless you plan to learn MySQL in depth, there is little advantage in choosing the Multifunctional Database option, which requires an extra 30MB of disk space.

If you choose Multifunctional Database, you will need to make a simple text edit to the MySQL configuration file later, as described in "Changing the default table type on Windows Essentials."

5. The next dialog box will be grayed-out if you are upgrading or if you chose Non-Transactional Database Only in the preceding step. Skip to step 6.

   If you chose Multifunctional Database, you need to tell MySQL where to create the files for the InnoDB engine. InnoDB stores data in a single **tablespace** that acts as a sort of virtual file system. InnoDB files, once created, cannot be made smaller. The default location for the tablespace is C:\Program Files\MySQL\MySQL Server 5.0\data. If you want to locate the tablespace elsewhere, the drop-down menu offers some suggested alternatives. When you have made your choice, click Next.

6. Leave the next dialog box at its default setting of Decision Support (DSS)/OLAP and click Next.

7. The next dialog box sets the networking options and SQL mode. The important settings are in the top half. Make sure that Enable TCP/IP Networking is checked and leave Port Number at the default setting of 3306. The lower half of the dialog box lets you choose whether to run MySQL in strict mode. This option is new to MySQL 5.0 and may cause problems with some PHP scripts. Although Strict mode is the recommended default, you should deselect it before clicking Next.

8. MySQL has impressive support for most of the world's languages. The next dialog box invites you to choose a default character set. In spite of what you might think, this has no bearing on the range of languages supported—all are supported by default. The character set mainly determines the order in which data is sorted. Unless you have a specific reason for choosing anything other than the default Standard Character Set, I suggest that you accept it without making any changes, as shown. You can always change it later. Click Next.

9. The recommended way of running MySQL is as a Windows service, as shown. If you accept the defaults as shown in the top half of the next dialog box, MySQL will always start automatically when you boot your computer and run silently in the background. (If MySQL has already been installed as a Windows service this section will be grayed-out.) If, for any reason, you don't want MySQL to start automatically, uncheck the Launch the MySQL Server automatically option. You can easily change this option later (see the later section "Starting and stopping MySQL manually on Windows").

The lower half of the dialog box gives you the option to include the bin directory in your Windows PATH. This option enables you to interact directly with MySQL and its related utilities at the command line without the need to change directory every time. You won't need to do this very often—if at all—but selecting this option makes life a little more convenient if the occasion ever arises. By the way, bin stands for binary; it has nothing to do with the Windows Recycle Bin. Click Next.

If you get a warning message like this, it means that MySQL is already installed as a Windows service. If you click Yes, the wizard will continue happily, but then fail at the final hurdle. (I know—I found out the hard way.) You must click No and choose a different name from the drop-down menu in the Service Name field.

10. A fresh installation of MySQL has no security settings, so anyone can tamper with your data. MySQL uses the name **root** to signify the main database administrator with unrestricted control over all aspects of the database. Choose a password that you can remember, and enter it in both boxes. Unless you access your development server from a different computer over a network, leave the Enable root access from remote machines check box unchecked.

Do *not* check Create An Anonymous Account. It will make your database very insecure.

If you are upgrading an existing version of Windows Essentials and want to keep your current root password, deselect the Modify Security Settings check box.

Click Next when you have finished.

11. At long last, everything is ready. Click Execute. If you have installed a software fire-wall, such as Norton Internet Security, it will probably warn you that MySQL is trying to connect to a DNS server. You must allow the connection; otherwise, MySQL will never work.

12. Assuming that all was okay, you should see this screen, which confirms that everything went smoothly. MySQL should now be running—even if you selected the option not to start automatically (the option applies only to automatic start on bootup).

13. If you want to change the configuration at a later date or remove MySQL as a Windows service, launch the Configuration Wizard from the Windows Start button by choosing Programs ➤ MySQL ➤ MySQL Server 5.0 ➤ MySQL Server Instance Config Wizard. You will be presented with the dialog box shown here.

This dialog box gives you the option to change the various settings by going through all the dialog boxes again or removing the server instance. This second option does not remove MySQL from your system, but it is intended for use if you no longer want Windows to start MySQL automatically each time you boot your computer. Unfortunately, it removes not only the automatic startup, but also the configuration file. The section "Starting and stopping MySQL manually on Windows" offers a less-radical solution.

Changing the default table type on Windows Essentials

The instructions in this section are required only if you selected Multifunctional Database in step 4 of "Configuring MySQL Windows Essentials."

The Windows Configuration Wizard sets InnoDB as the default table storage engine for a multifunctional database. To work with blogging engines, you should reset the default to MyISAM. All it requires is a simple change to the MySQL configuration file: my.ini.

1. Use Windows Explorer to navigate to the folder in which MySQL was installed. The default is C:\Program Files\MySQL\MySQL Server 5.0.

2. Locate the file called my.ini, and double-click it. The file will open in Notepad, ready for editing.

3. Approximately 80 lines from the top you should find a line that reads as follows:

```
default-storage-engine=INNODB
```

Change it to the following:

```
default-storage-engine=MyISAM
```

4. Save the file and close it. To make the change effective, restart MySQL. MySQL will now create all new tables in the default MyISAM format. To use the InnoDB format for a database, you can change the table type in phpMyAdmin, the graphical interface for MySQL that you will install later in the chapter.

Starting and stopping MySQL manually on Windows

Most of the time, MySQL will be configured to start up automatically, and you can forget about it entirely. There are times, however, when you need to know how to start or stop MySQL manually—whether for maintenance, to conserve resources, or because you're paranoid about security (a physical firewall is probably a much better solution).

1. Select Control Panel from the Windows Start menu. Double-click the Administrative Tools icon and then double-click the Services icon in the window that opens.

2. In the Services panel, scroll down to find MySQL and highlight it by clicking once. You can now use the video recorder–type icons at the top of the panel to stop or start the server, as shown. The text links on the left of the panel do the same.

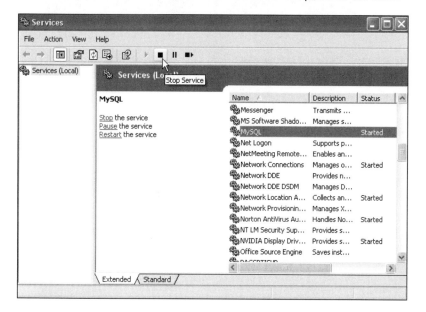

3. To change the automatic startup option, highlight MySQL in the Services panel, right-click to reveal a context menu, and choose Properties.

4. In the dialog box that opens, activate the Startup type drop-down menu and choose Automatic, Manual, or Disabled. Click OK. That's all there is to it.

Using the MySQL monitor on Windows

Although most of your interaction with MySQL will be through your blogging engine or phpMyAdmin, it's useful to know how to access MySQL the traditional way through the MySQL monitor (or the Command Line Client, as it's called in Windows Essentials). It's also a good way to test that your installation went without problems.

To start a session From the Windows Start button, select Programs ➤ MySQL ➤ MySQL Server 5.0 ➤ MySQL Command Line Client. This will open the Command Line Client and ask you for your password. Type in the root password that you chose in step 10 of the section "Configuring MySQL Windows Essentials" and press Enter. As long as the server is running—and you typed your password correctly—you will see a welcome message similar to the one shown here.

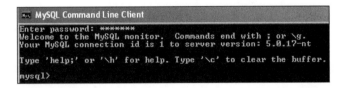

If you get your password wrong, your computer will beep and close the window. If you find this happening repeatedly, even though you're sure you typed in your password correctly, there are two likely explanations. The first is that your Caps Lock key is on—MySQL passwords are case-sensitive. The other is that the MySQL server isn't running. Refer to the previous section on how to control MySQL manually before doing too much damage by banging your forehead on the keyboard.

> *Being unable to connect to MySQL because the server isn't running is probably the most common beginner's mistake. The MySQL server runs in the background, waiting for requests. Opening the Command Line Client does not start MySQL; it opens the MySQL monitor, which is a channel for you to send instructions to the server. Equally, closing the Command Line Client does not stop MySQL. The server continues running in the background until the computer is closed down or until you stop it manually.*

Ending your session After you finish working with the MySQL monitor, type exit or quit at the mysql> prompt, followed by Enter. The MySQL Command Line Client window will automatically close.

Now take a well-earned rest while I get the good Mac folks sorted out. Skip ahead a few pages to the section "Using MySQL with phpMyAdmin (Windows & Mac)."

Setting up on Mac OS X

After leafing through so many pages of Windows instructions, you might be surprised that this section is considerably shorter. It's shorter because Apache and Perl are preinstalled on Mac OS X. PHP is also preinstalled, but the default version is not suitable for working with the latest version of MySQL. Fortunately, an excellent Mac PKG file is available for free download, which will provide you with a full-featured, up-to-date version of PHP 5.

Most of the setup is done through the familiar Mac interface, but you need to edit some configuration files. Although these are ordinary text files, they are normally hidden, so you can't use TextEdit to work with them. Instead, you need a specialist text editor, such as BBEdit, which is capable of editing hidden files.

If you don't own a suitable text editor, I suggest that you download a copy of TextWrangler from www.barebones.com/products/textwrangler/. TextWrangler is a cut-down version of BBEdit; it has fewer features, but is perfectly adequate for what's required here—and it's free. All the instructions have been tested on both BBEdit and TextWrangler.

> *These instructions have been tested on Mac OS X 10.3 and 10.4. They do not cover Mac OS X Server, which uses a different version of Apache, and comes with MySQL preinstalled. I have assumed that if you have the skill to run the server version of OS X, you should be able to handle the configuration without further assistance.*

Using Apache on Mac OS X

Although I have told Windows users to install Apache 2.0, the default version of Apache that comes preinstalled with Mac OS X (even Tiger) is Apache 1.3. It's an excellent web server still in widespread use, and it does everything you need for developing blogs and other dynamic websites on your Mac. What's more, because it's preinstalled, all you need to do is switch it on. Make sure that you're logged into Mac OS X with Administrative privileges and you're ready to go.

Starting and stopping Apache

1. Open System Preferences and select Sharing in Internet & Network, as shown.

2. In the dialog box that opens, click the lock in the bottom-left corner, if necessary, to allow you to make changes, and enter your password when prompted. Highlight Personal Web Sharing on the Services tab, as shown in Figure 2-5, and then click the Start button on the right. A message will appear, informing you that personal web sharing is starting up. After it's running, the label on the button changes to Stop. Use this button to stop and restart Apache whenever you install a new version of PHP or make any changes to the configuration files. Click the lock again, if you want to prevent accidental changes.

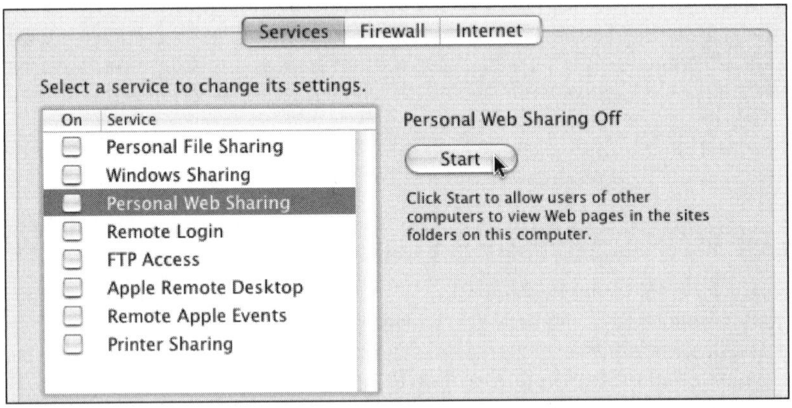

Figure 2-5. The Apache web server on a Mac is switched on and off in the Sharing section of System Preferences.

3. Open your favorite browser and type `http://localhost/~username/` into the address bar, substituting your own Mac username for *username*. You should see a page like that shown in Figure 2-6, confirming that Apache is running. That's all there is to it.

Figure 2-6. Confirmation that Apache is running successfully on Mac OS X

Sometimes, Macs seem to develop a personality of their own. If you have a local network, you might discover that the `localhost` *part of the URL changes to something like* `deathstar.local` *or whatever you have called your computer. I have two Macs, one called "Power Book" and the other called "David Powers' Mac Mini." These rather uninspired names translate to* `power-book.local` *and* `david-powers-mac-mini.local` *(illegal characters, such as apostrophes, are removed, and spaces are replaced by hyphens). The advantage is that I can access sites on my PowerBook from the Mac Mini and vice versa. However, for testing on the same machine,* `localhost` *is much shorter to type. After you use* `localhost` *a few times, your Mac will probably give up trying to be so clever and accept the shorter version. You can also use* `127.0.0.1` *as a synonym for* `localhost`.

Where to locate your web files

As the message in Figure 2-6 indicates, the place to store all your web files, including any blogs that you decide to test, is in the Sites folder in your home folder. You need to keep them there not only for the sake of tidiness but also because Apache needs to process (or **parse**) PHP and CGI scripts before it can display the output in your browser. Unlike ordinary web pages, you can't just double-click them in Finder and expect them to pop up in Safari or your default browser. To view a page that uses PHP and/or CGI on your local computer, you must enter the correct URL in the browser address bar in the same way as you access a site on the Internet.

The address for the top level of your Sites folder is http://localhost/~*username*/. Any subfolders are accessed by adding the folder name to the end of the URL. If you plan to test each of the blogging engines in the rest of this book, it's a good idea to create a subfolder for each one in Sites.

If you're the only person using the computer, you might prefer to locate all your files in Macintosh HD:Library:WebServer:Documents. It works exactly the same way, but instead of needing to include a tilde (~) followed by your username in the URL every time, you use just http://localhost/ as the address. If you test it now, you will see the same screen as shown in Figure 2-4. It makes no difference whether you use the central location or your own Sites folder. Just choose whichever is more convenient for you.

Using PHP on Mac OS X

Although Mac OS X comes with PHP preinstalled, it's a very cut-back version and is not automatically enabled. What's more, enabling it is nowhere near as straightforward as switching on Apache. To make matters even worse, the engine underlying Mac OS X is Unix, and without a solid understanding of Unix, installing PHP the traditional way can turn into a nightmare if anything unexpected happens.

Now the good news. The Mac PHP community owes a great debt of gratitude to a software engineer called Marc Liyanage, who creates precompiled packages for all major upgrades of PHP. The only drawback is that these packages involve a large download (about 28MB). Even if you have a slow Internet connection, the large download is worth it. You get a full-featured version of PHP that works "straight out of the box." If you run into problems, there's a searchable support forum on Marc's website, on which answers tend to be fast and accurate. It should be your first port of call in case of installation problems.

> *PHP relies heavily on the availability of external code libraries. It is essential that you have installed all the latest Apple system software updates before proceeding.*

Downloading and installing a precompiled PHP package

1. Marc Liyanage creates different packages for Apache 1.3 and Apache 2. The default installation in Mac OS X at the time of this writing is Apache 1.3, but it's important to check whether it's the same in your case. In Finder, open the Utilities folder in Applications and launch Terminal.

2. A window like the one shown here opens.

```
  ⊖ ○ ○              Terminal — bash — 80x24
Last login: Fri Dec 23 09:23:15 on console
Welcome to Darwin!
Vigor19:~ davidpowers$ ▊
```

It doesn't look very impressive, but if you've ever worked on a Windows or DOS computer, it should be familiar as the Command Prompt, and it performs the same function. All instructions to the computer are inserted as written commands at what's known as the **shell prompt**. This is the final line in the screenshot and it looks something like this:

Vigor19:~ davidpowers$

The first part (before the colon) is the name of your Macintosh hard disk. The tilde (~) is the Unix shorthand for your home directory (or folder). It should be followed by your username and a dollar sign. As you navigate around the hard disk, your location is indicated in place of ~. All commands in Terminal are followed by Return.

3. To find out which version of Apache is running on your Mac, type the following command:

httpd -v

After pressing Return, you should see a window similar to the one shown here.

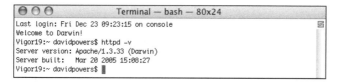

```
  ⊖ ○ ○              Terminal — bash — 80x24
Last login: Fri Dec 23 09:23:15 on console
Welcome to Darwin!
Vigor19:~ davidpowers$ httpd -v
Server version: Apache/1.3.33 (Darwin)
Server built:   Mar 20 2005 15:08:27
Vigor19:~ davidpowers$ ▊
```

This window tells you the version of Apache and the date it was built. You need the first two numbers of the server version—in this case, 1.3—to ensure that you download the correct PHP package.

4. Go to www.entropy.ch/software/macosx/php/, scroll about halfway down the page, and select the version of PHP 5 for Mac OS X 10.3/10.4 that doesn't require a commercial license for PDFLib (unless you have a license key) and that also matches the version of Apache running on your computer. Read any installation instructions on the site because they contain the most up-to-date information about special requirements or restrictions.

5. When the download is complete, the disk image should automatically mount the contents on your desktop. If it doesn't, just double-click it. The Extras folder contains either the commercial or the noncommercial version of the PDFLib library, neither of which is required for this book. Copy the Extras folder to your hard disk and explore it later. Double-click the PHP PKG file and follow the instructions onscreen.

6. Your upgraded version of PHP will become available as soon as you restart Apache, but before you do that, you need to make a minor change to the PHP configuration file php.ini.

Configuring PHP to display errors on Mac OS X

Marc Liyanage's package for PHP uses a version of php.ini that automatically turns off the display of error messages. Although no one likes seeing error messages, when using PHP for development, it's essential to see what's gone wrong and why.

1. Open BBEdit or TextWrangler. From the File menu, choose Open Hidden, and navigate to Macintosh HD:usr:local:php5:lib:php.ini. Because php.ini is a protected file, you need to select All Files from the Enable drop-down menu at the top of the Open dialog box, shown here. Click Open.

2. When php.ini opens in your text editor, you'll see that it's a long text file and that most lines begin with a semicolon. This means they are comments; the configuration commands are on lines that don't have a semicolon at the beginning.

To make it easier to identify the correct place in the files you edit, choose Preferences from the BBEdit or TextWrangler menu, and then select Text Status Display. Make sure that the Show Line Numbers check box is selected. Close the Preferences dialog box, and scroll down until you see the command shown on line 353 in the screenshot alongside.

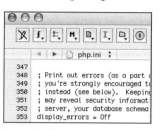

3. The icon of pencil with a line through it (shown at the top left of the screenshot) indicates that this is a read-only file. To edit it, click the pencil icon. You will see the prompt shown here.

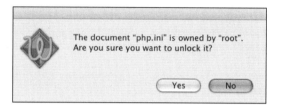

4. Click Yes and change the command shown on line 353 as follows (use the line number only as a guide—it might be different in a later version of PHP):

display_errors = **On**

5. About 10 lines further down, locate the following command:

log_errors = On

Change it to

log_errors = **Off**

6. From the File menu, choose Save, and enter your Mac administrator password when prompted. Close php.ini.

7. Restart Apache. You're now ready to test your PHP installation.

> *If you ever need to make further adjustments to your PHP configuration, follow the same procedure to edit php.ini, and restart Apache for the changes to take effect.*

1. Open a blank file in TextWrangler or BBEdit, and type the following line of code:

   `<?php phpinfo(); ?>`

2. Save the file in the Sites subfolder of your home folder as index.php.

3. Open a browser and enter the following URL in the address bar:

   `http://localhost/~`*username*`/index.php`

   Use the name of your Mac Home folder (the one identified by a little house icon in the Finder sidebar) in place of *username*.

4. Press Return. You should see a screen similar to that shown in Figure 2-7. This screen not only confirms that PHP is installed and running but it also provides masses of detail about the way the installation has been configured. You don't need to concern yourself with this information unless you start developing websites with PHP on a serious basis, but this is the page you will always be asked to display if you ever need to check why PHP doesn't work as expected.

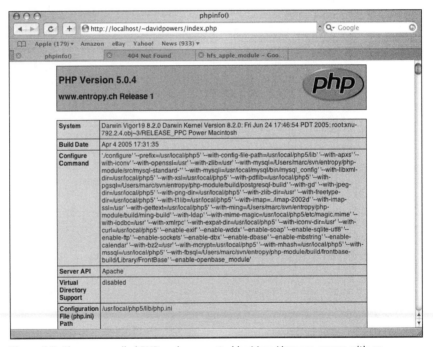

Figure 2-7. The precompiled PHP package created by Marc Liyanage comes with an impressive range of features.

At the time of this writing, PHP 5.0.4 is the most up-to-date, stable version of PHP available as a Mac package. Marc Liyanage creates the packages on a voluntary basis, so there is always a delay following the release of a new version of PHP. Although Windows users have been recommended to install PHP 5.1, everything required for this book is supported by PHP 5.0.4. So don't worry that you're missing out on anything.

Enabling support for CGI scripting on Mac OS X

Movable Type also requires CGI scripting to be enabled on your web server. The excellent news is that it's already turned on by default in Mac OS X. There are only two things you need to know to get CGI scripts to work on your computer:

- Where to locate CGI scripts
- How to set the correct permissions

Deciding where to locate CGI scripts

CGI scripts should normally be run in a separate folder from the rest of your web files. Because they are handled in a different way from ordinary files, Apache needs to know both where to find them and how to handle them. If you locate all your websites in Macintosh HD:Library:WebServer:Documents, everything is already configured—just place all your CGI files in Macintosh HD:Library:WebServer:CGI-Executables. The folder already exists, and you don't need to make any changes to your Apache configuration. The URL for your CGI scripts is automatically http://localhost/cgi-bin/. However, if you want to keep your web and blog files in the Sites subfolder of your home folder, you need to make some changes to your personal Apache configuration file.

Configuring Apache to support CGI in your home folder

1. Launch BBEdit or TextWrangler, and choose File ➤ Open Hidden. Navigate to Macintosh HD:private:etc:httpd:users:*username*.conf, where *username* is your Mac long username. If you cannot select the file, make sure that the Enable drop-down menu at the top of the Open dialog box is set to All Files. Click Open.

2. Unlike the main Apache configuration file, which contains more than 1000 lines, your personal configuration file will probably contain only a few lines, similar to the file in the following screenshot.

3. Place your cursor at the end of the file and press Return to enter a new line. You will be presented with a warning saying that the file is owned by root and asking you to confirm that you want to unlock it. Click Yes.

4. Insert the following directive. Make sure that you copy it correctly—Apache is very fussy about the correct mixture of uppercase and lowercase. Also make sure that there is no space in SetHandler. Use your own Mac username in place of *username*.

```
<Directory "/Users/username/Sites/cgi-bin/">
  Options ExecCGI
  SetHandler cgi-script
</Directory>
```

5. Choose File ➤ Save. Enter your Mac administrative password when prompted.

6. Restart Apache, as described earlier.

7. Create a subfolder called cgi-bin in the Sites folder of your home folder, which is where you should store all CGI scripts.

Creating a test CGI script

1. With BBEdit or TextWrangler still open, choose File ➤ New.

2. Type the following script into new file:

```
#! /usr/bin/perl

print "Content-type: text/plain\r\n\r\n";
print "Yes, it does really work!\n"
```

3. Save the file as mactest.cgi either in Macintosh HD:Library:WebServer: CGI-Executables or in the cgi-bin folder of your Sites folder.

Setting the correct permissions for CGI scripts

Because CGI scripts contain code that needs to be executed, simply saving them in the correct folder is not enough. You need to set the right permissions for Apache to be able to run them. Unfortunately, you can't do this by using the Get Info panel from Finder, but you need to do it at the command line in Terminal.

Changing permissions in Terminal

1. After saving a CGI script, open Terminal (Applications ➤ Utilities ➤ Terminal) and change directory to the folder in which your CGI scripts are stored. The command will be

```
cd /Library/WebServer/CGI-Executables
```

Or if you are using the cgi-bin folder in your Sites folder, it will be

```
cd ~/Sites/cgi-bin
```

2. Change the permissions on the CGI script by typing chmod 755 followed by the filename. So, in the case of the test file you have just created:

chmod 755 mactest.cgi

3. If you need to change more than one file, you can do them simultaneously by using the following command:

chmod 755 *.cgi

4. You can now check that CGI scripts are working by loading mactest.cgi into a browser. You should see a reassuring message similar to the screenshot shown here.

5. If you are using the cgi-bin folder in your Sites folder and don't see the message—or if you see the raw script—try running the script in Macintosh HD:Library:WebServer:CGI-Executables.

If you get a message about an internal server error, open BBEdit or TextWrangler ➤ Preferences and choose the Text Files: Saving category. Make sure that Default Line Breaks is set to Unix and then create a new version of the file.

Setting up MySQL on Mac OS X

MySQL is available as a Mac PKG file, so everything is taken care of for you, apart from some minor configuration.

> It's important to note that when upgrading an existing installation of MySQL, the Mac installer will not move your data files. You must first create a backup, as described at the end of this chapter, and then reload them.

Downloading and installing MySQL

1. Go to http://dev.mysql.com/downloads/.

2. Select the link for the recommended Generally Available release of MySQL database server and standard clients. Scroll down to the Mac OS X downloads section and choose the standard installer package. Make sure that you get the right one—there are separate packages for Panther and Tiger. As you can see from the screenshot in the next step, the PKG filename includes not only the MySQL version number (in this case 5.0.17) but also the version of OS X for which it has been compiled (osx10.4). The size of the download file is approximately 20MB. (If you are still using Jaguar, you cannot use MySQL 5.0; you need to download the most recent version of MySQL 4.1 instead.)

3. When the download is complete, the disk image will mount the contents on your desktop. If this doesn't happen automatically, double-click the DMG icon.

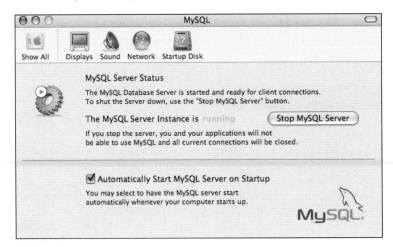

4. Double-click the mysql-standard-x.x.x.pkg icon to start the installation process (the precise name of the file will depend on the version downloaded). The Mac OS X installer opens. Follow the instructions onscreen.

5. Open a Finder window and drag the MySQL.prefPane icon onto Applications ➤ System Preferences. A MySQL control panel installs in your System Preferences. A dialog box appears, asking whether you want the control panel to be available just to yourself or to all users. Make your choice, and click Install.

Once installed, the control panel opens automatically and should start the MySQL server. Occasionally, the first-time startup incorrectly reports The MySQL Server Instance is running, but the button on the right side of the control panel still says Start MySQL Server. Click the button and enter your Mac administrator password when prompted. If this fails to solve the problem, restart your computer. Before restarting, I recommend that you select the option to have the MySQL server start automatically whenever your computer starts up, as shown here.

Automatic startup works without a hitch on Mac OS X 10.3 (Panther), but there appears to be a problem on 10.4 (Tiger). Even if you select the automatic startup option, you need to open the preference pane and click Start MySQL Server. *Hopefully, this bug will have been eliminated by the time you read this.*

The installation process adds a MySQL icon to the Other section of System Preferences, as shown. Use this icon whenever you need to start or stop the MySQL server.

6. You can now discard the disk image, although it's a good idea to keep the ReadMe.txt in case of problems.

Adding MySQL to your PATH

Most of the time, you will access MySQL through your blogging package or phpMyAdmin (introduced later in this chapter), but there will be times when you need to access it directly in Terminal. To avoid having to type out the full path to the correct directory every time, you can add it to the PATH in your environmental variables. If you have a new installation of Panther or Tiger, Terminal will use what is known as the "bash shell." If you have upgraded from Jaguar using Archive and Install, you will almost certainly be using the "tcsh shell." The only way to make sure is to open Terminal (in Applications ➤ Utilities) and check the title bar. It will either say Terminal — bash, as shown in the following screenshot, or Terminal — tcsh. Use the appropriate set of instructions.

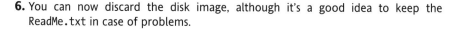

Amending PATH in the bash shell

1. Open BBEdit or TextWrangler.

2. From the File menu, choose Open Hidden and browse to your home folder. If there is a file called .profile (with a period as the first character), as shown in the screenshot, highlight it, and click Open.

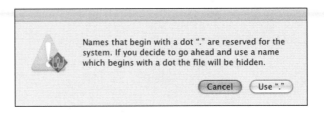

3. The file will exist only if you have already made changes to the way Terminal operates. If .profile doesn't exist, click Cancel, and open a blank file.

4. If you have opened an existing version of .profile, add the following code on a separate line at the end. Otherwise, enter it in the blank page.

```
export PATH="$PATH:/usr/local/mysql/bin"
```

5. Select File ➤ Save, and save the file as .profile in your own home folder. The period at the beginning of the filename should provoke the warning shown in the screenshot.

6. Select Use "." and close your text editor. The next time you open Terminal, the MySQL program directory will have been added to your PATH.

Amending PATH in the tcsh shell

1. Open Terminal and enter the following command at the shell prompt:

```
echo 'setenv PATH /usr/local/mysql/bin:$PATH' >> ~/.tcshrc
```

Make sure that you copy everything exactly, including the quotes and spacing as shown.

2. Press Return and close Terminal. The next time you open Terminal, the MySQL program directory will have been added to your PATH.

Securing MySQL on Mac OS X

Although you have a fully functioning installation of MySQL, by default it has no security. Even if you're the only person working on your computer, you need to set up a similar system of passwords and user accounts as on your hosting company's server. There's one important account that exists by default on all MySQL servers. It's called root and it is the main database administrator with unlimited powers over database files. When you first install MySQL, access to the root account isn't password-protected, so you need to block this gaping security gap. The MySQL root user, by the way, is totally unrelated to the Mac OS X root user, which is disabled by default. Enabling root for MySQL has *no* effect on the OS X root user.

> *If you have just added MySQL to your PATH, you must close and reopen Terminal before embarking on this section. Otherwise, Terminal won't be able to find MySQL.*

Setting the MySQL root password

1. Open Terminal and type the following command:

```
mysql -u root
```

The command contains three elements:

- mysql: The name of the program
- -u: Tells the program that you want to log in as a specified user
- root: The name of the user

2. You should see a welcome message like this:

```
○ ○ ○          Terminal — mysql — 80x24
Last login: Fri Dec 23 17:24:50 on ttyp1
Welcome to Darwin!
Vigor19:~ davidpowers$ mysql -u root
Welcome to the MySQL monitor.  Commands end with ; or \g.
Your MySQL connection id is 15 to server version: 5.0.17-standard

Type 'help;' or '\h' for help. Type '\c' to clear the buffer.

mysql>
```

3. The most common problem is getting an error message like this instead:

```
○ ○ ○          Terminal — bash — 80x24
Last login: Fri Dec 23 17:21:40 on ttyp1
Welcome to Darwin!
Vigor19:~ davidpowers$ mysql -u root
ERROR 2002 (HY000): Can't connect to local MySQL server through socket '/tmp/mys
ql.sock' (2)
Vigor19:~ davidpowers$
```

It means that mysqld, the MySQL server, is not running. Use the MySQL control panel in System Preferences to start the server.

Another common problem is for Terminal to report command not found. That means you have either mistyped the command or that you haven't added the MySQL program files directory to your PATH, as described in the previous section.

4. Assuming that you have logged in successfully, as described in step 2, type the following command at the mysql> prompt:

```
use mysql
```

5. This command tells MySQL that you want to use the database called mysql, which contains all the details of authorized users and the privileges they have to work on database files. You should see the message Database changed, which means MySQL is ready for you to work on the files controlling administrative privileges. Now enter the command to set a password for the root user. Substitute *myPassword* with the actual password you want to use. Also make sure you use quotes where indicated and finish the command with a semicolon.

```
UPDATE user SET password = PASSWORD('myPassword') WHERE user = 'root';
```

6. Next, remove anonymous access to MySQL:

```
DELETE FROM user WHERE user = '';
```

The quotes before the semicolon are two single quotes with no space in between.

7. Tell MySQL to update the privileges table:

```
FLUSH PRIVILEGES;
```

The sequence of commands should produce a series of results like this:

```
●●●                Terminal — mysql — 80x24
Last login: Fri Dec 23 17:24:50 on ttyp1
Welcome to Darwin!
Vigor19:~ davidpowers$ mysql -u root
Welcome to the MySQL monitor.  Commands end with ; or \g.
Your MySQL connection id is 15 to server version: 5.0.17-standard

Type 'help;' or '\h' for help. Type '\c' to clear the buffer.

mysql> use mysql
Reading table information for completion of table and column names
You can turn off this feature to get a quicker startup with -A

Database changed
mysql> UPDATE user SET password = PASSWORD('foED') WHERE user = 'root';
Query OK, 2 rows affected (0.31 sec)
Rows matched: 2  Changed: 2  Warnings: 0

mysql> DELETE FROM user WHERE user = '';
Query OK, 2 rows affected (0.04 sec)

mysql> FLUSH PRIVILEGES;
Query OK, 0 rows affected (0.24 sec)

mysql>
```

8. To exit the MySQL monitor, type exit, followed by Return. This simply ends your session with the MySQL monitor. *It does not shut down the MySQL server.*

9. Now try to log back in by using the same command as in step 2. MySQL won't let you in. Anonymous access and password-free access have been removed. To get in this time, you need to tell MySQL that you want to use a password:

```
mysql -u root -p
```

10. When you press Return, you will be prompted for your password. Nothing will appear onscreen as you type, but as long as you enter the correct password, MySQL will let you back in. Congratulations, you now have a secure installation of MySQL.

Using MySQL with phpMyAdmin (Windows and Mac)

Once your blogging package has been set up, it will communicate directly with your database. Before you can get to that stage, though, you need to perform a few administrative chores. Although you can do everything using MySQL monitor, it's a lot easier to use a graphic interface called phpMyAdmin. Many hosting companies provide it as the standard interface to MySQL, so it's useful to experiment with it on your own computer to get a feel for how it works.

As the name suggests, phpMyAdmin is a PHP-based administrative system for MySQL. It has been around since 1998 and constantly evolves to keep pace with MySQL developments. It works on Windows, Mac OS X, and Linux, and it currently supports all versions of MySQL from 3.23.32 to 5.0. phpMyAdmin is open source and is free.

Downloading and installing phpMyAdmin

1. Go to the project's website at www.phpMyAdmin.net and download the latest stable version. The version number of phpMyAdmin is frequently followed by pl and a number. The "pl" stands for **patch level** and indicates a fix for a bug or security problem. The files can be downloaded in three types of compressed file: BZIP2, GZIP, and ZIP. Choose whichever format you have the decompression software for. In the case of Windows users, this is most likely to be ZIP (3.4MB). Mac OS X users should be able to choose any format. BZIP2 is the smallest download (1.9MB).

2. Unzip the downloaded file. It will extract the contents to a folder called phpMyAdmin-*x.x.x*, where *x* represents the version number.

3. Highlight the folder icon and cut it to your computer's clipboard. On Windows, paste it inside the folder designated as your web server root (C:\htdocs, if you followed my example). If you're on a Mac and want phpMyAdmin to be available to all users, put the folder in Macintosh HD:Library:WebServer:Documents, rather than in your own Sites folder.

4. Rename the folder you have just moved to this: phpMyAdmin.

5. Like Apache and PHP, phpMyAdmin uses a text file to store all the configuration details. Prior to version 2.7.0 (released in December 2005), this was called config.inc.php and it was necessary to make the changes directly inside that file. Beginning with version 2.7.0, this file has been renamed config.default.php, and should no longer be edited. Instead, you store your own personal configuration details in a new file, which should be named config.inc.php.

   Although this sounds challenging, it's actually quite straightforward. Instead of searching through a file more than 800 lines long to find the right command, you store your settings in a very short file—and if you upgrade to a later version of phpMyAdmin, all you need to do is move the file to your new installation.

   So, open a text editor (such as Notepad on Windows or TextWrangler on Mac OS X) and get ready to create the file.

   > *By the time you read this, phpMyAdmin may include a script to automate the creation of config.inc.php. Creating it by hand isn't difficult, though. Just remember that PHP is case-sensitive, so copy the commands carefully. Sample files for typical setups are available in the download files for this chapter.*

6. If you are the only person who uses your computer and you don't need to password-protect access to phpMyAdmin, type the following code into a blank document:

```php
<?php
$cfg['Servers'][$i]['extension'] = 'mysqli';
$cfg['Servers'][$i]['password']  = 'mysqlRootPassword';
?>
```

   Use your own MySQL root password in place of *mysqlRootPassword*. I find this the most convenient way to work on my development computer, but it may not be appropriate for everyone because it gives anyone using your computer full access to all your MySQL databases, including the power to alter and delete existing data.

7. If your circumstances dictate the need to password-protect access to phpMyAdmin, use the following code instead of that shown in step 6:

```php
<?php
$cfg['Servers'][$i]['extension'] = 'mysqli';
$cfg['Servers'][$i]['auth_type'] = 'http';
?>
```

You will be prompted for a username and password each time you launch phpMyAdmin. Log in the first time as root. After setting up individual user accounts and privileges as described later in the chapter, you can log in with a different username, but your privileges will be limited to those granted to that particular user.

8. Save the file as config.inc.php in the main phpMyAdmin folder.

9. Open a browser and enter http://localhost/phpMyAdmin/ in the address bar (on a Mac, if you put phpMyAdmin in your Sites folder, use http://localhost/~*username*/phpMyAdmin/).

    If you used the code in step 6, you should see the phpMyAdmin welcome screen right away, as shown in Figure 2-8.

    If you used the code in step 7, enter root as the username and your MySQL root password when prompted.

10. In the unlikely event that phpMyAdmin reports that it cannot auto-detect the correct URL, add the following line (shown in bold) to config.inc.php:

```php
<?php
$cfg['PmaAbsoluteUri'] = 'http://localhost/phpMyAdmin/';
$cfg['Servers'][$i]['extension'] = 'mysqli';
```

On a Mac, use http://localhost/~*username*/phpMyAdmin/ if you put phpMyAdmin in your Sites folder.

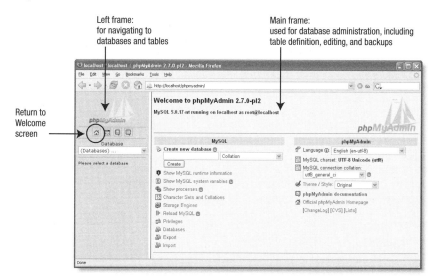

Figure 2-8. phpMyAdmin is a very user-friendly and stable graphical interface to MySQL.

11. If you opted for the http login method in step 7, you will find two more options listed at the bottom of the MySQL section of the front page, just beneath Import (as shown in the screenshot). These are self-explanatory: They allow you to change your login password and to log out of phpMyAdmin once you have finished.

> *If you get a message saying that the server is not responding or that the socket is not correctly configured, make sure that the MySQL server is running. If you still have problems, load* index.php, *the PHP test file that you created earlier, into your browser and check that the mysql and mysqli extensions are listed in your PHP configuration.*

Setting up your blog database with phpMyAdmin

phpMyAdmin is a frames-based web interface to MySQL. As shown in Figure 2-8, the left frame is used for navigation and stays onscreen at all times. The main frame on the right displays screens that allow you to create databases, define tables, browse through records and edit them, perform backups, and much more. However, I plan to concentrate only on those areas that you need to get your blog up and running:

- Creating a database
- Creating a user account for the database
- Giving the user account the necessary privileges
- Backing up and moving a database to another server

The Database drop-down menu in the left frame is the main way to navigate through phpMyAdmin. Each name in the list is a hyperlink that can be used to load details of a particular table into the main frame. On a brand new installation of MySQL, the drop-down menu contains just three entries:

- information_schema(16)
- mysql (17)
- test (-)

The first entry, information_schema, is a virtual database created automatically by MySQL, and it contains details of all your databases. It's a read-only database, so any attempt to edit it will result in an error. (It's new to MySQL 5.0, so you won't see it if you're using an earlier version of MySQL.) The mysql database controls user access to all your databases, so don't make any changes while exploring. In fact, you should normally never work directly inside the mysql database because phpMyAdmin has a much more user-friendly interface for administering user accounts.

Each blogging engine uses a different database structure, so you will need to set up a separate database for each one. In the following pages, I'll show you how I set up everything for a WordPress blog (WordPress is covered in detail in Chapter 5).

Creating a new database

1. If it's not already open, launch phpMyAdmin in your browser.

2. Type the name of your new database in the Create new database field at the top left of the Welcome screen, shown here. Collation determines the sort order of records, but the default setting is fine for English and most West European languages. Click Create.

> **Welcome to phpMyAdmin 2.7.0-pl2**
>
> MySQL 5.0.17-nt running on localhost as root@localhost
>
> **MySQL**
>
> Create new database ⓘ
> wordpress   Collation ▾
> Create

3. phpMyAdmin then presents you with a screen reporting that the database has been created and giving you the opportunity to create a new table. Most blogging engines do that for you automatically. So let's move straight on to setting up the necessary user accounts to work with your new database.

> *You will find detailed instructions for how to define database tables in Chapter 7, when you come to design a blog of your own.*

Creating a user account and setting the privileges for the blog

1. Return to the phpMyAdmin Welcome page. Click the home icon (the little house on the left of Figure 2-8).

2. Click the Privileges link in the left column of the Welcome screen (it's the seventh item below Create new database). The User overview screen opens. If you have never worked with MySQL before, you should have only one user: root. Click the Add a new User link halfway down the page.

3. In the page that opens, enter the name of the user account that you want to create in the User name field. Select Local from the Host drop-down menu, which automatically enters localhost in the next field. Selecting this option means the user can connect to

> **Add a new User**
>
> Login Information
>
> | User name: | Use text field: ▾ | davidsblog |
> |---|---|---|
> | Host: | Local ▾ | localhost |
> | Password: | Use text field: ▾ | ******* |
> | Re-type: | | ******* |
> | Generate Password: | Generate   Copy | |

MySQL only from the same computer. Then enter a password in the Password field and type it again for confirmation in the Re-type field. The Login Information table should look like the screenshot shown alongside.

4. Beneath the Login Information table is one labeled Global privileges, which give a user privileges on all databases, including the mysql one (which contains sensitive information). This is insecure, so leave the Global privileges table unchecked, and click the Go button at the bottom of the page.

5. The next page confirms that the user has been created, and displays many options that you can edit, beginning with the Global privileges table again. Scroll down below to the section labeled Database-specific privileges. Activate the drop-down menu, as shown here, to display a list of all databases on your system. Select the name of your blog database.

6. The next screen allows you to set the privileges for this user on just the selected database. Click Check All, and then deselect GRANT. The Database-specific privileges table should look like the screenshot. Click the top Go button, as shown.

phpMyAdmin frequently offers you a variety of options on the same page, each of which normally has its own Go button. Always click the one at the foot of or next to the section that relates to the options you want to set.

7. phpMyAdmin presents you with confirmation that the privileges have been updated for the user account. The page also displays the Database-specific privileges table again, in case you made a mistake and need to change anything. Assuming that everything is okay, you're ready to blog!

Editing a user account's privileges

1. If you ever need to make any changes to a user's privileges, launch phpMyAdmin and click the Privileges link on the Welcome screen.

2. Locate the name of the user account in the User overview table, and click the Edit Privileges icon to the right of the listing, as shown. You can also delete users by selecting the check box to the left of the User column and then selecting the method of deletion in Remove selected users before clicking Go. The default method just deletes the users, so they remain active until the privileges table is reloaded or the MySQL server is restarted.

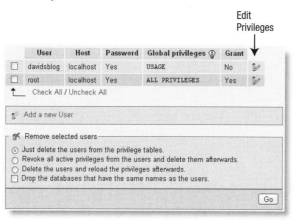

Backing up and transferring your blog to another server

You can't just copy a MySQL database file from your hard drive and upload it to your website, which can be very confusing. Even if you find the right files (on Windows, they're located in C:\Program Files\MySQL\MySQL Server 5.0\data), you are likely to damage them unless the MySQL server is turned off. Anyway, most hosting companies won't permit you to upload the raw files because it would also involve shutting down their server, causing a great deal of inconvenience for everyone.

Nevertheless, moving a database from one server to another is very easy. All it involves is creating a backup dump of the data, and loading it into the other database with phpMyAdmin. The *dump* is a text file that contains all the necessary Structured Query Language (SQL) commands to populate an individual table or even an entire database elsewhere. phpMyAdmin can create backups of your entire MySQL server, individual databases, selected tables, or individual tables. To make things simple, the following instructions show you how to back up only a single database.

> *These instructions do not work until you actually have some data in your database. Bookmark this section to come back to later after you have worked with at least one of the other chapters.*

Creating a backup

1. Launch phpMyAdmin and select the database that you want to back up from the drop-down menu in the navigation frame.

2. When the database details have loaded into the main frame, select Export from the tabs along the top of the screen, as shown here.

3. The rather fearsome looking screen shown in Figure 2-9 opens. In spite of all the options, you need to concern yourself with only a few.

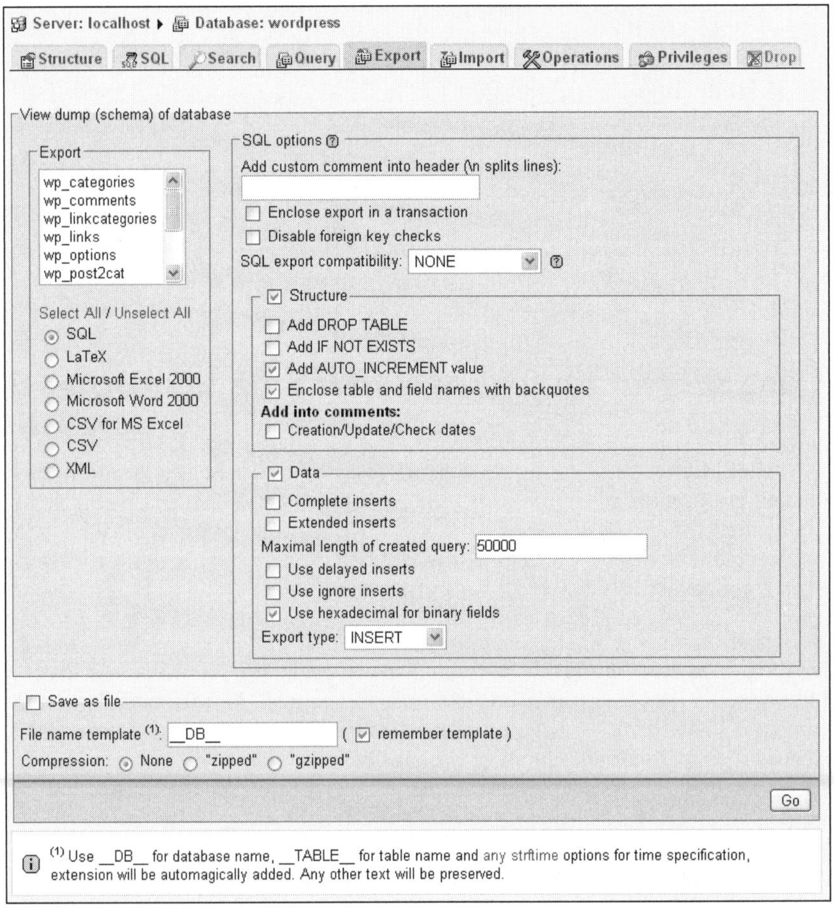

Figure 2-9. phpMyAdmin offers a wide range of choices when exporting data from MySQL.

4. The Export section on the left of the screen lists all the tables in your database. Click Select All and leave the radio buttons on the default SQL.

5. If the database has *never* been transferred to the other server before, the only option that you need to set on the right side of the screen is the drop-down menu labeled SQL export compatibility. The setting depends on the version of MySQL running on the other server (only the first two numbers, such as 3.23, 4.0, 4.1, or 5.0 are important):

- If the other server is running the same version of MySQL, choose NONE.
- If transferring between MySQL 4.1 and MySQL 5.0 (in either direction), choose NONE.
- If the other server is running MySQL 3.23, choose MYSQL323.
- If the other server is running MySQL 4.0, choose MYSQL40.

6. If the database has *already* been transferred on a previous occasion, select Add DROP TABLE in the Structure section. The existing contents of each table are dropped and are replaced with the data in the backup file.

7. Put a check mark in the box alongside Save as file at the bottom of the screen. The default setting in File name template is __DB__, which automatically gives the backup file the same name as your database. So, in this case, it will become wordpress.sql. If you add anything after the final double underscore, phpMyAdmin will add this to the name. For instance, you might want to indicate the date of the backup, so you could add 20060228 for a backup made on February 28, 2006. The file would then be named wordpress20060228.sql.

Loading data from a backup file

1. Upload the SQL file to your remote server. (This isn't necessary if you are transferring data to a new installation of MySQL on your local computer.)

2. If a database of the same name doesn't already exist on the target server, create the database, but don't create any tables.

3. Launch the version of phpMyAdmin, which is used by the target server, and select the database that you plan to transfer the data to. Click the Import tab in the main frame. The Import tab was added in phpMyAdmin 2.7.0. If your hosting company uses an earlier version of phpMyAdmin, click the SQL tab. At the bottom of the screen that opens, you will find a dialog box similar to that shown in step 4. It works in the same way.

4. Use the Browse button to locate the SQL file and click Go. That's it!

Import

File to import

Location of the text file   [   ]   [Browse...]   (Max: 2,048KB)

Character set of the file: [utf8   ▾]

Imported file compression will be automatically detected from: None, gzip, zip

Partial import

☑ Allow interrupt of import in case script detects it is close to time limit. This might be good way to import large files, however it can break transactions.

Number of records(queries) to skip from start [0   ]

Format of imported file   **This format has no options**

◉ SQL

[Go]

Now the fun starts

You should now have a fully functional local test environment in which you can experiment with the different blogging engines in the remaining chapters. The advantage of testing locally is that it gives you an opportunity to sort out any glitches in your web page before unleashing them on a—hopefully—admiring public. Of course, your PHP/MySQL setup is not only useful for working with the content of the rest of this book, I hope you'll be inspired by your blogging experience to explore creating other projects that maximize the potential of dynamic, database-driven sites. As you'll discover, once your content is stored in a database, you can display it in many different ways. It also becomes fully searchable, unleashing many more possibilities than a traditional static website.

by Andy Budd

What this chapter covers:

- Installing and configuring Movable Type
- Designing a custom blog template to implement in Movable Type
- Structuring the markup for the custom template
- Using Movable Type templates
- Installing Movable Type plug-ins

Movable Type (MT) is one of the oldest and most established blogging tools around today. While it might be a little quirkier than some of its newer competitors, it provides its users with a great deal of power and flexibility. In fact, as well as powering tens of thousands of blogs, Movable Type is starting to be adopted as a full-fledged content management system, powering everything from small brochure sites to corporate intranets.

In this chapter, I'll be showing you how easy it is to create your own blog from scratch using Movable Type. After a brief introduction, I'll begin by showing you how I came up with the design for a sample Movable Type blog. Next, I'll explain how the basic eXtensible Hypertext Markup Language (XHTML) template was constructed and how the design was turned from a Photoshop comp into Cascading Style Sheet (CSS) layout. Then it will be time to get your hands dirty as I walk you through the Movable Type installation and configuration process. With Movable Type up and running, I'll demonstrate how to build your own custom template pages and implement the new design. And finally, for those with an inquisitive mind, I'll set a couple of homework tasks for extra credit. If you want to follow along, you can download all the designs and source code for this chapter from www.friendsofed.com.

Movable what?

Movable Type started life in September 2001 as the personal project of Ben and Mena Trott. Mena's personal site had fast outgrown her existing software, so the pair decided to build its own. Originally intended for a few friends and colleagues, when Movable Type 1.0 was released a month later, its popularity was amazing. What started as a hobby quickly turned into a full-time job and, nine months later, Six Apart was born (see Figure 3-1). Six Apart now employs more than 70 people and develops two other blogging tools: TypePad and LiveJournal. Movable Type, however, continues to be the cornerstone of the business.

One of the reasons for Movable Type's huge success was its flexibility. At the time it was developed, most of the popular blogging tools were hosted solutions. These systems were simple to set up but difficult or impossible to customize. By comparison, Movable Type was a little trickier to use but gave authors much greater control over their sites. With a basic knowledge of the Web, you could tweak the default templates or create your own to produce a completely unique and personalized site. As such, Movable Type became the blogging tool of choice for many web professionals and hobbyists who enjoyed dabbling with a bit of code.

Movable Type is built using a programming language called Perl—a very popular language at the time. One of the most powerful features of Movable Type is an architecture that allowed Perl developers to write their own plug-ins, which build on the core functionality of Movable Type and allow site owners an even greater degree of flexibility. Plug-ins allow you to do anything from checking your spelling to turning your blog into a full-fledged Amazon shop. Perl isn't as popular as it once was, however, so some developers are switching to PHP-based blogging software instead. However unless you plan to write your own plug-ins, the fact that Movable Type is written in Perl probably won't make any difference to you.

Figure 3-1. Movable Type is one of several blogging products from Six Apart.

Because of Movable Type's long history, it has a very large and active community of users. Consequently, there are numerous sites and resources out there to help everybody from the complete beginner to the Movable Type pro. If you're struggling with a problem, there is a good chance that somebody else has already solved it. A quick Internet search will usually offer up the answer, but failing that, there are numerous forums and mailing lists dedicated solely to Movable Type.

Movable Type was originally free and supported by user donations. However, with the launch of Movable Type 3.0, Six Apart has introduced a new licensing system. You can still download a free copy of Movable Type, limited to one author and three blogs. Although this limit should be fine for most people, if you need more flexibility, the basic personal license is relatively inexpensive and also gives you free technical support. The new licensing model did put a few noses out of joint and caused some people to switch to different blogging systems. However, there is something to be said for having a team of dedicated developers there to answer questions and fix bugs, and this can really be achieved only through some form of licensing system.

Over the last couple of years, there has been an influx of new blogging tools to the market. Many of these tools build on the foundations set by Movable Type and attempt to address some of Movable Type's perceived weaknesses. Some of these tools seek to tackle the licensing issue, while others aim to organize content and presentation in new and interesting ways. All these new systems have their advantages and are starting to develop a loyal and growing community of users. But because of their relative newness, bugs are still being ironed out and plug-ins can be a little thin on the ground. These tools are ideal for early adopters who don't mind getting their hands dirty and knocking out their own plug-in where none exists. And to be fair, some of the communities are so active that if you suggest a useful plug-in one evening, somebody might have written it by the morning. However for flexibility, stability and the sheer number of resources available, Movable Type is still a hard platform to beat.

Installing Movable Type

Getting Movable Type up and running is a little more involved than using a hosted solution such as Blogger. However it's not too difficult, and if you've ever installed a Common Gateway Interface (CGI) script before, you should find this next section fairly straightforward.

Downloading Movable Type

The first thing you need to do is download the latest version of Movable Type from www.sixapart.com/movabletype/pricing (see Figure 3-2). Although there are several paid licenses, you can still download a free version that limits you to one author and three blogs. Unless you're planning to start some kind of collaborative blog, this free license will be fine for most people.

Clicking the Download Now link takes you to the license agreement page. After you read and accept the license, you'll be asked to log in using your **TypeKey** password. (If you don't know what that is, you probably won't have one, so you'll need to register.) TypeKey is a free online identification service run by Six Apart. The idea behind TypeKey is to reduce comment spam and anonymous or fraudulent postings by having a centralized comment login. If you run a Movable Type blog you can set it up to allow comments from registered TypeKey users automatically, while holding back other comments for moderation. Not too many people have a TypeKey password, but Six Apart is trying to change that by making new Movable Type users register for a password before they can download the latest version of Movable Type. It doesn't take very long, so go ahead and register.

After you register, you'll be taken to the download page. Assuming that you're installing Movable Type for the first time, you should download the full version. After you download and unpack the files, open up the index.html page in your browser and follow the link to the installation instructions. The documentation for Movable Type is quite good, so spend five or ten minutes becoming familiar with the installation instructions. I am assuming that you're installing Movable Type on a typical Linux server and will use MySQL as your database. If you don't already have an empty MySQL database set up, go ahead and do that now, noting the database name, hostname, username, and password. Chapter 2 contains information on installing MySQL and using phpMyAdmin to create databases. You can call your database whatever you like for the purposes of this chapter.

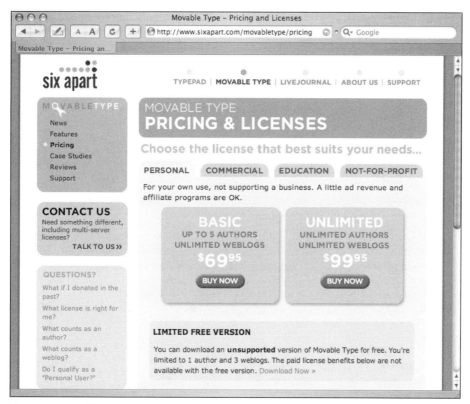

Figure 3-2. Movable Type pricing page

Configuring and installing Movable Type

First, you need to fill in some configuration details, so locate the file called mt-config.cgi-original, rename it to mt-config.cgi, and open it up in a text editor such as BBEdit. Near the top of the file you will see the following line of text.

    CGIPath http://www.example.com/cgi-bin/mt/

This URL is where you intend to install the Movable Type application, and is also the directory you'll access to administer your blog. You can install Movable Type into the cgi-bin, as created in Chapter 2, but if you are using a remote server that involves a little more configuration, so I'd avoid doing that. If you're using a remote server, you might be forced to use cgi-bin by your host, however. When using a local test server, cgi-bin is the best option; follow the instructions for a remote server when you are ready to use Movable Type in earnest. On a remote server, I tend to install Movable Type into a folder called movabletype, although you might want to make the directory name less guessable.

    CGIPath http://www.your-site.com/movabletype/

> *If you want to use the* cgi-bin *directory, change your settings as appropriate (use* localhost *if you are using a local server):*
>
> CGIPath http://localhost/cgi-bin/mt/
>
> *You also have to uncomment the following line:*
>
> # StaticWebPath http://www.example.com/mt-static
>
> *Movable Type contains some static files and images in its* mt-static *directory that you don't want to pass to the CGI script, as would happen if you are using the* cgi-bin *directory. Therefore, you have to tell Movable Type where to find these files and actually place them in the location specified with the* StaticWebPath *setting. Copy the* mt-static *directory to Apache's root, whether that's local or remote.*
>
> *You can now follow the rest of the instructions, though instead of moving the Movable Type files to the* movabletype *directory, you should move them to the* cgi-bin/mt *directory, remembering to omit the* mt-static *directory.*

Now you want to set up Movable Type so that it uses your MySQL database. Locate the following lines of text in mt-config.cgi:

```
# ObjectDriver DBI::mysql
# Database <database-name>
# DBUser <database-username>
# DBPassword <database-password>
# DBHost localhost
```

You should uncomment these lines by deleting the # and then fill in the details of your MySQL database.

```
ObjectDriver DBI::mysql
Database jennys_blog
DBUser jenny
DBPassword password
DBHost localhost
```

Assuming that your server is set up in a standard fashion, that's all you'll need to edit. Save mt-config.cgi and then close the file.

Windows paths on local servers

If you are a Windows user and testing on a local server, you have to change the paths at the top of all the .cgi files to point to your Perl installation, as explained in Chapter 2. If a piece of functionality does not work as described in this chapter and you get a 500 internal server error, it is very likely that you need to supply this path to your Perl files:

```
#! c:\perl\bin\perl.exe -w
```

Installing on a local server

To work with MySQL, you have to ensure that your Perl installation has the DBI and DBD::mysql modules installed (they provide the database functionality). If you are not sure, check the lib directory of your Perl installation. If it does not contain a DBI directory or a DBD directory, they are not installed. To be honest, this is only likely on Windows because most other operating systems come with Perl and MySQL connectivity built in. To install them on Windows, execute the following:

```
> ppm
ppm> install DBI
ppm> install DBD-mysql
```

Now copy all the Movable Type files to their final position, whether in the movabletype directory in Apache's directory structure or in the cgi-bin/mt and mt-static directories (remembering that only the latter should be in Apache's directory structure).

Installing on a remote server

If you're using a remote server, you have to upload all these files, so open up your favorite FTP application and connect to your server. Create a folder called movabletype (or cgi-bin/mt, if using that directory) in the desired location and start uploading the files. Your FTP client will probably handle the transfer mode automatically, but if it doesn't you'll need to make sure that the images are uploaded in binary mode and that everything else is uploaded in ASCII mode. There are a reasonable number of files to upload, so unless you're on a super-fast connection, you might want to take this opportunity to make yourself a cup of tea.

After the files are uploaded, you need to make sure that the permissions for the cgi scripts (the files ending in .cgi) are correct. The permissions need to be set so the owner (that's you) can read, write, and execute them while your group and other users can only read and execute them. In your FTP program you'll set these permissions through a permissions or an info window resembling the one shown in Figure 3-3.

After the files are successfully uploaded or moved to your local server, open your browser and go to a file named mt-check.cgi in the directory into which you installed Movable Type. In my case, it is located here:

www.my-site.com/movabletype/mt-check.cgi

As the name suggests, this file checks your server to make sure that all the correct Perl modules are installed. If you followed the instructions in Chapter 2, you should be OK. The page lists all the required modules and whether they are installed. If everything is correct, you'll see this message at the bottom of the page: Movable Type System Check Successful.

Figure 3-3. Info panel showing file permissions

You're now almost there. You just need to run a quick initialization script to set up the database tables and then you can take your first look at Movable Type. In your browser, access the file mt.cgi directory. If your system and configuration files have been set up correctly, you'll be told that you are about to finish the installation. If you have any errors at this point, check that you have all the required modules loaded, your file permissions are correct, and you entered the correct info in the config files. Windows users should check that the path to Perl is correct in mt-upgrade.cgi before continuing because the installation process uses this file.

Click the Finish Install button and watch while Movable Type works with the database. Congratulations, you successfully installed Movable Type!

Running Movable Type for the first time

So let's look at Movable Type for the first time. To do this, click Login to Movable Type on the final installation page, which takes you to the main Movable Type login page. The address you'll come to whenever you want to do anything with Movable Type is www.yourserver/movabletype/mt.cgi (or http://localhost/cgi-bin/mt/mt.cgi). As such, it's probably a good idea if you bookmark this page. Because this is the first time you log in, use the username Melody and the password Nelson. You'll be greeted with the screen shown in Figure 3-4.

The first thing you'll want to do is change the default username/password and add your own user details. Click the username at the top of the screen (in this case, it's Melody) and fill in your details. Remember to change the username and password to one you'll remember. Movable Type allows you to set up multiple blogs, but for this example you'll work with just one blog. Go to your main blogs homepage by selecting First Weblog from the drop-down menu at the top of the screen.

You'll want to customize your blog, so choose Settings from the menu on the left. Change the name of the blog to whatever you want.

Next, click the Publishing tab. This section determines where your blog will actually live on your site. If your blog will be your primary site, you'll probably want it at the root of your site; otherwise, you might want to put it in a directory called blog. The archive will be where all your old posts are stored and again, where that lives depends on how you want to organize your site.

```
Local Site Path: /usr/home/yourname/public_html/
Site URL: http://www.your-site.com/
Local Archive Path: /usr/home/yourname/public_html/archive
Archive URL: http://www.your-site.com/archive
```

Your core setup will probably look something like this. You should make sure that the local paths always reside in your web server's directory structure.

After you're done, save your changes. Changing these settings will not automatically create these directories, so you should create them on your sever after you finish. Now go back to the General tab and familiarize yourself with some of the options. If you like, create a short description for your blog. Later on, you'll use this for the intro text on your homepage. You'll also probably want to set the default post status to "publish" in the New Entry Defaults tab; otherwise, you'll have to remember to do this manually for each entry you write. After you're happy with your settings, save the changes. Now click on the rebuild site button in the left-hand menu and choose to rebuild all the files. Once the files have been rebuilt, click on the View your site link.

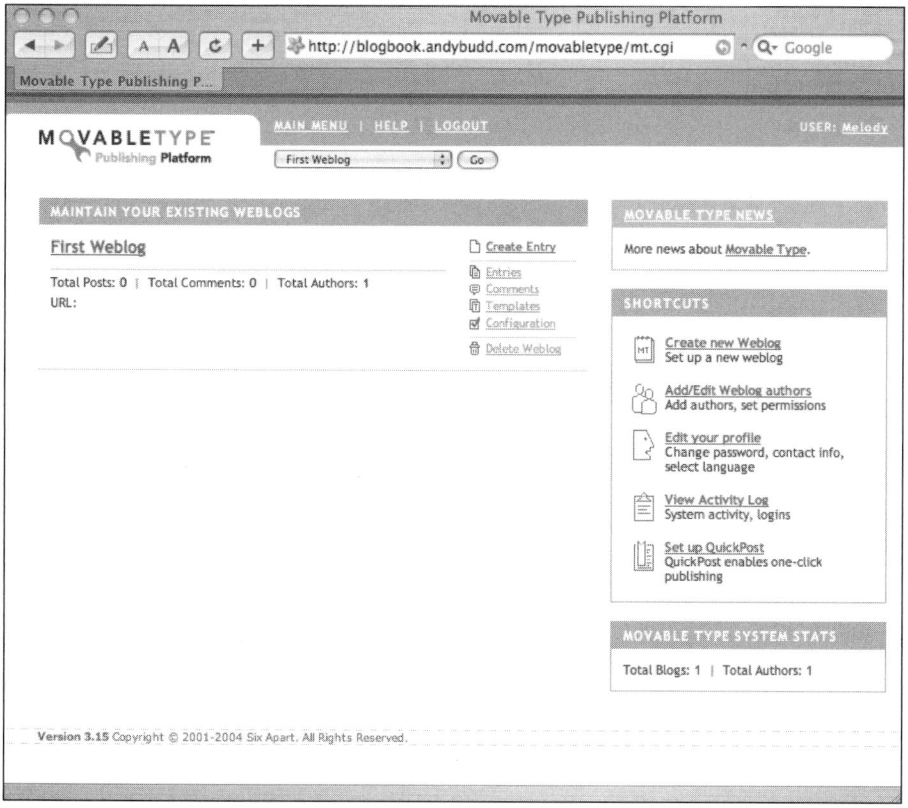

Figure 3-4. Homepage at first login

OK, so the default design is less than inspiring, but the blog is now up and running. Now you'll add some content to your new blog. Go back to the blog admin homepage and select the new entry menu item. Make a classic "Hello World" post, save the entry, and then go back to your blog homepage to see the result. Add a couple more posts, and your homepage should look something like the one shown in Figure 3-5.

Figure 3-5. Default blog with content

As you can see, I added a picture to one of these posts using the file upload option. Spend the next 10 minutes becoming familiar with the Movable Type interface. Try uploading a picture, and editing and deleting an entry. Try posting a comment and see what happens. By default, comments are held for moderation, but you can change the default behavior by selecting the Anyone check box in the Immediately publish comments from section of the Feedback tab in the blog settings section. When you're happy that you understand how Movable Type works, you can move on to the fun part—setting up your own custom design and templates.

The design

Design is the fun part of any project, but good design is more than just creating pretty pictures. It's about solving problems in a visual space. Often the best designs are so simple that you hardly notice them. They just seem to work. For my sample blog, I wanted to keep the design as simple as possible, allowing the content to take center stage. As such, I opted to keep design elements to a minimum, using a small number of graphic devices to provide the visual interest. If you want to see how this design took shape or create your own themes, I included the original Photoshop files among the downloads for this chapter.

3

Planning and the design brief

Most professional design jobs start with a discovery phase in which you learn as much as you can about your clients, their goals and objectives, what they like and dislike, their target market and how they want to be perceived. If you're lucky you'll receive a design brief, although you'll usually have to create one from client surveys, meetings, and phone calls. If you're designing for yourself, you'll already have thought about much of this stuff (but it never hurts to get your ideas down on paper).

The discovery phase helps define the problem, set boundaries, and provide hints to possible solutions. Without boundaries, the project will lack purpose and there is a good chance that you'll end up sitting in front of a blank canvas wondering what to do next. Alternatively, you'll end up creating numerous designs that never quite hit the mark because you're not exactly sure what the mark is. This is particularly true of personal projects, which have the tendency to fill up all the available time and drag on forever.

The purpose of this project is to create a standard design that anyone can use for a blog. The design needs to look modern, stylish, colorful, and fun. Blogs are personal sites, so it's important to let the author's personality shine through. As such, the design needs to be highly customizable to account for the widest range of styles and tastes possible.

Most blog content follows a standard format, with the latest post or posts forming the main focus of the page, and content such as links taking a subordinate role. This has led to the emergence of a typical blog style comprising a large branding image at the top, a central column for the main content, and a smaller side column for the secondary content. This style usually favors fixed widths and is generally centered in the browser window. Some people feel this style has been overplayed and is stifling creativity, and to some degree they are correct. However, this style has evolved because it suits the purpose well, making it a sensible choice when designing a generic blog template.

Kick-starting the design process

Many people get their design inspiration from paintings, books or music. Before I put mouse to canvas I like to seek inspiration from the Web. With client work I will usually ask clients for a list of their main competitors and well as sites they particularly like and dislike. I'll also look for examples of well-designed sites, either directly from my client's sector or, if I can't find any, from a similar or related sector. I also keep a full bookmark list of sites I like, divided into sections such as color, layout, simple, corporate, and so on.

To kick-start the creative process for this design I started looking though my list of favorite sites. Out of 200+ sites, about 60 jumped out as having a feeling close to what I wanted to convey (color, typography, imagery, layout, or something more ephemeral). I spent quite a while flicking between designs, allowing concepts to slowly form in my mind. Now thinking creatively, I started looking at various blogs to see how different designers approach the design problem. One of my main points of reference was the new blogger templates created recently by a host of well-known designers. These templates also needed to achieve a high degree of flexibility and universal appeal, so I was interested to see how the designers achieved this.

With a relatively fixed layout, it became apparent that the design's individuality would come from two areas: the color scheme and the main branding image. To demonstrate the design's flexibility I decided to come up with one basic "design" but two themes. I'm a huge fan of photography and believe that a powerful photo can make or break a design. So my next stop was Stock.xchng (www.sxc.hu), a free stock photography resource (see Figure 3-6). Free stock resources such as Stock.xchng or iStockPhoto (www.istockphoto.com) are great for personal project or for comping. However, for client work I always recommend getting your stock imagery from a professional stock library (it can guarantee that all the required permissions, such as model releases, have been obtained).

Figure 3-6. Stock.xchn—A great source of free stock photography for personal projects and comping

I chose to create a "masculine" and a "feminine" theme, and rather stereotypically decided that one would be blue and the other pink. I started searching Stock Exchange on the keywords "blue" and "pink"–downloading any images that I thought looked interesting. Because blogs are personal sites I thought it would be nice to get a picture of a real person in the branding image, so I started another keyword search for "men", "women", "boys" and "girls". I found it was much more difficult to find interesting pictures of men than of women, so I needed an alternative. Doing a final keyword search on "toys", I came across a few cool action figure pictures, which I downloaded and added to my collection. With 36 pictures to choose from (examples are shown in Figure 3-7), I felt confident that I knew where I was going and that it was time to start the visual design.

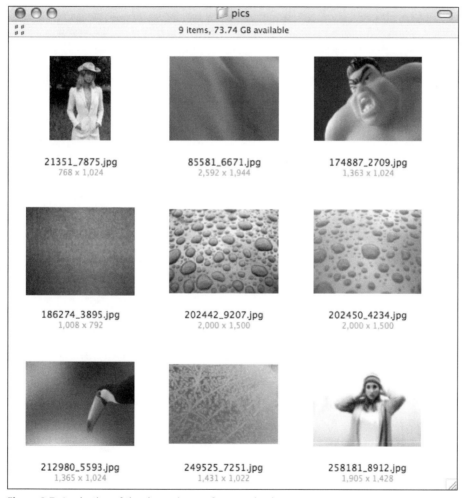

Figure 3-7. A selection of the chosen images from stock.xchng

Finally, the design!

To begin, I created a new Photoshop document, 1000 pixels wide by 800 pixels tall. Gradients are all the rage at the moment, so I created a layer filled with a subtle gray gradient to act as the background of my design. On top of that, I added another layer for the content area. This layer contained a white rectangle, 720 pixels wide and slightly shorter than the height of the canvas. I chose the width of 720 pixels because it fits nicely on most browsers at a resolution of 800 by 600 without horizontal scrolling. To help define the content area, I gave this layer a subtle drop shadow. I then started adding some sample content, an intro paragraph, a sample post, and some ancillary links. Also I created a large space for a branding image and filled that with a gradient as well. The result can be seen in basic-blog-template.psd (see Figure 3-8).

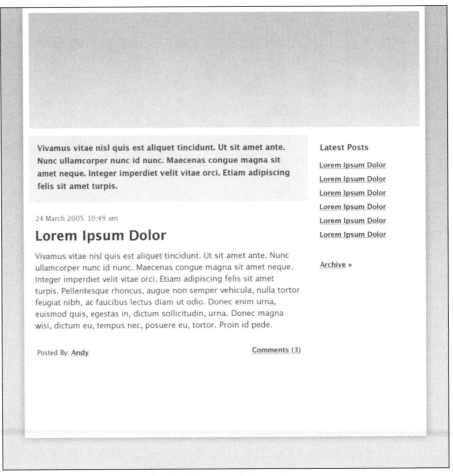

Figure 3-8. Basic design concept: basic-blog-template-psd

With the basic layout in place I started thinking about the color. So I created two color variations: one pink, one blue. Both these themes can be seen in final-blog-template.psd (and are also shown in Figures 3-9 and 3-10).

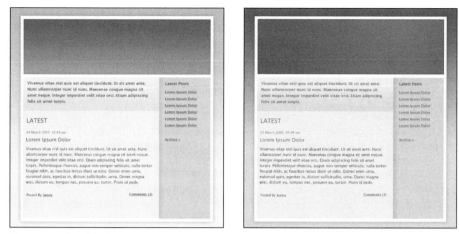

Figure 3-9. The pink theme   **Figure 3-10.** The blue theme

After playing around with several photos, I settled on two images. For the pink theme, I found a compelling image of a girl in a hat. The picture felt both fun and personal—just the type of picture I'd expect to see branding somebody's personal site. For the blue theme, I found a cool picture of a toy sumo wrestler, and thought the name of the picture, Angry Sumo, would make an excellent name for a blog. I traced the outline of each image using the pen tool, turned it into a selection, and then shrunk and feathered the selection by a couple of pixels before copying and pasting the cutout into my design. Next, I tweaked the images' curves so they'd fit better with the color schemes, and gave them a subtle glow. Finally, I overlaid a floral wallpaper pattern on the pink branding gradient to give it a rich luxuriant feel, and added a diagonal line overlay on the blue gradient to give it a slightly more technical feel. See the final versions in Figures 3-11 and 3-12.

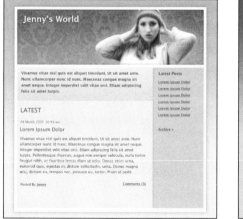   

Figure 3-11. Pink theme—final   **Figure 3-12.** Blue theme—final

Of course, these two themes are just ideas. You could choose to use a solid color or a background pattern instead of a gradient. And you could have lots of fun playing with the header graphic, choosing a variety of graphic or photographic images from a stock library, or creating your own montages.

XHTML and CSS

Most popular blogging tools choose to control layout and design using CSS. This is a very sensible approach because the separation of design from markup allows the systems to be much more flexible. Rather than the visual style being distributed across many templates, it can be controlled from a few simple CSS files. You don't have to be a CSS expert to tweak the design of your Movable Type blog, but a basic level of knowledge will definitely help. If you want to follow along with the examples in this next section, all the files can be found in the `html-templates` folder among the downloads for this section.

Creating the markup

Now the design is finished; it's time to build the XHTML template. If you were using a table-based approach, you'd probably look at the design and break it down into table cells. However, mixing structure and presentation is never a good idea. Instead I'll be using XHTML for structure only and will control the presentation using CSS. As such, to create the underlying XHTML, the design needs to be broken down by meaning instead of layout.

If you look at the design, the first thing you'll notice is the centered white panel where everything lives. Within this panel there is a branding image and a content area. The content area can be divided into the main content and the secondary content. In Figure 3-13, I also added a footer area, which is an option that isn't used at the moment, but might come in useful later on.

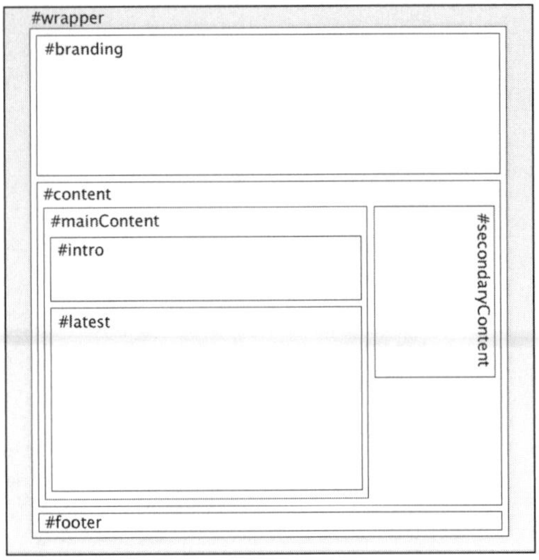

Figure 3-13. Markup outline

Translated into XHTML, it looks something like this:

```
<div id="wrapper">

<div id="branding">
</div><!-- close branding -->

<div id="content">

<div id="mainContent">
</div><!-- close mainContent -->

<div id="secondaryContent">
</div><!-- close secondaryContent -->

</div><!-- close content -->

<div id="footer">
</div><!-- close footer -->

</div><!-- close wrapper -->
```

Basic XHTML structure

CSS-based layouts tend to use quite a few named structural div tags. To help identify which named element a particular closing tag refers to, I comment them. This is purely personal taste, and they can be stripped out when the site goes live. However, during development these comments can be extremely useful.

Now the basic structure is in place, let's look more closely at the main content and secondary content areas. As you can see from the design, the main content area can be further broken down into an intro and a latest posts section. The intro will be a small bit of blurb on the homepage about the site, while the latest posts section will contain the most recent blog entries. If you knew that the intro was only ever going to be one paragraph, you could apply the intro id to a p tag instead of a div tag. However, to keep things as flexible as possible, it's probably best not to make too many assumptions.

```
<div id="mainContent">
<div id="intro">
</div><!-- close intro -->

<div id="latest">
</div><!-- close latest -->

</div><!-- close mainContent -->
```

The main content area can be broken down into an intro block and a latest posts block.

Latest posts block

The latest area will display the headline "latest" and then one or more entries. Because each entry is a separate thing, I wrapped each one in a div with a class of "entry". I gave the time and date of the entry a class of "date" and who posted the entry a class of "author". I also gave the comments link a class of "comment".

```
<div id="latest">
<h2>Latest</h2>

<div class="entry">
<p class="date">24th March 2005 10:49am</p>
<h3><a href="">Lorem Ipsum Dolor</a></h3>
<p>---<p>
<p class="author">Posted by: <a href="#">Andy</a></p>
<p class="comment"><a href="#">Comments (3)</a></p>
</div>

</div><!-- close latest -->
```

Secondary content block

The secondary content area is pretty simple. After the headline, there is a list with an id of latestNav that contains links to the most recent entries. Following that is a link to the archive section that contains all the old entries. Of course, you can add other things to the secondary content area, in which case you might want to divide them up by placing each chunk of content into its own div.

```
<div id="secondaryContent">
<h2>Latest Posts</h2>
<ul id="latestNav">
<li><a href="#">Lorem Ipsum Dolor</a></li>
---
</ul>

<p><a href="#">Archive &raquo;</a></p>
</div><!-- close secondaryContent -->
```

By marking up the document semantically and giving elements meaningful ids and class names, you created an excellent foundation to which you can apply your styles. You've now seen how the markup was created. Let's now take a look at the layout and styling.

Layout and styling

When I'm styling a template I usually keep all the styles in the head of the document for easy access. However, after the styles are 90 percent there, I split the CSS off into one or more external style sheets for easier maintenance. I do most of my CSS development using Safari, although another standards-compliant browser such as FireFox does just as well. When I want to test the layouts in different browser/OS combinations I turn to the excellent BrowserCam (see Figure 3-14).

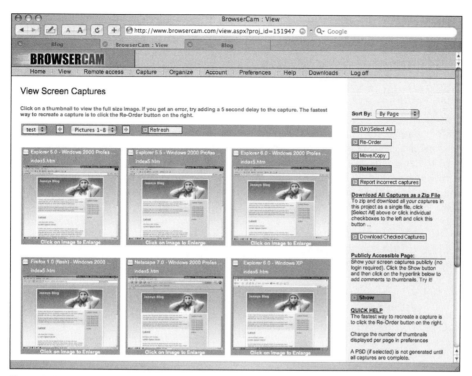

Figure 3-14. Browsercam screenshot

> *BrowserCam is a very useful service that allows you to preview your designs on a variety of browser/OS combinations. It is a subscription service, but you can register for a free trial at* www.browsercam.com.

You can edit the site's stylesheet by going to the templates tag on the left side of your blog config screen. Select the Indexes tab if it is not already selected and then click Stylesheet. You can add the styles directly to the main index page by selecting Main Index instead of Stylesheet. For the purposes of this chapter, I placed all the markup and styles in separate HTML files for you to download.

The first thing I'll do is zero down all the margins and padding using the universal selector. This procedure really helps when laying out a page because you don't have to worry about default settings. Using this method requires explicitly setting your desired margin and padding on all the elements. This can end up bloating your CSS slightly so, depending on how complicated the styles get, I might delete this rule later on and deal with the defaults on a case-by-case basis.

```
* {
    margin: 0;
    padding: 0;
}
```

95

Next I want to center the wrapper in the middle of the page. To do this, I set the width of the wrapper and then set the left and right margins to auto.

```
#wrapper {
    margin: 0 auto;
    width: 720px;
}
```

Unfortunately, this doesn't work in Internet Explorer (IE). Luckily, IE misinterprets text-align, aligning everything instead of just the text. This can be used to your advantage to center the wrapper in IE. Using text-align: center also centers all the text so it is manually corrected by adding text-align: left to the wrapper. I also added a minimum width to the body to avoid any problems if the browser window is scaled smaller than the width of the wrapper.

```
body {
    min-width: 720px;
    text-align: center;
}

#wrapper {
    margin: 0 auto;
    width: 720px;
    text-align: left;
}
```

Finally, I set the default font for the design and set the main background image. I also set the background color on the wrapper to be white and added some margin and padding.

```
body {
    min-width: 720px;
    text-align: center;
    font: 76%/1.6 "Lucida Grande", Geneva, Verdana, sans-serif;
    background: #fceff7 url(images/bg.gif) repeat-x;
}

#wrapper {
    margin: 50px auto 0 auto;
    padding: 10px 0;
    width: 720px;
    background: #fff;
    text-align: left;
}
```

Rather than embed the branding image in the XHTML, I'm applying it using the CSS. This procedure gives you much greater flexibility and allows you to swap out the branding image by just changing one line in the CSS, rather than doing a find and replace on every page on the site. You'll notice that I'm creating the 10-pixel gutter around the sides of the branding area by applying a margin to it. It would seem to make more sense to add this gutter to the wrapper div as a padding instead. However doing this brings into effect Internet Explorer's "Box Model Bug"; to avoid this it's generally better to apply margins to child elements than padding to parent elements that have a defined width or height.

```
#branding {
    width: 700px;
    height: 200px;
    margin: 0 10px 10px 10px;
    background: url(images/branding.jpg);
}
```

Now let's look at the content area. First, I want to add the 10-pixel gutter to the left and right of the content area. The content area is to be broken into two columns with the main content on the left and the secondary content on the right. Although there are various ways to do this, I find floating to be the most effective method. By setting the desired widths, floating the main content left and the secondary content right, it is possible to create a very simple two-column layout.

```
#content {
    margin: 0 10px;
}

#mainContent {
    width: 510px;
    float: left;
}

#secondaryContent {
    width: 190px;
    float: right;
}
```

If you look at the template, you'll notice that the wrapper no longer seems to enclose the floated content because floated elements are taken out of the flow of the document and essentially take up no space. I want the wrapper to extend around all the content; to do this, the floated content needs to be cleared. Clearing is a complicated topic, but applying clear to an element adds the total height of all the preceding floated elements to the cleared element's top margin. Normally, people would add an empty element after the floats and apply a clear to that. Luckily I already have an element I can clear—in the form of the footer div.

```
#footer {
    clear: both;
}
```

A quick check in Firefox reveals that the problem isn't completely solved. Firefox has a rather annoying bug whereby it doesn't clear empty floats. To solve this problem, you need to either add some content to the footer or give it a nominal height.

```css
#footer {
    height: 1px;
    clear: both;
}
```

The layout is now almost finished. The last thing I'll do is apply colored backgrounds to help define the content areas. For the intro area I'll be adding a horizontally repeating gradient as a background image. The background for the latest area is even simpler because it's just a solid color.

```css
#intro {
    background: #fddaef url(images/intro-bg.gif) repeat-x;
}

#latest {
    background: #fbeef6;
}
```

Adding the background image for the latest posts area is a little more complicated. If you add the background directly to the secondary content area, it will stop where the secondary content stops. However, I want the image to extend all the way to the bottom of the wrapper, creating a column effect. To do this you need to apply the background image, aligned right, to one of the secondary contents parent elements. You could apply it to the wrapper, but then the background would tile down the whole of the right side of the wrapper. Instead it would make more sense to apply the background to the content div.

```css
#content {
    margin: 0 10px;
    background: url(images/secondary-bg.gif) repeat-y right;
}
```

Unfortunately when you do this, nothing happens. At least you can't see anything happening. The problem is that the content div doesn't actually contain its two floated children: the mainContent div and the secondaryContent div. You could add an empty element at the end of the content div and clear that, however that is just adding unnecessary markup. Instead I've simply floated the content element as well, letting the cleared footer div take care of the rest.

```css
#content {
    margin: 0 10px;
    float: left; /* so the bg expands */
    background: url(images/secondary-bg.gif) repeat-y right;
}
```

Looking at the template in Internet Explorer for Windows, you'll notice something odd happening. The left and right margins on the content area now seem to be 20 pixels wide rather than the specified 10 pixels. This is because of an IE/Win bug known as the IE Double Margin Float Bug, which doubles the margins on floated elements. Luckily, this bug can be fixed simply by giving the element a display property of inline.

```
#content {
    margin: 0 10px;
    display: inline /* fixes the IE double margin float bug */
    float: left; /* so the bg expands */
    background: url(images/secondary-bg.gif) repeat-y right;
}
```

And that's the basic layout finished. If you open up basic-layout.html in your favorite browser, you should see something like Figure 3-15.

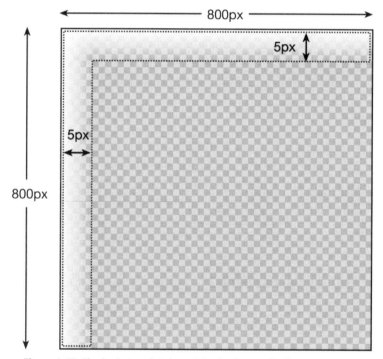

Figure 3-15. The basic template layout: basic-layout.html

The rest of the work is essentially cosmetic. Adding margins and padding, setting text, headline and link styles. I won't bore you with the details, but Figure 3-16 shows a screenshot of the tidied-up XHTML/CSS template `basic-template.html`.

Figure 3-16. Tidied-up version of the template `basic-layout.html`

Where's the drop shadow?

If you've been paying attention, you might have noticed that the final template is missing one crucial element from the original designs: a drop shadow. There are several ways to accomplish drop shadows, and each has its good and bad points. If there is a solid background color, you can create a 10-pixel-high image whose background matches the background color. You can then apply it as a repeating background image to the wrapper. However, your design calls for a graduated background, so you can't use that method. Another method is to create a really long background image and apply that to the wrapper. Unfortunately, you have no idea what the maximum page length it likely to be, but it could be fairly long. A long enough image, perhaps 2000 pixels, would have a big file size and seem a little over the top just for a nice drop shadow effect. The other problem that both these methods have is the need to create a separate image for each color theme. Wouldn't it be good if you could create one drop shadow that worked, no matter what the background was?

Well, as a matter of fact you can, using a file format known as PNG. You see, 24-bit PNGs support alpha transparency, allowing you to create drop shadows that act just like real shadows. The majority of recent browsers support PNG alpha transparency, with one notable exception: Internet Explorer. However, Microsoft has some proprietary CSS that allows you to enable alpha transparency support in IE 5.5 and above. It will involve a couple of "hacks" and using nonstandard code, but you can minimize the impact of it by using another Internet Explorer-specific technology: conditional comments.

Going into this in detail is beyond the scope of this book, but if you look at `final-template.html`, you'll see that I altered the XHTML and CSS slightly by using PNGs to produce the drop shadow. I then created a special stylesheet for IE 5.5 and above that uses the Microsoft proprietary code to enable alpha transparency. Because this doesn't work in IE 5.0, I created another stylesheet that removes the drop shadow for IE 5.0. You can see the final template in Figure 3-17.

Figure 3-17. Final template with transparent drop shadow: `final-template.html`

It's now much easier to skin the design by simply changing the background image or color. For instance, you could add a different gradient, or possibly a patterned background, and not have to worry about changing the drop shadow to match. Cool, huh?

Movable Type templates

Movable Type is essentially a specialized template engine. You create an XHTML template page and then add Movable Type template tags where you want the content to appear. So for a template that displays an individual blog entry you'd probably want to add tags for the title of the entry, the content, and when it was posted. When Movable Type processes that template, it will strip out the template tags and replace them with the content of your actual entry. Besides replacing individual chunks of content, template tags also allow you to perform simple logic such as displaying a comment form only if comments are allowed on a particular entry.

Movable Type has many different template tags, all of which are detailed in its excellent documentation. Movable Type template tags look similar to HTML tags, although all single tags start with the prefix $MT, and pairs of tags start with the prefix MT. Most are sensibly named so it's pretty easy to figure out what each one does.

```
<h2><$MTEntryTitle$></h2>
<MTDateHeader>
  <h2 class="date-header"><$MTEntryDate format="%x"$></h2>
</MTDateHeader>
<$MTEntryBody$>
<p><$MTEntryDate$></p>
```

Many template engines do the processing each time a page is requested, and such a system is said to be **dynamic**. However, a busy site with many page requests can put a lot of pressure on the template engine. Instead, Movable Type creates static HTML pages through a process called **rebuilding**. Each time you change a template, you need to rebuild it to see the change take effect. Although this process decreases the system overhead, rebuilding can take a bit of time, especially if you have lots of entries associated with that template. If you're making a series of changes to the templates, the constant rebuilding can get a little frustrating, and it is not uncommon to forget to rebuild and then wonder why the change hasn't taken effect. Luckily, most of the template tweaking will be done when your site is relatively new, so you don't have to worry about rebuilding lots of pages of content.

Main index template

Although Movable Type comes with a number of default templates, I'll show you how to build your own based on the XHTML template created earlier. The first is the Main template, which powers the blog homepage. To edit it, click the templates link on the left side of the blog config screen. Select the Indexes tab if it is not already selected and then click Main Index. Select All and delete the existing content.

The first thing I'll show you is how to make the title of the main page the name of the blog, which you can do by adding a Movable Type template tag called MTBlogName inside the <title> element. In this case, I'm using the encode_html attribute of this tag to make sure no unencoded entities such as ampersands appear in the title:

```
<title><$MTBlogName encode_html="1"$></title>
```

Most blogs publish an XML feed to allow visitors to keep track of the latest posts. Movable Type comes installed with a number of templates for different feed formats, such as RSS1.0, RSS 2.0, and Atom. You could add links to these feeds using relative paths, but it makes life a little easier if you use absolute paths. Rather than entering the paths by hand you can use the MTBlogURL template tag. I did the same for the stylesheet URL.

```
<!DOCTYPE html PUBLIC "-//W3C//DTD XHTML 1.0 Strict//EN" ➥
"http://www.w3.org/TR/xhtml1/DTD/xhtml1-strict.dtd">
<html xmlns="http://www.w3.org/1999/xhtml">
<head>
<meta http-equiv="Content-Type" content="text/html; ➥
charset=iso-8859-1" />
<title><$MTBlogName encode_html="1"$></title>
<link rel="alternate" type="application/atom+xml" title="Atom" ➥
href="<$MTBlogURL$>atom.xml" />
<link rel="alternate" type="application/rss+xml" title="RSS 1.0" ➥
href="<$MTBlogURL$>index.rdf" />
<link rel="alternate" type="application/rss+xml" title="RSS 2.0" ➥
href="<$MTBlogURL$>index.xml" />
<link rel="EditURI" type="application/rsd+xml" title="RSD" ➥
href="<$MTBlogURL$>rsd.xml" />
<style type="text/css"><!--
@import url("<$MTBlogURL$>styles-site.css");
-->
</style>
</head>
```

Besides being used for the page title, I want the name of the blog to appear as the top-level heading in the branding section of the page. It is quite a common convention to link the site name or logo to the homepage, so I did that as well.

```
<div id="branding">
<h1>
  <a href="<$MTBlogURL$>" accesskey="1"><$MTBlogName encode_html="1"$>
  </a>
</h1>
</div><!-- close branding -->
```

The first piece of real content on the homepage is an introduction to the site. This intro text can be drawn from the description you added when configuring your blog using the MTBlogDescription tag.

```
<div id="intro">
<p><$MTBlogDescription$></p>
</div><!-- close intro -->
```

Now it's time to get to the core of this template—the latest entries. If you remember, the latest posts area looked something like this:

```
<div id="latest">
<h2>Latest</h2>
<div class="entry">
<p class="date">24th March 2005 10:49am</p>
<h3><a href="">One entry</a></h3>
---
content
---
<p class="author">Posted by: <a href="#">Andy</a></p>
<p class="comments"><a href="#">Comments (3)</a></p>
</div>

</div><!-- close latest -->
```

On the homepage I'll display the last six entries posted. To tell Movable Type to loop through several entries, you need to use a container tag called MTEntries. In this instance, I'll use the lastn attribute to specify the last six entries. If I didn't specify this, Movable Type would display posts from the number of days specified in the blog config preferences section. Unlike most Movable Type template tags, container tags like MTEntries need to be closed.

```
<div id="latest">
<h2>Latest</h2>

<MTEntries lastn="6">
<div class="entry">
<p class="date">24th March 2005 10:49am</p>
<h3><a href="">One entry</a></h3>
---
content
---
<p class="author">Posted by: <a href="#">Andy</a></p>
<p class="comments"><a href="#">Comments (3)</a></p>
</div>
</MTEntries>

</div><!-- close latest -->
```

Within the MTEntries tag, you can add tags that will display information about each entry. The first thing I'll do is add the date and time the entry was made using the MTEntryDate tag, which has many formatting options (so check with the documentation to see what they all mean). I'll add the entry title using MTEntryTitle and a link to the full article using MTEntryLink. As you can see, a pattern is starting to form. Movable Type template tags are very sensibly named, so it's easy to tell what each one does. The main text of the entry is added using MTEntryBody, the author using MTEntryAuthorLink, and the number of comments made about this entry using MTEntryCommentCount. Adding a few more template tags, the latest post area looks like this.

```
<div id="latest">
<h2>Latest</h2>

<MTEntries lastn="6">
<div class="entry">
<p class="date"><$MTEntryDate format="%B %e, %Y %I:%M %p"$></p>
<h3><a href="<$MTEntryLink$>"><$MTEntryTitle$></a></h3>
<$MTEntryBody$>
<p class="author">Posted by: <$MTEntryAuthorLink$></p>
<p class="comments"><a href="<$MTEntryLink$>#comments"> ➡
Comments (<$MTEntryCommentCount$>)</a></p>
</div>
</MTEntries>

</div><!-- close latest -->
```

The navigation list in the secondary content area is created in a similar way.

```
<div id="secondaryContent">
<h2>Latest Posts</h2>
<ul id="latestNav">
<MTEntries lastn="6">
<li><a href="<$MTEntryLink$>"><$MTEntryTitle$></a></li>
</MTEntries>
</ul>

<p><a href="<$MTBlogURL$>archive/">Archive</a></p>
</div><!-- close secondaryContent -->
```

And that's the main template done. Easy wasn't it? You can see this template by opening up `main.tmpl` in the `MT-Templates` folder that accompanies this chapter. Save the template and then rebuild it. When you go to your blog homepage you should now see your slick new design rather than the slightly tired looking default layout (see Figure 3-18).

Figure 3-18. Main template

Master archive index template

If you look at the list of templates you will see one called Master archive index, which is the main page for navigating through older posts. The default template will display a list of every post you've ever made on the site. This is fine for a new site, but after you've been posting for awhile, the list can get very long and unwieldy. Instead of displaying every post, I'll display a list of months. Clicking one of these months will take you to a page containing links to every post made that month. To create this template, I can reuse most of the main index template by removing the intro and latest areas, as well as the content in the secondary content area. The main content area on the archive index page will look something like this:

```
<div id="mainContent">

<h2>Monthly Archives</h2>
<ul id="monthlyArchiveList">
<li><a href="#">March 2005 (4)</a></li>
<li><a href="#">Feb 2005 (8)</a></li>
<li><a href="#">Jan 2005 (6)</a></li>
</ul>

</div><!-- close mainContent -->
```

Similar to the MTEntries container tag, you can use the MTArchiveList container tag to display a list of all the default archive pages. In this case, I only want to display monthly archives so I define it by using the archive_type attribute. You can then display a link to the individual archive page using MTArchiveLink and display the number of posts in that archive using MTArchiveCount.

```
<h2>Monthly Archives</h2>
<ul id="monthlyArchiveList">
<MTArchiveList archive_type="Monthly" lastn="5">
<li>
  <a href=" <$MTArchiveLink$>"><$MTArchiveTitl$e> ➥
 (<$MTArchiveCount$>)</a>
</li>
</MTArchiveList>
</ul>
```

When you post an entry, Movable Type allows you to assign one or more categories to that entry. As such, it would be really useful to display a list of entries by category as well as by date. This can be done in a similar way by substituting archive_type="Monthly" with archiveType="Category".

```
<h2>Category Archives</h2>
<ul id="categoryArchiveList">
<MTArchiveList archive_type="Category" lastn="5">
<li>
  <a href=" <$MTArchiveLink$>"><$MTArchiveTitle$> ➥
 (<$MTArchiveCount$>)</a>
</li>
</MTArchiveList>
</ul>
```

You have to define the categories yourself from the categories menu, so add some categories now, and then assign categories to your test entries. If you have been following along, your new master archive index should now look like `master-archive.tmpl`. Replace the old archive template code with your new template code. Before you save and rebuild, you'll notice a field called output file which is the name and location of the file this archive will output. By default, the file is called `archive.html` and is placed at the root of your blog. However I find that it makes more sense to have this file as the index file of the archive directory, so change the field to read `archive/index.html`. Now you can access your blog archive by clicking the archive link on the homepage. It should look something like Figure 3-19.

Figure 3-19. Master archive index template

Category and date-based archives

If you look at the main templates page, you'll see that it is split into sections. The section called archives is the location for storing the templates for the different types of archives. The category and date-based templates will be very similar because I want them both to display a list of all the entries in that archive.

```
<ul id="archiveList">
<MTEntries>
<li><a href="<$MTEntryPermalink$>"><$MTEntryTitle$></a></li>
```

```
</MTEntries>
</ul>
```

With the date archive I want to add a little navigation widget at the top of the main content section to allow people to move forward and backward through each month. MTArchivePrevious is a container tag that displays the contents only if there is a previous archive. Any archive tags within this container tag will display info from the previous archive. Likewise, MTArchiveNext does the same thing for the next archive in the sequence.

```
<p id="archiveNav">
<MTArchivePrevious>
<a href="<$MTArchiveLink$>">&laquo; <$MTArchiveTitle$></a> |
</MTArchivePrevious>
<a href="<$MTBlogURL$>">Main</a>
<MTArchiveNext>
 | <a href="<$MTArchiveLink$>"><$MTArchiveTitle$> &raquo;</a>
</MTArchiveNext>
</p>
```

Unfortunately, Movable Type doesn't give you the ability to navigate through category-based archives in the same way. Luckily, there is a plug-in called "Supplemental Category Tags" that does the trick. As I mentioned previously, Six Apart has a plug-in directory that contains many useful plug-ins. The directory is located at www.sixapart.com/pronet/plugins/, and you can download this particular plug-in from www.sixapart.com/pronet/plugins/plugin/supplemental_ca.html or http://bradchoate.com/weblog/2002/10/31/mtcatx.

Installing a Movable Type plug-in is very straightforward. First, you need to download and unpack the plug-in. This particular one comprises two main files: catx.pl and catx.pm. If you navigate to the Movable Type directory on your web server, you'll see a directory called plugins. Place catx.pl in this directory. Still in the Movable Type home directory, you'll see another directory called extlib. Create a new directory here called bradchoate (the author of this plug-in) and place catx.pm in it. It's as simple as that.

This plug-in makes a couple of new template tags available, including MTCategoryPrevious and MTCategoryNext. You'll notice that they look very similar to the tags used in the previous example, except that they relate to categories instead of archives. Using a similar method to the archive widget, it's now possible to create a category navigation widget, allowing you to navigate between categories.

```
<p id="archiveNav">
<MTCategoryPrevious>
<a href="<$MTCategoryArchiveLink$>">&laquo; <$MTCategoryLabel$></a> |
</MTCategoryPrevious>
<a href="<$MTBlogURL$>">Main</a>
<MTCategoryNext>
 | <a href="<$MTCategoryArchiveLink$>"><$MTCategoryLabel$> &raquo;</a>
</MTCategoryNext>
</p>
```

109

If you save the Category template, rebuild the site and then navigate to a category archive, you should see a screen similar to Figure 3-20.

Figure 3-20. Category archive

Most of the main templates are out of the way. The individual archive template works in a similar way to the main index template, except that it shows only one entry instead of six. The default template uses quite a bit of logic, mostly revolving around comments. For my version of this template, I essentially just copied this information from the default template. Most of the default special templates relate to comments as well and are easy to customize. If you want to have a look at these templates, they can all be found in the MT-Templates folder you downloaded for this chapter. After these templates are updated by pasting in the new code, saving the changes and rebuilding the file, your custom blog will be finished.

Summary

Hopefully, this chapter has given you a brief overview of how to create a custom blog design from scratch and then turn that design into a Movable Type–powered blog. The whole project took a couple of weekends, so it's a little more involved than using a hosted solution. However if you enjoy messing around with design and code, it's a lot more fun. Also you'll end up with your own distinct-looking blog rather than a cookie-cutter design.

I tried to keep the templates as simple as possible and hope they will provide you with a starting point for more customization and experimentation. Looking at other people's blogs should give you plenty of inspiration, as should looking at the plug-in directory. Some of the plug-ins you'll definitely want to look at include MT-Blacklist for comment spam control and Markdown for easier entry markup.

Quite a few bloggers publish a list of interesting links as well as their main posts. You can do this quite easily by setting up a very basic second blog and then using a plug-in such as Multiblog or Otherblog to bring those links into your main blog. If you're looking for a project to test out your new Movable Type skills, this is a good place to start.

3

4 EXPRESSIONENGINE

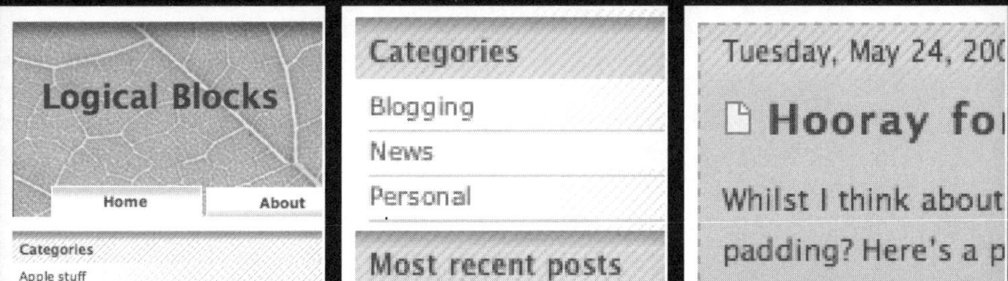

by Simon Collison

What this chapter covers:

- Obtaining and installing ExpressionEngine (EE)
- Introducing ExpressionEngine and how it works
- Designing and implementing a custom blog using ExpressionEngine

Way back in early 2004, the creators of an alternative blogging tool—a robust but limited young fellow called pMachine—introduced a new heavyweight with minimal fanfare but maximum power.

That new force was **ExpressionEngine (EE)**. Easily out-punching its rivals; those smart enough to realize its potential swiftly embraced this feature-rich system. Regrettably, those at the top of the blogging pyramid were slow to switch over to EE, so it still feels like a "well-kept secret."

If given an inch, I'd take a mile and spread my evangelical pitch across four volumes, extolling the almost unlimited virtues of EE over any other system. I'd explain that with a little manipulation, EE can be the only Content Management System (CMS) you'd ever need; how it can be bent and twisted to power complex magazine sites, music sites, and relational databases; and how it can even be configured to wake you up and make you tea in the morning. I will tell you that EE stands out as the most flexible, modular, and malleable publishing system available today. Whether creating a personal blog or building a ridiculously complex client website, EE can be manipulated to suit your needs. Use it as your base for any future projects and you'll never have to say "No" ever again.

With the capability to post from mobile phones or email, unlimited levels of membership and associated privileges, photo galleries and plug-in forums, tick-of-a-button data modeling and much, much more, EE really is becoming the tool of choice for web developers who need the stability of a robust and secure publishing platform coupled with the ability to extend it beyond their wildest dreams.

As it stands, I've been given only half an inch, so with this chapter you'll be concerning yourself with the basics of EE. You'll learn some pretty cool stuff, though. After you gain an understanding of how EE works and how you can manipulate its simple tag system and templates to personalize your structure, you'll learn how to mold the Cascading Style Sheets (CSS) to place your design stamp on the blog. You might only be building a blog—but what a blog it will be! They'll come from miles around to marvel at your ticked-off links (what?), drool over your smart comments (eh?), and swear as you stop them from posting spam comments linking your blog to their online casinos and penile enhancement drugs. Figure 4-1 shows what your site will look like.

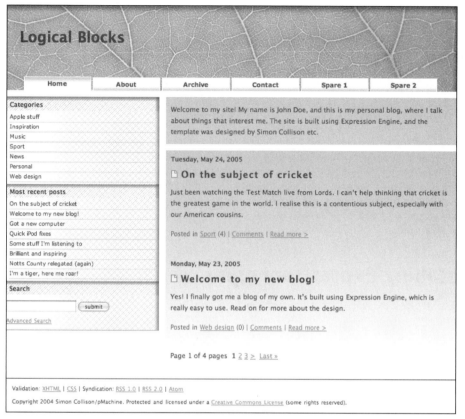

Figure 4-1. How the finished design will look

Design brief

Your brief is to build a blog that sits well on any browser or platform, is accessible to all users, and has at its foundation a well-oiled publishing engine that is easily managed and maintained, and ensures that you won't be facing a painful rebuild of any kind in the future.

If it comes as standard, I won't go into it. Thus, there are no lengthy discussions about DOCTYPE, CSS column layout, or the dos and don'ts of <hn> tag use. Instead, you'll take my Logical Blocks templates as a base, leaving much of the layout structure intact.

Your blog will be clean, neat, and solid. Information will be carefully spaced and placed into sensible hierarchies. Image use will be mostly subtle, making use of CSS background images that are easily replaced. The template you build will create a leaf theme, using green and yellow images alongside tweaked CSS to make your site look fresh and zesty. Yum!

About the template

The template that you will be styling is a blog template with the potential to be so much more. Throughout this chapter, you might spot areas for further exploration, but primarily you'll be building a rigid series of templates with very stylish CSS. Key to all this is a desire to avoid repetitive tasks and make EE work very hard on your behalf.

You'll come to grips with the modular nature of EE before defining some straightforward structure. Around this you'll sprinkle some flexible minimal markup before applying the eye-catching styling and images. The template will contain special tags with their own variables and parameters, allowing you to take one piece of information and treat it differently across your whole site. You'll employ simple conditional tags that protect you from extra work as you add sections later on. You'll create a blog that makes very smart use of embedded templates without hammering your server. In essence, you'll be thinking so far ahead that all you'll ever have to worry about in the future is the actual content of your blog articles.

Installing ExpressionEngine

The step-by-step lead up to running the Installation Wizard ensures that even the greenest of bloggers can quickly get up and running.

Requirements

Chapter 2 of this book showed you how to set up the PHP/MySQL/Apache environment. To run EE, your web server must have the following:

- At least 6 MB of space
- PHP version 4.1 or newer
- PHP must have XML support
- MySQL version 3.23.32 or newer

> If you are using a remote server, your hosting account must have CREATE, ALTER, and DROP grant privileges (for tables) for MySQL.

To take advantage of the image thumb-nailing feature (not used in this chapter), your server must support one of the three image-manipulation protocols: GD, ImageMagick, or NetPBM.

How to buy a copy

Yes, how to *buy* a copy. EE is not free. Unlike all the other tools in this book, this one costs $99.00 for a noncommercial license and $249.00 for a commercial one. Buy more, and you'll get reduced prices, but it still might seem way too steep to readers of this book.

So why include it? Well, you're buying unrivalled feature-rich software; the greatest customer support you could dream of; and access to hundreds of plug-ins, modules, and add-ons to take your designs to the stars and back. EE is the serious choice for anyone looking to build more than just a blog. This is the tool that can be your basis for a career in web design. Get to know its powers now and you'll be arming yourself for the terrors of working for clients in the future. With EE under your belt, you'll be ready to tackle even the wildest demands—be they your own or those of future colleagues or collaborators. If you end up building large magazine sites for good money, you'll begin to see the EE price tag as pretty cheap when it comes to project overheads.

You can purchase EE from the pMachine shop (https://secure.pmachine.com/index.php?ACT=EE) and then download a zip of the files from https://secure.pmachine.com/download.php after you have received purchase notification and license information and have logged in to the pMachine site.

Trial version

The folks at EE understand that the license cost can put off many potential customers, so luckily they allow you to run a trial version (www.pmachine.com/ee/trials) for 30 days on their server (for which you'll pay an extra $10.00 only if you decide not to buy it once the trial expires). All the base features are available, and the great thing about this trial version is that there is no database to install, there is no FTP work to be done, and you'll be building with your own secure Control Panel in minutes.

If you prefer to install the trial version on your own server, there is a downloadable trial available with encrypted source files (so you can't edit, copy, or extend the base functionality), although this expires after just 14 days. Be sure to check the server requirements on the EE trial pages.

> *You might have to install the Zend Optimizer (www.zend.com/store/products/zend-optimizer.php) before you use the 14-day trial. It's a free download that allows your PHP installation to work with the encrypted files.*

Either way, if you're frightened about spending a week's wages on a publishing tool without trying it, one of these trial options is for you. It's also very easy to move from the trial version to a fully licensed site without losing any of your customization (http://eedocs.pmachine.com/upgrade_from_trial.html). Be wary, though. Spend a few hours with EE and you will never look back. Start saving now.

In December 2005 a streamlined version called EE Core was released for bloggers who do not need membership features, photo galleries or technical support.. Core is in itself a very strong product, and is equipped with everything required for this chapter.

Installing

Assuming that you have purchased the full version of EE, you'll need to install it on your server. The following order of installation jobs is my suggestion (and is slightly different from that suggested in the EE documentation). The list assumes that you already downloaded the system files to your computer, unzipped them, and can see the folder structure on your computer.

1. Rename the system folder

The **system** folder is the true engine of EE. I recommend that you rename it admin.

2. Place the files on your server

First, delete the following files from inside the admin folder: the updates directory, and update.php. Those files are used only during system upgrades and will be provided with any future versions. Double-check to make sure that no existing files on your server share the name of any EE files or directories. Select *all* EE files and folders that are contained within the EE root folder and copy them to the root of your web server (this process might involve an FTP client if you are using a remote server). Your blog will then have a URL of http://localhost/index.php. Alternatively, if you have been following all the examples in this book, you can copy the EE root folder to your server document root. It would be more useful if you renamed this folder to EE or something similar first. This will result in a URL of http://localhost/EE/index.php.

3. Set file permissions

If you are using a remote server, you'll need to ensure that certain files and folders are writable to EE. You must not skip this step by assuming that everything will be fine. It won't. Local servers will be fine.

> *Most FTP programs allow you to set permissions using a dialog box with nine check boxes. Different combinations of these boxes will give you different permissions. Typically, you will highlight the file or directory you want to set permissions on, and then open the permissions menu, in which you'll click the appropriate check boxes. 666 means read and write access for everyone. 777 means read, write, and execute access for everyone.*

Without exception, you will need to set file permissions as follows:

Set to 666:

- path.php
- admin/config.php
- admin/config_bak.php

Set to 777:

- images/avatars/uploads/
- images/captchas/
- images/member_photos/
- images/pm_attachments/
- images/signature_attachments/
- images/uploads/
- admin/cache/

4. Create the database

Setting up a database is usually a straightforward affair. In common with the rest of this book, I recommend that you use PhpMyAdmin (www.phpmyadmin.net) to set up your database. Call your database weblog.

5. Install the Logical Blocks theme

EE installs with a default theme, but it's unlikely to suit you and won't be any good for the tutorial in this chapter. You need to choose the Logical Blocks theme by following these steps:

1. Visit the EE Template Library (http://templates.pmachine.com).

2. Choose the Logical Blocks Templates/Themes.

3. Use the Download link to download a ZIP file containing the theme.

4. Unzip the theme to the themes/site_themes/ directory.

After you finish, you should have a themes/site_themes/logical_blocks/ directory on your server. Be aware that you won't be able to switch template themes after installation. It's unlikely that you'll ever need to because you'll be happily playing with the Logical Blocks template set as a basis for whatever you end up building.

6. Run the Installation Wizard

Point your browser at the install.php file at http://localhost/install.php. You'll see the official installation preparation steps, which are somewhat similar to this list. At the top and bottom is the link asking you to continue—and you should.

There are a few confusing terms and questions on the wizard page, but those lovely EE folks have informed you when to care and when not to. Typically, only the items discussed as follows should concern you and only in rare cases do you need to worry about the extras.

7. Define settings and user account

Most likely, the wizard will have already completed most of these fields for you. All you'll probably have to do here is submit your email address as webmaster.

Next, enter your Database Settings in the required fields.

The page will also ask you to create your Admin Account, requiring a username, a password, your email address, a Screen Name (your author name that will appear on your site), and the name of your site.

8. Choose the appropriate template

Finally, in the spirit of making life easy, EE offers more than 20 template models, which you can see in action at http://templates.pmachine.com/. To follow many of the steps in this chapter, you need to select the most excellent Logical Blocks template, which was installed previously. You'll be reworking much of the design, but at least we'll all be starting on the same page.

9. You're all but done

Click the submit button, and in a whirl the system will be installed, your database tables will be populated, and a success page will appear, inviting you to check out your **Control Panel** (shown in Figure 4-2) and your actual blog.

Very important: All that remains is to delete the install.php file from your server for security purposes.

> *If for some reason your installation didn't go smoothly, scroll to the bottom of the Installation Instructions* (www.pmachine.com/expressionengine/docs/installation.html) *page for some troubleshooting tips.*

How does ExpressionEngine actually work?

Get to know the EE Control Panel because it will be your cockpit for the foreseeable future. To begin with, you'll learn about the Templates functions. In subsequent sections of this chapter, you'll learn more about some other key Control Panel tools, such as Publish, Edit, and Admin. Sections such as Communicate (the email module) and Modules won't be relevant for this chapter, although I recommend that you find some time to explore the wonders within them.

The Control Panel homepage (see Figure 4-2) shows you an overview of activity to date. Typically, you will see two columns with the latest posts and comments linked on the left, and stats and a notepad on the right. After install, you'll see one sample entry is automatically added to your site.

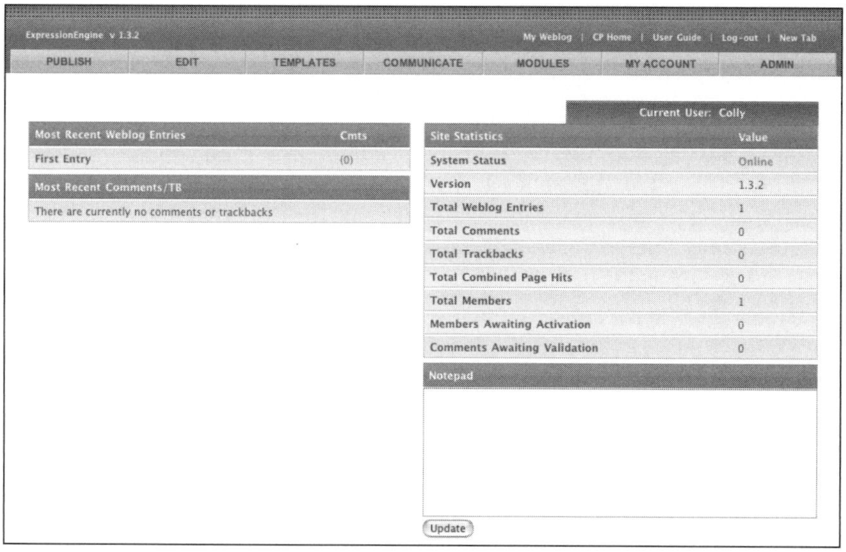

Figure 4-2. Control Panel homepage

Before you set about defining your blog structure, it is worth delving into how EE's **template system** actually works. Brilliantly, everything is self-contained, edited through a browser, and very, very flexible.

Templates

When you click the Templates menu item, you see the screen shown in Figure 4-3.

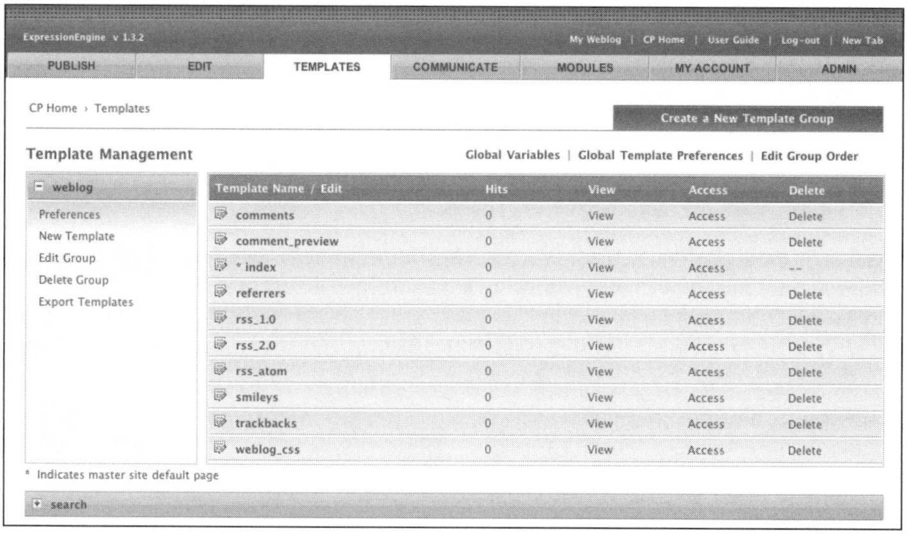

Figure 4-3. Template Management screen

You'll find two template **groups** already available, namely weblog and search (refer to Figure 4-3). Each group contains at least one template, each of which at this stage can be thought of as a complete page (made up of <head>, <body>, and all the other things you expect from a web page). This is EE structure in its simplest form.

EE URLs most likely look strange to you. The EE authors were careful to avoid using query strings (such as www.localhost/index.php?id=2&page=1), in which question marks and ampersands are used to fetch database information). The main reason was to make URLs easier for search engines to understand. So, all EE queries flow through the index.php file, and the work is done in the background. After the index.php part comes segments named and specified by you.

So how come you get to name these segments? Well, EE templates are stored in template *groups* that you create and define based on the site sections you need. The following description should help you understand the correlation between URL segments and template groups.

Look at a typical EE URL. In this example, you'll notice two additional words after the index.php segment. These are *not* directories, even though they look like directories. They are references to EE templates and groups created by you.

    http://localhost/index.php/*weblog/archives*

In this example, *weblog* is the template group, and *archives* is the actual template. These are templates and groups that *you* create. Sure, EE has some basic structure after install, but nobody is dictating anything to you here—you decide the structure and you structure with templates. Creating a new template group with its own templates inside creates new URLs to build your site. So, if you created a new group called blog and inside that you made a template into which you'd place an archive of all your articles, you might end up with a URL such as this one:

    http://localhost/index.php/*blog/archives*

Clicking to read more about each would require an individual article page, perhaps a new template called more. Dynamically, the EE system would use this more template to render the selected article, and automatically add the title of the selected case study to this URL:

    http://localhost/index.php/blog/more/*my_first_article*

Thankfully, there are a number of shortcut **tags** you can use to avoid typing out such long strings as you build, which will also make it easy to move your entire site to a different domain with the minimum of fuss. In fact, you'll never have to type the http:// localhost/index.php part anywhere in the templates.

> *It is important to understand this URL concept before moving on. Knowing the name of the template group and the template will allow you to adjust URLs in your browser to view pages in progress, long before you link to them from any other pages.*

Be aware that, by default, all template groups contain an index template, which you cannot delete, but can fully customize. This template is useful for creating shorter URLs for particular groups, essentially forming that group's homepage. The following two URLs lead to the same destination:

```
http://localhost/index.php/blog/index
http://localhost/index.php/blog
```

So, you'll have different template groups for different sections. You might have a portfolio group, an image gallery group, a journal group, and so on—each containing specific templates, or pages. On a typical site, you might then assign a template group to a particular section, or **weblog**.

Blogs, custom fields, and categories

Upon install, a blog called weblog1 is already created for you. It will contain one sample article and three sample **categories**, and you write your entries using basic entry fields. Before you go on, it is worth learning a bit more about all of these.

Blogs are the sections of your site and contain the information to be displayed. This is in contrast to templates, which specify how that information is displayed. In other words, the content is separated from the site's design. Blogs are of course tied in with templates. If you were to create several blogs (sections), such as one for your journal, one for your portfolio, one for album reviews, you should create a template group for each, naming them after your blogs. Thus, entries from your reviews blog should appear on your reviews group templates. This is not essential, but if you end up building big websites with EE, this modeling will really make sense of your structuring.

Sticking with the preceding example, you might create a blog called blog. In that blog you would place your blog entries, or case studies. By calling these entries into your blog templates, you determine how they are rendered on the site. You can define a set of custom entry fields, such as "Intro", "More detail", "Related links", and so on, to actually enter the data for the different parts of a page, just like any other web form. After you have entered data using these fields, you can control how the data is displayed on a field-by-field basis. For example, you could display the "Intro" field's text on one page and link to another page that contains all the other fields' text, formatted as you like it.

Finally, you can categorize the blog entries into areas such as "Family", "Work", "Observations", and so on. You'll learn how to do this later in the chapter.

> *Earlier, I suggested that you can think of templates as pages, and this is mostly true. Yet, this limits the way in which EE can really save time and effort and increase flexibility. This is where embeds can help.*

Embeds

In this chapter, you will create some templates that are not "pages" at all. Rather, these will be **embeds,** which are chunks of information that can be inserted into multiple pages where the same content is desired, for example page headers or footers, navigation menus, and so on. When you change the content of these embeds, this information will be automatically updated in every page that the embeds are included in. External JavaScript and CSS files work in a similar way, in that they are called into a template using a file reference, but the actual code remains external. Making one change to your CSS file affects all pages referencing it, and this method helps us understand template embeds. Many web designers use server-side includes in the same way, where there is a file that exists elsewhere on the server that is pulled into a full web page where necessary (something easily achieved using PHP). Thankfully, EE's embeds make this process incredibly simple and keep everything self-contained within the Templates area of the Control Panel.

> Brilliantly, you can place an embed in an embed, in an embed, and so on. Sure, there are a few rules to watch out for, but for now just celebrate and think about what you'll do with all that time you'll be saving.

Rest assured that later in the chapter you'll learn step-by-step how to create simple embed templates to get EE working hard on your behalf.

So, if you understand the preceding ideas but want to read more, check out the *EE User Guide*, which can be found at www.pmachine.com/expressionengine/docs. Otherwise, go and make a pot of tea because when you come back, you'll be getting down to some serious hard work.

Structuring your blog

In this section you can forget the theory, for it's time to get practical. Later you'll get to play with the CSS, but first you'll work through modeling your blog's structure. To start with, you'll create a new homepage and full article page before moving on to categories and customized entry fields. After that, you'll define a few preferences and adjust some EE tags to refine template performance. Finally, you'll make your comments system a bit smarter and carve the templates into embeds for easier site-wide management. Keep an eye on the walk-through steps to ensure that you don't miss a trick. In this section, you'll come to grips with the following:

- Turning the system off: Working privately so that only you as the logged-in administrator can see the site taking shape at the URL.
- Defining Template Group and Template: Creating your first editable template and using this as a basis for your site's URL structure.
- Editing templates: How to manage templates and fine points of editing.

- Redefining categories: Taking the default categories and changing them to suit your needs.

- Defining custom blog fields: Extending the default data fields to get more out of publishing.

- Specifying groups for your blog: Extending the functionality of the blog area by assigning categories in which to archive items and defining a custom set of data fields to hold the information.

- Default blog and preferences: Ensuring that the blog works the way you want it to.

Turning the system off

First things first: You need to switch the system off. Yes, off. EE allows you to prevent snoopers from viewing your build. As Super Admin, you can still view your site by logging in to the Control Panel and then calling up http://localhost/index.php in your browser. Go to Admin ➤ System Preferences ➤ General Configuration and switch the system off (see Figure 4-4).

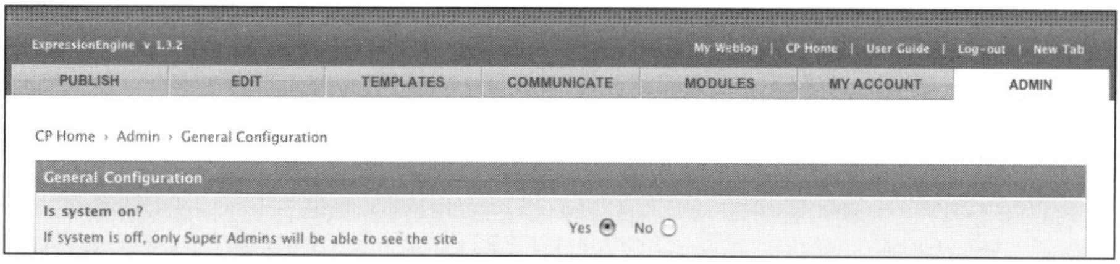

Figure 4-4. Be sure to switch the system off.

Defining Template Group and Template

1. Make your way to Templates from the main menu. On the right side of the bread-crumb menu, click Create a New Template Group.

2. In the box (see Figure 4-5), type a name for what will be your main template group by using a single word with no spaces (underscores are allowed). Remember, this name will form the basis of many of your site's URLs. Call it blog.

3. Opt to copy the weblog template group by selecting weblog from the drop-down box, which will make a full copy of the files and preferences of the default weblog template group. You do this primarily because it illustrates a very useful feature of EE, but also means you have a back-up group of the templates as they were installed, just in case you ever need them.

4. Click Make the index template in this group your site's homepage, which will force this template group's index file to be your site homepage, making the following two URLs identical:

   ```
   http://localhost/index.php/blog/index
   http://localhost/index.php
   ```

5. Click Submit, which will create the template group and take you back to the template group page.

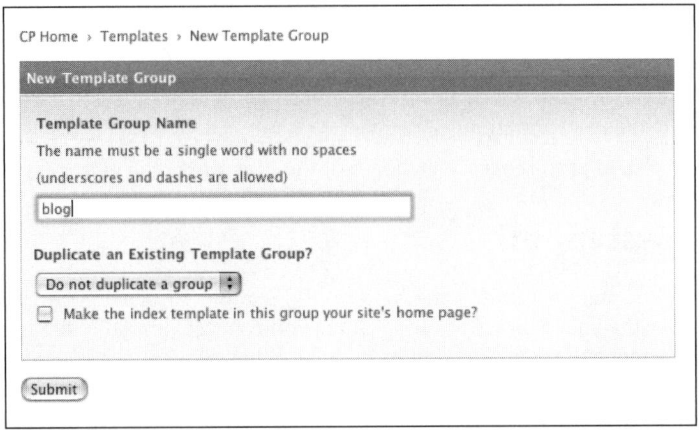

Figure 4-5. Create a New Template Group.

So you now have a new template group (blog) and homepage (blog/index) defined. You'll now see three groups, including your blog group on the Template Management screen. Click on blog to instantly expand and show all templates in the group (see Figure 4-6). There are quite a few choices and bits of info for each template, including hits for that page. You can also View a template in a new window, use Access to ban certain member groups from seeing it, and Delete it. Ignore most of these and the other options for now.

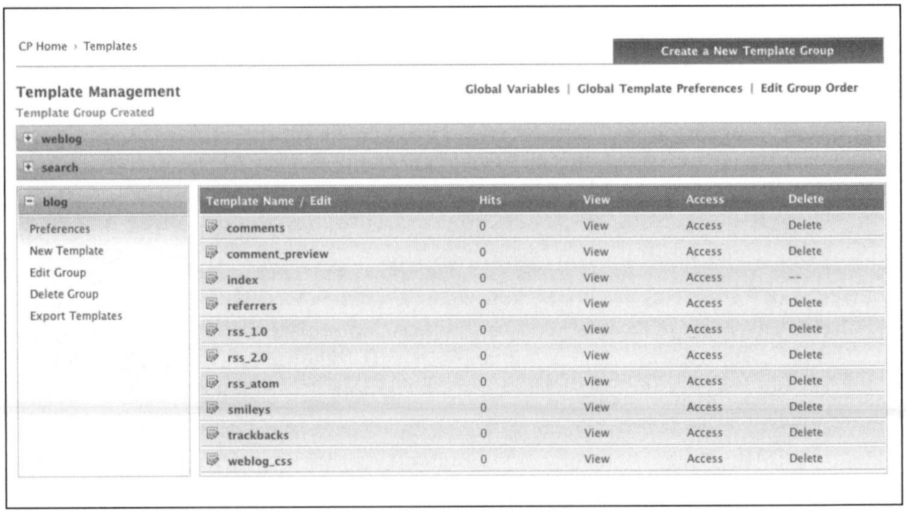

Figure 4-6. The blog template group expanded

Editing templates

Each template name is a link to an editable version. For example, you would click the index link to view and edit the source code (see Figure 4-7). Remember that this represents a full page, so you could edit the head information and all the body code right there. Remember this because you'll be in these templates rather a lot later in the chapter.

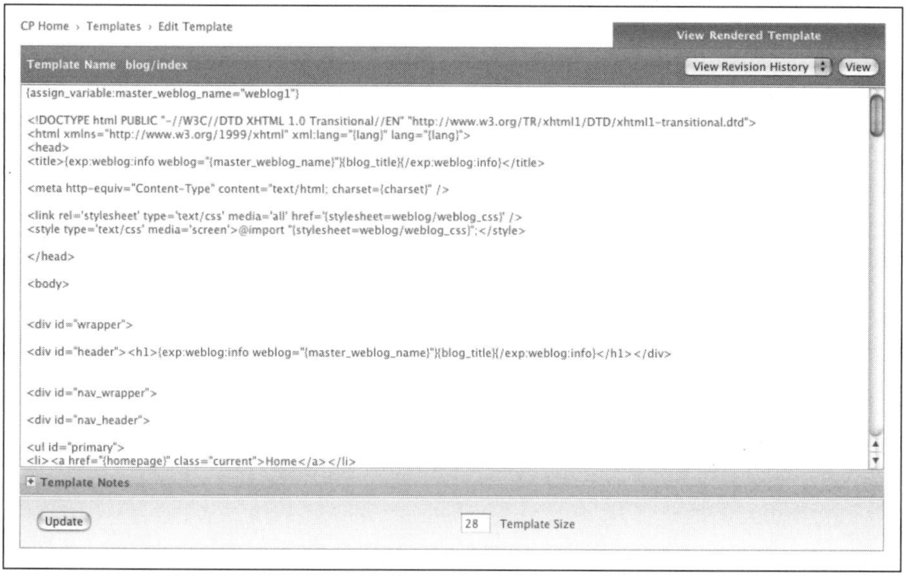

Figure 4-7. Editing a template

Redefine the categories

The default categories are unlikely to suit your needs. Naturally, it's easy to edit and add categories using EE. Follow these steps to change the categories:

1. Go to Admin from the main menu, and in Weblog Administration, select Category Management.

2. Rename the category group, by selecting Edit Group, and call the group Blog. Click Update to make the change. This will also take you back to the Category Management screen.

3. Now, select Add/edit Categories. From here, you can delete any unwanted categories, grab the **category ID** (not required for this tutorial), or customize the order (see Figure 4-8). For now, keep them alphabetical and select one to edit by clicking the Edit button.

4. In the required Category Name field, rename the category using plain English (any number of words) to whatever you need. (You will not need to specify a category image or description for this tutorial.)

5. As EE allows you to nest categories, you can also opt to make the category the "child" of a "parent" category by selecting another from the Category Parent drop-down menu. For example, you could create a category called Apple and make it the parent of child categories Software, Hardware, iPods, and Downloads.

6. Now add more categories. Select Create a New Category to the right of the breadcrumb menu on the main category page. The form is the same as the one for editing. Create a category called Movies before creating child categories Adventure, Horror, and Comedy. You can assign the parent to a child category when you create the child category.

7. Repeat this process and keep editing categories/parents/children until you're happy with your initial blog categories. Try Music, News, and Family as other parents, and assign your own children to these.

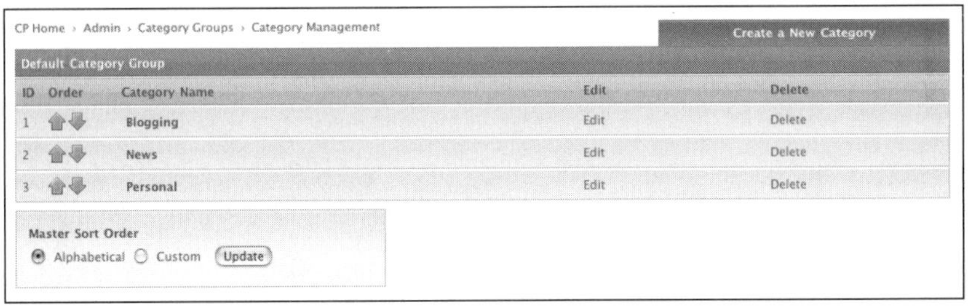

Figure 4-8. Managing categories

Define custom blog fields

The final chunk of prep is to define **custom entry fields** for your blog (see Figure 4-9). Possibly the most powerful element of EE, the ability to customize a blog with its own unique unlimited entry fields and then to decide whether to use that set on all or just selected blogs is what makes EE a great CMS tool. Once you gain experience, you can use EE **conditionals** and more-complex standard PHP to add, combine, and check the contents of your fields for very powerful results.

Brilliantly, each field can be further tweaked. Do you want your new field to be a text input, text area, or drop-down? Is it searchable? Is it required? How will you format it: XHTML, auto <BR>, or none whatsoever? In this tutorial, you'll use XHTML for text inputs and text areas, and no formatting for drop-downs.

I won't let you use auto <BR> because it's not big, not clever, and not appropriate for a site that is built using web standards because break tags are like presentational dinosaurs that litter otherwise clean markup (and can be avoided with <p> tags and a little CSS).

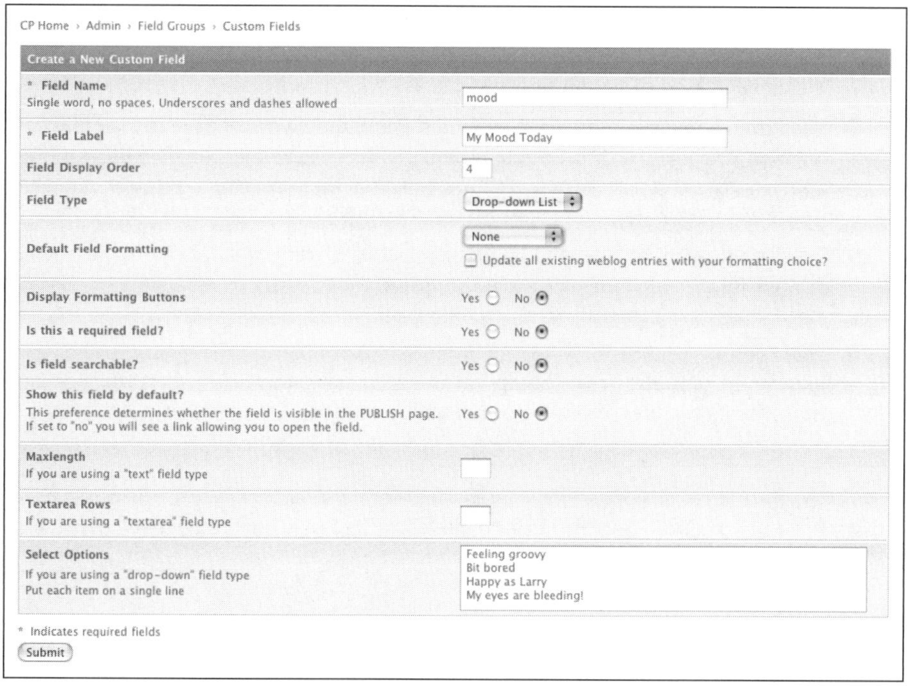

CP Home › Admin › Field Groups › Custom Fields

Create a New Custom Field

* **Field Name** Single word, no spaces. Underscores and dashes allowed	mood
* **Field Label**	My Mood Today
Field Display Order	4
Field Type	Drop-down List
Default Field Formatting	None ☐ Update all existing weblog entries with your formatting choice?
Display Formatting Buttons	Yes ○ No ⦿
Is this a required field?	Yes ○ No ⦿
Is field searchable?	Yes ○ No ⦿
Show this field by default? This preference determines whether the field is visible in the PUBLISH page. If set to "no" you will see a link allowing you to open the field.	Yes ○ No ⦿
Maxlength If you are using a "text" field type	
Textarea Rows If you are using a "textarea" field type	
Select Options If you are using a "drop-down" field type Put each item on a single line	Feeling groovy Bit bored Happy as Larry My eyes are bleeding!

* Indicates required fields

Submit

Figure 4-9. Creating a new custom entry field

Set the mood

By default, there are three fields: Summary, Body, and Extended. The Title field cannot be removed or edited, and there is no reason why you need to. Anyway, now you will refine your custom entry fields, removing Extended and adding a new field called My Mood Today:

1. Go to Admin from the main menu and in Weblog Administration, click Custom Weblog Fields.

2. Only Default Field Group exists, and you need to click Add/Edit Custom Fields to remove/add fields.

3. Delete the extraneous Extended text field. You do not need it, and removing it will keep your published pages clean and simple. You can just use the Body field for your extended article text. Still, it's useful to create a new field here, just so you know what's what.

4. On the right of the breadcrumb menu, click Create a New Custom Field (refer to Figure 4-9). Let's see. Why not create a field to tell your readers what mood you are in?

5. Field Name is the variable name you will place in the template to show the data. Type mood.

6. Field Label is the plain English label or sentence that will show on the Publishing page. Type My mood today.

7. Decide what kind of field it needs to be. Try a Drop-down List.

8. If you then choose None for Default Field Formatting, you are free to style the data however you want in the template, and I recommend this for drop-downs. Text inputs and text areas benefit from being XHTML-formatted because data line breaks will have paragraph tags appended nicely.

9. The drop-down doesn't need to be searchable or required, so skip to the Select Options bit. Very simply, add each option on a line of its own: Feeling groovy, Bit bored, Happy as Larry, My eyes are bleeding!

10. Click Submit. Hey Presto! A field of your own. Once back at the main menu of your field group, you also have the option of rearranging the field order, which is very useful for larger sites and for blogs in which you forgot to add seven fields.

> *Opting to* Display Formatting Buttons *in Weblog Preferences allows you to override the Default Field Formatting choice in the* Publish *page on a per-entry basis.*

While you're here, you can edit the Summary field to allow people to search it. Click the Edit button for Summary and then set the Is field searchable? radio button to Yes.

Specify groups for your blog

By *groups*, I mean custom entry fields groups, such as the custom entry fields group you edited just now, and category groups, such as the Blogs category group. There is also something called a *status group*, but you don't need it in this chapter. Groups add extra power to each blog area, extending the capabilities of each and modeling the data it contains.

For example, without assigning groups to a blog, you wouldn't have any fields in which to enter your data or categories in which to archive the articles, so your pages would be blank. Likewise, if you created a new category group for a blog, without assigning it to the blog, you couldn't place articles into those categories or make use of the custom fields you defined for it.

It's useful to know where this is all done, and you need to make sure that the correct groups are assigned to your blog before you continue.

1. Go back to Weblog Administration ➤ Weblog Management from the Admin menu, and you'll see your blog listed.

2. Select Edit Groups, and EE will show you which groups are assigned to that blog (see Figure 4-10). A new blog has no groups assigned until you select them. Yours will show the Default groups already assigned. Job done.

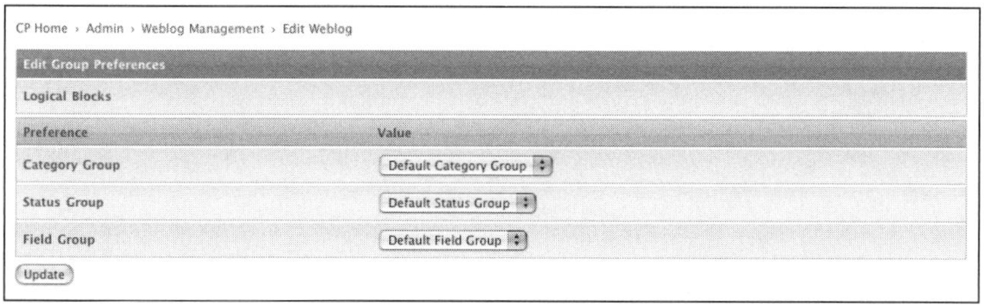

Figure 4-10. Assigning groups to a blog

For future reference, remember that you can assign one group (categories or custom fields) to many blogs, or have unique groups for each.

Default blog and preferences

As a newbie, rather than creating a new blog, you're better off developing with the default weblog1. The user-friendly Full Section Name is whatever name you gave your blog on install, but weblog1 is the vital variable you use to show results from a particular blog in your templates.

1. Go to Admin from the main menu and select Weblog Management from the Weblog Administration menu.

2. To the right of your Full Section Name, click Edit Preferences and you will be shown a myriad of new and exciting preferences unique to that blog (see Figure 4-11). Select General Weblog Preferences.

3. There are some key changes to be made in here. For a start, rename the blog Full Weblog Name. Call it Blog, and give it a short description.

4. This next bit is very important. Although EE is flexible enough to let you place data from any blog on any template anywhere, you should still define the path settings for the blog. To do so, expand the Path Settings node. Indicating the correct paths to templates here will ensure that your search results and Really Simple Syndication (RSS) feeds will work for you later on. You must point to your homepage (blog/index) and your article page (blog/more) as shown in Figure 4-12.

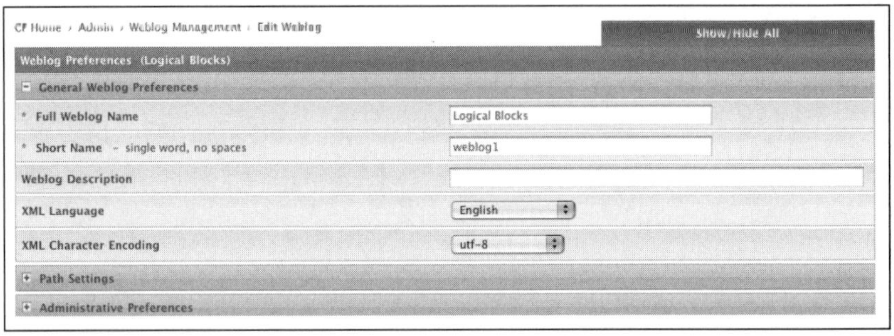

Figure 4-11. A section of the Weblog Preferences page

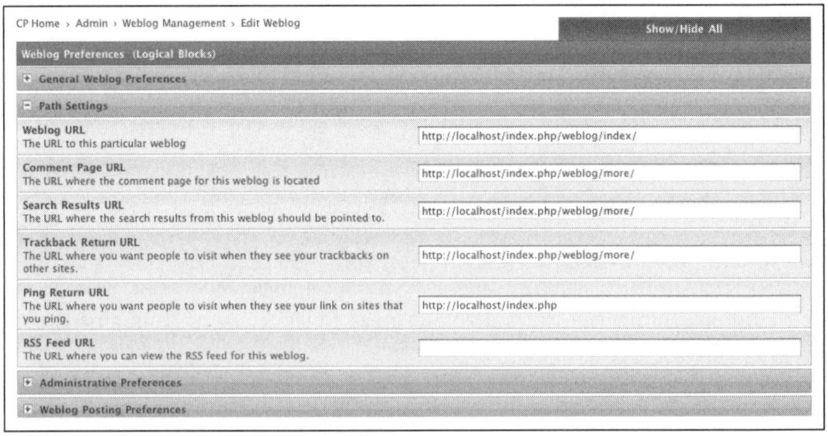

Figure 4-12. Defining path settings for your blog

While you are there, you might as well define a few other preferences. Most are set appropriately for a blog, but it is worth noting a few here. Open the Administrative Preferences node:

1. You can select from which custom entry field the search results will show an excerpt. Ensure that "Summary" is selected in the appropriate drop-down box.

2. Also, leave Allow Comments and Allow Trackbacks selected, so all your articles will be available for such unless you override on composing.

3. That will do for now. Click Update to save the preferences for weblog1.

Nice work, soldier

Understanding template groups, blogs, custom fields, and categories is key to a successful EE site, and although you edited only what was already there, it should be clear how to replicate it to define a whole new blog that might have its own unique groups or share those of another blog. Time for another cup of tea and maybe a cookie because next you'll be getting it on with the code.

Template customization

Now it's time to think about the actual scaffold of your blog. In the previous section, you worked through the data modeling, a vital part of the process that now needs to be reflected publicly via the page templates. Earlier in the chapter, you learned how EE templates work and how careful template naming creates sensible URLs. You're now aware that all template work happens within the Control Panel. In short, this is where the fun really begins.

In this section, you'll cover the following areas of template customization:

- Templates: A description of the templates you'll need to create.
- EE tags: How simple tags represent both default data and your own custom data and how to make the best use of such tags.
- Path variables: Working with simple path tags to replace long-winded absolute links and learning how this can help if you to move the site to another server.
- Conditionals: Handling variable data. If something equals x, do y. If y is empty, do z, and so on.
- Smarter conditionals: How to handle comments and comment totals and make EE work harder for you.
- Categories: Earlier you created some custom categories, but how do you show them on your public pages?

Over the next few sections, you'll be concentrating on two templates from your blog template group: index and more. You'll work at refining the index template with EE tags and semantic markup. Finally, you'll work out which areas of it are suitable to be made into embed templates for use on several or all templates.

> *EE allows you to store the changes you make to your templates, so if you make a glaring error or don't realize that you trashed the markup until several moves later, you can opt to open up a previously saved version of that template and copy it all, or the part that you wrecked, back into the latest version. Go to Global* Template Preferences *from the Templates section, and find the* Maximum Number of Revisions to Keep *preference. If you set this to* 5, *only the most recent 5 revisions will be saved for any given template. By all means set it to store up to 50 revisions, but be aware that each stored revision adds weight to your database.*

Templates you'll need

Your working site needs four main pages. Most of them will be obvious, but just to clarify, here's a basic description of the templates you'll need.

Index template

Think of this as your homepage. The **index template** is the default page in which the initial action happens. It shows titles and short bursts of your latest posts, has a list of your categories, and should also include a description of what visitors can expect to find within the site.

More page

Possibly the most important page of your website, the **more page** shows full articles by combining the data from all the custom fields into a seamless article (title, intro, main body of text, other custom elements). It shows just the selected entry by default and is not designed to show multiple entries. It is considered the most important template because it is normally full of articles that visitors land on via search engines, RSS feeds, and links on other blogs.

About page

You want to tell people who you are, right? Often you'll give important information about yourself in your articles, but it's important to collate some friendly facts in one easily accessible place: the **about page**. You can also use this template to introduce your blog at greater length. Why do you blog? What will you blog about? What can potential readers expect from you?

Contact page

The readers love you. They want to send you free things, or possibly want to offer you a job or something dirtier! Without a contact, they'll move on to someone else, so provide a simple **contact page** with a form that has your email address hidden within to prevent email spamming.

You'll see how to create these templates later in the chapter.

A number of other default pages will be available after install. Standard EE templates for search results, RSS feeds, archives, and so on already exist, and after you master template editing through your four main pages, you'll probably want to spend some time ensuring that these other templates fit the mold. Regrettably, there isn't enough space in this chapter to cover those modifications, but you should be armed to deal with the job after you've soaked up the advice on these pages.

Understanding EE tags

All EE tags are housed inside curly brackets and most can be customized using combinations of available variables. Let's look at a few. To view a template's code, click its name in the Template Management screen. So, to work with the blog template group, go to Templates from the main menu and expand the blog node. You can then work with each template, as described in the next few sections.

{master_weblog_name}

In your index template, you'll find the following at the very top. Click the template's name in the expanded blog node to view this:

```
{assign_variable:master_weblog_name="weblog1"}
```

This statement is placed at the very top of each template in the blog group that needs to find information from weblog1, your "Blog" blog. Making this statement saves you having to specify this blog in future EE tags; you'll just use {master_weblog_name} in its place. This is useful if you copy this template for use with another blog. All you do is alter the opening variable definition to inform all tags containing the {master_weblog_name} variable to look at that blog.

{exp:weblog:entries}

Next is the {exp:weblog:entries} tag, which represents a PHP routine designed to find all the data you published to a particular blog. Scroll to the blog <div> halfway into the index template and find the tag. The format is as follows:

```
{exp:weblog:entries weblog= ➥
"{master_weblog_name}" orderby="date" sort="desc" limit="15"}
    Data pulled from the weblog here
{/exp:weblog:entries}
```

First, notice the closing tag: {/exp:weblog:entries}. Most core EE functions require opening and closing tags. Second, look at some of the **parameters** inside the opening tag. The three shown give you some idea of how you can customize the results. You can order results by date, a particular custom field, or title. Perhaps you want to sort in ascending order? Limit to 5, 10, 46 entries?

You can opt to show results from one, two, or more defined categories by specifying the category ID (as discussed in the "Redefine the categories" section earlier), using category="2", using category="2|3|6", and so on. You can also specify which categories not to include by using category="not 4|6", which excludes categories 4 and 6.

The offset parameter is useful for breaking up entries into dynamic groups, perhaps showing a lot of detail from one entry by using limit="1" in one {exp:weblog:entries} tag; then closing that chunk and opening a new chunk using "offset=1" limit="5" in the {exp:weblog:entries} tag to show just the preceding entry titles, for example. I can't even begin to tell you how many more parameters exist for you to go crazy with because I have other things to do with my life.

Showing data inside the {exp:weblog:entries} tags

Remember creating/editing some custom entry fields earlier ("Define custom blog fields," steps 1–10)? Now you will add some EE variables inside the {exp:weblog:entries} tags to show the data.

Field name variables

To add a field to a template, you use a tag with the same name as the field, like so: {fieldname}. So, for example, adding the {summary} field name variable will show the contents of the Summary field from the selected blog. If when you edited that Custom Entry Field you selected XHTML for Default Field Formatting, you leave it as is. If you opted for no formatting, you could add paragraph tags to the variable:

```
<p>{summary}</p>
```

1. Remember the My Mood Today field you created in steps 1–10? You gave it the field name mood, so show it as follows:

```
<p><strong>My mood today:</strong> {mood}</p>
```

What if you sometimes don't fill that field in? Perhaps you'll leave that field blank when you write a new article and you consider it an optional piece of information.

2. If you don't want to display fields when they have been left empty for a particular blog entry, you'll also need to remove the related markup. To do this you add a conditional that checks to see whether that field is empty in the database:

```
{if mood != ""}<p><strong>My mood today:</strong> {mood}</p>{/if}
```

Here the {if} statement contains a comparison operator (the != bit), which stands for "not equal to" and tests to see whether the mood field is not empty (the "" bit). If it's empty, the code enclosed within the {if} statement will be ignored, so the mood information will not be displayed. Similar syntax can also be used to see whether a value is equal to another and produce a particular result based on that. If this excites you, go grab a good PHP book and check out the possibilities of comparison operators.

Place this code in the index template just below the {body} tag and remove the {extended} tag. Remember that you removed this field earlier in the chapter so there is now no need for its tag.

Some key {exp:weblog:entries} variables

There are quite a few key variables in use here, placed into the template by the EE chaps. Their aim is to provide you with all major variables so all you have to do is remove the ones you don't need.

{date_heading}

The {date_heading} tags display the dates that entries were published. However, again, EE has a clever trick to pull out of the bag here. If two or more are published on one date, that date will only show once, above the latest entry. Next time an article is published on a different date, it will show the new date above it. EE date formats use standard PHP date variables http://uk.php.net/date, and are customized by editing the %d,%m,%y variables and similar.

```
{date_heading}
<div class="date">{entry_date format=' %l, %F %d, %Y'}</div>
{/date_heading}
```

Data variables

The {title} variable is, as you expect, the title of the entry. Note the path variable in the hyperlink. You'll learn about those in a short while.

```
<h2>a href="{title_permalink=weblog/index}">{title}</a></h2>
```

Change the weblog link to blog, so you're using this blog's title. You'll be doing this throughout this section:

```
<h2>a href="{title_permalink=blog/index}">{title}</a></h2>
```

Custom entry field variables

By default, EE templates show the original field variables that are created with the blog.

1. Remember that you deleted the {extended} field earlier.
2. You only need {summary} in the index template because you'll show the full entry when you click through to the more template.

{categories}

The posted section performs a few tasks. If you were building a site allowing users to sign up for whatever reason or if you wanted to link to your User Profile, you'd use the link as shown in the {categories} section.

The {categories} tags list all categories in which the article was archived on submission and uses another path variable to create a link that will append the category ID to the URL to make your index template show only entries from that category.

```
Posted by <a href="{profile_path=member/index}">{author}</a>in
{categories}<a href="{path=SITE_INDEX}">{category_name}</a>
{/categories}
```

For your blog, remove the author link code because users will know whose blog they are visiting.

Conditionals

Next, you'll see more EE conditionals. The {if allow_comments} conditional checks to see whether you are accepting comments for the article; if you are, it will execute the code within, showing the total comments so far and adding a link to the more template. You'll learn a couple of tricks later to make this part work better for you.

```
{if allow_comments}
  ({comment_total}) ➡
  <a href="{url_title_path="blog/more"}">Comments</a>
{/if}
```

Pagination

The {paginate} variable looks at how many articles you have set in the {exp:weblog:entries} limit parameter and creates a Google-style set of page links (Page 1 of 4: 1|2|3|4, etc.):

```
{paginate}
  Page {current_page} of {total_pages} pages {pagination_links}
/paginate}
```

If you set the limit parameter to show five entries, after the fifth this tag will create links to the next page(s) of five, adding a variable to the URL to offset entries on the index template. See, this one template is starting to do a lot of work.

Path variables

The default template install misses a few of the tricks that make EE great, and now is a perfect time to make use of some of them. Path variables are a great feature that the EE documentation needs to make a bigger meal out of. Essentially, you'll never have to type your full URL with path variables. The following variable will substitute http://localhost/index.php:

```
{path="SITE_INDEX"}
```

Now this is great. When you finally move the site to a live web server or if you ever move to another server, all you need to do is change the paths as defined in General and Weblog Preferences.

You can add the template group and template name you specify, and this will automatically include your base site path.

```
{path=template_group/template}
```

The preceding variables can be used anywhere and are particularly useful for navigation.

Furthermore, if you use the following tag to link to your more template, EE will be sure to add the title of the entry to the URL. The URL title is created automatically when you publish an article, with some clever EE code-smithery replacing spaces and irregular characters with dashes or underscores via the medium of PHP:

```
{title_permalink="blog/more"}
```

That actually renders as `http://localhost/index.php/blog/more/my_article_title`.

Smarter conditionals

If you have data in the {body} field of an article, you create a link to the more template to show it, but it is worth adding a bit more flexibility here. I suggest that you prepare your template as follows:

1. If you need to use only the {summary} field, and there is nothing extra to show on the more template, add a conditional to see whether {body} is empty; if so, the link will be removed.

2. Remember the {if} statement you used earlier to check whether {mood} was empty or not? Here, you use a similar statement for {body}, wrapped around the {title} variable. It has to be used twice so that both parts of the link markup are conditional:

```
{if body != ""}
  <a href="{title_permalink="blog/more"}">{/if}{title}{if body != ""} ➠
</a>
{/if}
```

Replace the code that displays an <h2> version of the title:

```
<h2 class="title">
  <a href="{title_permalink=weblog/index}">{title}</a>
</h2>
```

Using this code can prevent users from viewing the article on its own and deny access to any other features you might provide on the more template. It is ideal for short posts, quick links, or stuff that's not that important to you.

Smarter comment totals

In the default template is the following code:

```
{if allow_comments}
  ({comment_total}) <a href="{url_title_path="weblog/comments"}"> ➠
Comments</a>
{/if}
```

That is fine, but what if there are no comments or only one? Wouldn't it be better to have it say "No comments" rather than "0 comments", or "1 comment" rather than the terrible "1 comments". Instead, you use {if} conditionals to test whether {comment_total} is less than, greater than, or equal to one, and show the appropriate result:

```
{if allow_comments}
  {if comment_total < 1}no comments{/if}
  {if comment_total == 1}
    <a href="{title_permalink="blog/more"}"> 1 comment</a>
  {/if}
  {if comment_total > 1}
    <a href="{title_permalink="blog/more"}"> {comment_total} comments ➥
</a>
  {/if}
{/if}
```

Notice also that EE allows {if} statements inside {if} statements. You first test to see whether comments are allowed and then test for the quantity inside that.

Sort out the sidebar

By default, EE puts certain tags into the sidebar <div> that you won't need for this tutorial. Because you are building a personal blog, you need to remove the following conditional aimed at checking whether a user is logged in or not:

```
<h3>Members</h3>
<ul>
  the conditional code
</ul>
```

Showing your category list

Next, the categories you defined earlier are called in to the sidebar. The {exp:weblog:categories} tag requires the blog to be defined, and by adding the style="nested" parameter, EE will automatically create an unordered list, indenting child categories inside their own list(s). The great thing here is that this type of list is semantic, and you can define multilevel list styles later to control each list. In the following snippets, note that the paths have been pointed to your blog template group:

```
<h3>Categories</h3>
{exp:weblog:categories weblog="{master_weblog_name}" style="nested"}
  <a href="{path=blog/index}">{category_name}</a>
{/exp:weblog:categories}
```

Also, you can add show_empty="no" to the {exp:weblog:categories} code to show categories only after they contain at least one article.

Using article titles as headlines

Now this is where you can start to define exactly what you want to show in the sidebar. Use {exp:weblog:entries} tags to show a set number of headlines from your blog:

```
<h3>Most recent posts</h3>
<ul>
  {exp:weblog:entries orderby="date" sort="desc" limit="15" ➡
                                weblog="{master_weblog_name}"}
    <li><a href="{title_permalink=blog/more}">{title}</a></li>
  {/exp:weblog:entries}
</ul>
```

Note that here you do need to add unordered list markup. The <ul> and </ul> tags come outside of the {exp:weblog:entries} tag to avoid being looped. The <li> </li> tags are within, and they will be multiplied however many times you specify in the limit parameter.

Using parameters, you can show the most commented articles using the orderby= "comment_total" parameter. For a full list of available parameters, see the *User Guide* (www.pmachine.com/expressionengine/docs/templates/weblog/parameters.html).

So, the index template should be working a bit harder for you now, and the concept of EE tags should be clearer. The final thing to do is change all the links to the weblog blog to links to the blog blog, as you have done with all the examples so far. After that, index is complete as a template, and you need not do anything else to it. Still, there must be a few sections of the code that you want to use on other pages or might need to edit later on. It's time to consider embeds.

Make it easier with embedding

After you are happy with the index template, you can think about turning some of the chunks into **embeds**—blocks of code that can be included in other pages and make site-wide editing much easier.

Embed the main navigation

I guarantee that you'll want to change your main navigation menu regularly. Perhaps you'll want to link to your new photo galleries section or maybe change the order of the nav items. This can be a real pain in the markup, so having your main navigation exist as an embedded template makes great future-thinking sense. Later in this section you'll make the actual menu more dynamic, and when you do, you'll be glad you only need to change the one file. Here's how to create the embed:

1. Select Templates from the main menu.

2. Click Create a New Template Group and create a group called includes.

3. Do not duplicate a group nor make the index template your homepage. Just give the group a name and submit.

4. Next, create a new empty template in the include group and call it main_nav. This empty template will soon power the main menu on every page.

5. Go back to the blog/index template, and find the following menu code:

```
<div id="nav_wrapper">
  <div id="nav_header">
    <ul id="primary">
      <li><a href="{homepage}" class="current">Home</a></li>
      (all nav links)
      <li><a href="#">Spare 2</a></li>
    </ul>
  </div>
</div>
```

6. Copy that code and type the following in its place:

```
{embed="includes/main_nav"}
```

7. Save the blog/index template.

8. Navigate back to your new includes template group, and open main_nav.

9. Paste the menu code you copied a few moments ago into it and save the template (save Figure 4-13). You have just created your first embed.

Just think, you can now edit the main menu for every page that has the {embed="includes/main_nav"} marker. Thus, if you need to rename a menu tab, add another, or change a path, you only need to edit the includes/main_nav template.

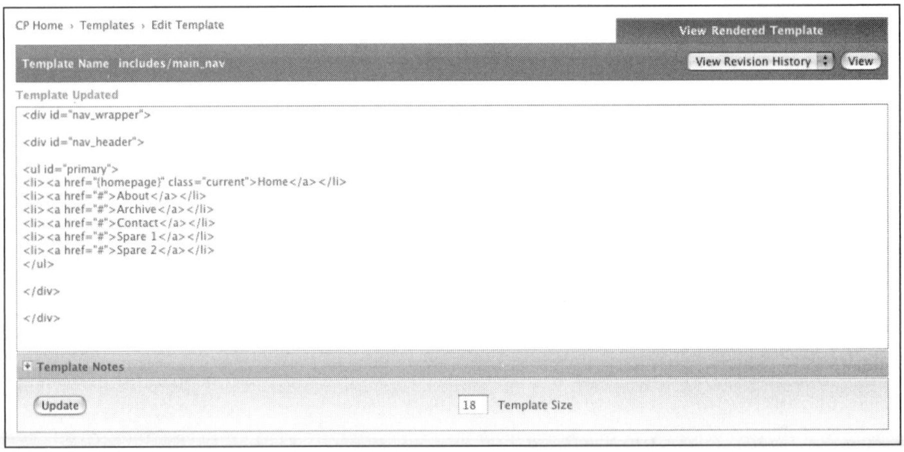

Figure 4-13. Your new main_nav template

Use your <head>?

Some EE users turn all the <head> information into an embed, which can be very useful, but be aware that you might need to redefine the <title> element on subsequent pages. So, you leave <title> and anything else that might not be the same on every template and make an embed of the following head data:

```
<meta http-equiv="Content-Type" content="text/html;
charset={charset}" />
<link rel='stylesheet' type='text/css' media='all' ➥
        href='{stylesheet=weblog/weblog_css}' />
<style type='text/css' media='screen'>@import
"{stylesheet=weblog/weblog_css}";</style>
```

Then, if you want to change the CSS reference, add metadata, a link to external JavaScript, or anything else, you can still edit the embed to inform all your EE pages in one move. Your <head> will then look more like this:

```
<head>
  <title>
    {exp:weblog:info weblog="{master_weblog_name}"} {blog_title}
    {/exp:weblog:info}
  </title>
  {embed="includes/head"}
</head>
```

A bit on the side

Now that you're coming to grips with embeds, you should add an embed to your sidebar <div>.

1. Create a blank template called sidebar in your includes group

2. Add {embed="includes/sidebar"} somewhere in the sidebar <div>, which will allow you to add content to every page's sidebar if you need to flag something up. Later, you could use this embed to show the latest images added to your Image Gallery.

That's it! Your index page is now complete. The full code for the revised index page is available to download from www.friendsofed.com. Let's leave the index page now, and start building the rest of the blog.

More page

Before you start creating other templates, you need to create your blog/more template. The more template will show your entire article, combining all the data from your Custom Entry Fields into one seamless entry.

Open the blog group, and you will see a menu of five options next to the group name.

Click New Template and you'll get some juicy options (see Figure 4-14).

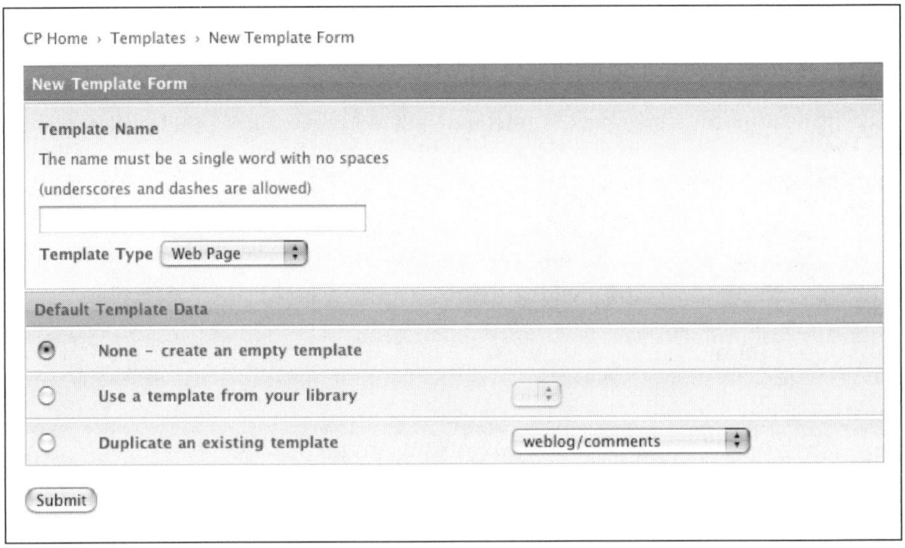

CP Home › Templates › New Template Form

New Template Form

Template Name
The name must be a single word with no spaces
(underscores and dashes are allowed)

Template Type [Web Page ▼]

Default Template Data

⦿   None – create an empty template

○   Use a template from your library   [▼]

○   Duplicate an existing template   [weblog/comments ▼]

(Submit)

Figure 4-14. Create new templates

Name the new template (more). By default, EE will show Template Type as Web page on the drop-down menu.

Rather than create an empty template, select Duplicate an existing template, and from the drop-down menu, select weblog/index.

Submit it, and EE will automatically place a clone of that template in your blog template group, called more.

1. Remove the login code as you did in the index template.
2. Replace the same code you removed from the index template with the same embeds—that's main_nav, sidebar, and any others you created earlier. For example, all the navigation links will be replaced with {embed="includes/main_nav"}, and you'll insert {embed="includes/sidebar"} in the sidebar just as you did on the index template.

3. Also, you need to reflect your Custom Entry Fields on the more page between the {exp:weblog:entries} tags, so add {mood} plus your {body} field below the {summary} field, thus creating a full article.

4. Remove some of the extraneous tags that EE places between the {exp:weblog:entries} tags, such as the path link around the title, as you are already on the page, and the member profile_path around the {author} variable. The code to remove is bold in the following listing:

```
<h2 class="title">
  <a href="{title_permalink=weblog/index}">{title}</a>
</h2>
{summary}
{body}
{extended}
{if mood != ""}<p><strong>My mood today:</strong> {mood}{/if}
<div class="posted">
  Posted by <a href="{profile_path=member/index}">{author}</a> in
  {categories}
    <a href="{path=SITE_INDEX}">{category_name}</a>
  {/categories}
  <br />
  {if allow_comments}({comment_total})
    <a    href="{url_title_path="weblog/comments"}">Comments</a>
&#8226;
  {/if}
  {if allow_trackbacks}({trackback_total})
    <a href="{trackback_path="weblog/trackbacks"}">
      Trackbacks
    </a>  &#8226;
  {/if}
  <a href="{title_permalink=weblog/index}">Permalink</a>
</div>
```

Note that the {exp:weblog:entries} tag has only one parameter, limit="1", because you need to show only the selected article, and the URL will inform the page which article to show. Make sure that any paths specified point to the correct template group and template (blog/index or blog/more). Again, the full code is available from www.friendsofed.com.

Add more sample articles

You will have noticed that a sample article appeared after you installed EE. It makes sense at this stage to edit this and make it a little longer, and also to fill in the My Mood Today field. From the main menu, select Edit, and then select the only available article. Look at the structure of the Edit form (as shown in Figure 4-15) and the various options available to you. Move the article to a more relevant category or try making some of the words bold or italic using the formatting toolbar.

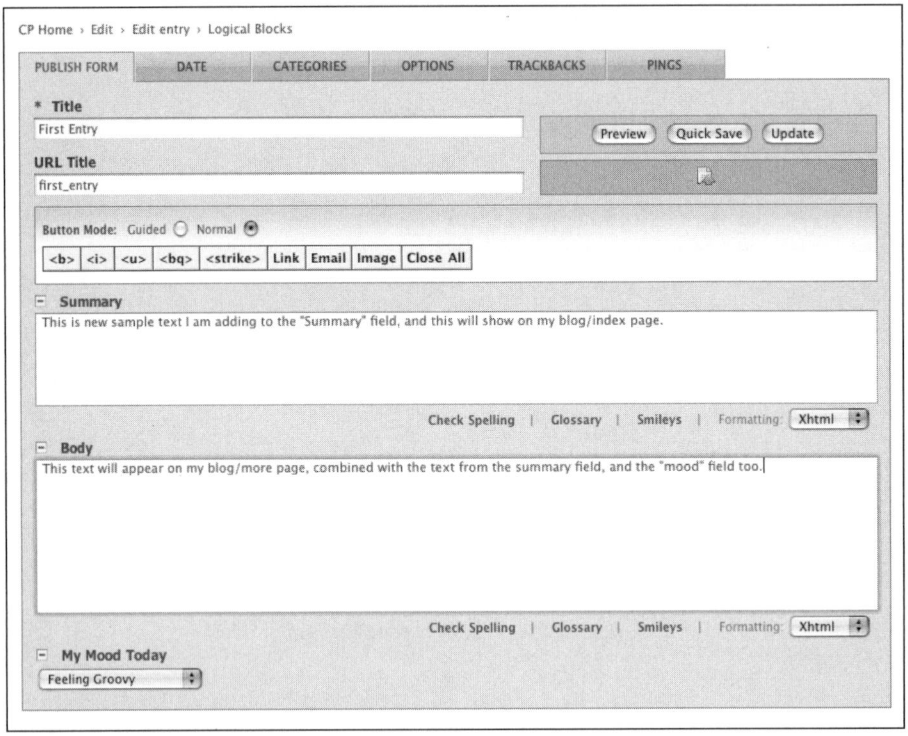

Figure 4-15. Editing the sample entry

Next, add a brand new article. From the main menu, select Publish. You will see a blank version of the form you were just editing. The format is self-explanatory, so go through each field adding sample data (a short blurb, main body text, category, and so on), and then Publish it. Repeat this process until you are happy that you have enough test data for your needs. If you can't think what to write, add some Lorem Ipsum text, pasted from a typical generator, such as www.loremipsum.net. This is what the pros do. Notice that the template tags you looked at in the *Understanding EE tags* section are now beginning to work for you on the blog/index and blog/more pages, with headlines being added to the sidebar, and articles showing chronologically in the main column (as shown in Figure 4-16.)

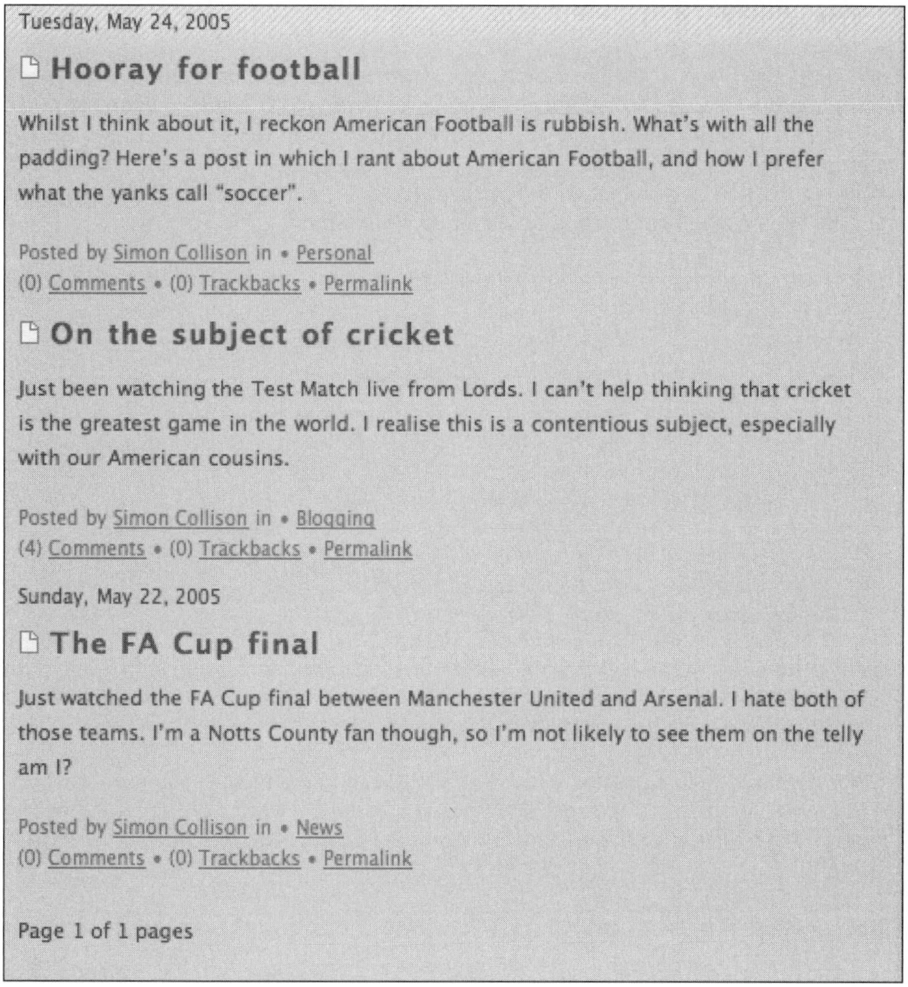

Tuesday, May 24, 2005

Hooray for football

Whilst I think about it, I reckon American Football is rubbish. What's with all the padding? Here's a post in which I rant about American Football, and how I prefer what the yanks call "soccer".

Posted by Simon Collison in • Personal
(0) Comments • (0) Trackbacks • Permalink

On the subject of cricket

Just been watching the Test Match live from Lords. I can't help thinking that cricket is the greatest game in the world. I realise this is a contentious subject, especially with our American cousins.

Posted by Simon Collison in • Blogging
(4) Comments • (0) Trackbacks • Permalink

Sunday, May 22, 2005

The FA Cup final

Just watched the FA Cup final between Manchester United and Arsenal. I hate both of those teams. I'm a Notts County fan though, so I'm not likely to see them on the telly am I?

Posted by Simon Collison in • News
(0) Comments • (0) Trackbacks • Permalink

Page 1 of 1 pages

Figure 4-16. Your blog is starting to fill up.

Further improvements

By now, you will have a working blog with a multientry page showing your sample entries (the blog/index page) and your full article (the blog/more) page. Great, but although you know that the process of building these pages is unique and very flexible, visitors won't be seeing anything out of the ordinary yet. In the next section you'll learn a few more clever EE tricks to enhance your articles and get a little interaction going with your readership.

Sort the menu out

Later, in the CSS section, you'll be swapping pretty menu tabs around depending on which section you are viewing. As it stands, this would require you to have a unique menu for every section (one for about, one for blog and so on), and you'd have to add class= "current" to whichever was the active tab. This is cumbersome and makes a mockery of turning your menu into an embed template. There is a better way. Here, you'll maximize your one menu embed template to do all this work for you.

1. Go back to the menu include you created earlier in the `includes` template group (includes/main_nav).

2. Remove `class="current"` from the home link because you'll be using a more dynamic method of highlighting the active page shortly.

3. You now need to add the paths to the new templates as follows:

```
<li><a href="{homepage}">Home</a></li>
<li><a href="{path=blog/about}">About</a></li>
<li><a href="{path=blog/archives}">Archive</a></li>
<li><a href="{path=blog/contact}">Contact</a></li>
And so on for any other main pages you
ambitious folks might have created
```

Suddenly, you have a navigable blog. Woo-hoo! Still, you can further refine the main menu. Because you're using the exact same menu on every page, it's not possible to add an id to a particular element to show it as selected.

No worries. Do something better. In the `includes/main_nav` template, you use conditionals to look at the URL and return a selected class based on it. The URL is informing the template which section you're viewing and using the appropriate CSS to style the navigation tab.

Segments

The {segment} variable is particularly powerful. Lots of URLs have more information after the www.yoursite.com part—often, directories such as www.yoursite.com/tools/ list_generator or similar. Remember that EE URLs do not have directory references like that, but by now you know that there are template group and template references in the URLs, such as http://localhost/index.php/blog/about, and you can think of them as segments. In the following URL there are two such available segments after the index.php part:

```
http://localhost/index.php/blog/about
```

You can think of these as:

```
http://localhost/index.php/{segment_1}/{segment_2}
```

Thus, you can use a conditional to see where you are. Here you'll add some clever code to test for this and return a given value. If {segment_2} does equal "about", class="current" is added to the link, which will make the tab stand out as selected. If {segment_2} does not equal "about", nothing is added, and the tab remains a standard tab. Let's do it:

1. Open the includes/main_nav template you created earlier, which contains your basic main navigation.

2. Replace each menu list element with the following code—adjusting the segment conditional to about, contact, or whatever—and also adjust the paths accordingly. For each navigation link, you will have code like this:

```
{if segment_2 == "about"}
  <li><a href="{path=blog/about}" class="current">About</a></li>
{/if}
{if segment_2 != "about"}
  <li><a href="{path=blog/about}">About</a></li>
{/if}
```

Note that the code for each nav link is the same, except for the home link. Because URLs for the homepage will not have any segments after the index.php/blog/ part, all you need is a conditional that looks for the lack of a second segment, as follows:

```
{if segment_2 == ""}
  <li><a href="{path=SITE_INDEX}" class="current">Home</a></li>
{/if}
```

Although your menu uses more lines of code, it is one menu that works for every page, making EE work that much harder so you don't have to. Here's the full code for the main sections you created:

```
<div id="nav_wrapper">
  <div id="nav_header">
    <ul id="primary">
      {if segment_2 == ""}
        <li><a href="{path=SITE_INDEX}" class="current">Home</a></li>
      {/if}
      {if segment_2 == "about"}
        <li><a href="{path=blog/about}" class="current">About</a></li>
      {/if}
      {if segment_2 != "about"}
        <li><a href="{path=blog/about}">About</a></li>
      {/if}
      {if segment_2 == "archives"}
        <li><a href="{path=blog/archives}" class="current">Archives ➥
</a></li>
      {/if}
      {if segment_2 != "archives"}
        <li><a href="{path=blog/archives}">Archives</a></li>
      {/if}
      {if segment_2 == "contact"}
        <li><a href="{path=blog/contact}"
class="current">Contact</a></li>
      {/if}
      {if segment_2 != "contact"}
        <li><a href="{path=blog/contact}">Contact</a></li>
```

4

```
            {/if}
          </ul>
        </div>
      </div>
```

That is one smart menu you have made. Go and make another cup of tea and think about how useful segments might be to you in the future.

Comments and comments form

OK. So far, you created a brand new template group (blog), tweaked the Weblog Preferences for weblog1, removed any unwanted EE tags and variables, refined your categories, and carved up regular chunks into embeds. You're also now in full control of your two main templates: index and more. Now you can look at making things a little smarter, making your blog work much better than anyone else's. You'll start by making your comments "clever."

1. By default, the **Comments** and **Add a Comment** headers will show up even if you aren't allowing comments on the article, so you add the {if allow_comments} conditional around each header:

```
{if allow_comments}
  <div class="main"><h2 class="title">Comments</h2></div>
{/if}
```

2. Below the **Comments** header, you should add the following to check for comments, and if the total is less than one, your message will be displayed:

```
{exp:weblog:entries weblog="weblog1"}
  {if comment_total < 1}
    <p>There are no comments yet for <em>{title}</em>.</p>
  {/if}
{/exp:weblog:entries}
```

Clever comments

EE is already configured to show any comments added in response to your article, but there are a couple of cool style changes you can make, and at this stage it's a good idea to add this markup. Basically this will force EE to style alternating comments with different background colors, but always render any you add as author with yet another color. Obviously, replace "reader@bloghandbook.com" with your own email address.

Add the following to blog/more (the CSS classes are already defined in the weblog_css template that you'll be learning more about in the next main section):

```
{exp:comment:entries sort="asc"}
{if email != "reader@bloghandbook.com"}
  <div class="{switch="commbox|commboxalt"}">
{/if}
```

```
{if email == "reader@bloghandbook.com"}
  <div class="commbox_author">
{/if}
{comment}
  <div class="posted">
    {comment_date format='%d/%m'} at {comment_date format='%H:%i'}
    from {url_or_email_as_author}</div>
  </div>
{/exp:comment:entries}
```

If you are logged in, EE will know that it is you commenting by matching your email address to the one specified previously and will use `<div class="commbox_author">` around your comment. Otherwise, guests will have either "commbox" or "commboxalt" used behind their comments. If you know the email addresses of regular contributors, you can also add further conditionals for them to display an icon or color for their comments.

Try to understand some of the other devices coded into the template. Note that an `{if logged_out}` conditional is used to ask nonmembers to fill in some personal info, and that for you as author only the main comment text area will show on the rendered page. Also, it'll be worth your while learning about devices such as Captcha and Smileys, which warrant more focus than this chapter allows.

Create some other useful templates

Every blog worth its salt needs an about page and a contact page, which are very easy to create by cloning existing templates. Here, you'll go back to the Templates menu and create two new templates in the blog group: contact and about. When creating them, you will opt to copy the blog/index template.

Create the contact template

Follow these steps to create the new template:

1. Open the blog group; you'll see a menu of five options next to the group name.
2. Click New Template.
3. Name the new template (contact). By default, EE will show Template Type as Web page on the drop-down menu.
4. Rather than create an empty template, select Duplicate an existing template and from the drop-down menu, select blog/index.
5. Submit it. EE will automatically place a clone of that template in your blog template group, called contact.
6. Open the contact template, and replace the {exp:weblog:entries} information with the Contact form tags available at http://eedocs.pmachine.com/modules/email/contact_form.html. Change the <title> element and any other headings accordingly. You just created your contact page (http://localhost/index.php/blog/contact).

Create the about template

These steps are very similar to the previous list, although here you'll be placing an embedded template within your new about page:

1. Open the blog group, and again you will see a menu of five options next to the group name.

2. Click New Template as you did for your contact template.

3. Name the new template (about). As before, EE will show Template Type as Web page on the drop-down menu.

4. Select Duplicate an existing template and from the drop-down menu, select "blog/index".

5. The system again places a clone of the blog/index template in your blog template group, this time called about.

6. Open the about template and replace the {exp:weblog:entries} information with {embed="includes/about_intro"}.

7. Next, go to the includes group and create a blank template called about_intro. Into that template add whatever information you want to use to describe yourself, making use of <p> tags, <strong> tags, or whatever standard formatting you might want to style it up with.

8. Change the <title> element and any other headings. You have just created your about page (http://localhost/index.php/blog/about).

Catch your breath

Obviously, this has been a whirlwind tour of the markup side of things. There are a thousand more great tags, parameters, variables, and workarounds that you can use here, and I do advise you to take some time to read the *User Guide* to see whether there are more devices that will suit your blog. It might also be worth having a break because when you resume, you'll be coming to grips with the CSS and images. It is probably time you put the kettle on again.

Styling using CSS

So far you've looked at the structure of the data to be displayed in your blog, but what about making it look great as well as read great? The good news here is that the default EE templates are styled using CSS, possibly the greatest thing ever to happen in web design.

To the uninitiated, in simple terms CSS means having one file containing all the color, typographic, and layout properties that are applied to every template of your website. Change a font property once to have it applied everywhere. Tired of your main content being on the left? Move it to the right with one simple CSS command. Adapting the CSS and images of this template is the key to making the blog your own, and getting this right will get your blog noticed.

CSS is a vast and vital subject, and it is not possible to explain the ins and outs of CSS in this chapter, so I recommend that you grab a copy of *Cascading Style Sheets: Separating*

Content from Presentation, Second edition (Briggs et al.; Apress, 2004) to learn more. In this section, the focus is on some of the more flexible and influential styles, plus a few useful tips and tricks that might make all the difference.

Before you begin

Let's not beat around the bush. CSS is difficult to master, and some of the concepts can take awhile to sink in. For this reason, the CSS you'll work with is minimal, but feel free to experiment. Just make sure that you keep those template revisions on!

In this section, there is quite a lot to cover, including the following:

- Where is the CSS?
- Ensuring that CSS affects the templates: If your templates can't see your CSS, they won't be styled.
- Understanding the layout: a guide to key structural containers and how they fit together to organize your content.
- Reconfiguring the masthead: how to join the header and main menu.
- CSS inheritance: how one declaration affects another and when to spot knock-on effects.
- Understanding the sidebar links: what makes the whole line become a clickable link and how these links can be adjusted.
- Ticked-off visited links: a guide to creating the versatile and hugely popular ticked-off links, in which a background image is used as a visual indicator of pages already visited.
- Styling comments: When structuring your blog/more page, you added markup to highlight comments owned by yourself and assigned alternate background colors to the containers. Here you learn more about styling these comments.
- Optional extras: making use of the hidden strip at the top of every page.

Where is the CSS?

So, "Where's this magical CSS?" you wail. Well, the CSS file is located in the weblog templates and is called weblog_css. You open and edit it as you would any other template, If you are saving template revisions, they will also apply to weblog_css, so you can always take a few steps back if you screw up.

Ensuring that your CSS affects your templates

The rules within weblog_css are applied to the templates because a reference link to the file is embedded in every template. The following code snippet shows the entire head section of the index template with the CSS link highlighted:

```
<!DOCTYPE html PUBLIC "-//W3C//DTD XHTML 1.0 Transitional//EN"
"http://www.w3.org/TR/xhtml1/DTD/xhtml1-transitional.dtd">
<html xmlns="http://www.w3.org/1999/xhtml" xml:lang="en" lang="en">
<head>
```

```
<title>Logical Blocks</title>
<meta http-equiv="Content-Type" content="text/html; charset=utf-8" />
<link rel='stylesheet' type='text/css' media='all' ➥
href='http://localhost/index.php?css=weblog/weblog_css' />
</head>
```

If you decide to leave the default CSS template intact and want to create your own, you duplicate the weblog_css template, replace weblog_css with the name of your new template, and then work with that new template instead. Whichever template you specify in the head of the template will control all the styling in the body section of the template.

If you have a tab-enabled browser such as Firefox or Safari, it's worth having three tabs open during CSS work: one for the blog/weblog.css template, one for a template it is applicable to, and one for the rendered site itself. This allows very swift editing and removes the need to continually navigate through the Control Panel template pages. You might prefer to refer to source code, rather than EE templates, when editing CSS because it allows you to view pure markup, classes, and ids without all the EE tags and parameters, which can be a hindrance when you need a bit of thinking space.

It's impossible to discuss every CSS id and class here, but it's worth stopping and admiring a few, especially the ones that have immediate influence on your site structure.

Understanding the layout

The diagram shown in Figure 4-17 illustrates the juxtaposition of the key CSS blocks you'll look at over the next few pages. Each key block will be looked at in turn, and you will learn a few CSS tips and tricks that will transform the look of your blog without having to open or edit any of the previous templates you worked on. You dealt with the content; now you'll deal with the presentation.

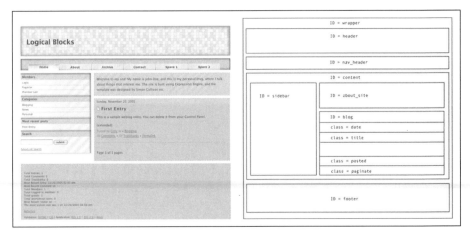

Figure 4-17. Diagrammatical overview of main CSS structure alongside finished site

#wrapper

The first CSS declaration is the wrapper, which appears immediately after the body of the HTML is opened, and this id centers the design in the browser window. Note that the final closing <div> on all of your templates closes this wrapper.

```
<div id="wrapper">
```

The only significant note here is the 10px padding that operates inside the wrapper. This creates the broad white border around the content, enclosed by a 1px gray border. This padding pushes the masthead down by 10px. I suggest retaining the left, right, and bottom 10px padding, but you can adjust the top padding above the masthead by locating the #wrapper id in the CSS template and replacing the padding reference with the following:

```
padding: 10px 10px 10px 10px;
```

This works like a clock face: top, right, bottom and left. Adjusting the first 10px reference will move the masthead and following content up or down. Note that the gray 1px border increases the set width from 750px to 752px—that's compensation for 1 pixel on each side. If all padding settings are the same, you can further shorten the statement to padding: 10px;.

Sorting out the masthead and navigation

Let's begin at the beginning. Your site title is held within the <h1> tags. You can locate the <h1> CSS and change the font, size, weight, color, and so on—or use the header graphic to display your title.

```
<div id="header"><h1>Logical Blocks</h1></div>
```

If you do use a graphic title, you might have the <h1> text sitting on top, which is no good. So, add the following to your CSS file in place of the existing <h1> CSS:

```
h1 {
  display:none;
}
```

The display:none attribute ensures that as long as the CSS file is available, the <h1> does not show. Remove the CSS as some users do and you lose the background image with its graphic title, but the <h1> disguise goes with it, rendering the text. Some argue that this is poor use of the most important <hn> tag; others think it a key accessibility tool and useful for good search engine placement. I go with the latter. Andy Budd talks about proper use of hn tags on his website (www.andybudd.com/archives/2004/07/heading_for_trouble), and Dave Shea has collected several image-replacement methods and offers concrete advice over at Mezzoblue (www.mezzoblue.com/tests/revised-image-replacement).

Locate the Logical Blocks images

The next few sections refer to the default background images used to decorate the installed template. All the default images are installed into the themes/site_themes/ logical_blocks folder, and you can quickly make the template your own simply by opening them in Photoshop and reworking them to your own design. Note, however, that the text refers to a number of optional images that have been added to the www.friendsofed.com website for you to download. You are welcome to download all these images in one group and overwrite all the default files to instantly change the look of your blog (this depends on how much or how little you are prepared to do).

Two choices of header layout

By default, the Logical Blocks masthead and navigation blocks appear separated (see Figure 4-18.) Although they are controlled by two different ids, it is simple to adjust this situation to suit your needs, for example, making them appear not separated, as shown in Figure 4-19. Here you have two simple options to make this design your own. You'll start by taking the first steps toward the Leaf design.

Option 1: Replace the images

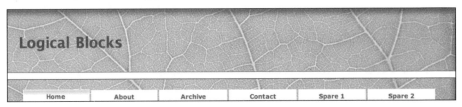

Figure 4-18. Option 1: Swapping the default images for your own or the provided substitute images

You can simply replace the default background images (lb_header.gif and lb_menuback.gif) with your own images or the two samples provided for you at www.friendsofed.com: lb_header_leaf.jpg and lb_menuback_leaf.jpg. These images are the same size as the default images and are designed not to tile. Whichever approach you take, be sure to place your images in the root/themes/site_themes/logical_blocks directory and change the references to lb_header.gif and lb_menuback.gif in #header and #nav_wrapper.

Option 2: Close the gap and join the images

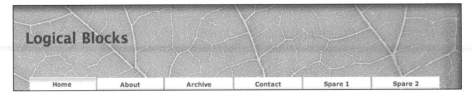

Figure 4-19. Closing the gap, and using composite images

Option 2 fits nicely with the Leaf design. With Option 2, you can resize the containers to hold taller or shorter images, or remove the space between them to combine the two images and make a composite header with navigation tabs lining its base. This method will require your two images to match up, so the bottom of the lb_header.leaf.jpg will match the top of the lb_menuback_leaf.jpg. Let's look at the default CSS for the header:

```
#header {
  margin: 0 0 10px 0;
  color: #030;
  height: 100px;
  width: 750px;
  border: 1px solid #663;
  background: ➡
    url({site_url}themes/site_themes/logical_blocks/lb_header.gif);
}
```

The margin properties make use of CSS shorthand again, and a significant attribute is the 10px bottom margin, which creates the white space dividing header from navigation. Notice that if a CSS value is 0, you need not add px to it. Note also the height property, which works perfectly in all browsers, and I suggest that you make your masthead equal to the specified 100px. If you do decide to use a masthead image that is taller or shorter than 100px, be sure to edit the height reference in the #header id accordingly.

With that understood, you can now hack the CSS for the header. Note the change to margin, and the border-bottom rule in addition to the existing all sides border declaration. Also, the image reference has changed to reflect the new image file:

```
#header {
  margin: 0 0 0 0;
  color: #030;
  height: 100px;
  width: 750px;
  border: 1px solid #663;
  border-bottom: 0px;
  background: url({site_url}themes/site_themes/ ➡
                        logical_blocks/lb_header_leaf.gif);
}
```

So, you removed the 10px space between the two elements and also removed the bottom border of the header. Next, look at the default nav_wrapper CSS. There are many elements powering the actual navigation tabs, displayed simply by the presence of the unordered list menu in the template. You need not worry about that right now; let's just look at the navigation wrapper:

```
#nav_wrapper {
  padding: 20px 0 0;
  border-left: 1px solid #336;
  border-right: 1px solid #336;
  border-top: 1px solid #336;
  background: url({site_url}themes/site_themes/ ➡
                        logical_blocks/lb_menuback.gif);
  font: bold 10px 'Lucida Grande', Verdana, Arial, Sans-Serif;
}
```

4

Removing the top border will ensure that the lb_menuback_leaf.gif images sits flush with the lb_header_leaf.gif image in the header. Also of note is the padding. A 20px padding-top is applied using CSS shorthand, and this can be adjusted to reduce the distance between masthead and menu tabs. If you alter this padding, you should alter your lb_menuback_leaf.gif accordingly. Here's the revised CSS:

```
#nav_wrapper {
    padding: 20px 0 0;
    border-left: 1px solid #000;
    border-right: 1px solid #000;
    background: url({site_url}themes/site_themes/ ➥
                        logical_blocks/lb_menuback_leaf.jpg);
}
```

You will now have your #header and #nav_wrapper blocks joining visually, with two background images joined. You can upload into Photoshop and refine these images and then put them back in the root/themes/site_themes/logical_blocks directory if you desire.

Tabs

I mentioned that many elements power the actual menu **tabs**. Controlling a horizontal menu list is a tricky thing. It is simple to force the list items to sit horizontally using display:inline, but to apply link, hover, selected state images and alternative link colors and weights requires a number of properties to be applied. Some of these help your menu display well on older browsers, too.

For the Leaf design, you need to replace the selected.gif, tab.gif, and tabover.gif images in the root/themes/site_themes/logical_blocks directory. Three alternate tab images that reflect the Leaf style (selected_leaf.gif, tab_leaf.gif, and tabover_leaf.gif) are provided at www.friendsofed.com for download. Alternatively, remove the image references in the CSS (by removing the url(...) part) to leave just color references:

```
background: #CCC;
```

Note that rather than specifying the light gray as #CCCCCC, you use #CCC, which is nice and short. It is possible to abbreviate any hexadecimal reference if it has three equal groups of numbers or letters following the format #aabbcc or has no variation such as #aaaaaa. In this situation, you need to specify each character only once, so a nice orange such as #ee9933 can be abbreviated to #e93. As for grabbing your own colors, the Dreamweaver and Photoshop palettes are perfect, or visit the WC3 documentation at www.w3schools.com/css/css_colors.asp for a bit more information.

You want more?

You might want to have more than six menu tabs, and there isn't room for seven or eight. In this case, find the #nav_header ul#primary a, #nav_header ul#primary span, #nav_header ul#primary a.current statement, and adjust the width declaration of 102px to suit your needs. You need to make the width of each button smaller if you want to include more.

> *The CSS mentioned here is typical of the various navigation styles, in that many classes are grouped together as they have equal properties. Be aware that making one change will affect several link states on your menu.*

A word of caution

Be sure that you're still saving template revisions here (Admin ➤ Template Preferences) because menu customization has you tweaking all the various nav styles, and it is easy to stray from a working model into a mess that fails on some browsers. Work step-by-step, pixel-by-pixel, and never make more than two moves before saving and checking the results.

#content

The #content id does little more than hold the sidebar and the main column together. Just think of it as important stitching that just happens to have a 10px margin between the previous navigation and the columns it contains. Edit that 10px setting to tighten the stitching:

```
#content {
  margin: 10px 0;
}
```

Inheritance

CSS is full of shorthand, and once you understand how this works hand-in-hand with markup, you can save a great deal of time and effort, and avoid "overdeclaring" classes. Perhaps the best example of this efficiency is **inheritance**. Let's say you are using an unordered list in your sidebar, and another one in your main content, and you want to style each differently. You might add a unique indicator to the <ul> or <li> items for each, but it bloats the markup and will make redesigning your site much more difficult.

Who owns what?

The key here is that one list lives inside your #sidebar column, and the other lives inside your #blog column. So, in the CSS you can assign a set of list styles to each id, so your list markup contains no class declarations because you specified in your CSS that a list within a certain id should look a certain way. Here's how it works for your sidebar links:

```
#sidebar ul {
  list-style-type: none;
  margin: 0;
  padding: 3px 5px;
  border: 0 solid #CCC;
  color: #666;
}
```

```
#sidebar li {
  border-bottom: 1px solid #CCC;
}
#sidebar li a:link {
  color: #333366;
  line-height: 150%;
  text-decoration: none;
  ...and so on.
```

You'll notice that rather than a plain <ul> or <li> before the styling attributes, #sidebar is declared for each part, followed by the <ul> or <li>. The sidebar now owns this style, and the styles will not apply to an unordered list outside of the sidebar.

#sidebar

This is the left-aligned column containing categories, headlines, search tools, and so on. A background image is set to repeat vertically (repeat-y), tiling from the right to create the faint diagonal lines behind the content, and a <h3> assigned to the sidebar carries its own background image for the darker gray headings. The CSS for each is shown here (note that they are not listed together in weblog_css):

```
#sidebar {
  float: left;
  color: #333;
  text-align: left;
  margin: 0 11px 15px 0;
  border-top: 1px solid #999;
  border-bottom: 1px solid #999;
  background: url({site_url}themes/site_themes/ ➥
                  logical_blocks/lb_diags_white.gif) repeat-y right;
}
#sidebar h3 {
  width: 249px;
  height: 16px;
  margin: 0;
  color: #336;
  text-decoration: none;
  display: block;
  text-align: left;
  background: url({site_url}themes/site_themes/ ➥
                       logical_blocks/lb_diags_h3.gif) right;
  padding: 6px 0 0 5px;
}
```

You should find it easy to edit the lb_diags_white.gif and lb_diags_h3.gif images to apply your own stamp on the sidebar.

1. To further the Leaf design, an image called lb-diags_h3_leaf is available on www.friendsofed.com for you to upload and replace.

2. Also, you will need to change the font color of the h3 text, from #336 to #330. Adjust the CSS as follows:

```
#sidebar h3 {
    width: 249px;
    height: 16px;
    margin: 0;
    color: #330;
    text-decoration: none;
    display: block;
    text-align: left;
    background: url({site_url}themes/site_themes/ ➥
                            logical_blocks/lb_diags_h3_leaf.gif) right;
    padding: 6px 0 0 5px;
}
```

Having just discussed your #sidebar list styling, let's take that and turn it into something really cool.

Understanding the sidebar links

Notice that the sidebar links are clickable for the whole sidebar width because the CSS declaration display:block is used in conjunction with a set width, specifying a sensitive area longer than the actual link text. That will come in very useful.

Next, notice the yellow background as you hover over the links. This effect is not specified in your sidebar link states, but is inherited from the default link states specified much earlier in the stylesheet:

```
a:link {
    text-decoration: underline;
    color: #666;
    background: transparent;
}
a:hover {
    text-decoration: underline;
    color: #900;
    background: #FFC;
}
a:visited {
    text-decoration: underline;
    color: #666;
    background: transparent;
}
```

Confused? Don't be. Notice that the background property is not specified in your sidebar links. If it were, whatever the value, it would be implemented. However, because the property remains undeclared, the sidebar links inherit the background style from the default links (see Figure 4-20).

Figure 4-20. Sidebar links with background color on hover state

To make things work smoothly, you need to make the following tweaks in weblog_css:

1. For your Leaf design, you need to change the a:link and a:visited color declarations from #666 to #330, almost the same as you did in the #sidebar h3 declaration.

2. Look for all link declarations in the CSS and make the same adjustment to keep your links consistent.

That should help you refine the sidebar links as they stand, but wouldn't you rather make a bigger impact? It's time to get ticked-off.

Ticked-off visited links

It's easy to show a user which links they have visited. Usually you would set the a:visited link class to a different text color to indicate this. Everybody does that, but using just one CSS background image, you can create an image trick to do this for you (see Figure 4-21). What about a tick appearing to the right of all visited links or an arrow appearing on hover to further entice the user to follow that link?

Figure 4-21. Ticked-off visited links

First, create the background image. Be very careful to keep the dimensions as specified in Figure 4-22. You will use CSS positioning to shift this image up and down by the appropriate number of pixels, showing a tick or arrow as required. For example, the hover state specifies the image be moved up by 20 pixels, thus hiding the first 15px bar and 5px space of the image and making the bar with the arrow visible on rollover. For a visited link, everything moves up 40 pixels, making the bar with the tick viewable instead.

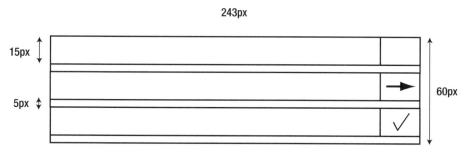

Figure 4-22. Dimensions for ticked-off background image

The CSS is pretty simple and is making full use of the display:block and set width discussed earlier. Just replace the #sidebar ul and list links styles with the following. Be sure to enter the correct path to your ticks image:

```
#sidebar ul {
  list-style-type:none;
  padding:3px;
}
#sidebar li a {
  display:block;
  line-height:150%;
  width:243px;
  background:URL(http://localhost/images/ticks.gif);
  text-decoration:none;
}
#sidebar li a:link, a:active {
  color:#336;
}
#sidebar li a:hover {
  color:#000;
  background-position: 0 -20px;
}
#sidebar li a:visited {
  background-position: 0 -40px;
}
```

After you have an understanding of how the image and CSS positioning are combining to create the effect, try resizing the image rows and adjust the CSS accordingly. For more information about this technique, to copy the code and to see it in action, visit www.collylogic.com/index.php?/weblog/comments/ticked_off_links_reloaded. Some bloggers have been very creative with this method, and remember that you can make use of the whole background width, not just the far-right area. Go mad.

#about_site

The #about_site id is used to house the Welcome to my site! introduction (see Figure 4-23) and can be removed without breaking the layout (although I suggest you keep it in and use it to introduce your blog). It has the same attributes as the #blog id, but sits on its own because you can't declare an id twice.

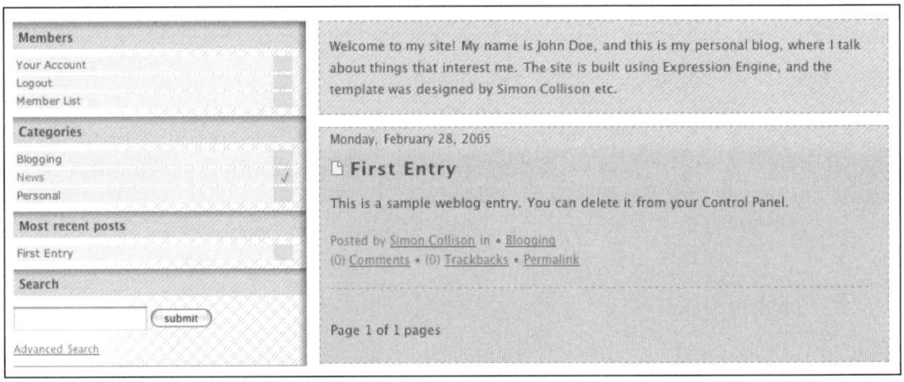

Figure 4-23. Alignment of #sidebar, #about_site, and #blog

#blog

You can think of #blog as your main column, for it is where your articles will be displayed. There is one notable declaration in the CSS:

```
background: #CCC url({site_url}themes/site_themes/ ➡
                    logical_blocks/lb_diags_grey.gif) repeat-x;
```

You'll notice that the background is a flat gray, but a diagonal image (lb_diags_grey.gif) is used along the top of the box. This is achieved by declaring a background color for the whole box and a tiled image set to repeat horizontally along the top by using repeat-x. Simply editing the color reference and adjusting the image will immediately transform the look of your design. You can easily remove either the image reference or the color reference from the background attribute to simplify things.

The #blog id has no padding to set the text in from the margin. This was done specifically to avoid width issues for those new to CSS, which can be caused by left and right padding increasing box width in older browsers. The **box model hack** (www.tantek.com/CSS/ Examples/boxmodelhack.html) solves such problems, but if you are new to CSS, just forget it. Instead, the main class, with its left and right margins, holds the text inside the #blog box. The main class also avoids the use of padding to keep things clean. It does mean you're starting with extraneous classes in your markup, though, so if you feel confident, read about the box model hack, apply padding to #blog, and remove the main class.

Be aware of the posted class, which allows you to control the look of the comments total, trackbacks total, and entry date as they appear below your article summaries. Also note the use of a <h3> header for the date headings and a <h2> for the article titles. Particularly useful is the <h2> link, defined in the stylesheet to inherit not only the standard <h2> formatting but also the formatting of the title class and the default link states, giving you numerous ways of controlling the look of your titles. It might seem clunky, and that's because it is, but let's say it's there to further illustrate the idea of mass inheritance combined with laziness.

For the Leaf design, you must download the image fadeout_leaf.gif from www. friendsofed.com. The fadeout_leaf.gif is a 20px by 400px image that is repeated horizontally behind your content to create a subtle green gradient. Notice the changes to the background declaration in the CSS for both #about_site and #blog:

    background: #FFF;

becomes . . .

    background: #FFF url({site_url}themes/site_themes/ ➡
                        logical_blocks/fadeout_leaf.gif) repeat-x;

Behind #about_site, you will see the gradient more as a block because it isn't too high a box, whereas on the longer #blog, the gradient is more apparent. These simple images do a great job of defining content areas without cramping the design and help keep paragraphs in context.

Finally for #about_site and #blog, remove the border declarations that were creating the dashed borders. They can now be considered as extraneous detail and are best removed. Also ensure that the background-color declaration is white; that's #FFF.

4

Styling comments

The final notes for the main column refer back to the {if} conditionals you might have used to control the look of comments, based on whether or not you are the author. Remember that the markup contained a switch conditional ensuring that comments are contained inside alternating colored boxes, as shown in Figure 4-24, by using the classes commbox and commboxalt.

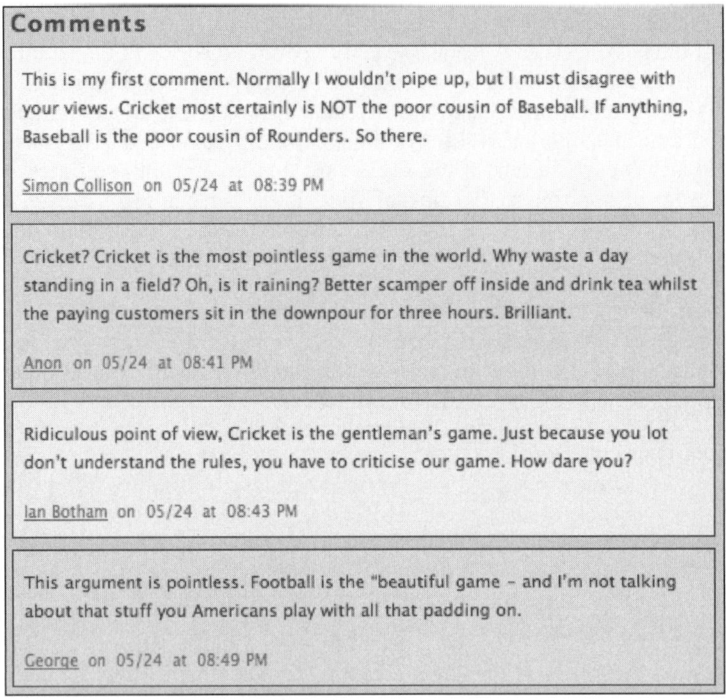

Comments

This is my first comment. Normally I wouldn't pipe up, but I must disagree with your views. Cricket most certainly is NOT the poor cousin of Baseball. If anything, Baseball is the poor cousin of Rounders. So there.

Simon Collison on 05/24 at 08:39 PM

Cricket? Cricket is the most pointless game in the world. Why waste a day standing in a field? Oh, is it raining? Better scamper off inside and drink tea whilst the paying customers sit in the downpour for three hours. Brilliant.

Anon on 05/24 at 08:41 PM

Ridiculous point of view, Cricket is the gentleman's game. Just because you lot don't understand the rules, you have to criticise our game. How dare you?

Ian Botham on 05/24 at 08:43 PM

This argument is pointless. Football is the "beautiful game – and I'm not talking about that stuff you Americans play with all that padding on.

George on 05/24 at 08:49 PM

Figure 4-24. Alternating comments

Locate these styles in weblog_css and adjust them as desired:

```
.commbox {
  background: #EDEAEB;
  border: 1px solid #ddd;
  padding-left: 7px;
  padding-right: 7px;
  margin-bottom: 7px;
}
.commboxalt {
  background: #FAF6F7;
  border: 1px solid #ddd;
  padding-left: 7px;
  padding-right: 7px;
  margin-bottom: 7px;
}
```

Duplicate one of the styles, rename it commbox_author, and adjust the background-color. This class will then be used for every comment you make as site author:

```
.commbox_author {
  background: #CCC;
  border: 1px solid #ddd;
  padding-left: 7px;
  padding-right: 7px;
  margin-bottom: 7px;
}
```

#footer

Another important section is the #footer. It is unlikely that you'll want to remove this container for site statistics, RSS links, and credits, so it is worth explaining a couple of key changes.

Note the following style in weblog_css:

```
#footer p {
  margin: 10px 0 5px;
}
```

Here, CSS is used to define paragraph tags that are used inside the #footer. This inherited paragraph definition allows you to treat paragraph tags differently for that section. If you don't need to style them differently, simply remove the #footer p definition, and they will adopt your standard p definition.

For your Leaf design, you need to remove the border properties from the #footer CSS, essentially removing the dashed border, and thus keeping your main page elements consistent, simple, and clean.

Optional

The original Logical Blocks design featured a blue block right at the top of the page (see Figure 4-25) called #eeheader_temporary. This is an ugly name for a temporary device used to announce that the template was a competition entry. This is worthy of mention because while the markup for this was removed in the official EE release, the CSS is still lurking in weblog/weblog_css and it might be something you want to use to display a strap-line or simple links.

Figure 4-25. The shockingly named #eeheader_temporary block

Look near the top of weblog_css for a set of CSS styles belonging to the #eeheader_ temporary class. Besides the container, there is a set of link styles that apply only to that block. To make use of this optional extra, place the #eeheader_temporary id markup directly above the "wrapper" id:

```
<body>
  <div id="eeheader_temporary">
    Your link or strap-line goes here.
  </div>
  <div id="wrapper">
```

How does it look?

There is so much more you can delve into when it comes to styling your blog—much more than can be covered here. Again, do take time to identify the default classes in the Logical Blocks template and reference them against their definition in the stylesheet. As soon as you are comfortable with editing and swapping CSS rules, you can easily begin creating your own.

At this stage your blog should be looking pretty smart (see Figure 4-26), even if it still looks a bit like the installed template. Still, given time you can start ripping out default sections, shifting columns around, and experimenting with alternative menus and text rendering. Before you do though, whet your appetite with some other EE highlights worthy of a brief mention.

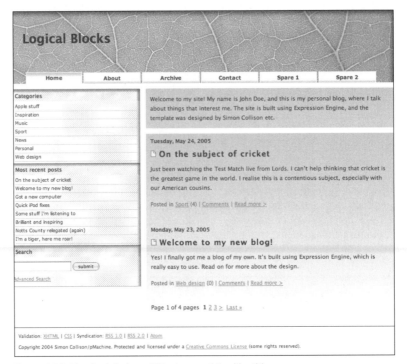

Figure 4-26. The final design will look something like this.

Strengthening your EE blog

Here are a few ways to further improve your already fantastic blog. You should explore them after you work your way through the rest of this chapter.

Plug-in baby

The approachable PHP base of EE means it's easy for anyone to build plug-ins for the engine. Many come preinstalled, and you can use the Plug-in Manager in Admin to keep track of your plug-ins. To grab new ones and keep an eye on new releases, be sure to visit http://plugins.pmachine.com/ regularly. Particular recommendations include the excellent **CSS Switcher**, the fabulously **Acronym** plug-in **Time Of Day** (exchanges timestamps for custom messages; for example, "Posted during breakfast"), and **No Follow** (a tool that renders comments left by spammers unrankable by search engines and thus pointless). Plug-ins are easily installed and are free. Check the release notes for each plug-in for specific details.

Query caching

Where to begin with this one? **Query caching** (or **Johnny caching**, as it is known in our office—sorry) caches the output of your database, saving each query (a dynamic connection made in the search for data) as a text file. When your visitors access your web pages, the cache files are examined to see whether the queries have been cached. If they have, EE uses the cached data instead of querying the database, preventing the server from being overloaded. There are a number of ways to enable caching, be they specific to a single template, a group, or the whole site. I highly recommend spending some time exploring these options (http://eedocs.pmachine.com/general/caching.html).

Image Gallery module

This module gels seamlessly with the rest of your site by using similar template structure, tags, and conditionals. But it treats your images as if they were articles, allowing comments, gathering stats—and all controlled by the admin panel. Setup instructions are clear, and if you were happy setting up standard blog prefs, you'll be fine. This module is comprehensive and a sheer joy to use (www.pmachine.com/expressionengine/docs/modules/image_gallery/control_panel/index.html).

Support

If you are struggling, consult the **EE Knowledge Blog**, (www.pmachine.com/expressionengine/knowledgeblog).

If you can't resolve your problem there, place your faith in the **EE user forums** (www.pmachine.com/forum). Search for an answer and you'll find it. Ask a question and you'll receive a response within 6–12 hours. The EE team does not sleep, apparently.

Ready for launch

Ready to launch? Sure? OK, switch the system on, allowing access to all. Check that your design hangs together appropriately in all the browsers you have access to and run it through an XHTML validator (see http://validator.w3.org for a good example) to seek out the pesky gremlins. In particular, watch out for non-SGML characters such as ampersands (&), curly quotes, or unclosed <div>s.

Hopefully you will fast become an EE aficionado, and will already have an eye for all the possibilities. Establishing your blog with EE is the smart move because the engine is constantly being upgraded, with more and more functionality being developed and the promise of more great modules on the horizon. If there is something you want to achieve, the chances are it is doable with EE. As you gain more experience, you will learn how to develop your own tags and methods of implementation and work out how to do what at first might not seem possible. With this in mind, you could end up using EE to build complex magazine and business sites, sacking off the day job, and becoming a site architecture whiz kid. Trust me, it's all there waiting for you.

Summary

Grab your tea and treat yourself to another cookie because I'm about to massage your ego. If you have followed this chapter religiously, you will have ridden a very steep learning curve, coming to grips with the power of content management over traditional static page building. The CSS techniques you employed are great foundations for further exploration, and you should now be in a position to begin experimenting with your own style combinations to further customize your pages.

Most importantly, you have a very sexy blog—or at least the beginnings of one. What's more, you opted to build it with the most malleable, well-structured blogging tool available. You'll never look back and I predict that in a short time you will be shuffling stuff around your templates like peas around your plate. Enjoy your blog.

5 **WORDPRESS**

Full Frontal K2 Testing Actio

Dashboard **Write** Manage Links Presentation

Write Post **Write Page** Write Note

Write Page

Page Title

Colophon

Discussion

☐ Allow Comment
☐ Allow Pings

Page Content

This is our great colophon page.

Aren't we great! Yeah I thought so too.

Recent Flickr

www.**flickr**.com

Default Template
Archives
Links
✓ Colophon Templat
Send to a Friend
colophon

by Chris J. Davis and Michael Heilemann

What this chapter covers:

- Downloading and installing WordPress
- Understanding the theme system
- Using Kubrick, the default theme that ships with WordPress
- Taking advantage of advanced theme customization

In this chapter we'll take a look at the open-source personal publishing platform WordPress. We'll look at where to get WordPress, how to install it, and of course—the meat and potatoes of this chapter—how to leverage the power of the theme system to create your own custom theme that can be packaged and made available to the wider world.

First, let's take a moment to get to know the two guys who are driving this bus of fun. Michael Heilemann is currently a resident of Copenhagen, Denmark, and runs the blog Binary Bonsai (http://binarybonsai.com), which first saw the light of day in 2002. Chris J. Davis hails from Nicholasville (affectionately known as NickVegas), Kentucky, and helms the Ship of Sillyness anchored off the shore of Sillyness Spelled Wrong Intentionally (www.chrisjdavis.org). We've both been using WordPress since its very first release in May 2003 and before that we used b2 (http://cafelog.com/), the predecessor of WordPress.

When Michael is not busy blogging, toying with his site, or writing for this book, he works full-time as a 3D graphics artist and level designer for a Danish computer game company. Chris spends his time as a husband and father, as well as the webmaster and web developer for a small private university in Central Kentucky USA.

Both Michael and Chris have extensive experience with self-publishing on the Internet, going back as far as 1996 or so, encompassing several personal sites (http://binarybonsai.com/archives/2005/01/02/chest-of-nostalgia/) during years spent as professional HTML monkeys and designers during the dot-com boom.

Michael and Chris are also responsible for two popular templates for WordPress and other Content Management System (CMS) platforms: Kubrick from Michael, which has since become the default template for WordPress; and Persian from Chris. Whenever *Kubrick* is mentioned in this chapter, we're referring to the template, not to the late visionary, Stanley Kubrick.

You can dig up more dirt yourself at http://binarybonsai.com/colophon/ and www.chrisjdavis.org/colophon/. For now, let's concentrate on getting on with the matter at hand: installing and customizing WordPress.

Before we venture forth into the wide wonderful world of PHP, Cascading Style Sheets (CSS), and Hypertext Markup Language (HTML), we should let you in on a dirty little secret: Michael couldn't write PHP to save his life. The first and most important lesson we can impart to you is this: Templating in WordPress does not require a degree in differential equations; it requires only the willingness to learn and experiment.

Now this isn't to say that those of us who *are* skilled in PHP-foo will be bored. The theme system is flexible enough to give us the room to do some truly amazing things, as Chris will demonstrate a little later.

As a testament to the real power available to the theme, authors Michael and Chris have their personal sites: Binary Bonsai (http://binarybonsai.com) and Sillyness Spelled Wrong Intentionally (www.chrisjdavis.org). Each of us has a very different skill set, but we have managed to mold our sites to our hearts' desire. If you learn nothing else from this chapter, learn this: You don't have to be a programmer to work with themes in WordPress.

WordPress is surrounded by an incredibly lively and dynamic community that constantly supports and drives the development of the project. Thanks to the dedication of an ever-growing group of developers, there is a veritable smorgasbord, a cornucopia if you will, of plug-ins, templates, and documentation at your fingertips. A good place to start when you are stuck is the support forums (http://wordpress.org/support/) or the Codex (http://codex.wordpress.org).

Inside this chapter

This chapter is divided into three sections. In the first section we'll take a look at how WordPress works and what we consider best practices when hacking the system. We'll also cover WordPress's famous "five-minute install."

In the second section we'll break down the default WordPress Kubrick template and take a look at how each of the parts works, which will prepare you for making your own theme.

In the last section we'll cover a few of the more-advanced tricks that can be used when using templates. These tricks give the theme author with a little PHP knowledge a very powerful weapon.

If we have done our jobs well, at the end of this chapter you should have the tools to forge ahead and create your own template, incorporating advances hitherto unknown in the field of blog template design!

Rules of engagement

Because of the nature of the universe, we can't be there to answer questions and offer situation-specific advice. However, as luck would have it, there is a land far, far away filled with rivers of chocolate, fluffy bunnies to frolic with, and WordPress support. Okay, maybe not the first two, but there is definitely WordPress support to be found.

WordPress support

This might seem like an odd section to add to a chapter on template design, but here's the thing. WordPress is in essence an open-source project, created and maintained by a group of people in its spare time. And because WordPress is available for free, there are few resources to maintain a formal support system. Thus, all WordPress support is maintained by a most generous community.

The reason we're bringing this up is to highlight the "get and give" nature of an open-source community.

If you swing by the WordPress forums looking for a solution, keep your eyes open for problems to which you might hold a solution. Your three minutes spent typing it out might save someone else hours of troubleshooting. And in the process, you might learn a thing or three.

Understanding the WordPress Codex

Throughout this chapter, we will refer numerous times to the WordPress Codex: an online documentation site that is constantly under development and open for anyone to edit. This chapter couldn't have been written had it not been for the Codex, nor could we have created our sites as easily without it.

The Codex is your number one resource to understanding the inner workings of WordPress.

Dealing with code

Be adventurous; don't be afraid to break things. There is no better teacher than trial and error, but experience shows that although being adventurous will usually get you results, you're probably also going to end up in a good deal of dead ends. So whatever you do, make sure you back up as often as possible! You'll regret it if you don't; we guarantee it.

Make use of community members; they're a hardy bunch with infinite knowledge. We cannot stress enough the gift that the WordPress community is. Dive in and ask questions—you will get answers.

If you find that WordPress doesn't do something you want, take a moment to look around and ask questions before you decide to create something yourself. Reinventing the wheel is never a good idea. Decide exactly what you need to get done and then have a look around you to see whether you can find a plug-in that already has the functionality you're looking for. If not, and you are gifted in code-foo, please write something and share it. If your code-foo skills are weak, get to know some people with PHP and Structured Query Language (SQL) experience and swap favors. Collaboration is one of the hallmarks of open-source design and production.

In the end, writing a template is about ideas first, code second.

Sharing

WordPress is obviously free of charge and will remain so for all eternity because of the license under which it was created. This idea of sharing for the sake of it is a strong notion, which should be enforced by the community—that's you—whenever possible.

Even if whatever you want to share isn't necessarily done, put it out there with a disclaimer and let people rip it apart and build new things from it. Odd collaborations can lead down some very interesting paths.

And again, even if you're unsure of the quality of what you're putting out there, the worst thing that can happen is that someone might point out your mistakes, giving you the opportunity to learn from them.

Maintenance

5

Websites are like any other part of life, be it your car, roses in the backyard, or your teeth. Without attention and a little love, they start to go all "wonky" on you. So every few months, set aside an hour or two to run through the checklist (http://codex. wordpress.org/WordPress_Site_Maintenance), and you're probably less likely to run into any problems.

And let us re-emphasize the part about backing up your files and database. Don't just think about doing it. Do it!

Introducing WordPress

WordPress is an open-source personal publishing platform released under the GPL license and maintained by a group of volunteers, which is available to anyone free of charge.

As the term *open source* implies, all the WordPress source code is freely available to anyone to do with pretty much as they please, as long as they follow the terms of the GPL license (bundled with each download).

Although WordPress is used mainly as a blogging system, its simple structure and flexible underlying architecture allow for some pretty wicked customization. This wicked customization is what we'll dive into in this chapter.

Downloading and installing WordPress

If you already have a WordPress installation up and running, you can obviously skip this section—unless, of course, you're on a really boring train ride across whichever continent you happen to be in and this is the only thing you brought with you to read (if so, you're free to continue).

Now, WordPress is renowned for its five-minute install, which—you guessed it—takes no more than five meager minutes from start to finish (as with all things, your mileage may vary). The five-minute install is so renowned, in fact, that in the readme.html file that accompanies WordPress 1.5 Strayhorn, it is the first thing mentioned after Matt's introduction.

Here in its entirety is the seven-step installation guide from the readme.html file, which should make installation a relative breeze. Please make sure that you have your database username and password ready because you will need them.

This is assuming that your server fulfills the requirements of PHP version 4.1 or greater as well as MySQL version 3.23.23 or greater, which it should, of course, because you installed PHP 5.1 and MySQL 5.0 back in Chapter 2. Didn't do that? Well, go back and do it, people . . . we'll wait. Now assuming that you have passed the server requirements test, you need to download WordPress. The latest and greatest version can be found at http://wordpress.org/download/.

At this point, you have two choices: upzip and upload to a remote server, or use your own machine locally. The following steps are largely the same, regardless of where you are testing—with the exception, of course, that if you're using a remote server you would upload to it and create the MySQL database there via phpMyAdmin.

Unzip the package into your web server root, as outlined in Chapter 2. For this chapter, we assume that you're running MacOS X and you're using /Library/WebServer/Documents as your server root. The ZIP file is set up to produce the following directory structure: /Library/WebServer/Documents/wordpress, so the root of the web application on your test server will be http://localhost/wordpress/. If you are using a remote server and want to maintain this structure, upload the wordpress folder to the server.

If you want WordPress to be the main application, make sure you move the contents of the wordpress directory (including any subfolders) into the server root and then delete the wordpress directory. This means that you can reach WordPress at http://localhost/. If you are using a remote server, you can, of course, simply upload the contents of the wordpress folder to the server.

Anyway, before you get to that stage, you have a few more things to do:

1. Open up wp-config-sample.php with a text editor and fill in your database connection details. We recommend creating a new database via phpMyAdmin, called wordpress, by following the steps outlined in Chapter 2. For those who don't want to flip back, go to http://localhost/phpmyadmin/. (Mac users might notice that when you type in localhost/a/path/ your browser URI field will show something more like this: somename.local/a/path/. You see this because your Mac is using the computer name that was set in the Sharing Preferences panel. There is nothing to worry about.) Figure 5-1 is a shot of what the screen looks like.

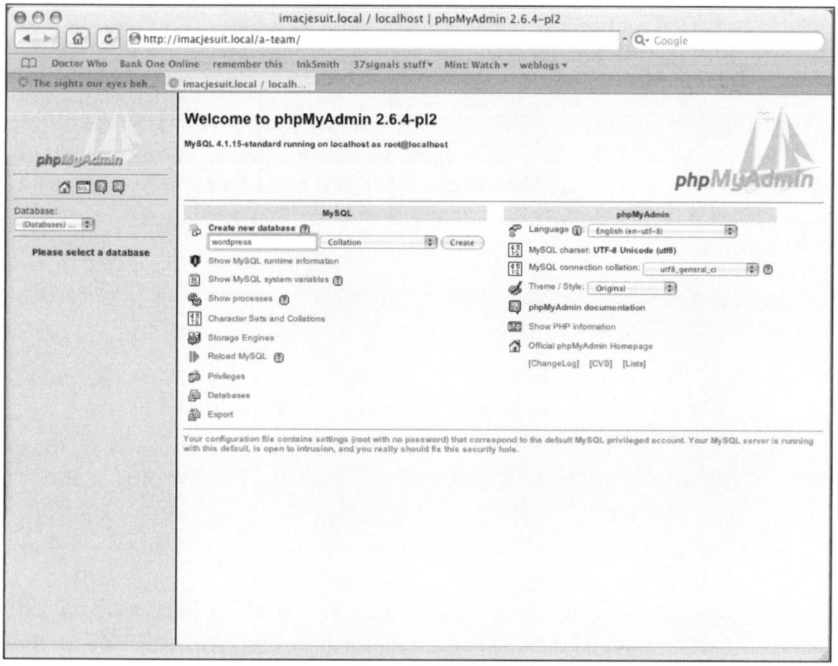

Figure 5-1. Creating a new database called wordpress with phpMyAdmin

2. Save `wp-config-sample.php` as wp-config.php.

3. If you are working on a remote server rather than a local server, upload everything to your server via your favorite FTP client. Otherwise, just skip to step 4.

4. Launch `/wp-admin/install.php` in your browser (this will be `http://localhost/wordpress/wp-admin/install.php` if you accepted the defaults when unzipping, or `http://localhost/wp-admin/install.php` if you are running WordPress at the server's root). Then sit back and relax as WordPress entertains you with its clever banter. WordPress will create the tables needed for your blog and let you know when everything is ready to go. There are only two steps, so pay attention or you might miss it! If there is an error, double-check your `wp-config.php` file and try again. If it fails again, please go to the support forums with as much data as you can gather.

5. Note the password given to you. We recommend that you open the `wp-login.php` link in another window or tab, copy and paste the randomly generated password into the password field, and log in.

6. The moment you have logged in, go on to Users and then Profile, and update your password with something meaningful.

Please note that if you're upgrading from a previous version of WordPress, the installation procedure is slightly different, and you will be better off consulting the `readme.html` file, which is bundled with WordPress 1.5. Also, if you're upgrading from a previous version, by all means back up your files and database before you venture forth!

177

Regardless of what you do, I suggest that you at least skim the readme.html, which is located in the wordpress folder. If nothing else, changes might have been made since the time of this writing.

After you log in, the first page that you see is known as the Dashboard. In a nutshell, the Dashboard is an overview of your blog and contains aggregated news from around the WordPress world. From this initial screen you can see whether you have any comments in moderation; how many posts, comments, and categories you have; and which sites are linking to you.

You will see the following menu options available when you are in the admin area of WordPress:

- **Write:** This is really the point of blogging, isn't it? From this menu you can create posts and pages to add to your WordPress-powered blog.

- **Manage:** The Manage menu item takes you to an overview of all the posts, pages, comments, and categories that have been created on your blog. It also allows you to delete and edit them.

- **Links:** Guess what this does? By clicking this you can add, edit, or delete links for your blogroll.

- **Presentation:** One of the most powerful features of WordPress, and the whole reason for this chapter, the Presentation tab is where you manage your themes and templates.

- **Plugins:** It is a debate about which is more powerful: plug-ins or themes. The bottom line is that they are both essential parts of your WordPress experience. You will find the tools to activate and manage your plug-ins here.

- **Users:** WordPress has a powerful and flexible user system that allows for granular control of "rights" for your users. In this area you can create, promote, and delete users who are on your blog.

- **Options:** The proverbial kitchen sink, friends. Here you set your blog's name, create the tagline, decide whether you accept new users, select how you want to syndicate your site via Really Simple Syndication (RSS), and choose how many posts to show on your index page. Just to name a few.

- **Logout:** Well, if you want to log out of the admin area, click here.

Click View Site in the header area of the admin area. You will be taken to http://localhost/index.php, which should look similar to Figure 5-2. You might see http://localhost/wordpress/index.php instead, depending on where you unzipped to. From now on, we assume that you placed the files in the root of the web server, not in a wordpress subdirectory.

Figure 5-2. Default layout of a new WordPress installation

Now that we have covered installation and your first login, let's take a look at how WordPress operates.

Mechanics of WordPress

WordPress uses PHP to handle creating, editing, and displaying your content. At its core, it has a number of functions that do the dirty work for you. There are quite a lot of these functions, and more are added with every new iteration. In this section, we will cover how WordPress displays your blog posts by looking at WordPress's URI, its use of pretty permalinks, The Loop, and templates.

Displaying your blog posts

Let's take a moment to look at how WordPress knows when to do what. It all begins with a little ditty known as URL. (URL is short for Uniform Resource Locator, which is incorrect. It is actually URI, Universal Resource Indicator. Thank a misprint for the current confusion.)

A URL is, of course, the address of the page you're trying to access. In the case of Michael's blog, the URL for one of his entries might look something like this: http://binarybonsai.com/archives/2005/02/25/its-another-world/.

Before we go on, it's important to note that although this is how the URL is presented to us, it is not the physical address of that bit of content. WordPress can serve content in a variety of ways. The directory-like structure that you see is commonly referred to as *pretty permalinks* (http://codex.wordpress.org/Introduction_to_Blogging#Pretty_Permalinks).

The way pretty permalinks are set up has to do with "rewriting" URLs. (Rewriting URIs is beyond the scope of this chapter, but if you want to know more about it, you can find it covered at length in the WordPress Codex: http://codex.wordpress.org/Using_Permalinks.)

Without pretty permalinks, the link to the preceding entry would instead have been http://binarybonsai.com/index.php?p=1441, which works just as well in terms of retrieving the information. However it isn't quite as user-friendly, nor is it as cool as the pretty permalink version. However, the non–pretty permalink tells us much more about how WordPress functions, which is what we are interested in at the moment.

The ?p=1441 is in fact a parameter passed to index.php, and it is here in index.php that the magic happens. The variable type in this case is p (which stands for post), and the value is 1441. The Loop, which will be covered in detail a little later, now knows that we are requesting a post with the unique ID of 1441 (that is, the 1441st post on this site); it then scurries off to retrieve that post content from the database.

WordPress has a number of these variables that can be called in various ways. If for instance you want a list of all the entries from the year 2005, simply replace p with year and 1441 with 2005 to form www.chrisjdavis.org/index.php?year=2005, and voila, you have a complete list of all the entries created in 2005.

Another variable is monthnum, which—as the name implies—takes a month number as its value; it can represent any number from 1 to 12. For example, if you look up www.chrisjdavis.org/index.php?monthnum=5, the current month of May is retrieved from the database.

Now we know what you are thinking. Can I combine these variables in new and interesting ways? Of course you can! The parameters are tied together using an ampersand. Let's say you want the month of May from 2003: `http://binarybonsai.com/index.php?year=2003&monthnum=5`. Notice that the URL begins with a question mark for the first variable and then uses the ampersand to tie on each additional variable.

It's that easy.

After version 1.5 of WordPress, it is no longer quite as important to be able to parse these variables and make decisions based on them. Why? Because WordPress does most of the work for you through the use of conditional tags.

We will have a more in-depth look at conditional tags later in this chapter.

Advantages of pretty permalinks

The name says it all—prettified versions, or more correctly, human-readable versions of the more machine-readable default structure. There are a number of advantages to using pretty permalinks. `www.chrisjdavis.org/index.php?p=4` doesn't mean that much to us, but `www.chrisjdavis.org/this-great-post` does. Giving your readers meaningful content and context is what blogging is all about. Another huge advantage of using pretty permalinks is that your content will be more optimized for search engine indexing . . . very important in these days of SEO craziness and Google ranking.

Pretty permalinks provide an advantage called *peeling*. Take another look at the pretty permalink to the entry on the 1991 gaming classic, Another World: `http://binarybonsai.com/archives/2005/02/25/its-another-world/`. Very quickly you can discern the title of the entry (Another World) and the date on which it was published (February 25, 2005).

Furthermore, if you wanted to see what else was published on that exact date, you could simply peel the title, leaving only `http://binarybonsai.com/archives/2005/02/25/`, which would then show that in fact two entries were published on that particular day in February, 2005. You could go on to peel the day, which would leave you with an archive of the entries published during February. Peeling the month would give you a view of all the posts in 2005. And peeling one last time will take you to the archives page, a hub of sorts for further navigation into the archives of the Bonsai.

For your own site, this is a great way to maintain your directory structure, and we highly recommend that you spend some time understanding how to customize this rewriting. There are some great resources available in the Codex (`http://codex.wordpress.org/Using_Permalinks`). Luckily, WordPress makes the black magick that is mod_rewrite much easier to work with through template tags. You can find a listing of them on the aforementioned page.

> To work with permalinks, go to Options and then click Permalinks. It is likely that you will need to use a permalink pattern to follow the examples in this chapter. Use one of the examples shown on this page if you are not sure what you'd like at this stage. You also need to activate mod_rewrite in Apache. This is as simple as uncommenting the LoadModule line in /path/to/apache/conf/httpd.conf that refers to mod_rewrite.

The Loop

As mentioned in the last section, WordPress uses The Loop (http://codex.wordpress.org/the_loop) to fetch information in different ways, depending on what page you're on. As the name implies, The Loop is a bit of code that retrieves content depending on the information given to it and then keeps looping until all the appropriate content has been retrieved.

Let's take an example: Michael published 22 entries during February, 2005. If you were to load up the archives for February, 2005 on Binary Bonsai (http://binarybonsai.com/archives/2005/02/), The Loop would go to the database and cycle one by one through all entries published during February, 2005.

The Loop looks like this:

```php
<?php if ( have_posts() ) : ?>
<?php while ( have_posts() ) : the_post(); ?>

  <!-- loop content -->

    <?php endwhile; else: ?>
      <p>
      <?php _e('Sorry, no posts matched your criteria.'); ?>
      </p>
<?php endif; ?>
```

This is how WordPress retrieves entries and comments. So let's go back and break this down in English. The first bit of code says that if the database returned some posts, go on to the next line:

```php
<?php if (have_posts()): ?>
```

Now that we know we have posts, let's start displaying each of them:

```php
<?php while ( have_posts() ) : the_post(); ?>
```

After we have displayed all the data we have for each post, let's go ahead and stop:

```php
<?php endwhile; else: ?>
```

If there are no posts to show, show this paragraph instead:

```php
<p><?php _e('Sorry, no posts matched your criteria.'); ?></p>
```

Are we all done showing posts now? Good! Close up shop and move on:

```php
<?php endif; ?>
```

Most of the time, the purpose of The Loop is to retrieve entries so they can be displayed to the end user. This is done through the use of template tags, which fall within the loop. Anything put inside the loop will be executed/displayed for every entry on the resulting page.

Now before we move on to talking in detail about template tags, it's worth taking a look at The Loop from a slightly different angle. Normally, you would use The Loop for retrieving and displaying a set of entries or a single entry, based on either a period of time or some other unique identifier.

But say you're into reviewing and discussing books and you want to display a list of all the entries in the Book Reviews category that contain more than ten comments. You would turn to The Loop for that list.

Say that you want to have the headline of all the yearly, monthly, and category archive pages to include a count of the entries within that year, month, or category. Again, you would turn to The Loop to accomplish this.

Yes, in truth, The Loop is a wonderful tool.

Designing with WordPress

Designing is really the reason for you reading this chapter, isn't it? How can you leverage your CSS and HTML skills to create a beautiful usable layout with WordPress? Lucky for you it is easier than you might think. There are two main components to any design powered by WordPress: CSS and HTML, and the PHP-based templating system.

CSS and HTML

As with any design for the Web, everything starts with well-formed HTML and CSS. WordPress was built from the ground up to be a semantic publishing system with an eye to standards. This means that visually everything is powered by CSS. Let's take an example. Say you want to style your blog posts with an h1 tag that has a blue background and a gray, 5-pixel border to the left of the h1 tag. Here is the necessary code to make that happen; first we start with this CSS:

```css
H1
{
    background-color: # 8BCCF4;
    Border-left: 5px solid #ccc;
}
```

Then in our page, say, index.php, we would write this:

```php
<h1>
<?php the_title(); ?>
</h1>
```

And that's it. If you were now to load index.php in your browser, you would see the title of your posts styled as h1 tags per our rules defined in CSS. Everything in WordPress can be styled by CSS. The bit of PHP in the preceding snippet is one of WordPress's template tags.

So now is a good time to talk about template tags and template structure in WordPress.

Template structure

WordPress has a pretty sophisticated theme system, which allows you to change how it looks and operates. We'll be making use of this quite a bit throughout this chapter. And although it might seem slightly complicated at first, it yields quite a bit of power that can make for a more dexterous blog in the long run.

Perhaps the best thing about the theme system is how easy it is to change the face of your blog in one fell swoop—at the click of a button.

We will be using the default theme that ships with WordPress for most of our examples. It is called Kubrick, after the late visionary movie director. Although there are many reasons why we will use this theme as our foundation, the most important is that it will always be available to everyone because it is the default WordPress theme. Also it is widely used and has already been through the hands of thousands of users, so support is usually very close at hand. And of course, Michael built the thing.

File structure

Kubrick comes as a package of a number of files and a directory for images. All these files work together, depending on what WordPress needs to serve up to the reader, and it might take three or four files to serve up a single page for a reader. We will look at each file that makes up Kubrick a little later in this chapter.

Now there's no reason why an entire theme can't fit into a single file. But once you gain a sense of the structure, the compartmentalized approach used in Kubrick makes it considerably smoother to take care of system-wide changes to the theme.

To integrate these various files, WordPress has been equipped with a range of functions for calling in the needed files (include tags) as well as functions for determining what kind of page it currently needs to show (conditional tags).

If you open up the index.php from the default Kubrick theme that comes with WordPress 1.5 in a text editor, you will see that the very first line of code contains a tag called get_header. This piece of code actually displays the contents of header.php. The last three lines of index.php are also include tags, namely get_sidebar and get_footer, and each one displays the contents of sidebar.php and footer.php, as you would expect.

Using these include tags makes it much easier to create a wide range of pages that all share the same structure, layout, and information. Using this technique, changing copyright information or something similar in the footer will immediately spread to all the pages on your site.

There are four include tags: get_header, get_footer, get_sidebar, and get_comments.

To make things smarter yet, conditional tags allow you to have a single file react differently depending on what it's supposed to be doing. Let's assume that you want to run a plug-in in the sidebar, but only when the user is viewing the frontpage—nowhere else. You simply wrap the plug-in code in a simple if statement such as this one:

```php
<?php if (is_home()) { ?> Plugin Code Goes Here <?php } ?>
```

This is extremely useful, as you will see later, in managing, for instance, a sidebar.php file that works across the entire site, yet behaves differently depending on what part of the blog the reader is in. So let's look at them in depth.

Template tags

Residing both in and out of The Loop, template tags are how WordPress brings information from the recesses of its database to be presented to the user. Examples of places in which you can make use of template tags include headlines, dates, entry content, permalinks, and so on.

Many template tags can be configured, using parameters passed to WordPress through the template tag's syntax, allowing for a degree of customability. Where a default template tag might look something like this: `<?php the_title(); ?>`, you could also pass it some variables like this: `<?php the_title('<h3>', '</h3>'); ?>`.

Each template tag has a different set of possibilities when it comes to customizing; time spent studying the WordPress Codex on template tags (http://codex.wordpress.org/template_tags) is time saved later when you suddenly need to figure out how to employ some odd combination of template tags.

Here's a loop from the frontpage of our default template:

```php
<?php if (have_posts()) : while (have_posts()) : the_post(); ?>
  <div class="post">

    <h2 id="post-<?php the_ID(); ?>">
      <a href="<?php the_permalink() ?>" rel="bookmark"
         title="Permanent Link to <?php the_title(); ?>">
         <?php the_title(); ?></a>
    </h2>

    <small><?php the_time('F jS, Y') ?>
<!-- by <?php the_author() ?> --></small>

    <div class="entry">
      <?php the_content('Read the rest of this entry &raquo;'); ?>
    </div>

    <p class="postmetadata">Posted in <?php the_category(', ') ?>
      <strong>|</strong> <?php edit_post_link('Edit','
```

```
                  ','<strong>|</strong>'); ?>
                  <?php comments_popup_link('No Comments &#187;',
                  '1 Comment &#187;', '% Comments &#187;'); ?>
              </p>

              <!-- <?php trackback_rdf(); ?> -->

          </div>
      <?php else : ?>

          <h2 class="center">
            Not Found
          </h2>

          <p class="center">
            <?php _e("Sorry, but you are looking for
              something that isn't here."); ?>
          </p>

          <?php include (TEMPLATEPATH . "/searchform.php"); ?>

      <?php endif; ?>
```

The following template tags are called in the previous PHP code: the_ID, the_permalink, the_title, the_time, the_author, the_content, the_category, edit_post_link, comments_popup_link, and trackback_rdf. Their purposes are as follows:

- the_ID

  Every entry on your site, whether it is a post or a comment, has a unique numeric ID. It is rarely used anywhere but internally and merely helps the engine distinguish between pieces of information.

- the_permalink (http://codex.wordpress.org/Template_Tags/the_permalink)

  WordPress allows you to display single entries or posts; you use the_permalink to request these. The actual "look" of the permalink differs depending on the individual setup, as discussed in the Data Hierarchy section. What is returned via the_permalink is not a link, but a URL. To create a clickable link, you need to do something like this:

```
<a href="<?php the_permalink(); ?>" title="
    <?php the_title"><?php the_title(); ?></a>
```

- the_title (http://codex.wordpress.org/Template_Tags/the_title)

  Displays the title for a given post/entry.

- the_time (http://codex.wordpress.org/Template_Tags/the_time)

  This tag requires a bit more explanation than most of the other tags because it is quite configurable. At its core, it will print out the time of publication for the current entry. The time format differs depending on the individual WordPress setup, however. Furthermore, the_time can be configured either in the WordPress administration or right at tag level. (For example, <?php the_time('F jS, Y') ?> presents you with: February 8th, 2005.)

The thing to remember about the_time is its relationship with the_date: They both can output time and date. The way they differ is in how they behave when called. If you want the publication date to be displayed with every post you make, you use the_time. If you prefer to have the date show up only once per day, you should use the_date. You can also combine them in new and interesting ways—again, experimentation is your best friend.

- the_author (http://codex.wordpress.org/Template_Tags/the_author)

  WordPress natively supports multiple author environments. If you have more than one author on your site, you would use the_author to show who is posting what.

Looking up the_title() in the WordPress Codex (http://codex.wordpress.org/Template_Tags/the_title), you will see that it actually takes three parameters as well: the_title(*'before', 'after', display*). The first parameter, 'before', allows you to place some text just before the title. The 'after' parameter is, of course, the opposite. And the 'display' parameter is, as the Codex also explains, a Boolean value (meaning it can be true or false), which allows you to tell the_title whether it should simply write the entry's title directly to the place in your page that it is called, or if it should be **returned** for use in other PHP code.

We will be taking a closer look at returning later in this chapter. You can find out the specifics of each of the tags we have mentioned in the Codex as well. Now let's move on to a different type of template tag that WordPress offers.

Conditional tags

Conditional tags are used when you want to display different content depending on where you are on your site. Imagine that you want different content in your sidebar depending on whether the user is viewing the frontpage or an archived entry—this is where you would make use of conditional tags.

Basically, a conditional tag answers questions. Is the current page a search page? Is the current page an archive page? Is the current page an archive page for the Books category? Is the user trying to reach a non-existing page? You get the idea.

Through the use of conditional tags, you can tailor the display of information to what you think the reader should be seeing at any given time. In the case in which a user might be trying to reach a page that for some reason doesn't exist, it might be a good idea to provide that user with a set of options, such as a search form or a set of likely destinations.

Conditional tags are used within a PHP if-else structure, like so:

```
<?php if (is_home()) { ?>

This is the frontpage.

<?php } elseif (is_single()) { ?>

This is a permalink page
```

```php
<?php } else { ?>
```

This is not the frontpage or a permalink page.

```php
<?php } ?>
```

When the page is being served to the user, WordPress first checks to see whether this is the frontpage. That is, whether it is being loaded without any parameters (as discussed in the "Displaying your blog posts" section). If that is the case, WordPress stops there, and This is the frontpage will appear in the browser. If that isn't the case, it will move on to check whether the current page is a single page or if we are viewing a single article/post. If that's the case, This is a permalink page will be printed. And finally, if neither is the case, This is not the frontpage or a permalink page will be presented to the end user.

If-else, conditional PHP statements are fairly straightforward, but it is always a good idea to get better acquainted with your tools, so I recommend skimming over the documentation for if, else, and elseif at the PHP manual site (http://php.net/if). The versatility of the if-else conditional statements will get you a very long way.

Another very gnarly use of if-else conditional statements is combining them, like so:

```php
<?php if ( ( is_home() ) or ( is_single() ) ) { ?>
```

This is either the frontpage or a permalink

```php
<?php } ?>
```

This is great for saving some space and can alternatively be combined with something like this:

```php
<?php if (! is_home() ) { ?>
```

This is not home

```php
<?php } ?>
```

Whenever you place an exclamation point in front of a variable, it negates the variable. So in the preceding code, we are really saying that if this is *not* home, display the text This is not home, whereas if we are on the frontpage, it will not be shown.

Crafty use of these techniques can help keep the number of individual template files you will use to a minimum, but dramatically increases the complexity of each template file. There are trade-offs in everything, after all.

Include tags

A third type of template tag available in WordPress is the so-called **include tag**. WordPress themes are modular in design, having any number of theme template files. This modular design allows for some pretty exciting possibilities. At a minimum, a WordPress theme has to have a stylesheet, header, footer, sidebar, and index theme template.

You make use of include tags to construct your site from the modular pieces. Using this method you can create a single header, footer, and sidebar that can be included in any page you create for your WordPress-powered site.

The default include tags and the theme template files they look for include get_header (header.php, wp-header.php), get_footer (footer.php, wp-footer.php), get_sidebar (sidebar.php, wp-sidebar.php), and the odd one out, comments_template (comments.php or comments-popup.php, wp-comments.php or wp-popupcomments.php).

Conventional wisdom is to name your theme template files without the preceding wp-, but if you name them wp-something_or_other.php, they will still work.

At the most basic level, you could create a theme template which looked like this, and it would work as you would expect it to:

```php
<?php get_header(); ?>
Content goes here
<?php get_sidebar(); ?>
<?php get_footer(); ?>
```

Theme templating doesn't stop here, though. Let's say that you want to expand your template to have a third column with the new sidebar being a theme template file called sidebar2.php. You would simply place:

```php
<?php include (TEMPLATEPATH . '/sidebar2.php'); ?>
```

In your master theme page, this has the same effect as the default include tags. When viewed in a browser, sidebar2.php will be included in your page.

Content types in WordPress

By default, there are three types of content in WordPress: posts, pages, and comments. Each content type has its own unique features. Leveraging all three will give you the most robust and feature-full blogging experience. There are other content types that can be added to WordPress via plug-ins, such as Chris's CJD Notepad plug-in (www.chrisjdavis.org/cjd-notepad/), which allows you to create notes via the WordPress admin interface. This can be helpful when researching topics to blog about.

Enough with the shameless promotion. Back to the action: Let's talk about posts.

Posts

The bread and butter of any blog is the post content. A **post** is a single entry on your blog, tied to a category and a date. You could have three posts for one day on your blog, all in different categories, or just one post in one category. Posts live within your blog chronology, meaning they show up on your index.php page and are navigable by month, year, and day as well as category.

It is your posts that will drive the content and direction of your blog, as well as generate wider conversation through commenting if you choose to enable it.

Pages

WordPress was initially geared toward the chronological publication of journal-like entries (what have become known as blogs). Increasingly, the support forums were filled with people trying to manage and power their entire site with WordPress. What people were screaming for was more of a CMS than a blogging platform.

After some debate, it was decided that there would be real benefit in folding this kind of functionality into WordPress, and since version 1.5 these CMS-like features have been available from within the WordPress admin interface (to create a Page, go into the administration back-end of your blog, select Write and then Write Page).

These static posts are simply referred to as Pages (notice the capital P) and they are, in essence, the same as a post. Pages are stored in the database in the exact same way as posts and can have comments, and register pingbacks and trackbacks just like normal posts.

However, Pages differ from posts because they don't use the category system and they fall outside of the normal blog chronology. You also have the option of organizing Pages in a tree-like hierarchy and choosing a custom template on a per-Page basis. We will talk more about applying custom templates to Pages later in this chapter.

Although you can manually create links to your Pages, an easier way of going about this is to use wp_list_pages. This template tag outputs a linked, nested list of the Pages currently available on your site. You can read more about wp_list_pages here: http://codex. wordpress.org/Template_Tags/wp_list_pages. (You also can read more about the Page's functionality in the WordPress Codex at http://codex.wordpress.org/pages.)

Comments

Comments are one of the most exciting and community building aspects of blogging. Enabling commenting on your blog promotes conversation and exploration. Some of the most meaningful content on weblogs is in the comments, not necessarily in the posts themselves. WordPress has a robust commenting system, incorporating trackback, pingback, and per-post commenting.

Themes in WordPress 1.5

As of WordPress 1.5, all themes and plug-ins are stored in /wp-content/themes/ and wp-content/plugins/, respectively. This is important to note, since it is a life saver when you are trying to troubleshoot a broken theme or plug-in.

Both themes and plug-ins are activated through an admin interface located at wp-admin/themes.php and wp-admin/plugins.php. In these pages, you can see which plug-ins or themes are currently active and you can activate or deactivate plug-ins and themes.

WordPress ships with two themes installed: the original theme (pre–WordPress 1.5) by Dave Shea is labeled Classic, and Kubrick is labeled Default.

Kubrick

Kubrick is the code name for the template that comes with WordPress 1.5, nicknamed after the late director Stanley Kubrick. Michael designed the first version of Kubrick in July 2004, and it was officially adopted into WordPress with the 1.5 release in February 2005 (adopted so very proficiently into the new template system by Ryan Boren).

We'll spend a little time taking Kubrick apart so you can see how all that we have talked about applies to an actual theme.

Using Kubrick as a base for your own template is a good idea because it is likely to save you a lot of headaches and oversights, but there is no replacement for creating your own work of art from scratch. Take a look at Kubrick and learn the ropes; then try your hand at creating something from scratch.

The files

Kubrick comes bundled as 14 template files and a directory for images. Each file performs a specific task, and working together they grab, format, and display your blog content for all the world to see. Let's have a look at each of the files and what job it performs.

style.css

This is the only file that you absolutely have to have for your theme to really be called a theme. The rest of the functionality needed for WordPress to function is already present. Because this is the only file needed, it is also where the metadata about the theme goes. If you open the Kubrick `style.css`, you'll find the following lines at the top of the file, preceding the actual CSS information:

```
Theme Name: WordPress Default
Theme URI: http://wordpress.org/
Description: The default WordPress theme based
on the famous <a href="http://binarybonsai.com/kubrick/">
Kubrick</a>.
Version: 1.5
Author: Michael Heilemann
Author URI: http://binarybonsai.com/
```

This code is mostly self-explanatory, and when it comes time for you to create your own theme, you simply make a copy of the Kubrick directory, change this information, and voila—you're in business.

index.php

This is the file the user is presented with when viewing the frontpage of your site. By default, it shows a header, two columns, and a footer—with the main column containing a loop for displaying blog entries.

header.php

This file is inserted at the very beginning of every page.

footer.php

Similarly, this file is inserted at the very end of every page.

sidebar.php

The `sidebar.php` file contains all the things that belong on the sidebar. Who would've guessed, eh? Having it in a separate file allows us to make changes once and then register everywhere we include the file.

single.php

When calling up a specific entry, this is the file used.

page.php

WordPress comes with a functionality that will allow you to create Pages that behave in many ways like a static HTML page would. Say you wanted an About page for your blog: you could create it from within WordPress's administration back-end without ever having to toy with separate .html or .php pages. This can save you quite a lot of trouble in terms of aligning your design and layout across the entire site. Be aware, however, that you can't use PHP within a page's content (at least not without a third-party plug-in).

comments.php

This file is called from `single.php`, showing the comments, pingbacks, and trackbacks of the entry being called. Essentially it is also possible to use comments with the Pages function of WordPress (which makes it possible to create, for instance, a static About page for your blog), should the need arise.

comments-popup.php

Essentially performs the same function as `comments.php`, except it was created to work in a pop-up window instead of inline with the entry. We consider this template a leftover from bygone days and can't remember the last time we saw a WordPress-powered blog using it.

searchform.php

To make it faster and easier to make changes across the entire blog, the search form resides in its own file.

archive.php

When going back into the archives, such as when you're viewing a specific month, this is the template used. By default it calls the entries using the_excerpt instead of the_content, which makes for faster skimming through larger quantities of entries.

search.php

To make it easier to provide hints for searches, they are provided with their own template.

404.php

When WordPress can't find the data you're looking for, it will present you with this file. By default, there's nothing on the page other than a short remark, telling the user the obvious (Error 404 - Not Found). Michael has added a range of tools for the user on his site, making it easier to go from there to something that might be of some use (you can see it by going here: http://binarybonsai.com/gimme404).

archives.php

The Pages functionality in WordPress allows you to select a template for each page you create, and archives.php is one such template. It allows you to create a quick archives page that can act as a base for further exploration into the archives of your blog.

links.php

As with archives.php, links.php is a Page template, meant to make it easy for you to create a Page to display your links. It includes the necessary code for fetching your links from WordPress's Link Manager.

Taking a closer look at the code

If you open up index.php in your favorite text editor, you see a very large amount of code, which can be hard to decipher. So let's take a stab at demystifying it a bit. The Kubrick main template is comprised of header.php, footer.php, sidebar.php, and searchform.php. If you now open header.php, you can see where the complexities begin.

Just after the pingback code, there is a block of inline CSS. This CSS is there to help the average Kubrick user with adding a custom image to the header. From the Kubrick header.php file: "To accommodate differing install paths of WordPress, images are referred only here, and not in the wp-layout.css file. If you prefer to use only CSS for colors and what not, then go right ahead and delete the following lines, and the image files."

What this means in English is that because not everyone uses the same server, WordPress and thus your theme will be located in different places. On one machine it might be at /www/home/bob/wordpress/, whereas on another machine it might be at /vhosts/bobssite.com/wordpress/—you just never can tell.

To help with that problem, this block of CSS lets you explicitly set the path to an image by calling one of the theme-specific template tags:

```
background: url("<?php bloginfo('stylesheet_directory'); ?>
/images/kubrickheader.jpg") no-repeat bottom center;
```

When loaded in your browser, the preceding will be executed and displayed as follows:

```
background: url("http://www.bobssite.com/wp-content/themes
/default/images/kubrickheader.jpg") no-repeat bottom center;
```

Simple enough. If you know the path your images will take, you can move this block to the style.css file, removing it from header.php, which helps clean it up a little. That's it for the header; now let's open sidebar.php and see how Kubrick uses the conditional tags we spoke about earlier.

Around line 15 you will start to see where the conditionals come into play.

The first conditional we call is (is_404()). This tag handles situations when the user requests a page that doesn't exist, so you would place whatever text you want to show the user after the closing tag (?>) but before the next opening PHP tag (<?php).

```
<?php /* If this is a 404 page */ if (is_404()) { ?>
<?php echo 'Whoa, there aint nothing here hoss.'; ?>
```

Now when users look for something that is not on our site or has been removed, they will be shown that friendly bit of text and be called hoss. Next is the conditional tag (is_category()), which checks to see whether the user is browsing a category; if so, it displays the following message:

```
<?php /* If this is a category archive */
        } elseif (is_category()) { ?>
  <p>
    You are currently browsing the archives for
    the <?php single_cat_title(''); ?> category.
</p>
```

And next are (is_day()), (is_month()), and (is_year()) which return the appropriate text if the user is browsing a day (mysite.com/2005/05/21/), month (mysite.com/2005/05/), or year (mysite.com/2005/) archive.

```
<?php /* If this is a yearly archive */ } elseif (is_day()) { ?>
  <p>
    You are currently browsing the <a href="
    <?php echo get_settings('siteurl'); ?>">
    <?php echo bloginfo('name'); ?></a>
    weblog archives for the day <?php the_time('l, F jS, Y'); ?>.
  </p>
```

```
<?php /* If this is a monthly archive */ } elseif (is_month()) { ?>
  <p>
    You are currently browsing the <a href="
    <?php echo get_settings('siteurl'); ?>">
    <?php echo bloginfo('name'); ?></a>
    weblog archives for <?php the_time('F, Y'); ?>.
  </p>
```

```php
<?php /* If this is a yearly archive */ } elseif (is_year()) { ?>
  <p>
    You are currently browsing the <a href="
    <?php echo get_settings('siteurl'); ?>">
    <?php echo bloginfo('name'); ?></a>
     weblog archives for the year <?php the_time('Y'); ?>.
</p>
```

Next to last is a conditional tag that is returned if the user has searched our site; the content of the <p> element is the result.

```php
<?php /* If this is a monthly archive */ } elseif (is_search()) { ?>
  <p>
    You have searched the <a href="
    <?php echo get_settings('siteurl'); ?>">
    <?php echo bloginfo('name'); ?></a>
    weblog archives for <strong>'<?php echo wp_specialchars($s);
?>'</strong>.
    If you are unable to find anything in these search
    results, you can try one of these links.
</p>
```

This last tag is a great example of using conditional tags and the exclamation mark to negate a tag. What we are saying is *"Return this text if this is a paged result, but only if the pages variable is not empty."*

```php
<?php } elseif (isset($_GET['paged'])
            && !empty($_GET['paged'])) { ?>
  <p>
    You are currently browsing the
    <a href="<?php echo get_settings('siteurl'); ?>">
    <?php echo bloginfo('name'); ?></a> weblog archives.
</p>
```

This tag closes the elseif block, and allows us to move down our sidebar to other code that might need to be executed:

```php
<?php } ?>
```

Through the use of conditional tags, Kubrick can serve customized information for a number of scenarios out of one template file. If you were not using conditionals here, you would have to have a custom sidebar for each possibility or hard code the sidebar into numerous custom templates.

If you open archive.php, you see a similar use of conditional tags, this time allowing us to show different text based on whether we are viewing a category, monthly, daily, yearly, author, or paged archive.

Working with template pages

Don't be afraid to create new files if you need them. The ones that come with WordPress, especially `archives.php` and `links.php`, are merely examples from which you can take what you need and delete the rest.

Now that we have spent some time going over the types of tags that you can access in WordPress, let's move on to creating a custom template for our site.

Let's create a Colophon page, complete with a handy "email me" contact form. If you're not familiar with the term *Colophon*, you can think of it as an About Me page or a CV (curriculum vitae).

First, we need to create a Page inside WordPress's admin back-end. Go to Write ➤ Write Page (see Figure 5-3).

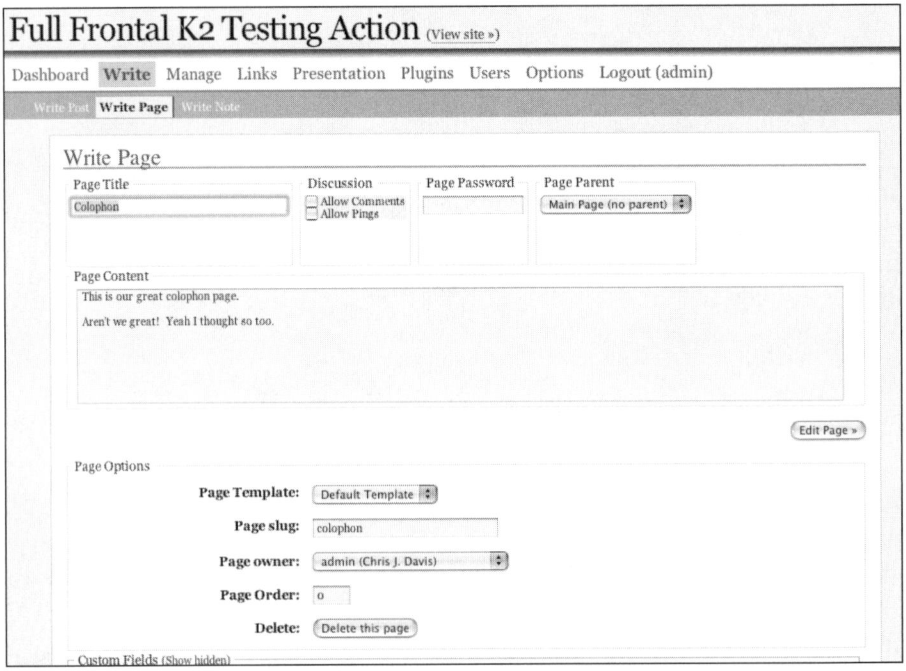

Figure 5-3. The Write Page screen, which is where all the magic happens

Title your new page Colophon, turn off comments and pings (not that it matters because we won't include the comments template in our custom Colophon template). Under Page Options, make sure that under Page Template it says Default Template.

Other page options

There are some other options you can set on this page. Although they don't play a role in our current exercise, it is worth mentioning them and what they do.

Page Content

Page Content allows us to add some text to the page, much as if we were writing a post. You could just type in the information you want on your page here.

Page slug

Ah, the Page slug. The single most useful feature on this page with the most bone-headed, unusable name. The Page slug allows you to set the URI for this page (or post, for that matter). For instance, we have entered colophon as our page slug so when we visit this page in our browser the URI will be http://localhost/colophon/. If we put nani-nani-boo-boo in the Page slug field, our URI would be http://localhost/nani-nani-boo-boo/ (and that is funnier, and funnier is good).

Page parent

One of the smoothest features of Pages is the child/parent relationship. In WordPress you can assign a page to be the child of another page. This really becomes powerful when you have multiple pages set as children of another page. If you leave a page as the child of the main page, you will get a result similar to that shown in Figure 5-4. You see that the Pages heading on the right contains the Colophon page because the Colophon page is still the child of the main page. If you were to pick another page as a child of the Colophon page, it would be listed under the Colophon link on the right. Note that the URI of the child page is derived from the parent page's URI. For example, adding another page with a page slug of more as a child of the Colophon page would give us http://localhost/colophon/more/.

At this point you would also want to set your page order.

Page Order

Page order really only comes into play when you have more than one page acting as a child to a parent page. Suppose that you have a page called Gallery, and then you have three pages that are children of that page. You would use Page Order to determine the order of the children, or which page is listed as the first child, which is the second, and so on.

Viewing the new Page

We finished our first step. Now click Create New Page.

WordPress should save the page to its database, reload the current page, and serve you with a link called Manage Pages. Click that link and you will see a list of the pages that you currently have in your database. Look for the one called Colophon, find it, and click the corresponding View link on the right side of the page. Of course, if you never created a Page in your WordPress install, it will be the only one listed here. Lucky you.

You should see a web page similar to Figure 5-4.

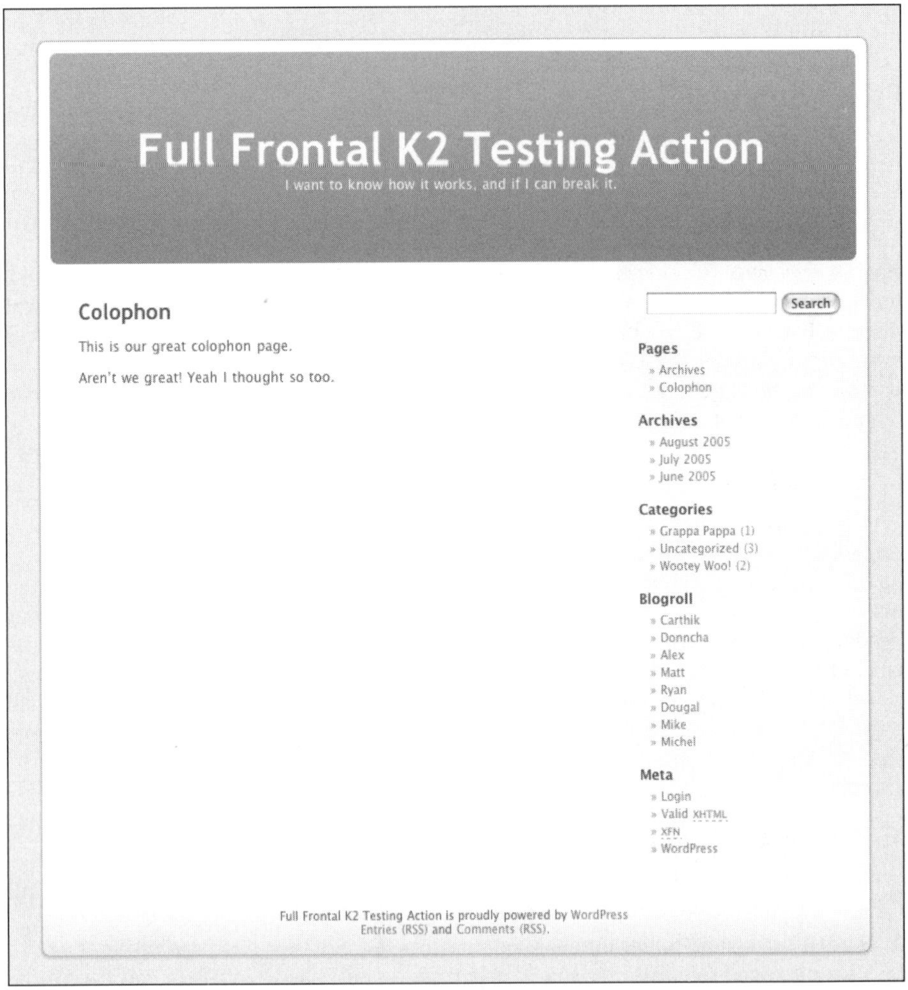

Figure 5-4. The Colophon page as your visitors would see it

That is to say, it works. It's not a particularly interesting page, but we're about to remedy that with a little bit of code magic. Open up a new blank document in your favorite editor and save it as colophon.php in your default theme folder. Now let's get on to adding some shine to this dull page.

Editing the Page

First, open up with the standard template file header. It is important to name your custom templates something descriptive because WordPress will label each one by reading the Template Name line.

```php
<?php
/*
Template Name: Colophon Template
*/
?>

<?php get_header(); ?>
<div id="content" class="narrowcolumn">
<?php if (have_posts()) : ?>
  <?php while (have_posts()) : the_post(); ?>
    <div class="post" id="post-<?php the_ID(); ?>">
      <h2><?php the_title(); ?></h2>
        <div class="entrytext">
            <?php the_content(); ?>
        </div>
      </div>
  <?php endwhile; endif; ?>
<form method="post" action="some-processing.php">
   <label for="nm">
     <small>Your name</small>
   </label>
<div>
   <input type="text" name="name" size="50" id="nm" />
</div>
   <label for="em">
     <small>Your email address</small>
   </label>
<div>
 <input type="text" name="email" size="50" id="em" />
</div>
     <label for="content">
  <small>Your message</small>
   </label>
<div>
<textarea name="message" cols="47" rows="10" id="ms">
   </textarea>
</div>
<p>
<input type="submit" title="Click here to
     send your message." value="Send" />
</p>
</form>
<?php edit_post_link('Edit this entry.', '<p>', '</p>'); ?>
</div>
<?php get_sidebar(); ?>
<?php get_footer(); ?>
```

The first five lines tell WordPress that this file is a Page template named Colophon.

After that step, we load the header and define a <div> tag with the "narrowcolumn" class (creating a 450px wide column, as defined in style.css). We load all the normal template tags that we use to call our post/page content.

After the php endwhile; endif; is where the fun begins. Here, we include the form and form elements that allow our readers to send us some e-mail. We're not covering the PHP that you need to process and send off the e-mails; that again is beyond the scope of this chapter. So we save the page again and make sure that the shiny new colophon.php page is in /wp-content/themes/default/, whether that is on the local machine or on a remote server. We then go back into the WordPress admin, and load Manage ➤ Pages and then select to edit the Colophon.

When the page loads for editing, notice the drop-down menu for Page Template (halfway down the screen). Now is the time to do something with that. If you click the drop-down menu, you should now see Colophon Template as a choice, as shown in Figure 5-5.

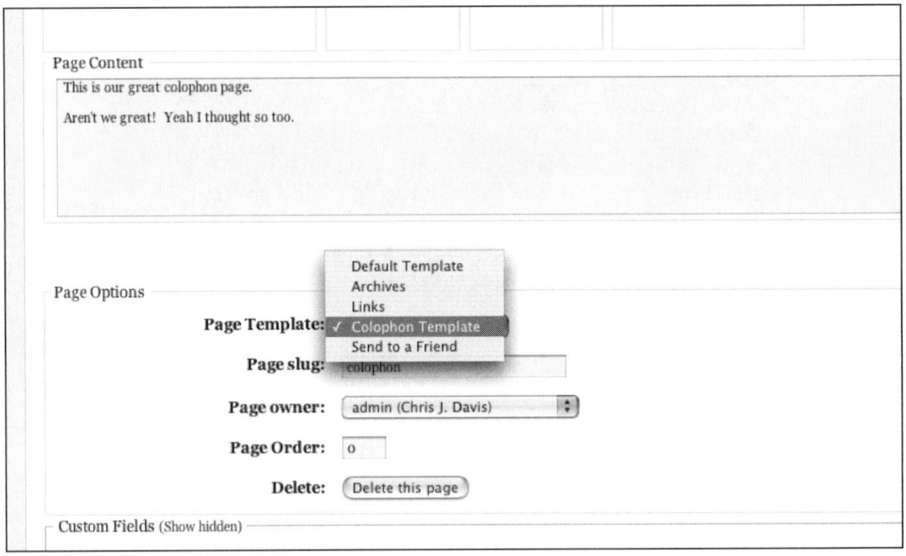

Figure 5-5. Applying the Colophon Template to our Page named Colophon in WordPress admin

Select Colophon Template from that menu, and then for the fun of it, go back up to the Page Content text area and add this to the end of the text: And hey, if you think we're great, leave me a message with this nifty contact form below! Save the page; the browser will reload the page with a message at the top that says Manage Pages. Click that link and then find your colophon page in the listing on the next page. Click View. When the page loads, you should see the screen shown in Figure 5-6.

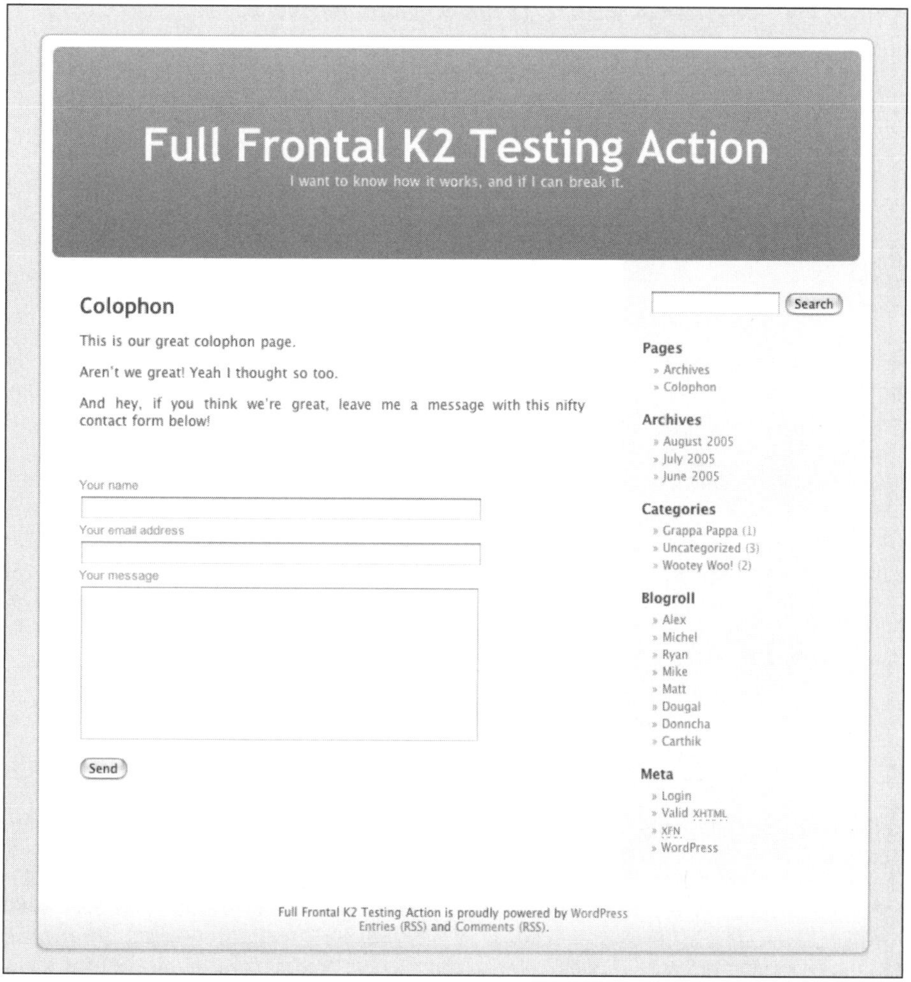

Figure 5-6. Your colophon page now with contact form!

Congratulations! You just created your first custom template for WordPress. This is a pretty simple example of what can be done if you leverage the theme system correctly. The code processing the contact form and shooting off the e-mail is in the code download, so go check it out.

Now let's look at customizing an existing template.

Customizing an existing template

Open up wp-content/themes/default/archives.php in your text editor, and let's get to work! (Make sure to open archives.php, not archive.php!)

Archives is a pretty basic template. Let's take a look at the code:

```php
<?php
/*
Template Name: Archives
*/
?>

<?php get_header(); ?>

<div id="content" class="widecolumn">

<?php include (TEMPLATEPATH . '/searchform.php'); ?>

<h2>Archives by Month:</h2>
  <ul>
    <?php wp_get_archives('type=monthly'); ?>
  </ul>

<h2>Archives by Subject:</h2>
  <ul>
      <?php wp_list_cats(); ?>
  </ul>

</div>

<?php get_footer(); ?>
```

Let's make this code a little more fun for us and usable for our visitors by making some quick edits.

For starters, we'll move the current monthly and category archives into a sidebar, we'll replace them with a list of the ten newest entries, and, heck, we'll throw in a list of the top ten most-commented entries (we'll refer to them as the "most popular" entries) for fun.

First, move the content of the widecolumn into its own sidebar div and rename the widecolumn div to narrowcolumn. (The difference between the narrowcolumn and widecolumn classes in the Kubrick template is that the widecolumn class is centered on the page, leaving no room for a sidebar; whereas the narrowcolumn is aligned to the left, leaving space to the right for a sidebar.)

We have to make a few changes to the content of the sidebar to make it validate and style correctly. The following is a good way to go about marking it up:

```php
<?php
/*
Template Name: Archives
*/
?>
```

```php
<?php get_header(); ?>

<div id="content" class="narrowcolumn">

<!--this is where our content will go -->

</div>

<div id="sidebar">
  <ul>
    <li><?php include (TEMPLATEPATH . '/searchform.php'); ?></li>

    <li><h2>Archives by Month:</h2>
        <ul><?php wp_get_archives('type=monthly'); ?></ul>
    </li>

        <li><h2>Archives by Subject:</h2>
          <ul><?php wp_list_cats(); ?></ul>
        </li>
        </ul>
</div>
<?php  get_footer(); ?>
```

Now this code is working (you should go ahead and test it, just to make sure). If you have a brand spanking new install of WordPress you probably won't see much change because you don't have any content that isn't in the current month. Don't worry, though, because when you do have months' and years' worth of content this will be a great trick to employ. Now we can move along to the main column of the Page.

We don't want to hard code the name of the Page into the HTML; instead we want to read the name of the WordPress Page. This is easily done because Pages (being little more than "static" blog entries) use the same Loop as your normal blog. Replace `<!-- this is where our content will go -->` with the following lines of code:

```php
<?php if (have_posts()) : while (have_posts()) : the_post(); ?>
  <div class="post" id="post-<?php the_ID(); ?>">
    <h2><?php the_title(); ?></h2>
      <?php edit_post_link('Edit Page', '<p>', '</p>'); ?>
      <div class="entrytext">
      <?php the_content('<p class="serif">Read the rest
            of this page &raquo;</p>'); ?>

      <?php link_pages('<p><strong>Pages:
            </strong> ', '</p>', 'number'); ?>
    </div>
</div>
<?php endwhile; endif; ?>
```

The Page now has a headline, which should read Archives, although the Page itself is probably rather empty. If you want to write a small introduction or a set of instructions for your Archives page, go right ahead and edit the Page content.

Regardless of how you end up using the various parts to form your template, starting out by looking at what Kubrick does is probably a good idea. The template files that make up Kubrick can be found at /wp-content/themes/default/).

Let's now talk about custom templates—and, more importantly, how we can bend them to our will.

Advanced templating in WordPress

Where do we turn when the techniques we have outlined are just not cutting it? What if we want just one of our Pages to have a blue background while the rest of them have white backgrounds?

What happens when we want to add a page to our site that doesn't have anything to do with our posts or categories?

Again we turn to templates, but this time to a lesser known subset of templates: **custom templates**.

Templates, posts, Pages, and plug-ins

There are a number of strictly defined templates in WordPress. But there is also another category of templates that can be anything, can be called anything, and can be applied to any Page you create in WordPress. The fun begins with custom templates.

It is a little-known fact that you can apply custom templates to blank Pages in WordPress. What this means is that you can create a completely blank Page in WordPress and then apply a custom theme template laden with code to it. As an example let's look at the archives page at Chris's site Sillyness Spelled Wrong Intentionally (www.chrisjdavis.org/archive/).

If you were to look at the page via the WordPress admin, the Page content area would be completely blank. If you then opened the custom template, you would see a whole mess o' code, and interestingly enough the_loop would be nowhere to be found. In fact, the only WordPress core code that you would find would be get_header(); and get_footer(); .

The rest is either embedded code or plug-in calls.

So let's get into some code

Our first step is to create the custom template that will be applied to the Archives page. Because we *do not* want to reinvent the wheel, we'll be making use of Shawn Grimes' Clean Archives plug-in (www.sporadicnonsense.com/files/srg_clean_archives_1.5.zip)

and Chris's Commenter Heat Map plug-in (www.chrisjdavis.org/hacks/1.5/cjd_comment_heat.zip). After you download these two plug-ins you need to place the *.php files in your Plugins folder located at wp-content/plugins/. After you have done so, load /wp-admin/plugins.php in your browser and activate it. When you load the Plugins Manager, things are pretty straightforward. Find CJD Comment Heat and SRG Clean Archives and click Activate in the right column for each one. You're now ready to move on to the next step. But before we go on, we'll talk a little bit about what each of these plug-ins does.

CJD Comment Heat

In a nutshell, CJD Comment Heat creates a "heat map" of the comments that have been made to your site. You can see an example of this plug-in at work on Chris's site: www.chrisjdavis.org/archive/#heat. As you can see, the image, powered by Gravatars (http://gravatar.com), becomes bigger when there are more comments made. If you mouse over the image, you'll see a tooltip telling you how many comments a user has made.

SRG Clean Archives

Clean Archives from Shawn Grimes is a plug-in that gives a clean, straightforward look at archives, broken out by month. You can see it in action over at Shawn's site: www.sporadicnonsense.com/archives/.

Using the plug-ins

First things first. Every custom template must start with the following code (this file is called new_archive.php):

```
<?php
/*
Template Name: Archives Template
Description: A template for my archives pages.
*/
?>
```

We call for our header.php file and start adding our content:

```
<?php get_header(); ?>
<div class="main">
  <h2>
    Here are the archives for <?php bloginfo('name'); ?>.
  </h2>
  <p>
  Search the archives.
  </p>
      <div class="search">
      <form method="get" id="searchform" action="/index.php">
    <input type="search" value="Search" name="search" id="s" />
    <input type="submit" id="submit" name="Submit" value="Go!" />
    </form>
</div>
```

We could have put some of this in the Page Content area of the Create Page screen, but for this demo we want to have everything in the template, so on we go:

```
<?php srg_clean_archives(); ?>
<h2>
Commenter Heat Map
</h2>
<p>
    Below is a heat map of the commenters here.
</p>
<?php cjd_comment_heat(); ?>
</div>
```

Notice the call to the plug-ins. Finally, we close with the footer call:

```
<?php get_footer(); ?>
```

That is the entire template; now we save it as new_archive.php, place it in /wp-content/themes/default/, and then log into the WordPress admin area to create a new Page.

Finally, we need to create a blank Page and link it up with the new template.

Let's go to Write ➤ Write Page and get down to business. We need to give our Page a title, let's say My Archives. We can skip down past the Page Content area to Page Options.

The first field should be Page Template, and in the drop-down box we should find Archives Template—select that, make sure you have my-archives as the Page slug, and click Create New Page. That's it. If you have installed and activated the plug-ins, when you load http://localhost/my-archives/ you should see your lovely new Archives page.

Let's continue our exploration of custom templates by looking at another little-known power hidden within the theme system: **per category templates.**

Hidden spiffiness abounds

Deep within the recesses of the WordPress code base lies dormant the power to create custom templates for each of our categories; what is astounding is how easy it is to create them. This sleeping giant merely awaits the correct filenames to wake and unleash untold shininess and spiffiness upon your visitors' heads!

This isn't a feature for everyone, but we think that for a select few it can be a breath of fresh air, not to mention a solution for many frustrations.

When you get down to brass tacks, this is a profoundly easy feature to exploit. All you need to know is the number of each category and what you want each category to look like. Let's look at how it can be used on Chris's site (www.chrisjdavis.org).

Context-sensitive information is the bee's knees

Giving information to the user that is both contextually correct as well as *useful* should be the goal of any webmaster. A prime opportunity to do this is when a reader is browsing your category pages.

You will find on Chris's site, where appropriate, a list of other resources specific to the category you are browsing in the left-aligned column. Two prime examples are the Tutorial (www.chrisjdavis.org/category/tutorials) and Web Standards (www.chrisjdavis.org/category/web-standards) categories. On each one, you find links to offsite resources.

Now this is a very limited example of per category templates. If you want, you can change every aspect of the way the Page is displayed, load alternate stylesheets . . . anything! The sky's the limit. But think before you go crazy, people. So what does one need to do to tap in to the power of per category templates? Glad you asked!

Let's write some code, shall we?

After the previous discussion, creating these templates will be a piece of cake. We'll start by making sure we actually have a category.php file to begin with. You will find it very helpful to have a good layout with which to browse categories, and your readers will, too. If you don't have one, simply open a new file in your favorite text editor and enter this code to get you started with a category template:

```php
<?php
/*
Template Name: Category Template
*/
?>

<?php get_header(); ?>
<div class="narrowcolumn">
<?php if (have_posts()) : while (have_posts()) : the_post(); ?>

<h3>
<?php the_time('l') ?>, <?php the_time('F') ?>
        <?php the_time('jS') ?>, <?php the_time('Y') ?>
</h3>
<h1>
<?php permalink_anchor(); ?><a href="<?php echo the_permalink(); ?>"
        rel="bookmark" title="Permanent Link: <?php the_title();
?>">
        <?php the_id(); ?></a> <?php the_title(); ?>
</h1>

<small>
<?php the_category(' ,'); ?>
</small>

<p>
```

5

207

```php
<?php the_content(); ?>
</p>

<?php endwhile; else: ?>

<p>
<?php _e('Sorry, no posts matched your criteria.'); ?>
</p>

<?php endif; ?>
</div>
<?php get_footer(); ?>
```

Simply save this code as category.php and place it in /wp-content/themes/default/.

Now that we have a category template file, we need to decide what we want to customize. Let's make this the Gorillas category. Heh, gorillas are funny.

Make sure to have more than the Uncategorized category to play with. Create a new category by going to the Dashboard and selecting Manage ➤ Categories. Call the category Gorillas and give it a description if you want. Finally click Add Category. Make a note of its ID because you'll need that in a second. You also need to have at least one post in a category before you can see it, so go ahead and add a post by clicking Write ➤ Write Post in the Dashboard. When you have written it, make sure you select the Gorillas category at the top right and then click Publish. You can now view the category from the frontpage of the blog.

You'll now create a template for the Gorillas category (with whichever category number you noted in the last paragraph), okay? Good. You need to have some links to gorilla resources on the Net offered to your visitors while they are in your Gorillas category listing.

First, we edit our previous template name section like so:

```php
<?php
/*
Template Name: Gorillas Category Template
Description: A template for the Gorillas Category.
*/
?>
```

Now usually we would want to just call <?php get_sidebar(); ?> and include the template file sidebar.php, but we want to add context-sensitive info, and the menu is the best place for it. So we will be hard coding this bit in this template between the closing div and before calling the footer:

```html
<div id="sidebar">
  <ol>
  <li>
   <a href="http://gorilla.com" title="gorillas">gorilla.com</a>
  </li>
  <li>
```

```
        <a href="http://www.kilimanjaro.com/gorilla/websites.htm"
                    title="Gorillas Help Site">kilimanjaro.com</a>
        </li>
        <li>
        <a href="http://kongisking.com"
                    title="really big gorilla">Kongisking.com</a>
        </li>
    </ol>
    </div>
```

The rest of the template is fine for our purposes, so we are ready to save this puppy and move on.

Now for the payoff—making it all work

Okay, so now we have created a template for our Gorillas category, complete with spiffy links about gorillas for our readers. We are ready to save this bad boy, but how does WordPress know to use this when Gorillas is called?

It is time to do something with that category number we found. All we need to do is save this file as category-*n*.php, where *n* is the number of your category. For example, if Gorillas is category number 18, we would save this file as category-18.php and place it in wp-content/themes/default/.

Easy-peasy, as they say. Believe it or not, that's all there is to it. The next time you load the Gorillas category you should see the template we just created.

Note that unlike Page templates, you don't need to assign this template to your category. WordPress just knows what to do when it finds a category template with a number attached in your theme directory.

Now let's talk about a seldom-used theme template: the Home template (home.php).

There's no place like Home

We talked about the different files that WordPress is hard coded to recognize. One of the template files that we have not talked about yet is home.php, which is used when index.php is called without any arguments passed to it.

That is a mouthful, isn't it? What that nonsense means is the following. When you load a site, say www.binarybonsai.com, the physical URI, or address, is www.binarybonsai.com/index.php. When you click a link to a specific post, say one that is number 732, the address becomes index.php?p=732. Now p=732 is an argument, or rather how we tell WordPress that we want to see post #732.

Most sites use some mod_rewrite magic so you don't see it, but (trust us) it is there. So home.php is used only when the physical address in the address bar of your browser is somesite.com/index.php.

And that matters to me WHY exactly?

Good question; glad you asked.

home.php is the front door of your blog. This is where you want to show users and visitors the most recent posts, your categories and how busy they are, and links to other blogs and sites that you think visitors will like. In other words, this is the place to inform and amaze your users and visitors. You can customize the information in home.php. You will already have seen index.php, which will give you some idea about what you can place on your frontpage. home.php is simply a customizable version.

Suppose we want to have the home page of our site contain some aggregated content, say some of our images posted to Flickr, and then the five newest entries of our weblog. In other words, we're providing fresh, rolling news for users and visitors so that they don't see the same old frontpage every time they pay a visit. And just to make things interesting, let's not call the_loop: `<?php if (have_posts()) : while (have_posts()) : the_post(); ?>` anywhere on that page.

What we're showing you isn't necessarily the best way to go about this; this course of action will demonstrate how powerful and completely disconnected from the core function of WordPress you can make home.php. Keep that in mind.

How am I displaying all this info if I am not hitting the database for it?

Simple. You're using the version of magpieRSS (http://magpierss.sourceforge.net/) that is bundled with WordPress to grab, parse, and style various RSS feeds.

What home.php gives you is the ability to have a WordPress-handled index page that can be more static in nature than a blog, with a blog behind the scenes. In essence, we move closer to using WordPress as a CMS instead of merely an elegant blogging platform.

Of course, you want to have the_loop included in the home template to simplify matters. We just wanted to emphasize the extreme flexibility of WordPress when using templates by going without it.

Let's write some code!

If this section is your first exposure to the RSS aggregation built into WordPress, don't go nuts with it! It is powerful and easy to use, but you take a hit in performance when using it.

We'll create a new document in our favorite text editor and call it home.php. We'll open up with the customary code:

```php
<?php get_header(); ?>
```

Here is the first new bit—we need to call the RSS functions and set a variable to today's date:

```php
<?php require_once (ABSPATH . WPINC . '/rss-functions.php'); ?>
<?php $today = current_time('mysql', 1); ?>
<div class="main">
```

```
<h2>
Recent Flickr
</h2>
```

We're not parsing RSS for the Flickr area because Flickr (http://flickr.com) provides a nice little solution for this already (http://flickr.com/badge_new.gne). We won't paste it all in here, but you can find the code easily enough on its website. If you've been living under a social software-proof rock lately, Flickr is the premier way to publish and share your photos with family and friends. Flickr incorporates tagging and commenting to create a unique user experience. Go and check it out!

OK. Here is where the fun begins. We're now ready to call and handle the first RSS feed:

```php
<?php
$rss = @fetch_rss('http://localhost/feed/');
if ( isset($rss->items) && 0 != count($rss->items) ) {
?>
```

What have we done so far? We're telling WordPress that we want to grab the RSS feed from our site; if the feed responds, move on (remember to change the URI to whatever your WordPress installation is: http://localhost/wordpress/feed/, for example).

```php
<h3>
Latest Posts on <?php bloginfo('name'); ?>
</h3>

<ol>
<?php
$rss->items = array_slice($rss->items, 0, 5);
foreach ($rss->items as $item ) {
?>
```

The preceding snippet says to grab the pieces of the RSS feed (publish date, author, title, content, and so on) and create an array from them. We then deal with each array in turn:

```php
<li>
<a href='<?php echo wp_filter_kses($item['link']); ?>'>
 <?php echo wp_specialchars($item['title']); ?>
<small>--
<?php echo human_time_diff( strtotime($item['pubdate'], time() ) ); ?>
<?php _e('ago'); ?></small>
</li>
<?php
}
}
?>
</ol>
```

Let's look at what is going on here. We are grabbing the link for the item returned and passing it through one of WordPress's many filters. This link allows us to load the post in

211

full at the site referenced. Because this is our own site, when you click on the link it will load the post using your single.php template.

Next, we grab the title that is returned, and then close the link tag, moving on to grabbing the publish date (when the item was published). Using human_time_diff, we calculate how long it has been since the item has been posted. That gives us the groovy human readable 21 days ago stamp.

After the block of RSS aggregation code, we just need to add these bits and we are done:

```
</div>
<?php get_footer(); ?>
```

We save this file as home.php and place it in /wp-content/themes/default/. When we visit http://localhost/ we should see home.php loaded instead of the default index.php (remember that you can have http://localhost/wordpress/ as the root of the WordPress installation). Check out the results in Figure 5-7.

Figure 5-7. Your blog running with home.php

And there you have it . . . a letter opener

All MST3K jokes aside, that's about it. You now see the potential that home.php has, freeing your site up to be just about whatever you want while retaining the flexibility and power that WordPress brings to the table. And again Michael and I want to stress that this is really only scratching the surface of the system. There are new, incredible features added to WordPress almost on a daily basis, not to mention all the great plug-ins and themes.

Summary

Congratulations! You should now be well on your way to mastering the theme system in WordPress. We sincerely hope that by now you are starting to see the power and flexibility available to you. With a little (or a lot of) CSS know-how you can make some spectacular designs. But remember this is just the tip of the iceberg. When you feel comfortable with the lessons learned in this chapter, hit up the Codex: http://codex.wordpress.org/ WordPress_Lessons#Designing_Your_WordPress_Site and stop by the WordPress IRC channel on irc.freenode.net, #wordpress. For instructions on how to use IRC, check out IRC Beginner: www.ircbeginner.com/.

Remember that personal publishing is about freedom—freedom to say what you want for the world to hear. Get to designing and join the global conversation.

5

6 TEXTPATTERN

Add a new User

	Login
User name:	Use text fi
Host:	Local
Password:	Use text fi
Re-type:	
Generate Password:	Generate

Welcome to Textpattern

Please choose a language:

English (GB)

Submit

My Site

My pithy slogan

First Post · 12 minutes ago by textpattern

Lorem ipsum dolor sit amet, consectetuer adipiscing elit. Donec rutrum est eu mauris. In volutpat blandit felis. Suspendisse eget pede. Class aptent taciti sociosqu ad litora torquent per conubia nostra, per inceptos hymenaeos. Quisque sed arcu. Aenean purus nulla, condimentum ac, pretium at, commodo sit amet, turpis. Aenean lacus. Ut in justo. Ut viverra dui vel ante. Duis imperdiet porttitor mi. Maecenas at lectus eu justo porta tempus. Cras fermentum ligula non purus. Duis id orci non magna rutrum bibendum. Mauris tincidunt, massa in rhoncus consectetuer, lectus dui ornare enim, ut egestas ipsum purus id urna. Vestibulum volutpat porttitor metus. Donec congue vehicula ante.

by John Oxton

What this chapter covers:

- Introducing Textpattern (TxP)
- Installing TxP
- Designing a blog
- Preparing images
- Adding content
- Creating a page template and archive section

Before we even begin with any of the technical stuff, let's get the introductions out of the way. To its mates, of which it has many, Textpattern is known simply as TxP. For the rest of this chapter, unless I am referring specifically to the textpattern folder on the server I will call it by its more informal name: TxP.

"So what is it?" It is much more than simply a tool for creating blogs; it is a complete content management system and with a thriving community of developers and designers behind it; there isn't much you can't get done with a copy of TxP. For me, this is reason enough to invest a little time getting to know it. But it is also the reason why it would be too much to try and explain it all in one chapter.

Instead, I am going to concentrate on some of the key features of TxP in the hope of giving you a solid foundation from which you can move onward and upward. I will introduce you to the simple TxP tags used to build templates and how TxP itself can help you work with those tags. Along the way, we will explore the two main TxP areas, content and presentation, and we will take a quick look at the admin features relevant to your blog. With all that done, we will dive straight in to design and build a blog with TxP.

A brief history

TxP has been around in one form or another since 2001. So it's hard to believe that it was only 2005 when the much-awaited first official stable released arrived in the form of Textpattern 4.

In the beginning, it was the creation for and of one man, Dean Allen (http://textism.com), but has since become the passion of thousands of users like me and the more technical folk, who are responsible for the forward movement of TxP.

This chapter and the future of TxP

During the course of writing this chapter, TxP was updated no fewer than three times, which made the task of writing all the more challenging, to say the least. TxP does seem to be undergoing an intense period of development at the time of writing, so it has been tough choosing what to write about and what to leave out. In the end I looked at TxP's history and what has remained consistent since the now infamous Release Candidate days, and those are the areas I have tried to stick with. In doing so, I am really touching only the tip of a very large and beautiful iceberg and I can't emphasize enough the importance of experimenting with TxP after you are done here. On more than one occasion, TxP has surprised me with its capabilities.

Supporting the cause

TxP is free to download and use, but there are a number of ways to offer a bit of financial support if you feel so inclined. The most obvious way is to host your blog on TextDrive servers. TextDrive is owned, in part, by TxP creator Dean Allen; if you do host with TextDrive, you have the opportunity to donate some money to the TxP cause during the registration process. At this stage, it is the easiest way to support the cause. Visit http://textdrive.com for more information.

Alternatively, there is a PayPal button on the main TxP site itself if you fancy making a one-off donation before or after you have downloaded the software.

The creative process

My approach may seem a little chaotic and perhaps even unorganized at times. It would have been easier to put together a super slick presentation, simply to make myself look good, but a new blog is very rarely super slick and organized. Furthermore, a good blog undergoes changes constantly as new ideas are formed and as you come to grips with your content management system.

I have tried to write as I remember first approaching my own blog (joshuaink.com) in TxP. So stick with it; even if it seems to be getting a little lost, it does come to a working conclusion!

Installation

In the following sections, I provide an in-depth, step-by-step guide to installing TxP. If you are feeling confident about the whole process after reading Chapter 2, you can skip this bit and consult the README.txt file shipped with TxP, which provides very concise instructions on getting up and running.

Download and unzip the core files

The latest TxP release can be downloaded from www.textpattern.com/download as a GZIP or a ZIP file. If you are in any doubt about which to choose, download the ZIP file because this is the most commonly supported format on both Windows and Mac. Both versions contain the exact same software.

After the download is complete, extract the files to the root of your development server, wherever it might be. In common with other chapters, I will assume that you did not leave the root folder of the ZIP file intact, so the TxP installation starts at http://localhost/, not http://localhost/textpattern-4.x/.

The root folder contains a number of files, as shown in Figure 6-1, and some—such as history.txt and README.txt—are not necessary for running TxP, but are worth a quick readthrough before you delete them. To complete a successful setup of TxP, you should have the files folder, the images folder, the textpattern folder, the index.php file, and the .htaccess file.

Figure 6-1. Contents of the unzipped Textpattern download

Note that, as with other chapters, you can have TxP stay alongside your other blog software if you wish. To do so, leave the `textpattern-4.x` folder intact at the root of your server (though renaming it txp is more practical). This means that you will have to add the txp to all the paths mentioned in this chapter.

The .htaccess file

The `.htaccess` file, as shown in Figure 6-1, is probably not visible if you are using a Mac but it was placed in your root folder when you unzipped the files.

If you want to check that it is present in the folder, there are a number of ways to show hidden files on a Mac (for example, using BBEdit or TextWrangler to open hidden files, as described in Chapter 2). Another method is to use TinkerTool (shown in Figure 6-2). As its name suggests, it lets you tinker with settings in relative safety. TinkerTool can be downloaded at www.bresink.de/osx/TinkerTool.html. After it's installed, fire it up and find the Show hidden and system files check box. Check the box, click the Relaunch Finder button on the bottom right, and you should now see the `.htaccess` file and probably also a `.DS_store` file (the latter has nothing to with TxP; it is a Mac system file and can be safely ignored).

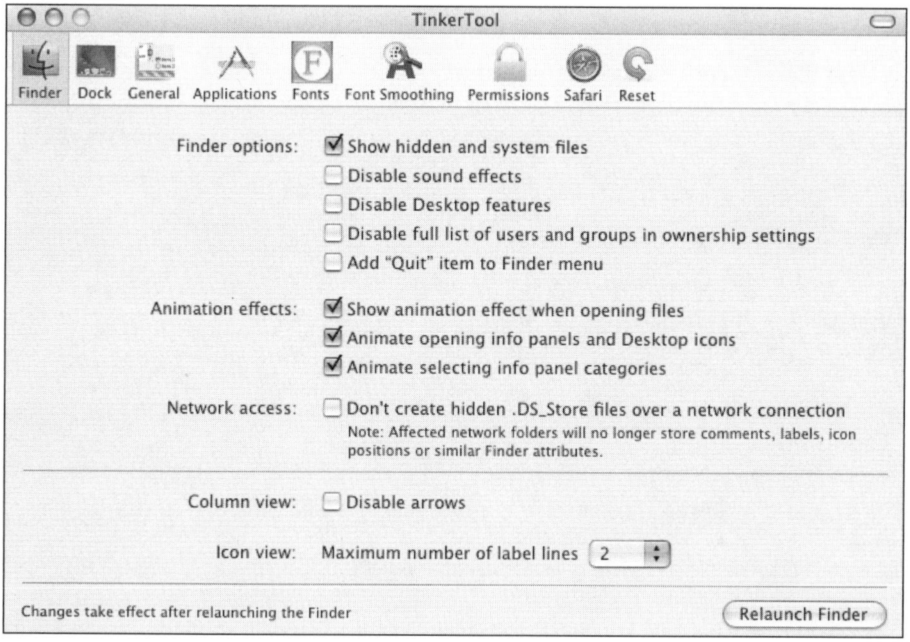

Figure 6-2. A shot of the TinkerTool interface

It is worth noting briefly that although using the .htaccess file simplifies things enormously, it is not absolutely essential for a site to run. For example, I recently found myself faced with the task of developing a commercial TxP site on a Zeus web server (www.zeus.com/) that does not use .htaccess. After the initial panic receded, I soon realized that although it required a little more thinking, the job could be done just as well without the .htaccess file. I don't want to go in to any depth here (that would confuse the matter at hand), but it is worth remembering.

Set up a database

Of course, David has already run through setting up phpMyAdmin in some detail in Chapter 2, and we'll follow his instructions to set up our TxP database, as shown in Figure 6-3. Fire up your browser and point it in the direction of your phpMyAdmin install: http://localhost/phpMyAdmin/. You will see on the opening page a form field with this label: Create new database. Enter your desired database name (let's call it mytxpblog), leave the drop-down menu set to Collation, and press the Create button. Remember to make a note of the database name: you'll need it shortly.

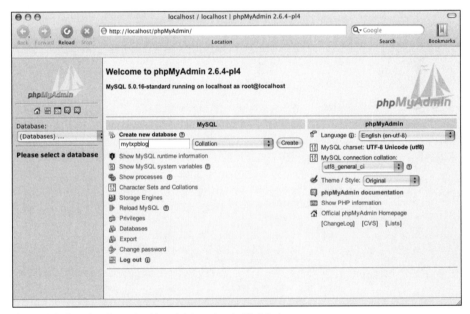

Figure 6-3. Creating the mytxpblog database in phpMyAdmin

You should now see a message confirming creation of the database, as shown in Figure 6-4.

Database mytxpblog has been created.

SQL query:
CREATE DATABASE `mytxpblog` ;

[Edit] [Create PHP Code]

Figure 6-4. Confirming the creation of the database

Locate the home icon just below the logo on the left side of the page, as shown in Figure 6-5, and return to the homepage.

Figure 6-5. Home icon within phpMyAdmin

From the list of options just under the Create new database form field select the Privileges link. When that page is loaded, look for the Add a new user link about halfway down the page. From here, you'll create a user account, the details of which you will need to remember for the TxP setup.

In the User name field, enter a username such as txpusername. Set the Host drop-down menu to Local.

Ensure that the Password drop-down menu is set to Use text field, choose a password such as mytxppassword, and retype it in the Re-type form field to be sure it's correct. The end results should look like Figure 6-6.

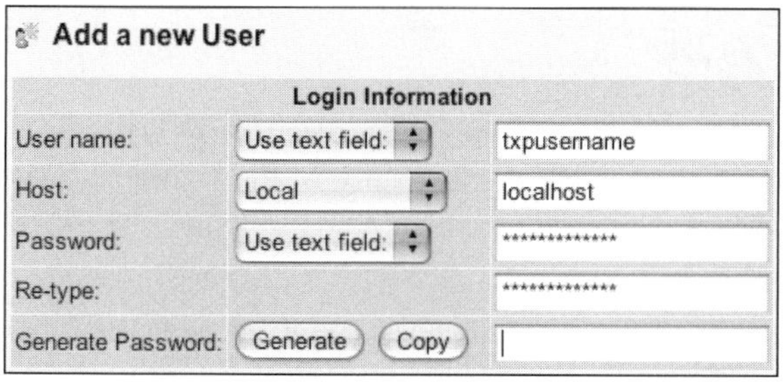

Add a new User		
Login Information		
User name:	Use text field:	txpusername
Host:	Local	localhost
Password:	Use text field:	*************
Re-type:		*************
Generate Password:	Generate Copy	

Figure 6-6. Configuring a database user

Skip straight over the Global privileges table and press Go. You should now see a new page with the heading You have added a new user. Scroll down the page to Database-specific privileges and choose mytxpblog from the list, as shown in Figure 6-7.

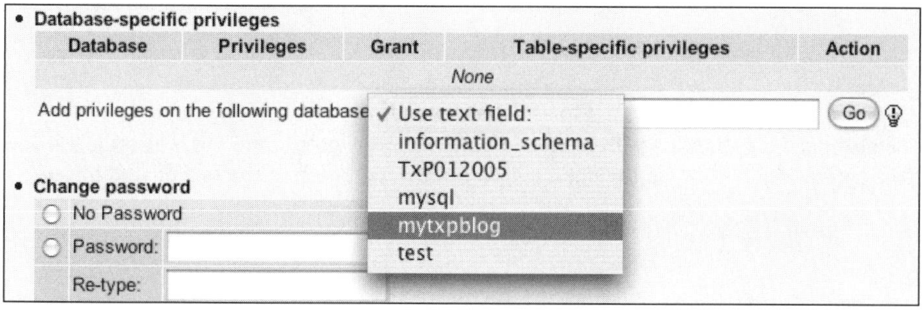

- **Database-specific privileges**

Database	**Privileges**	**Grant**	**Table-specific privileges**	**Action**
		None		

Add privileges on the following database ✓ Use text field:
information_schema
TxP012005
mysql
mytxpblog
test
    Go

- **Change password**
  - ○ No Password
  - ○ Password:
  - Re-type:

Figure 6-7. Choosing the TxP database

221

The page that loads presents you with a table of Database-specific privileges, as shown in Figure 6-8. Click Check All and then deselect GRANT. This done, press Go at the bottom right of the table.

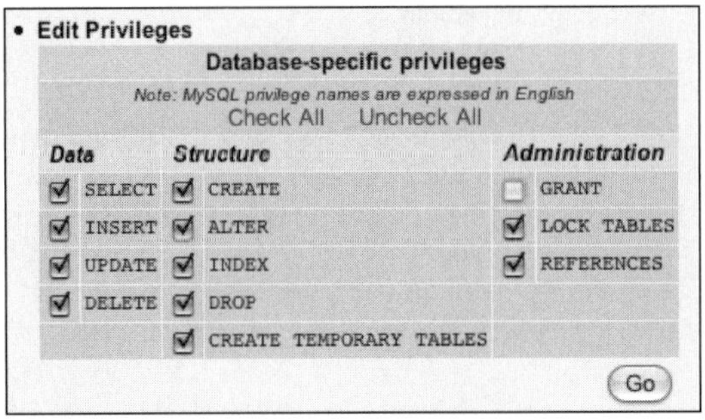

Figure 6-8. The database-specific privileges for our example

The page then refreshes with a message at the top along the lines of this: You have updated the privileges for 'txpusername'@'localhost'. That's it—job done. Time to get set up!

Running the Setup Wizard

In your browser you can now navigate to the textpattern directory, http://localhost/ textpattern/ where you will be presented with the first stage of the TxP Setup Wizard (this may be http://localhost/txp/textpattern/ or equivalent if you have installed TxP in a subfolder).

Choose your preferred language from the menu, as shown in Figure 6-9, and click Submit.

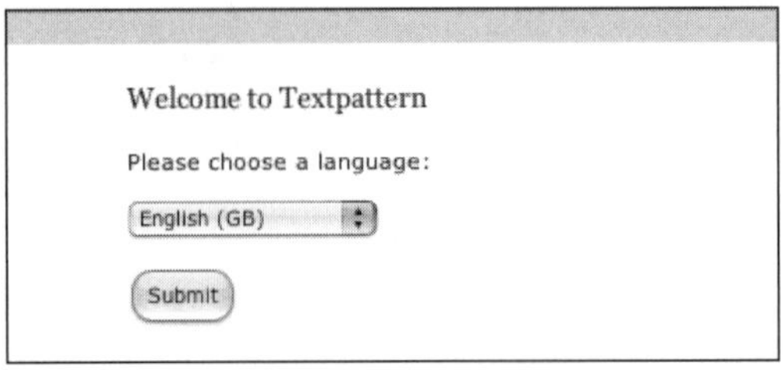

Figure 6-9. Choosing your preferred language

The next page presents you with a table for your database details and this is information you have noted while setting up the database. I'll run through each of the sections on this page.

MySQL

These form fields take the information from the database you set up using phpMyAdmin and are populated as follows:

MySQL login: txpusername

MySQL server: localhost

MySQL password: mytxppassword

mySQL database: mytxpblog

Unless TxP is sharing a database with something else you can safely leave the Table prefix form empty.

Site path

The Site path is the absolute path to the textpattern folder on your server. Because you are testing locally, there is an easy way to check this in your browser: cut and paste the contents of the site path form in to your browser and it will open up textpattern in your folder, as shown in Figure 6-10.

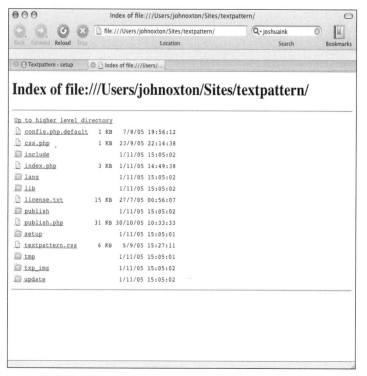

Figure 6-10. The contents of the textpattern folder on your server

Site URL

TxP will probably have picked this up as http://localhost. Again, you can check by pasting the URL into your browser; you should be greeted with the message config.php is not ok or not found. If you would like to install, go to [/subdir]/textpattern/setup/. Don't worry about this apparent error message; at this stage this is a good sign that TxP is in the right spot. If you have TxP in a subdirectory, you'll have the corresponding subdirectory appended to the site URL.

After you fill in all the forms and checked the Site path and Site URL, your page should look very much like Figure 6-11.

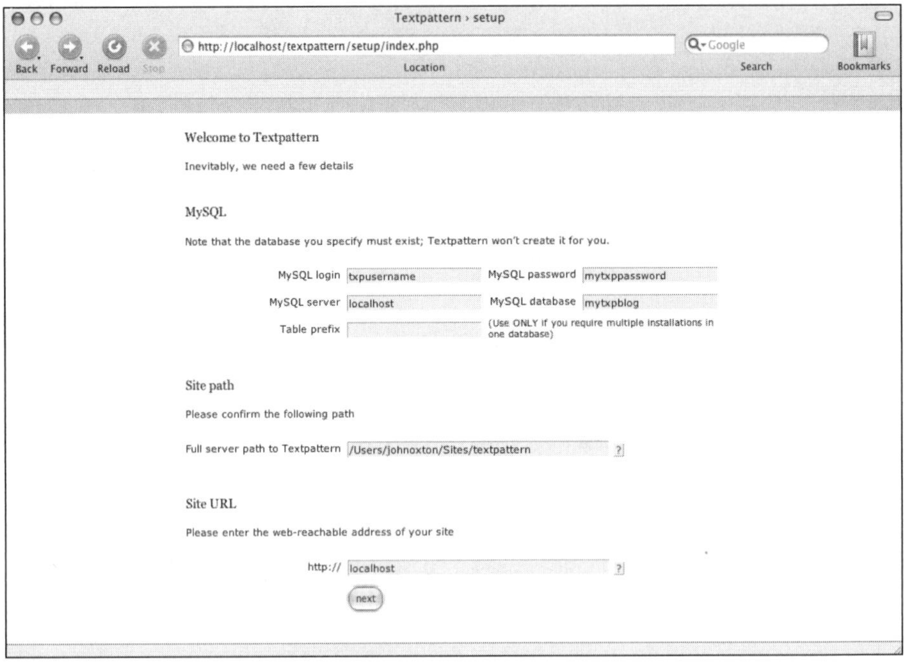

Figure 6-11. Completed configuration details

Press next, and (as long as all the details you filled in are correct) TxP will connect to the database and provide further instructions, as shown in Figure 6-12. If TxP fails to connect to the database nine times out of ten, there is simply a misspelling of either the login, password, or database details. In this situation press the back button on your browser, check the details you filled in, and press next to try again. If you continue to experience problems with all information present and correct I suggest revisiting Chapter 2 and double-checking your configuration.

TxP now needs you to do a little of the leg work. A text area, as shown in Figure 6-12, contains a snippet of PHP from which we will create the config.php file.

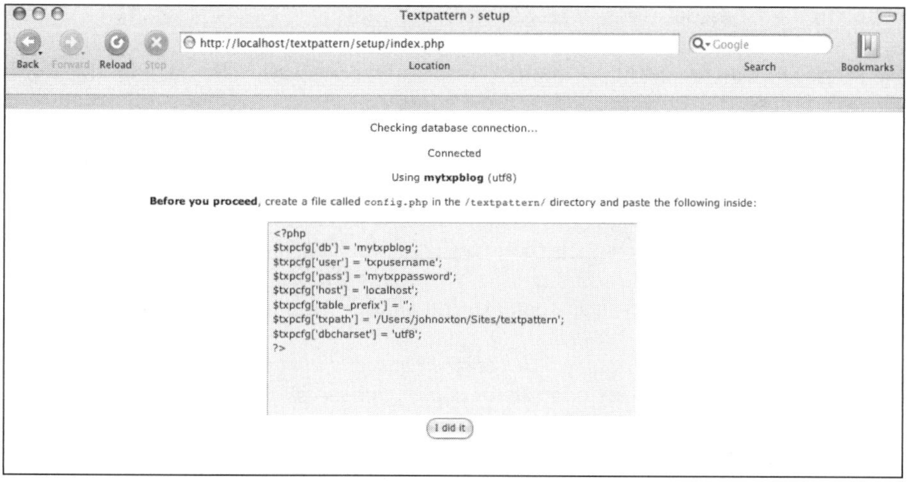

Figure 6-12. TxP gives you the details for your config.php file

Creating the config.php file

Open up your favorite text editor, such as Dreamweaver or TextWrangler, create a new blank file, cut and paste the PHP in the text area as instructed by TxP, and save it as config.php to the textpattern directory in the root of your server, as shown in Figure 6-13.

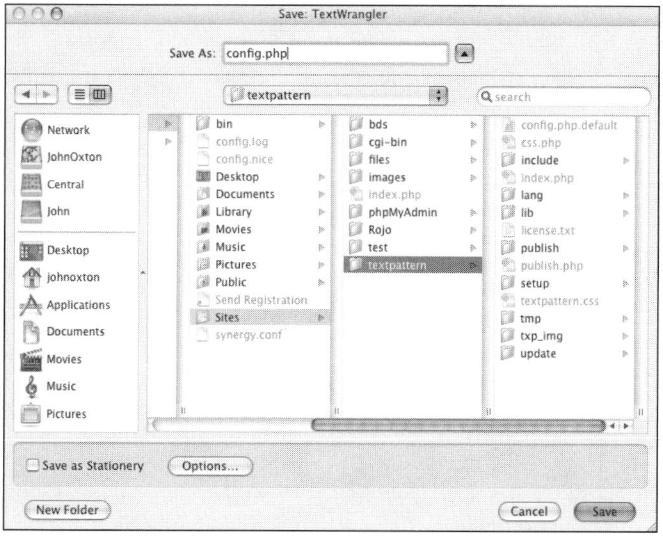

Figure 6-13. Saving the config.php file to the textpattern folder

Return to the TxP setup screen in your browser and press the I did it button. If all has gone well and again if TxP returns an error, retrace your steps and check for typos. You will get the message Thank you. You are about to create and populate database tables. Now you will be prompted to add your name and to choose a username and password. You should try and choose a strong username and password because this login area will be open to the world, and all that stands between your site and malicious attack are a good username and password. A good username might be something a little less obvious than just your name; maybe you could pick your mother's maiden name or the name of your pet dog when you were a child. To create a good password, don't use any names or dates that are relative to your life and add some unusual characters into the mix. So, for example, you could create a username of: *bobthegoldfish* and a password of: *n0nsen=5e*.

> *The only other important thing to say about your username and password is to keep it really safe. If you lose your TxP username and password it is not easy to recover. There is no* I forgot my details *option on the TxP login.*

The final screen of the Setup Wizard should now display this message: You should be able to access the main interface with the login and password you chose. Thank you for your interest in Textpattern with the words main interface being a link to the login.

To log in to Textpattern after this, simply visit http://localhost/textpattern, as shown in Figure 6-14.

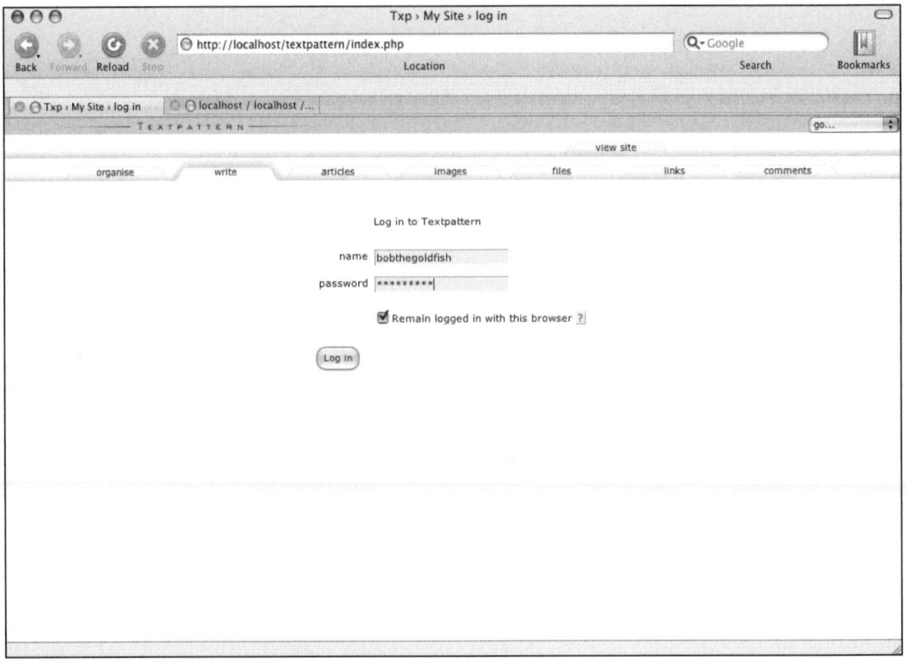

Figure 6-14. You have successfully installed TxP.

First login

The page you'll land on when you log in for the very first time is the Manage languages page (see Figure 6-15). Here you can install your language of choice to work with TxP if you changed your mind since installing it. To change the language, simply click the appropriate Install link to the right of the language you want; after a little loading time, the drop-down menu at the top of this area will now contain your language. After choosing the language you want in the drop-down menu, press Save to install your choice.

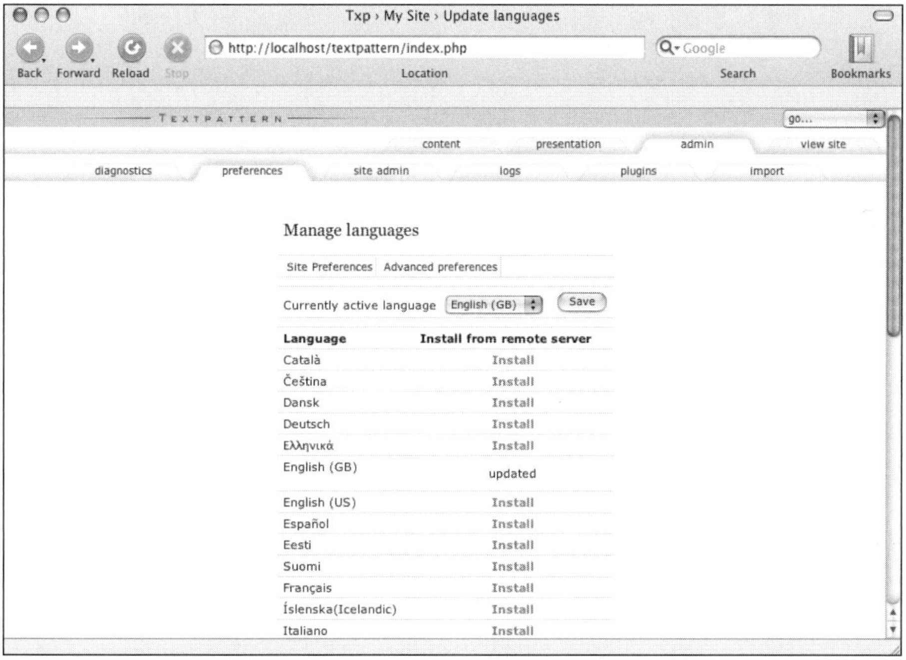

Figure 6-15. The Manage languages page

Did it all work?

Although the fact that you can log in to the TxP back end indicates that everything has gone well, it's a good idea to check the front end, too. Point your browser at the root of your site, most likely http://localhost, and you should be greeted with the default TxP layout and First Post, something along the lines of that shown in Figure 6-16.

Figure 6-16. Your blog's homepage

If you don't see this frontpage, it usually means that something is missing. That something is probably the index.php file from the TxP download. In this case, you should grab a copy from the TxP download ZIP file and drop it in place in the root of your server, overwriting the older version if need be.

Assuming that all is well on the front end, it's time for a more in-depth look at the back end.

Key TxP areas

There are three key areas of TxP and they are found on the top row of tabs in the back end, as shown in Figure 6-17:

- admin, in which you configure and control TxP functions to suit your needs
- presentation, in which you add HTML, <txp: /> tags, and styling to present your content
- content, in which you organize, add, and edit your content

The fourth tab, view site, simply opens up the front page of the site in a new browser window. Notice that when you click one of the tabs in the top row, different tabs become available on the bottom row. Let's look at each area in a little more detail.

Figure 6-17. The TxP admin area

Admin

You probably won't spend too much time in admin beyond setup, and even then there isn't a great deal to do. So while you take a look around this area I will run you through the basic changes that you may need to make to get up and running successfully.

Diagnostics

When you select the diagnostics tab, you'll be greeted with Pre-flight check and Diagnostic info. Any information given in red indicates items that need attention—useful information, indeed! I'll go through the three most common messages you might see, and how to fix them.

- /path to your server/textpattern/setup/ still exists. This message simply tells you that the directory /textpattern/setup/ still exists and might pose a security issue. If you open up the main textpattern directory on your web server, find the setup directory, and delete it, as shown in Figure 6-18, refresh the page and you'll see that this message should now be gone.

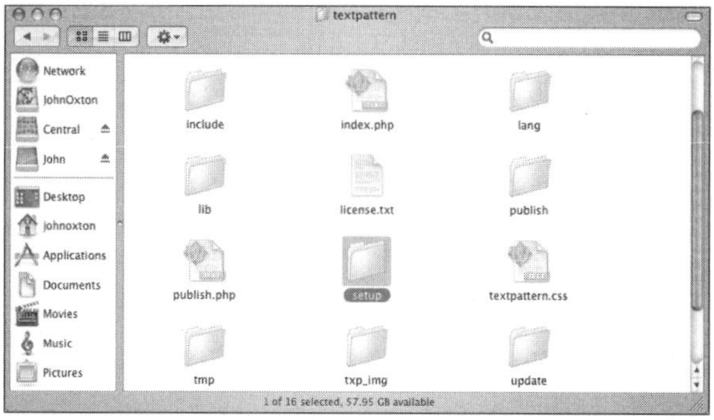

Figure 6-18. Deleting the setup folder from the textpattern folder

- Image directory is not writable: /path to your server/textpattern/images and File Upload Path is not writable: /path to your server/textpattern/files. If you plan to upload and share images and files using the tool provided by TxP (such as your homemade mp3s), you need to make these directories writable (even if you don't plan to, making the directories writable is a good habit to get into as part of the setup process). Usually this means you have change permissions to 777, which is simply a way of telling the server that the directories can be written to and executed as well as read. The easiest way to do this is to navigate to the directory in which the main textpattern folder resides (this is where the images and sites folders are also located) by using your command line/terminal/shell with the cd command (for example, using OS X terminal, found in Applications ➤ Utilities). At the prompt, enter cd /pathtoyourserver/ and then the following commands to change the permissions of your folders: chmod 777 files and then (after pressing Enter) chmod 777 images (and press Enter as shown in Figure 6-19). Return to the diagnostics web page and refresh the page. These messages should now be gone.

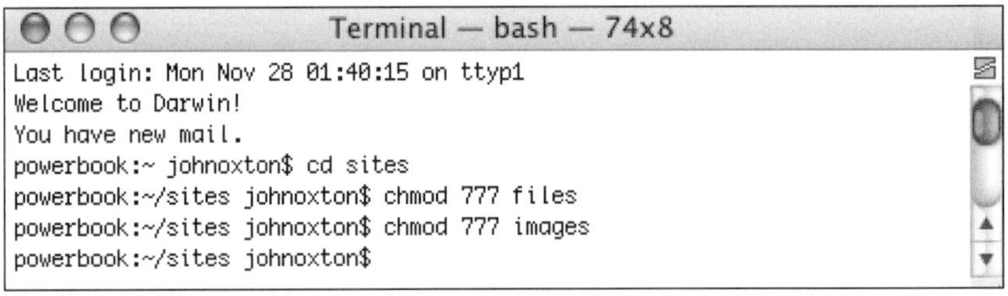

```
⬤ ⬤ ⬤              Terminal — bash — 74x8
Last login: Mon Nov 28 01:40:15 on ttyp1
Welcome to Darwin!
You have new mail.
powerbook:~ johnoxton$ cd sites
powerbook:~/sites johnoxton$ chmod 777 files
powerbook:~/sites johnoxton$ chmod 777 images
powerbook:~/sites johnoxton$
```

Figure 6-19. All diagnostic checks have been passed.

After you fix all these issues, your diagnostics page will display an All checks passed! message, and you are fine to continue on to the next tab: preferences.

Preferences

The preferences tab allows you to easily change the way your site works. When you click the preferences tab, you will arrive in the Site preferences area. But there are also two other pages, Advanced preferences and Manage languages, that are accessible via links at the top of the preferences page. You have already seen the Manage languages area, so no need to revisit it; however here is a quick overview of the other two pages:

Site preferences This page, which is the first area that opens when you click the preferences tab, lets you choose the basics of your site, such as your time zone, whether comments should be moderated or not, and how you want to present dates on your posts. You don't actually need to adjust anything here for your blog to work (it's designed to work right out of the box), but for this example you do need to change the permanent link mode so when you create an archives section you can give it a clean URL—such as /path to your server/archives/. To do this, look under the heading Publish for the drop-down menu labeled Permanent link mode and change the value from ?=messy to /section/title. Scroll to the bottom of the page and press Save. That's it—job done.

More about permanent link mode If you happen to find yourself on a server that doesn't allow you to use the /section/title Permanent link mode or any of the other "clean URL" options, don't panic; the ?=messy Permanent link mode can be used just as effectively. For example, where I suggest we will reach the archive section via /path to your server/archive/ you would simply replace this with /path to your server/index. php?s=archive. As the name suggest, it's perhaps, a little messier than we want, but it does show that TxP will run well on most server setups.

Advanced preferences It is unlikely that you will want to venture into advanced preferences until you get really comfortable with TxP. But there are a couple of things you should do straightaway that will stop the readers of your site who access your posts via RSS or Atom feeds from sending e-mails of complaint, in bold red letters no less. Let's do that now.

1. Scroll down to the area titled Publish.
2. Change the radio button for the Show comment count in feeds? option from yes to no.
3. Change the radio button for the New comment means site updated? option from yes to no.
4. Press Save at the bottom of your screen to save your settings.

What this process does is stop the RSS and Atom feeds from being updated every time someone adds a comment to your site. This is a potentially useful feature in some situations, but my experience has been that people find it very annoying: they have read and enjoyed your entry, but have another 200 plus feeds to get through before lunch, so the last thing they want is your feed hassling them every time you get a comment.

Presentation

Beginners to TxP often find the presentation area very confusing. Some of this confusion, I think, has to do with the way areas are named. For example, forms are not *forms* as you may understand them from using the web, and pages, as you will see, are quite a bit more than simply run-of-the-mill HTML.

For the lucky few, it all makes sense at first glance. But to those who find it all a little confusing to start with, I usually say, stick with it; the TxP developers have done their job well, and the fog will begin to clear as you work with the software. At that point, the sheer elegance of TxP will become apparent.

I'll now cover the basics of an enormously powerful area of TxP. After you understand it, you will be flying. We'll look at the options on the left side of the screen in the Creating an archive section and page template section.

Sections

Sections, as the name suggests, are the main areas of your site. Most sites have an about section, a contact section, and perhaps even a links section. This is probably the easiest way to understand sections initially.

Sections work with pages, which are discussed next, and together they allow you to build the skeleton of your site. Notice that TxP has a built-in section called Default that can't be

6

deleted. This section is used by TxP on the homepage, so when a visitor lands on your very first page (for example, http://myblog.com), TxP will use the Default section and its associated settings to present the front page.

Pages

You can think of *pages* as site templates. Every section can have its own page, or many sections can share one page (in this case, we need only a one-page template). This is one of TxP's key features that, when combined with sections, gives you the power to use one setup of TxP to run multiple designs very easily. Notice a long list of options on the left—they are links to help you generate TxP tags. (We'll be using some of these options along the way, so there will be more details a bit later.)

Forms

The name *forms* often causes confusion to new TxP users because most of us are familiar with forms as something used on the web for capturing information: logins, orders, and so on. TxP forms, though, are something completely different and have nothing to do with HTML forms. The easiest way to understand TxP forms is as storage boxes in which we can keep chunks of code. Forms are used in conjunction with pages, and I will show you how they work when we get to putting the site together.

Style

The style tab is where all the Cascading Style Sheets (CSS) are stored in TxP; we will be visiting this area extensively throughout this chapter. To the left of the main text area is a link that says Edit in CSS editor. As you might expect, this link opens up the stylesheet in TxP's built-in style editor. If you want to use this editor while following along with the examples in this chapter, go right ahead. I am not a fan of this editor, however, so you won't hear me mention it again.

Content

As the name suggests, the content area is where we go to add content. When you log in or click the content tab, you are taken to the write tab by default because it is the most logical place to start on a day-to-day blogging basis—this is where you make your daily entries. To the left you will see a tab marked articles that (as the name suggests) lists all the articles you have ever published. Although there are other areas within content, they are not needed for our blog. As I said in the beginning, it's been tough deciding what not to tell you. The content area is far and away the simplest area to figure out and after you have a good understanding of the fundamentals, working out the areas I have skipped over here will be a snap—really it will.

Question mark buttons

Finally note little question mark buttons to the right of many of the options within the TxP back end. They give you helpful tips about what actions will be performed by that particular option. Clicking them has no impact on your site, so feel free to click away.

Default design

During setup, you visited the front end of TxP and saw what is a deceptively simple design. In reality, there is a lot more going on than you might expect to give you everything you need to get a useful blog up and running.

First, though, let's take a quick look at a fundamental part of TxP: the txp tag. Open up a new browser window or simply click the view site tab, and enter the web address of your site so that you have a copy in front of you to show your changes.

Back in the TxP back end, the first stop is the admin area and you will find yourself in the preferences area by default. Let's just walk through a simple example of how TxP slots together.

The site name and the site slogan

In the preferences area of the admin area, under the heading Publish, you see a text field labeled Site name, as shown in Figure 6-20. You can change it to whatever you like and it will show up on your front page. Go ahead and change it to anything you like, scroll down the page, press Save, and then refresh the site front end—it will have been updated.

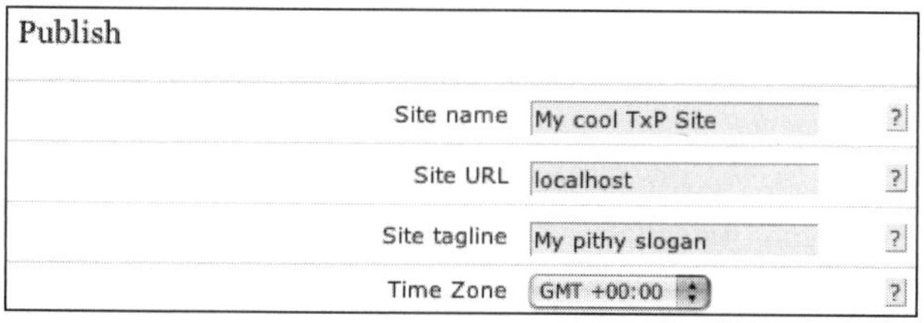

6

Publish		
Site name	My cool TxP Site	?
Site URL	localhost	?
Site tagline	My pithy slogan	?
Time Zone	GMT +00:00	?

Figure 6-20. Setting the site name and slogan

To see how this works, click the presentation tab and look through the default template code. You will see a `<txp:sitename />` tag, as shown in Figure 6-21. This is the TxP tag that pulls the information out of the admin area onto your site.

```
<!-- head -->
<div id="head">
<h1><txp:link_to_home><txp:sitename /></txp:link_to_home></h1>
<h2><txp:site_slogan /></h2>

</div>
```

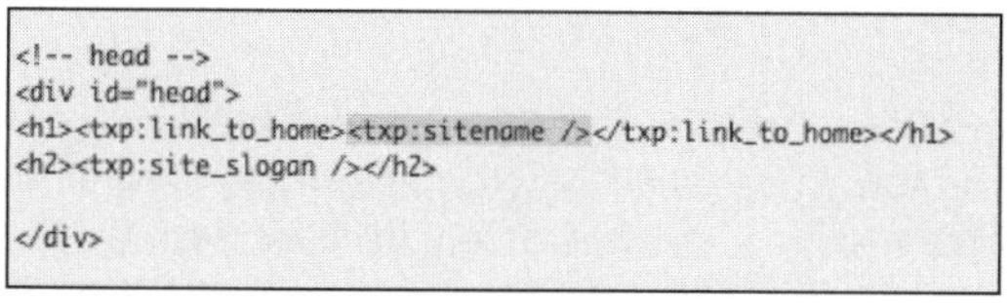

Figure 6-21. Displaying the site name in a template

The exact same situation applies to the site slogan in the preferences area of admin. You see a text field labeled Site tagline and the words My pithy slogan; in the default template code, we find a TxP tag `<txp:site_slogan />` that outputs My pithy slogan to the site. This example is perhaps one of the simplest examples of a TxP tag in action, but it does illustrate the principle of tags nicely. A TxP tag is essentially a set of instructions that TxP reads and takes action on. So by adding `<txp:sitename />`, you tell TxP to look at what name the site has been given in the preferences area and present it on the site.

It's your blog

Now that TxP is installed, you learned about the options available in the TxP management interface, and you had a quick look at the default TxP blog design, let's start to think about your own blog. Before you dive into reams of code, it is always best to do a bit of planning. So you first have to think about what you want from your blog and then consider its visual design. Only then can you start creating your masterpiece.

What is the purpose of your blog?

Until you define your blog's reason for existence it will be very difficult to get any kind of design going. If you don't already have a clear idea of what it is you want to blog about, it's worth spending a couple of days making some notes of your ideas about what you want to do to begin with and what you might want to do in the future. For example, do you want to add links to other sites? Will there be other sections, such as an About me section? How will you organize the archives or will you just have a search form instead?

For the sake of this exercise, let's assume that you want to keep things nice and simple: publish articles and receive comments back—that's it. For the sake of this exercise, let's go for a really simple one-column layout and give it our own little twist.

Designing your blog

Designing for yourself can be a frustrating experience for some: nothing is ever good enough, and nothing ever reflects your personality the way you would like. Some people will spend hours scouring stock photography sites, hoping to come across something that fits, but I find that process completely soul-destroying and have a tendency to go out for a walk or pace around the office, searching for an idea first and a way to implement it second.

On this occasion, I was thinking about how I would describe the basics of the page layout—the head, the foot, and the bit that goes in between—and I thought a stretchy person might be able to help me illustrate the point.

The next step was to take this rough idea and give it legs and hands (and a head, for that matter). I fired up my favorite graphics package, Macromedia Fireworks, and drew a schematic diagram to show where I wanted the bits of my design to go, as shown in Figure 6-22.

What I lacked were the practical drawing skills to make my idea a reality. Fortunately, I happen to be in touch with a very talented cartoonist by the name of Kev Adamson (www.kevadamson.com) and was able to recruit him to help give me what I wanted.

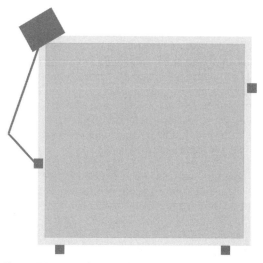

Figure 6-22. My schematic design, mocked up up in Fireworks

From my very brief note (worded roughly as "Kev, please make me a stretchy man") and my very dull gray box (refer to Figure 6-22) came back a work of art (see Figure 6-23). Not only did this help me get motivated but I was nowhere near as self-critical about the end results because someone else did such an important visual part of the site. Thus I was free to get on with the job at hand: getting a blog up and running. I think it is worth hunting down some talent for collaboration if you don't have the skills to bring your ideas to life. And if you can afford to do it, why not fork over the extra cash? You are sure to reap the rewards in extra traffic and all the opportunities that brings.

Figure 6-23. The finished illustration, compliments of
kevadamson.com

Integrating with TxP

This is the bit where it is all supposed to look well organized; where I take you through each step of getting this design to work in TxP with military precision, making it look like the well-planned job of a true professional. But what really happened before I started writing? Well I fiddled, and tweaked, and then fiddled some more, broke it a bit, and retraced my steps to fix the breakage. Basically, I made it up as I went along (I really do enjoy doing things this way, especially when it's all so new). As long as you take the time to review what went wrong and learn from your mistakes, this can be the most fun way to do it. Kids tend to do things this way, and hey, how happy are kids?

Let's not reinvent the wheel, though; as I have explained there is more to the default TxP design than meets the eye. All the information architecture is done for us, so all we need to do is add our design on top of it to make it our own.

Built-in code editing

TxP allows you to edit the CSS and Page templates using its built-in editors located under the presentation tab. Personally I prefer to use an external editor such as Dreamweaver because it gives me the option of undo, find and replace, line numbers, and code coloring. I also find it much easier to work with the code this way.

During the walkthrough of this build, that is the way I'll do it: cutting and pasting between my external editor and the relevant TxP interfaces. It is up to you how you do it, of course, and it is perfectly possible to edit directly in TxP. What is more important than how you decide to edit your code is to remember to press Save at the bottom of the page after you finish editing in TxP. It's easy to forget and can lead to much head-scratching as things fail to work.

Live design

At this stage, all we have is Kev's cartoon. Actually, that's all we need because the rest of the design is done purely via XHTML and CSS. We are, for want of a better term, going to go through a live design process.

The slicing of the image we'll come back to shortly, but first let's go and explore to see what we have in the way of XHTML to play with. Before we can plan how we will incorporate the cartoon using CSS, we need to know the ids and classes of XHTML elements and where they are in the structure of the page.

In the TxP back end, navigate to Presentation ➤ Style and you should see a sentence on the left that says you are editing CSS default.

Let's jump straight in and make some tweaks, I'll discuss the end result once we are done. Change the following:

```
#sidebar-1{
    float: left;
    width: 150px;
```

```
    \width: 150px;
    w\idth: 150px;
    margin-right: 5px;
    padding-top: 100px;
}
```

to:

```
#sidebar-1{
border:1px solid red;
}
```

Do the same to #sidebar-2 and #content, so we end up with this:

```
#sidebar-2{
    border:1px solid blue;
}
```

and this:

```
#content{
    border:1px solid green;
}
```

Add a black border to the #container <div>:

```
#container{
    border:1px solid black;
    width: 760px;
    \width: 770px;
    w\idth: 760px;
    margin: 10px;
    margin-left: auto;
    margin-right: auto;
    padding: 10px;
}
```

We want to remove the right alignment from the #sidebar-1 paragraph, so find the following code and delete it:

```
#sidebar-1 p{
    text-align: right;
}
```

Finally there is a <div> called #foot that also needs a border added:

```
#foot{
    border:1px solid yellow;
    clear: both;
    margin-top: 5px;
    text-align: center;
}
```

Remember to press Save at the bottom of the style page when you are done.

Admittedly, if you look at the site now it's not the prettiest layout, but you did it to give a strong visual clue about how we'll set about getting Kev's cartoon in place.

It's time to start tweaking the default page template. But wait, what is this <div> I talked about?

The div tag

XHTML <div> tags are simple containers for content, a bit like real-world boxes in which you store stuff. Unlike other elements that attempt to define the nature of the content contained within them, such as a paragraph (<p>) tag or a Level 1 heading (h1) tag, a <div> tag does not describe the nature of its contents at all. In this respect it is very much a blank canvas and therefore extremely useful. It is the norm to add an id or class attribute, or both, to a <div> to give some meaning to the contents it contains and to target it reliably with CSS.

As you have seen in the previous code, the TxP developers gave us a <div> tag with the id of foot (or <div id="foot"> as it appears on the page template) to let us know that the contents of that <div> tag belong at the foot of the page, as highlighted in Figure 6-24.

When naming a <div> tag using an id or class, you should always try and describe the nature of the content as opposed to the visual aspects of the <div> tag. For example <div id="foot"> is slightly better than <div id="greenBar"> because the id foot makes some attempts to explain the contents of the <div> tag, whereas the id greenBar, we assume, tells us instead something about its visual nature. Let's suppose you get fed up with green and change the actual color to red via the CSS; the id then becomes both meaningless and confusing because there is no longer a green bar present on the site.

I did say the id foot was only slightly better, though, and for this reason: The foot id works only because it relies on our understanding of what tends to go at the foot of most sites (copyright notices, back to top links, and so on). However, it is still questionable how sound it is, semantically speaking, because it describes the physical location of the <div> tag as opposed to its actual contents. Who knows, for some reason we might want to move the foot to the top of the page in the future (visit http://csszengarden.com to see plenty of examples of this sort of practice), rendering the id meaningless and confusing. What should we call it then? Well, there is no right answer but, although we will keep at as foot throughout this chapter, I have a tendency to call the <div> tag containing copyright notices and so on <div id="site-info">. Here's betting there are plenty of people who would disagree with that choice, though, and have their own ideas about the correct name.

The subject of semantics can and should absorb a bit of your time, and everyone has slightly different ideas, (although most agree on the core principles). Try not to lose sleep over it; this is your blog and as long as you understand what the <div> ids describe, that's what really matters for now.

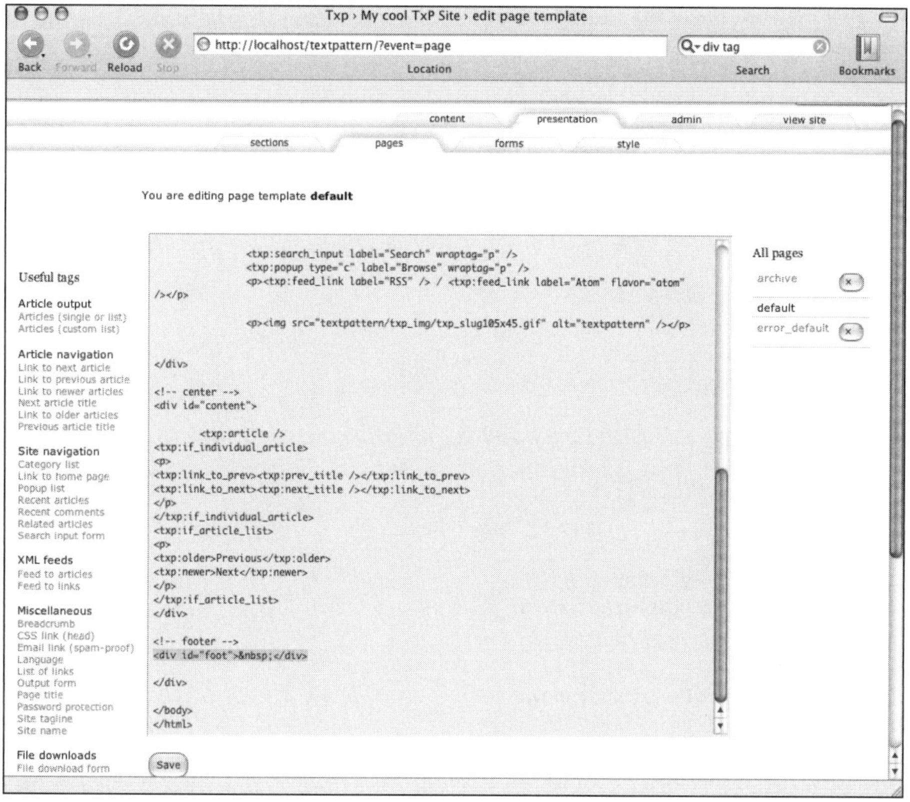

Figure 6-24. The foot `<div>` tag

And the difference between ids and classes? An id is unique, a bit like you, and must appear only once on any given page, whereas classes can appear as many times as you like.

So, that, basically, is a `<div>` tag. Let's move swiftly on, shall we?

Modifying the page template

We'll inherit most of the functionality present in the default page template, we are simply going to shift it around a little. So move out of Presentation ➤ Style and head to Presentation ➤ Pages. You will see a sentence that says You are editing page template default. This is the code you are going to edit.

This step will probably be the most tricky part of the whole process, so take your time. Before you start, you might also want to copy and paste the entire page template into your favorite editor and save it as something like pagecode.txt so that you have a backup should it all go wrong.

The first job is to move the sidebar-1 `<div>` tag underneath the content `<div>` tag, so highlight and cut the following code:

```
<!-- left -->
  <div id="sidebar-1">
  <txp:linklist wraptag="p" />
</div>
```

Then scroll down a little until you find the following:

```
</txp:if_article_list>
  </div>
  <!-- footer -->
<div id="foot"> </div>
```

Between the closing `</div>` and the opening foot `<div>` tags, paste the sidebar-1 code:

```
</txp:if_article_list>
  </div>
  <!-- left -->
  <div id="sidebar-1">
  <txp:linklist wraptag="p" />
  </div>
  <!-- footer -->
<div id="foot"> </div>
```

The next job is to move the TxP logo and the RSS/Atom links into the foot `<div>` tag. Find `<div id=" sidebar-2">`, locate the code that follows, and highlight and cut it to your clipboard:

```
<p><txp:feed_link label="RSS" /> / <txp:feed_link label="Atom" ➥
flavor="atom" /></p>
<p><img src="textpattern/txp_img/txp_slug105x45.gif" ➥
 alt="textpattern" /></p>
```

Scroll down to `<div id="foot">`, delete the ` ` and paste the preceding code in its place:

```
<!-- footer -->
  <div id="foot">
  <p><txp:feed_link label="RSS" /> / <txp:feed_link label="Atom" ➥
  ~flavor="atom" /></p>
  <p><img src="textpattern/txp_img/txp_slug105x45.gif" ➥
  _alt="textpattern" /></p>
</div>
```

Press Save directly below the default template text area.

Before we move on, there are two quick jobs to do. First, having already done this once, I have the benefit of hindsight and I know we'll need an extra `<div>` tag for our design to work, so let's add that now.

At the top of the content `<div>` tag, add a new `<div>` tag with an id of content-container and close it after the content `</div>` tag ends:

```
<!-- center -->
  <div id="content-container">
  <div id="content">
  <txp:article />
  <txp:if_individual_article>
  <p>
  <txp:link_to_prev><txp:prev_title /></txp:link_to_prev>
  <txp:link_to_next><txp:next_title /></txp:link_to_next>
  </p>
  </txp:if_individual_article>
  <txp:if_article_list>
  <p>
  <txp:older>Previous</txp:older>
  <txp:newer>Next</txp:newer>
  </p>
  </txp:if_article_list>
  </div>
</div>
```

After all this is done, remember to press Save. Let's take a quick look at your site now—it should look very much like that shown in Figure 6-25.

Figure 6-25. Your site so far

We'll leave it there for now. That gives us all we need to get the design well under way, although we'll be back to tweak the template later.

Before we move back to Kev's cartoon and the CSS, take two minutes to pop along to the World Wide Web Consortium (W3C) validator at http://validator.w3.org/ and check that there are no mistakes in the resulting XHTML code.

> *Because you're running from a localized setup, open up your site in the browser, choose* View ➤ Page Source *via the browser's toolbar, highlight all the HTML code, and copy and paste it into the* Validate by Direct Input *text area at the bottom of the W3C validator page. If you don't get a* Passed *validation* result, *retrace the previous steps and check for mistakes.*

Preparing the image

From here, we need to slice Kev's cartoon image into three parts: a head, a middle, and a foot. Figure 6-26 shows this process in Fireworks using the slice tool (it's very much the same process in Photoshop). We will then export these three slices and use them as backgrounds in our site.

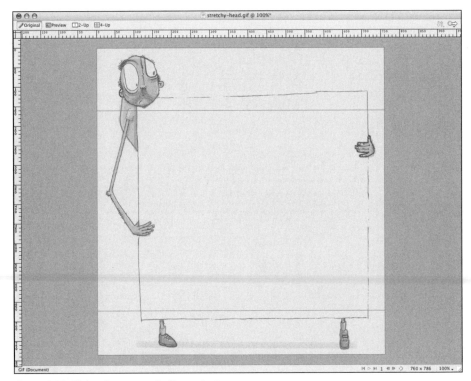

Figure 6-26. Slicing the cartoon in Fireworks 8

These images are available in the code download for this chapter on www.friendsofed.com (the filenames are stretchy-head.gif, stretchy-middle.gif, and stretchy-foot.gif).

Creating a color swatch

We will need some color to liven up our text, and one way to get colors is to extract them from the main image used throughout the design. I use Macromedia Fireworks to create color swatches for this very purpose, but if you use Photoshop you can read Andy Clarke's writeup at www.stuffandnonsense.co.uk/archives/arrangement_de_couleurs.html and get much the same effect.

To do this in Fireworks is really very simple. Open up the image you'll use in Fireworks (in this case, our cartoon) and choose File ➤ Image Preview in Fireworks 8 or File ➤ Export Preview in earlier versions. Make sure that the format is GIF and look for the arrow at the top right of the format menu. Here you will find the Save Palette function. When prompted, save to somewhere convenient as mycolours.act (or any name you can remember). Press Cancel in the image preview to take you back to the main Fireworks canvas. Figure 6-27 shows this process.

6

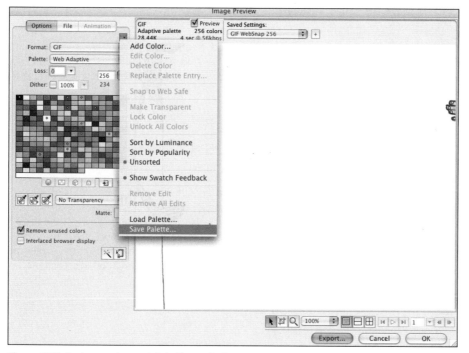

Figure 6-27. Saving a color swatch in Fireworks 8

To get the values of these colors, load them into Fireworks by opening the swatches window via Windows ➤ Swatches. Choose Replace Swatches, which is reached via the small menu icon located at the top right of this window, as shown in Figure 6-28.

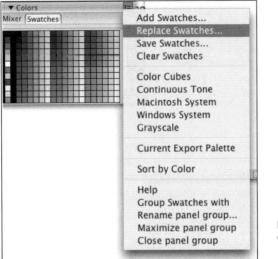

Figure 6-28. Loading color values

From here you can navigate to the .act file you created and load up your colors. Then draw a rectangle on a blank canvas and pick off the colors from your swatch to get the hex values, which can then be copied and pasted directly in your CSS file when you want to add color.

Uploading the image slices

There are two ways to load the image slices onto the server to be ready for use: place them manually into the images directory or use TxP's built-in image upload tool, located under Content ➤ Images. The problem with doing it via TxP's built-in image upload tool is that TxP will rename the image, giving it a numeric value. So although it is possible to add it via TxP, in this case it is probably easier and quicker to just export the image slices directly from the graphics editor into the images directory at the root of the server, or copying and pasting them there. That is exactly what I have done for this example, as shown in Figure 6-29.

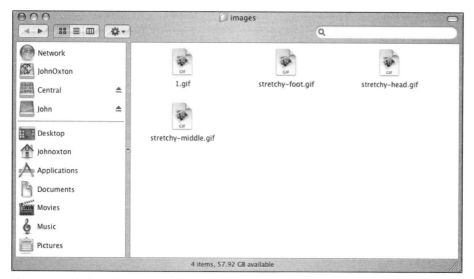

Figure 6-29. Placing the image slices in the web server's images directory

If you really do want to use TxP's image upload tool, you'll simply need to make a note of the number TxP gives the image and then use it accordingly in the CSS.

Adding the image slices to the design

The colored borders we added to the three <div> tags earlier on and the three image slices we have created should give some clue about what comes next. Let's choose Presentation ➤ Style and start adding our images via the CSS:

```
#sidebar-2{
    border:1px solid blue;
}
```

to this:

```
#sidebar-2{
    border:1px solid blue;
    background-image:url(../images/stretchy-head.gif);
}
```

And this:

```
#content{
    border:1px solid green;
}
```

6

to this:

```
#content{
    border:1px solid green;
    background-image:url(../images/stretchy-middle.gif);
}
```

Finally add the foot image, remembering to press Save at the bottom of the page when you're done.

```
#sidebar-1{
    border:1px solid red;
    background-image:url(../images/stretchy-foot.gif);
}
```

More thoughts on semantics

This is a good time to return to our discussion on semantics and <div> tags. Note that the titles of the images we just added suggest we are about to have a confusing situation in which the sidebars become a head and a foot. This is indeed the case. Much to my zealot heart's disgust, I have decided not to do anything about it right now because we will, out here in the real world, manage perfectly well with the ids we have. I offer to you the challenge of fixing these issues as a noble and worthy exercise to be taken on after we finish our work here.

Surely this is a cop out? Well, maybe, but I have at least tried to explain the principles. Changing the ids of these <div> tags right now would mean turning these two paragraphs in to a somewhat lengthier edit of the CSS and XHTML found in the default TxP install. So although we want to cover some ground within these two disciplines, this is a chapter of finite length whose focus is on TxP as a whole. Let's move on.

Making it work

The first thing to notice when looking at our site is that there isn't enough height on the <div> tags and the height just doesn't look quite right. To make it work, we'll add some height, which I worked out from the size of the slices themselves. While we're at it, we'll remove the borders from around the <div> tags. The resulting CSS code should be as follows (and as before, press Save when you're done):

```
#sidebar-1{
    background-image:url(../images/stretchy-foot.gif);
    height:113px;
}
#content{
    background-image:url(../images/stretchy-middle.gif);
    height:512px;
}
```

```
#sidebar-2{
    background-image:url(../images/stretchy-head.gif);
    height:160px;
}
```

Rogue white space and other undesirable behavior

Look at the design and notice that there is an undesirable gap between the head and the middle images. And the text doesn't fit within the confines of the design. Now might seem like the time to start worrying about it, but don't worry yet because there are bigger issues we have to deal with first. I just wanted to flag the problems now so that if you are following along step by step you know that it's fine to carry on. We'll fix these issues in due course.

A first look at a blog post

If all our blog posts were going to be exactly the same length as First Post, our work here would be simple. But you and I know that this won't be the case: websites need to stretch, at the very least, vertically. So, to highlight yet another problem that needs fixing, the contents of that First Post need to be extended (although we are bound to get a little distracted by some TxP features along the way).

Pop along to Content ➤ Articles and click on the words First Post. The post will open in the write tab. Notice that there is no HTML in this post—and for good reason. Click the Advanced Options link to the left of the text area. You'll see the title Use Textile and under that the heading article and a drop-down menu that by default contains the words Use Textile.

A brief look at Textile

First off, what is Textile? In short it's an easy way to write XHTML for people who don't normally trouble themselves with such things. Let me show you a quick example:

In XHTML we might write this:

```
<h1>My level 1 heading</h1>
<p>My first paragraph</p>
<p>My second paragraph</p>
```

Written in Textile that would look like this:

```
h1. My level 1 heading

My first paragraph

My second paragraph
```

6

What is immediately apparent is that Textile is easier and quicker to write. Paragraphs are created in much the same way as they are in word processing software—by pressing Enter twice—and there is no hassle remembering to close tags. Textile takes care of all that for you.

To the left of the post is a link titled Textile Help that lists commonly used Textile mark-up, whereas the More link at the bottom of the list takes you off to the main Textile website (http://textism.com/tools/textile) to receive a more in-depth look at the mark-up.

Of course, you can use XHTML to make posts if you want: simply change the drop-down menu under Advanced Option from Use Textile to Leave text untouched.

Adding some extra content

Armed with this knowledge of Textile, we can easily extend First Post to include more paragraphs. Simply copy and paste the first paragraph four times, ensuring that you press Enter twice between each paste. As ever, remember to press Save on the right of the post. Figure 6-30 shows the process.

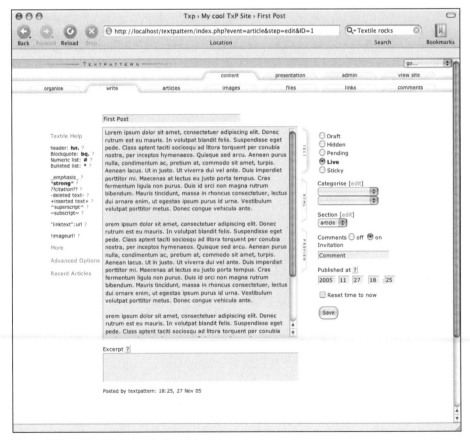

Figure 6-30. Adding more text to the site

As shown in Figure 6-31, all that extra text is overlapping the links at the bottom of the site (unless you happen to be looking in Internet Explorer (IE) on Windows, in which case the result will be slightly different but still a royal mess that needs sorting out).

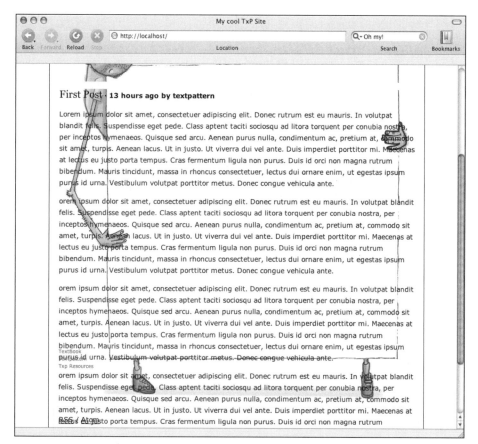

Figure 6-31. The site's a bit of a mess just now

Why a browser with good CSS support is important

It's at this point that we realize we've run in to real trouble. It's also at this point that we need a browser we can be fairly sure is playing nicely with the W3C specs—in this case the CSS 2.1 specs (www.w3.org/TR/CSS21). So we must abandon our beloved IE for now because its support for these specs is patchy, to say the least. We'll come back to the troublesome browsers only after we sort out the genuine problems. It's only by doing things this way that we can avoid RHI (Repetitive Head Injury).

If you wonder which browsers are good and which are not so good (or are surprised to learn that there are other browsers possibly better than IE), then pop over to http://browsehappy.com and get the details.

Allowing for content length

The first thing is to sort out the problem of the content overflowing the #content <div> tag vertically. The browser sees that we set the height to 512px and it is respecting that, but obviously the content is much higher so it is just flowing out of the <div> tag.

Another property in CSS, min-height, is exactly what we need. It tells the browser to make the <div> tag a minimum height of 512px (but if it needs to be higher, make it so). We kill two birds with one stone: we are guaranteed a minimum height of 512px for the background image but our content will push the <div> tag down if it needs more space. Let's put it into practice:

Comment out the height and then add min-height:521px to the #content <div> tag:

```
#content{
    background-image:url(../images/stretchy-middle.gif);
    /* height:512px; */
    min-height:512px;


}
```

That fixes the overflowing text, but now we have yet another problem: the background is repeating—not nice. It's easy to fix, though: update #content as follows:

```
#content{
    background-image:url(../images/stretchy-middle.gif);
    background-repeat: no-repeat;
    /* height:512px; */
    min-height: 512px;
}
```

Finally we need to deal with IE because it doesn't understand min-height. We'll use a hack called the underscore hack to give IE a height value while hiding this value from other browsers:

```
#content{
    background-image:url(../images/stretchy-middle.gif);
    background-repeat: no-repeat;
    _height:512px;
    min-height: 512px;
}
```

The underscore hack: sounds pretty nasty, doesn't it? In an ideal world we wouldn't have to use it, but sometimes IE needs a little nudge to help it along. There are numerous hacks and workarounds for IE, and nearly everyone who uses CSS has had to use a hack or a workaround at some point in their career. My advice is to use hacks only when there are no other options available, and be sure to use them sparingly.

For a more detailed look at the underscore hack, visit http://wellstyled.com/
css-underscore-hack.html.

We are making good progress. The next two issues to deal with are the obvious lack of a
background that joins up the design's head and foot no matter how long the blog post is and
the fact that the text itself is too wide for the design. To fix both of these problems we'll use
that extra `<div id="content-container">` that we added to the page template earlier.

We also need a graphic that will tile horizontally, so I went back to Kev's cartoon illustration and took out a slice that looked like it would tile nicely. The nature of the drawing
meant this process was trial and error, and it took two or three attempts before I got
anything I was happy with. This image is available in the code download for this chapter on
www.friendsofed.com: the filename is stretchy-tile.gif, and you should pop this in to
the images directory along with all the other stretchy gifs. Figure 6-32 shows the choice
we made.

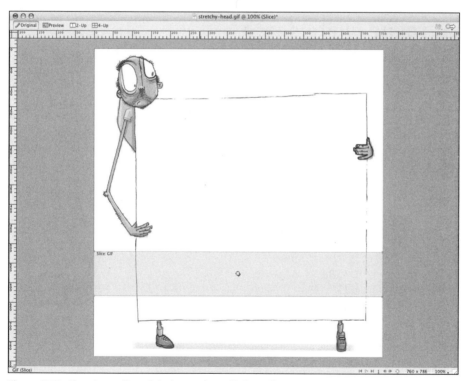

Figure 6-32. Choosing a slice of the image that will tile well

Just above the CSS for the #content, add the CSS for the tiled image:

```
#content-container{
    background-image:url(../images/stretchy-tile.gif);
}
```

While we're at it, add some padding to the #content:

```
#content{
    background-image:url(../images/stretchy-middle.gif);
    background-repeat: no-repeat;
    _height:512px;
    min-height: 512px;
    padding-left:155px;
    padding-right: 80px;
}
```

A look at the site now should reveal what looks like an almost complete design. You might be wondering which advanced mathematical formulas I used to get px values for padding-left and padding-right. The truth is that I used no formulas; it was simply a case of trial and error until it looked right. No golden ratios here, no sir.

That rogue white space

We spoke earlier about the rogue white space that is separating the head image and the middle image. Now is the time to tackle it. Fear not, we'll be coming back for the unsightly search box and the browse menu a little later.

Just to demonstrate how strange this white space problem is, do this: add border: 1px solid red; to the CSS for #content just as you did when we first started the layout, and you will see it cures the problem. Okay, remove the border; it's not going to help us, unfortunately.

I went about curing this by logical trial and error and found that adding padding-top:1px; to both the #content and #sidebar-2 CSS fixed the problem:

```
#content{
    background-image:url(../images/stretchy-middle.gif);
    background-repeat: no-repeat;
    /*height:512px;*/
    min-height:512px;
    padding-left:155px;
    padding-right: 80px;
    padding-top:1px;
}
#sidebar-2{
    background-image:url(../images/stretchy-head.gif);
    height:160px;
    padding-top:1px;
}
```

Great news but why did that work?

Finding out why strange CSS stuff happens is why the web standards community is invaluable; I sent a few e-mails to my fellow CSS designers, and Mike Stenhouse (http://donotremove.co.uk/) sent back a mail pointing out that it was the margins from the <h3> escaping the #content <div> that were causing the space problem. Never satisfied, I asked why this should be so. Dean Edwards (http://dean.edwards.name/) mailed back with a link that explains the anomaly much better than I could.

The explanation is far too detailed to cover in this chapter but, if you really must know how we just achieved that fix, visit www.researchkitchen.de/blog/archives/css-autoheight-and-margincollapsing.php and be prepared to have a headache at the end. Otherwise, accept it and move swiftly on.

To-do list

Up until now, we've been pretty casual about putting together our site. That's not always such a bad thing; it can help creativity just to go with the flow for awhile. A quick look at our site now shows that it's time to tidy up and think about getting this thing launched. It's at this point I usually get together a to-do list, so I'll do that right now:

- Deal with My Site and My Pithy Slogan.
- Move browse and search forms.
- Sort out links at the bottom of the page.
- Add some color to the text.
- Make the archive section.

Let's go through each of these in order.

My Site and My Pithy Slogan

Do we really want a pithy slogan? Probably not, so we'll just get rid of it. Go to the presentation area and then the default page template, and delete the site slogan code and its containing <h2> tags. You are looking for this: <h2><txp:site_slogan /></h2>. Don't forget your new best friend, the Save button, before moving on.

Returning back to the CSS, note that the #head, which relates to <div id="head"> and contains the code for the My Site heading in the page template, has a height applied and its no longer needed, so delete height:100px; leaving the code as follows:

```
#head{
    text-align: center;
}
```

That's already freed up some vital screen real estate. The next job is to make the heading a little smaller. Looking at the page template, this heading is a level 1 heading so let's knock the font size for <h1> down to 2em instead of 3em in the CSS.

```
h1{
    font-weight: normal;
    text-decoration:none;
    font-family: Georgia, Times, Serif;
    font-size: 2em;
}
```

That certainly frees up a bit of screen real estate, but it still looks too separate from the design. So we'll move it. Back to the default page template and find the following code. Highlight and copy the line that contains the <h1> and then delete the entire head <div>; that is, all the code that follows:

```
<!--head -->
  <div id="head">
  <h1><txp:link_to_home><txp:sitename /></txp:link_to_home></h1>
</div>
```

Scroll down to the content <div> and paste the <h1> in at the top:

```
<!-- center -->
  <div id="content-container">
  <div id="content">
  <h1><txp:link_to_home><txp:sitename /></txp:link_to_home></h1>
  <txp:article />
```

As is now our daily mantra, don't forget to press Save when you are done!

There are some who might say that moving the <h1> tag from the top of the page reduced the accessibility of the page and some who will say it doesn't really matter. Personally, I would have preferred to keep it at the beginning of the XHTML but have been willing to make the compromise to get the look I want.

To be honest, this is a big discussion and way out of the scope of this chapter, but the point I want to make is that moving the HTML around isn't something you should do lightly to solve your problems. You can degrade the accessibility of a page if you are not careful, and I mulled this over for awhile before deciding it would be OK.

Move browse and search forms

I don't like those ugly form elements at the top of my page; quite simply they distract from Kev's cartoon, so let's get rid of them. First, delete the code contained within the #sidebar-2 and add in a new link for an archive section. True enough, we haven't created the archive section yet, but we need to make these modifications before we do. So the following code:

```
<!-- right -->
  <div id="sidebar-2">
  <txp:search_input label="Search" wraptag="p" />
<txp:popup type="c" label="Browse" wraptag="p" />

</div>
```

becomes this:

```
<!-- right -->
<div id="sidebar-2">
  <p><a href="/archive">Browse the archive</a></p>
</div>
```

Of course, if you have TxP in a subdirectory, you should prefix /archive with the path to your installation (for example, href="/txp/archive"). Before we move on, but not before saving of course, let's move the Browse the archive anchor to the right. Back to the CSS, find the code for #sidebar-2; directly below it add the following:

```
#sidebar-2 p{
    float:right;
    margin-top:140px;
    padding-right:60px;
}
```

What we have done here is to target the <p> tag very specifically in the sidebar-2 <div> and float it to the right. Because we know the height of #sidebar-2 is 160px, we can make a good guess that a top margin of 140px will push it down to just below the top edge of the piece of paper being held by the man. 60px of padding is added to the right in the same way as we did for the #content <div>—to push the <p> tag inside the background graphic without ruining the illusion. You did remember to press Save, right? OK, that's the last time I'll mention it.

Sort out links at bottom of the page

Keen as I am to get on with making an archive section, we need to have this template completely finished beforehand. So let's take a quick trip to the bottom left of the page and look at the list of links found there—these are links out to other sites on the Web and are added to via the Content ➤ Links part of TxP. We aren't going to feature these links sitewide so we'll just get rid of them.

In doing so, we will essentially make the #sidebar-1 <div> redundant; its only purpose without any content is to show the graphical feet of the man, but we have the #foot <div> that can serve that purpose, so let's go ahead and delete the code that follows from the page template:

```
<!-- left -->
    <div id="sidebar-1">
    <txp:linklist wraptag="p" />
</div>
```

Using the existing CSS for #sidebar-1, you'll put the feet in the foot, so to speak, by moving the contents of #sidebar-1 to #foot. Copy the background-image and height code from #sidebar-1 and paste it within the #foot. While here, remove the yellow border code from the #foot, leaving the CSS looking as follows:

```
#foot{
    clear: both;
    margin-top: 5px;
    text-align: center;
    background-image:url(../images/stretchy-foot.gif);
    height:113px;
}
```

After this is done, you can safely delete any CSS for #sidebar-1 because you won't need it again.

What you should see now in the foot are the RSS/Atom links and the TxP logo to the left of the stretchy man's feet. We want to bring at least some of that in to our design.

We'll lose the TxP logo for now; we can add a credit somewhere else at a later date if we so wish. We need, then, to find and delete the following XHTML from the foot <div> in our default page template:

```
<p><img src="textpattern/txp_img/txp_slug105x45.gif" ➡
alt="textpattern" /></p>
```

Looking at the design, we see the RSS/Atom links are not aligned center within the foot <div>, and this is the effect we're looking for. You will see that there is already text-align:center to be found among the CSS code for #foot; we have a bug! After a bit of searching, I found that it is because of some CSS already in place that is overriding our new CSS:

```
p, blockquote, li, h3{
    font-family: Verdana, "Lucida Grande", Tahoma, Helvetica;
    font-size: 0.9em;
    line-height: 1.6em;
    text-align: left;
    padding-left: 10px;
    padding-right: 10px;
}
```

We no longer need the text-align:left; in the preceding CSS code, so locate it and delete it, leaving the following:

```
p, blockquote, li, h3{
    font-family: Verdana, "Lucida Grande", Tahoma, Helvetica;
    font-size: 0.9em;
    line-height: 1.6em;
    padding-left: 10px;
    padding-right: 10px;
}
```

The RSS/Atom links are now central, but they are sitting on top of the bottom line of the design. We want to move these links down a little to sit halfway between the two feet of the stretchy man. To do this, we target the <p> tag that contains them and add a little padding, which will push the whole paragraph downward. We do this by adding the following CSS to our styles; add it just under the styles for #foot:

```
#foot p{
    padding-top:40px;
}
```

The end result should look a little something like Figure 6-33.

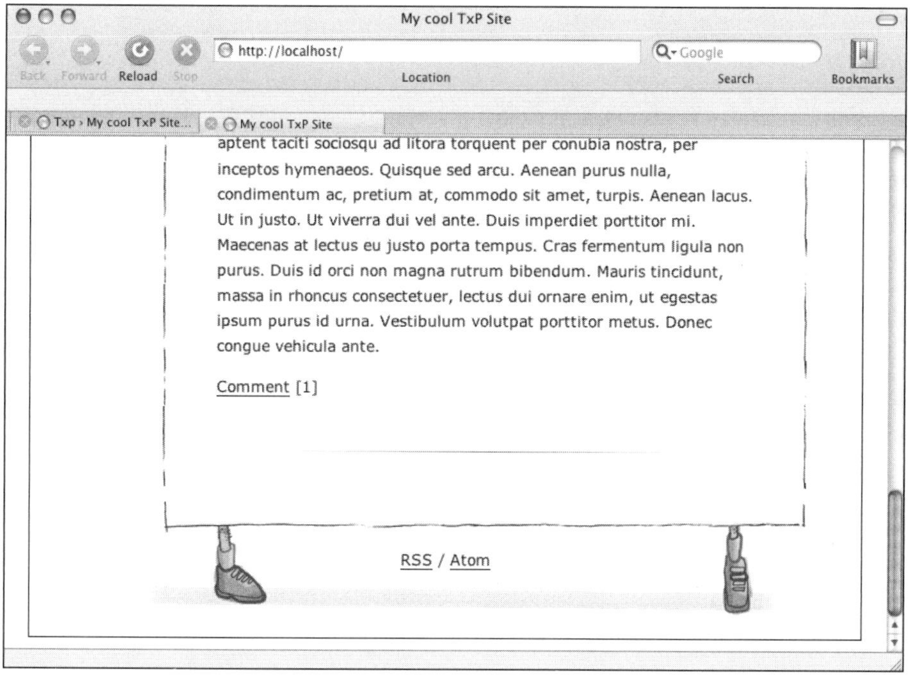

Figure 6-33. The results of all our hard work

Adding a little color to the text

Somewhere near the beginning of the chapter, while we were slicing up Kev's cartoon, we discussed extracting colors from the cartoon to bring a bit of color to our text. What we'll do, as we have done all along, is try and preserve as much of the original TxP CSS as possible and simply tweak it a bit to get the colors we want into the design.

If you look at your front page in your web browser and choose View ➤ View Source, you see that the site heading is contained within the following XHTML:

```
<h1><a href="http://mysite.com/">My Site</a></h1>
```

To target this specific tag, jump to the CSS and look for the following code:

```
h1 a, h2 a{
  border: 0px;
}
```

Directly below the code for the h1-a and h2-a, add the following:

```
h1 a{
   color: #99CC99;
}
```

This is the hex value of a light green I extracted from the cartoon, and I have targeted the anchor (represented by the <a>tag) and not just the heading. Had I simply targeted the heading, the anchor would have stayed its default color, and no change would have been noticeable.

Note that Browse the archive link is already colored red. This is CSS that ships as part of the default TxP design; our link just happens to have inherited it. I planned to pick a red for links from my color palette, but I think this color works well, so I'll use it for all links.

I need to locate the bit of CSS that relates to the Browse the archive link in the #sidebar-2 <div> and find the color value. Because I'll apply this style to all anchors, I'll also delete the code out because I no longer need it. So having noted the color #C00, delete the following from the CSS:

```
#sidebar-2 a, #sidebar-1 a{
   border: 0px;
   color: #C00;
}
```

Then locate the code for all anchors:

```
a{
   color: black;
   text-decoration: none;
   border-bottom: 1px black solid;
}
```

Changing the color from black to our new red color:

```
a{
 color: #C00;
   text-decoration: none;
   /* border-bottom: 1px black solid; */
}
```

The preceding code also shows how I chose to comment out the border in this instance and to leave text-decoration:none; in place, which serves the purpose of removing the underline effect of links. This was simply personal choice, but you might want to simply change the border color to match or remove both the border and text-decoration, which would mean all anchors would be underlined.

CSS shortcuts

I just want to stray off topic slightly, even though we don't have the page space to go into much detail about CSS shortcuts. Because you just used some, though, I thought I should give you a quick side-by-side comparison to see what they are. The CSS currently looks as follows:

```
a{
 color: #C00;
  text-decoration: none;
  /* border-bottom: 1px black solid; */
}
```

That code is full of CSS shortcuts; the long version of the code might look like this:

```
a{
    color: #CC0000;
    text-decoration: none;
    border-bottom-width: 1px;
    border-bottom-color: #CC0000;
    border-botttom-style: dotted;

}
```

I think that is pretty self-explanatory (with perhaps the exception of the color value). We can abbreviate hex values in this way: as long as the red, green, and blue hex pairs are the same we can go ahead and abbreviate. Looking back at the color we applied to the anchor on the <h1> tag, therefore, instead of writing it as color: #99CC99; we can abbreviate it to color: #9C9;. Back now to adding the color to our site design: coloring the anchors has had the effect of showing that the heading First post is in fact a link. Don't click it just yet; we'll be coming back to it next. Before we move away from colors, let's sort out the rollover effects for the links.

We need to add a rollover effect to our anchors so that when a user mouses over the link there is a clear indication that it is a link that can be followed. To do that, we add the following just below the CSS you just altered to change the color of all anchors:

```
a:hover{
color: #FFF;
background: #C00;
}
```

Click that First post heading and you will be presented with a bit of a mess; even worse, if you're using OS X you might get a page not found message. Fear not; we can fix all these things with a few quick tweaks under the hood. Choose Presentation ➤ Sections and look for the section with the name article, change the Uses page: archive to Uses page: default, and then press Save at the bottom of that section's settings. Go back to your site, refresh your browser, and all should now be as you would expect. If you scroll down to the bottom of the article, you will even see a comment and a comment form. Go ahead and leave a test comment for yourself.

Page not found?

If changing the page the article section uses hasn't finished the job and you are getting a page not found message, you need to make one of two changes.

Messy permanent link mode

This is the simplest and quickest way to solve your page-not-found problem, and if you find yourself working with TxP on a host that doesn't support the use of an .htaccess file (see the install notes at the beginning of this chapter), it is your only option. Open up the admin tab; in the preferences find the drop-down menu titled Permanent link mode and change it to ?messy. Scroll to the bottom of this page and press Save. Now when you refresh your site and try the link, you'll see a URL along the lines of http://localhost/index.php?=1. Although it solves the immediate problem, it means that a little bit of extra TxP knowledge is needed further down the line.

For example, with this option turned on, the link to Browse the archives will not work. To fix it, open up your template_head form, find the code for this link, and change it as follows:

```
<!-- right -->
<div id="sidebar-2">
<p><a href="?s=archive">Browse the archive</a></p>
</div>
```

You should now be able to browse your archives like everyone else.

To keep life simpler in the long run, we can tell Apache to allow the .htaccess file to work.

Modify the httpd.conf file

In Chapter 2 you set up your development server and you made a few adjustments to the httpd.conf file. You need to locate it again and open it up in your favorite text editor.

I just want to mention at this stage that I am no Apache guru—far from it—and when I first hit the page-not-found problem, I wasn't too sure why it was happening. Putting TxP into messy URL mode gave an indication that it probably had something to do with the .htaccess file not working as it should. A little bit of Googling lead me to fellow author Richard Rutter's excellent blog, in which I found an article explaining that OS X (the most likely platform to experience this problem) does not allow .htaccess by default. The moral of the story? Most problems are a quick Google search from being solved.

Anyway, to the specific fix. With your httpd.conf file open you need to do a find for AllowOverride None. Find is usually done by pressing Ctrl+F (or Apple+F on a Mac). We are searching for two of these statements and change them to AllowOverride All, the first being at about line 377:

```
# Each directory to which Apache has access
# can be configured with respect
# to which services and features are allowed and/or disabled in that
# directory (and its subdirectories).
#
# First, we configure the "default" to be a very restrictive set of
# permissions.
#
```

```
<Directory />
    Options FollowSymLinks
    AllowOverride All
</Directory>
```

The second is at about line 406:

```
# This controls which options the .htaccess files in directories can
# override. Can also be "All", or any
# combination of "Options", "FileInfo",
# "AuthConfig", and "Limit"
#
    AllowOverride All
```

When you have made these changes, you must restart your server and refresh the site in your browser for them to take effect.

What you should now see when you follow the Browse the archive link is a TxP-branded 404 page (the template for which can be found in Pages ➤ error_default), which indicates that our modifications have been successful. But we are still missing an actual archive section, so the next step is to create a simple archive purely with the tools available by default in TxP.

Creating an archive section and page template

Creating a section will take you just a few clicks. Choose Presentation ➤ Sections and right there at the top you will see a text input and a Create button. In this case, we want to create an archive section, so tap the word archive (all lowercase) into the text area and press Create. After the page has reloaded, scroll down and you will see it there—job done! Figure 6-34 shows the process.

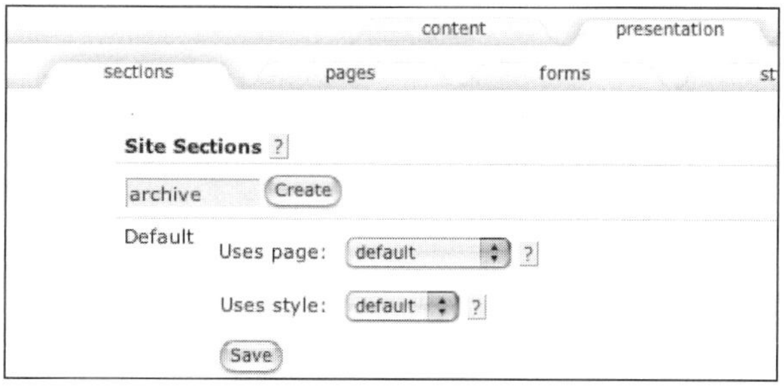

Figure 6-34. Creating the archive section

If you visit your site and click the Browse the archive link that you created a little earlier, you should now be taken through to the archive section that will, at this stage, just contain Kev's cartoon man holding his paper and the My Site heading. It won't take us long to sort this out, though. We'll cover some key TxP theory along the way.

Page template and TxP forms

We'll take the long route to a page template, but in doing so I'll introduce you more thoroughly to TxP forms (found under Presentation ➤ Forms). When you come to building bigger TxP sites, planning and forms are your very best friends and make updating that much simpler.

What you'll do is take a copy of the default page template and modify it slightly to create the archive page template. Before you do that, though, you'll create a set of forms allowing the two page templates that will result from this exercise to share code common to them both.

Jump to your default page template, as shown in Figure 6-35. From the very first line (starting with <!DOCTYPE html PUBLIC "-//W3C//DTD XHTML 1.0 Transitional//EN") highlight by dragging the cursor over and all the way down to the line that ends with the </h1> tag. Copy this text to your clipboard (Ctrl+C or Apple+C on a Mac).

You are editing page template **default**

```
<!DOCTYPE html PUBLIC "-//W3C//DTD XHTML 1.0 Transitional//EN"
        "http://www.w3.org/TR/xhtml1/DTD/xhtml1-transitional.dtd">
<html xmlns="http://www.w3.org/1999/xhtml" xml:lang="en" lang="en">
<head>
        <meta http-equiv="content-type" content="text/html; charset=utf-8" />
        <link rel="stylesheet" href="<txp:css />" type="text/css" media="screen" />
        <title><txp:page_title /></title>
</head>
<body>
<div id="accessibility">
    <a href="#content" title="Go to content">Go to content</a>
    <a href="#sidebar-1" title="Go to navigation">Go to navigation</a>
    <a href="#sidebar-2" title="Go to search">Go to search</a>
</div> <!-- /accessibility -->
<div id="container">


<!-- right -->
    <div id="sidebar-2">
      <p><a href="/archive">Browse the archive</a></p>
</div>


<!-- center -->
<div id="content-container">
<div id="content">
<h1><txp:link_to_home><txp:sitename /></txp:link_to_home></h1>
```

Figure 6-35. The contents of the template_head form

Select Presentation ➤ Forms and find the link that says Create new form. Click it and you'll see a blank text area. Paste the code you copied to your clipboard into the text area (Ctrl+V or Apple+V on a Mac). Now scroll down a little and find the text input titled Form name (required) and call this form template_head. Below that is a drop-down options menu titled Form type (required); choose misc from the list and select Save new. Look on the right side of the page after it reloads; you should now see your template_head in the list, probably at the bottom.

Go back to your default page template and select all the code from and including the line that starts with <txp:if_individual_article> and highlight everything right down to the end. Repeat the process as you did to create a form, but this time name it template_foot. Again, your new form should appear in the list on the right when you're done.

Let's just review before we do anything drastic. Your template_head should contain the following code:

```
<!DOCTYPE html PUBLIC "-//W3C//DTD XHTML 1.0 Transitional//EN"
        "http://www.w3.org/TR/xhtml1/DTD/xhtml1-transitional.dtd">
<html xmlns="http://www.w3.org/1999/xhtml" xml:lang="en" lang="en">
<head>
<meta http-equiv="content-type" content="text/html; charset=utf-8"
/>
<link rel="stylesheet" href="<txp:css />" type="text/css" ➥
 media="screen" />
<title><txp:page_title /></title>
</head>
<body>
<div id="accessibility">
<a href="#content" title="Go to content">Go to content</a>
<a href="#sidebar-1" title="Go to navigation">Go to navigation</a>
<a href="#sidebar-2" title="Go to search">Go to search</a>
</div> <!-- /accessibility -->
<div id="container">
<!-- right -->
<div id="sidebar-2">
<p><a href="/archive">Browse the archive</a></p>
</div>
<!-- center -->
<div id="content-container">
<div id="content">
<h1><txp:link_to_home><txp:sitename /></txp:link_to_home></h1>
```

And your template_foot should contain this:

```
<txp:if_individual_article>
  <p>
  <txp:link_to_prev><txp:prev_title /></txp:link_to_prev>
  <txp:link_to_next><txp:next_title /></txp:link_to_next>
  </p>
  </txp:if_individual_article>
  <txp:if_article_list>
  <p>
  <txp:older>Previous</txp:older>
  <txp:newer>Next</txp:newer>
  </p>
```

6

```
          </txp:if_article_list>
          </div>
          </div>
          <div id="foot">
          <p>
          <txp:feed_link label="RSS" /> / <txp:feed_link label="Atom" ➥
           flavor="atom" />
          </p>
          </div>
          </div>
          </body>
     </html>
```

If that is what you see, go back to your default page template, scroll to the bottom of that page, find the text input titled Copy page as:, type **default_backup** into that field, and press the Copy button. This gives you something to come back to if any of these form modifications go wrong and you need to start over.

You should still see at the top of your page the words You are editing page template default and from this template delete all the code except the <txp:article /> tag. Now you have one line of code, you need to pull those forms you just created to recover your design.

On the left of the page template text area is a list of useful tags. Scroll down to the set of links with the heading Miscellaneous and there you'll see an Output form link. Click it, and a pop-up window with a drop-down menu of form options and a Build Tag button displays, as shown in Figure 6-36.

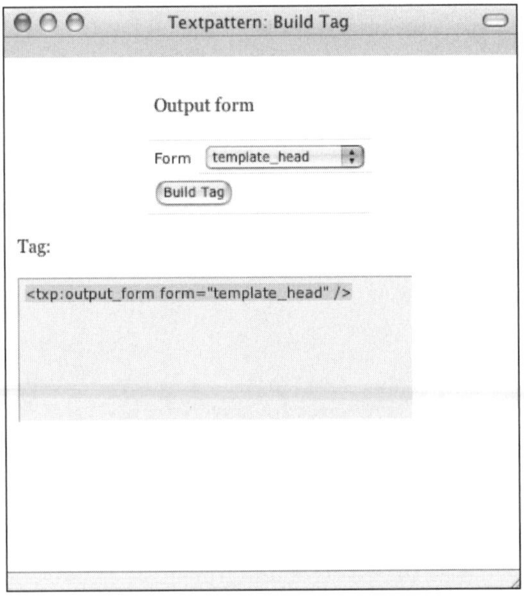

Figure 6-36. Building a tag with the help of TxP

Select template_head from the list and press Build Tag; then copy and paste the resulting tag into your default page template above the <txp:article /> tag. Paste it below the <txp:article /> tag, too, so you will have the following:

```
<txp:output_form form="template_head" />
    <txp:article />
<txp:output_form form="template_head" />
```

Obviously, we don't want the template_head twice, we need the template_foot, too, so edit the bottom tag accordingly, leaving the following:

```
<txp:output_form form="template_head" />
    <txp:article />
<txp:output_form form="template_foot" />
```

Press Save to update the site and pop to your browser, making sure that you are on the homepage as opposed to the archive page. Press Refresh and everything should be as it was before—nothing has changed on the surface, but things just got a little more flexible, as I will demonstrate in a moment.

Let's go straight ahead and create a new page template to use for the archive section. In fact, because we quite casually created our backup of the default page earlier, we already covered how this is done—but let's do it again anyway:

Making sure that the heading for the page template reads You are editing page template default, scroll down below the text area until you come to the text input titled Copy page as. Type **myarchive** into the text area and press Copy; it should appear on the list to the right. You now have an exact copy of your default template.

Click the myarchive link so the heading above the template reads you are editing page template myarchive and we can add our code to make the archive work.

> *A note of caution: always check the heading before you start editing templates to be sure you are editing the right one and always make a local copy as a text file or HTML file before you begin editing a template. I have been caught out on more than one occasion editing the wrong template and then pressing* Save *before realizing too late that the damage was done.*

Archive code

Remove the <txp:article /> tag from the myarchive template so only our <output_form /> tags remain. As its name suggests, this is the tag responsible for presenting our articles, but we don't want our actual articles on the archive page; we want a list of recent articles.

To do this, look at the list of links to the left of your page template; under the heading Site navigation, you will find a link for Recent articles. Clicking this link generates a pop-up window with a bucket full of options, more options than we really need for our simple archives. Set up your options as indicated in Figure 6-37 and press the Build Tag button. The label field will contain the word Recently; you can delete this, or you can leave it in place, it's up to you. Copy this tag to your clipboard and after returning to your myarchive page template, paste it between the `template_head` and `template_foot` tags and press Save.

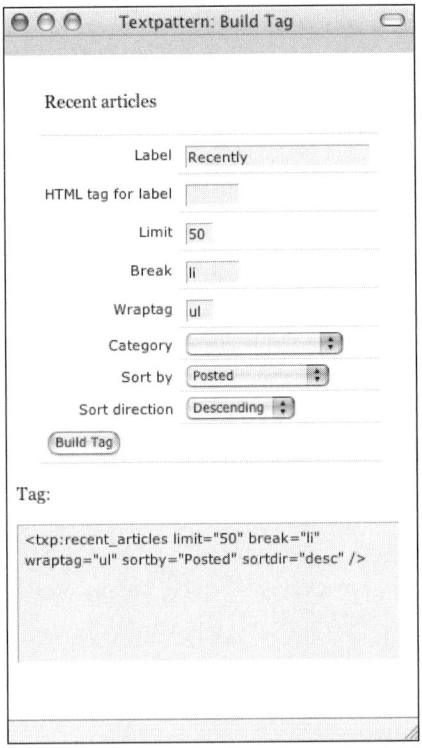

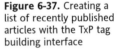

Figure 6-37. Creating a list of recently published articles with the TxP tag building interface

Here you have told TxP to output a list of the last 50 articles published on the site—and that's it. This is a very simple archive and although I was tempted to go into huge detail about a variety of ways this can be achieved, archiving is an area under rapid development in TxP and anything I write will likely be out of date by the time you are reading this. If you want more complex archiving, a search on any of the sites I list at the end of this chapter will likely turn up some interesting results.

Speaking of search, it is always a nice feature, and if a returning visitor remembers the heading or a keyword from a past article, there's a good chance it will show up.

To create a search, we return to the site navigation of our list on the left and choose Search input form, which generates yet another pop-up window with options. On this occasion, the default options set by TxP are fine for our purposes, so press Build Tag and copy and paste it to the myarchive template, sandwiching it between the template_head tag and the tag you just added for recent articles.

To review, the code in the myarchive page template should now look as follows:

```
<txp:output_form form="template_head" />
<txp:search_input label="Search" button="Search" size="15" />
<txp:recent_articles limit="50" break="li" wraptag="ul" ➥
sortby="Posted" sortdir="desc" />
<txp:output_form form="template_foot" />
```

If that's how it looks, press ever-necessary Save at the bottom to update the template. To make this template work with our archive, we now need to choose Presentation ➤ Sections and associate our archive section with the myarchive template. Once again, find the archive section, look for Use page drop-down options, select myarchive from the list, and press Save. If all has gone well, a refreshed visit to your archive section should now produce a search box and a list containing the first post. If you want to see it in action, go ahead and publish another post and see whether it shows up in the list.

Now that we have two working templates for our site, I just want to return to the forms we have created for them to share. They are pretty simple, but they do illustrate the power of TxP forms nicely. Let's say, for example, we created 20 different templates for 20 different sections of a big site and then we remember we forgot to add the links to allow browsers to auto-discover RSS feeds automatically. With our templates all sharing a common form, it is just a case of editing the shared form—in this case, template_head—by inserting the following code and pressing Save; all the templates are now bang up to date.

```
<!DOCTYPE html PUBLIC "-//W3C//DTD XHTML 1.0 Transitional//EN"
        "http://www.w3.org/TR/xhtml1/DTD/xhtml1-transitional.dtd">
    <html xmlns="http://www.w3.org/1999/xhtml" xml:lang="en" lang="en">
    <head>
<link rel="alternate" type="application/rss+xml" title="My great blog"
href="http://mydomain.com/rss/" />
```

I'm not sure about other TxP users, but I often find myself with <txp:output_form /> tags nested inside other forms. It all gets quite complicated, but a little planning and a little practice and forms will soon become some of your most useful allies.

A quick look at the default form

If you are feeling good about forms, have a look at the default form. It is the form that is presented to you when you click on the forms tab first of all. It is also the form that presents the articles in your blog—the form that the <txp:article /> tag draws from to present your posts. So let's just take a moment to walk through the tags. Before we do that, though, pop along to the content area and just make a note of the write tab's text areas. Figure 6-38 gives you a visual reference of how the default form and the write tab relate to each other.

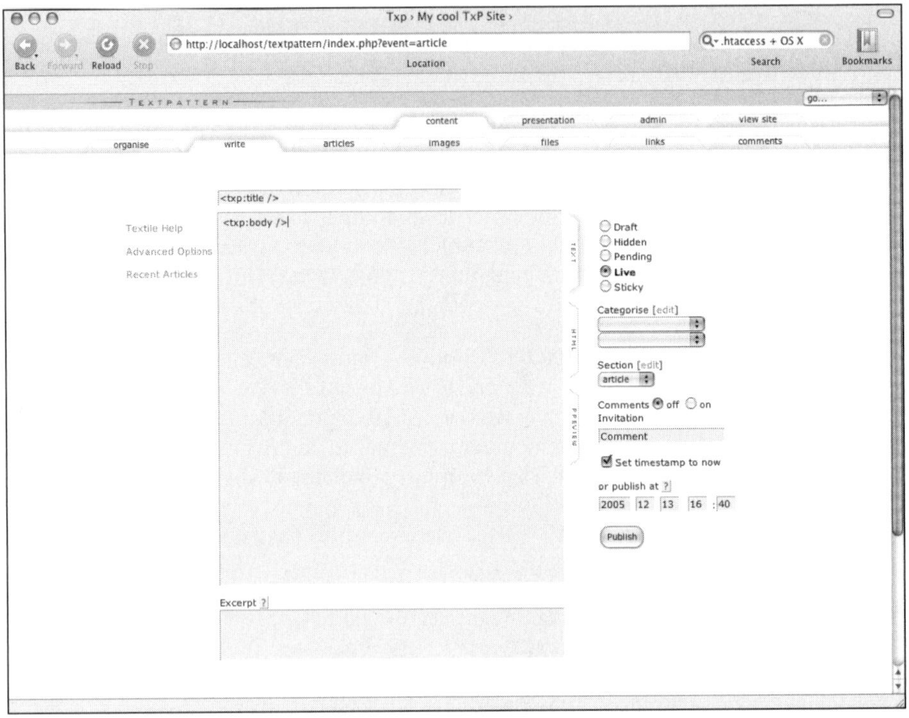

Figure 6-38. TxP tags inside the write tab, illustrating how the tags work

This first line of the default form, <h3><txp:permlink><txp:title /></txp:permlink> · <txp:posted /> by <txp:author /></h3>, is a mix of straight XHTML and TxP tags. The <h3> tag is, as you would expect, a level 3 heading, and anything we put in the first single-line text area in the write tab ends up formatted according to this first line of the form. We can see that the logically named <txp:title /> tag is wrapped in a <txp:permlink> tag. The easiest way to explain this is to pop along to your site and click the title of the First Post. The address in the browser changes to something along the lines of /path to your server/article/first-post. This is the article's permanent link, or *permalink* as it is often called. Basically, this is the link where the article can be found when it's a bit older and is no longer present on the front page of the site. The <txp:permlink> tag takes care of all of this automatically. The · is simply an HTML character entity reference that produces the dot between the heading and the author's name, which is taken care of by the <txp:author /> tag.

`<txp:body />` represents the second multiline text area of the write tab. Anything you write in this second text area is presented on the site using `<txp:body />`, a tiny tag that represents the bulk of your blog posts.

`<txp:if_comments><p><txp:comments_invite /></p></txp:if_comments>` takes care of the comments if you have them switched on. At the bottom of the articles on the front page you will see a link titled Comment [1]. Follow it and you can leave your own comment. There is more to discover about comments and TxP, but again this is an area under heavy development. What you have here does the job very well, but as you get more comfortable you might want to look around the various TxP sites I list at the end of the chapter for more information on controlling comments.

Finally we have the following:

```
<div align="center">
<img src="<txp:site_url />images/1.gif" ➥
style="height:1px;width:400px"
class="divider" alt="" />
</div>
```

This is simply some HTML that adds the horizontal line you can see below the Comment[1] link and the `<txp:site_url />` is a clever TxP tag that uses whatever your site URL is, for example, `http://foobar.com`, and produces an absolute path to the image.

The final job

Finally we have a blog, well almost. All throughout there has been a black border around your cartoon man; this was there for development purposes only, so it's time to remove it. Find the #container within the CSS and delete the `border:1px solid black`. And, of course, don't forget, hit Save when you're done.

Resources

There are many brilliant resources out there for TxP, but these are the sites I find myself at most often:

Textpattern forums

Have no doubt; this is where all the hard-core Textophiles hang out, but no need to be shy—they are a seriously great bunch of people. There is a massive archive of information here and I have had good experiences, from an almost live debug session with the man himself, Dean Allen, straight through to seeing a feature request I made turn into a step-by-step how-to guide within two hours. The original and still the best TxP resource.

`http://forum.textpattern.com`

Textpattern resources

As this site's title suggests, there is a wealth of TxP resources to find: tutorials, plug-ins, templates, tips, tricks, and—for the more advanced—a selection of mods. Not only that, but the site in itself is a showcase for just how powerful TxP is when it comes to managing many content contributors over many sections and categories.

```
http://textpattern.org
```

TextBook

The TextBook project is a superb and fast-growing wiki that goes into a lot of detail about the finer points of TxP. TextBook gets special thanks from me because I found it invaluable during the writing of this chapter. If you are interested in extending your TxP knowledge beyond blogging, this is the site to start at.

```
http://textpattern.net
```

Textgarden

There is a growing number of superb templates at the Textgarden. If the stretchy man in this chapter doesn't float your boat, worry not; you can grab another template here for free.

```
http://textgarden.org
```

TxP magazine

Last but by now means least: TxP magazine. Not so much a resource in the sense of the others—a growing library of TxP articles, tips, and tricks; some really good looking designs to be seen here too.

```
http://txpmagazine.kbbu.de/
```

Plug-ins

There are hundreds of plug-ins for TxP, and some are good, some not so good. You will find many listed at texpattern.org and until an official TxP plug-in repository becomes available this is the best place to start. Following is a list of links to my favorite TxP developer's websites whose plug-ins I have used often:

- www.wilshireone.com
- http://johan.galaxen.net
- http://thresholdstate.com
- http://compooter.org

- http://allinthehead.com
- http://greenrift.textdrive.com
- http://manfre.net

Summary

In writing this chapter I have really only skimmed over the top of the capabilities of TxP. It was more difficult deciding what not to tell you as opposed to what to cover. In writing this chapter, if I have achieved nothing more than giving you a little confidence to go off and explore the possibilities yourself, then I achieved my goals. Happy blogging!

6

7 WRITE YOUR OWN BLOG ENGINE

by Richard Rutter

What this chapter covers:

- Creating a content management system using PHP and MySQL
- Building an administration site to add and edit posts on your blog
- Building your own blog
- Making your blog searchable
- Automatically updating an RSS feed for your blog
- Migrating your blog from a development environment to a live server

The previous chapters have demonstrated the extensive capabilities of four off-the-shelf blog engines, so why on Earth would you want to write your own? Well perhaps you're a control freak looking for the ultimate in customizability. Or (more likely) you're looking to learn a new trick and have some fun along the way. This chapter will explain how a blog engine works and guide you through the steps of building your own. You will learn how to set up a database in MySQL and how to query that database using PHP. By the end of the chapter, you will have your own blog engine running on PHP and MySQL in a development environment and on a live server for all the world to visit.

A content management system

A blog engine is a specific form of content management system (CMS). A CMS (see Figure 7-1) takes in content (your blog post), stores it, and spits it out into templates for the end users (your readers).

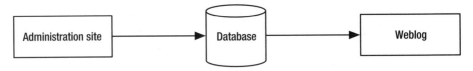

Figure 7-1. Site map of blog engine CMS and blog

A CMS moves away from static pages and into the realm of dynamic content.

The technology

Like the other blog engines in this book, your CMS will be built using free open-source software. Like TextPattern and Expression Engine, your CMS will be built using MySQL and PHP. MySQL is the database server used to store your blog posts, and PHP is the server-side scripting language used to put content into the database and pull it back out into your templates. I chose MySQL and PHP because they are free, fast, reliable, and easy to learn with vast amounts of documentation and help online.

Development environment

All this talk of databases and servers means you are now officially a developer, and every good developer needs a development environment. You could do all your work on a live web server, but life becomes much easier when you can try things out on your own machine, even without an Internet connection.

Before you go any further, you need to follow the instructions in Chapter 2 that explain how to set up a development environment. In particular, you will be using Apache, PHP, MySQL, and PHPMyAdmin.

Preparing the database

You now have all the tools in place to build your blog engine, so it's time to get down to some serious thinking. First, you need to plan how to store your blog in the database.

Related data in a database is grouped together in tables. Each table consists of rows and columns, similar to a spreadsheet. You can store all your blog posts in a single table; each post will take up a row with its various elements arranged in columns, for example, a Title column, a Summary column, and so on.

A database can contain any number of tables. So in addition to your table of posts, you could also have a table of categories. Although each table remains independent of the others, it is possible to extract information from many tables simultaneously by cross-referencing, or **joining**, tables. You will learn about joining tables later. For the time being, you need to work out how each blog post is structured, from a content point of view, to define the database table for your posts. Let us assume that each blog post comprises a title, a date, a summary, and the post itself. On this basis, the database table containing your blog posts will be structured as follows:

Field	Type of Information
title	Single line of text
date	Date and time post was created
summary	Short piece of text
post	Potentially long piece of text

To make life easier further down the line you will need to add two more fields to your table: an id field to provide a unique reference for each post and a timestamp so you can tell when any post was created or modified (this is in addition to the post date).

Creating your table

Before you can add a table to MySQL, you must first add a database in which to create your table. To do this, as with all other MySQL administration, you will use phpMyAdmin, which runs in your web browser. Launch the software by going to http://127.0.0.1/phpMyAdmin/. A suitable name for a database storing a blog is probably blog. To add a database called blog, type 'blog' into the Create new database field in the right frame and click Create, as shown in Figure 7-2.

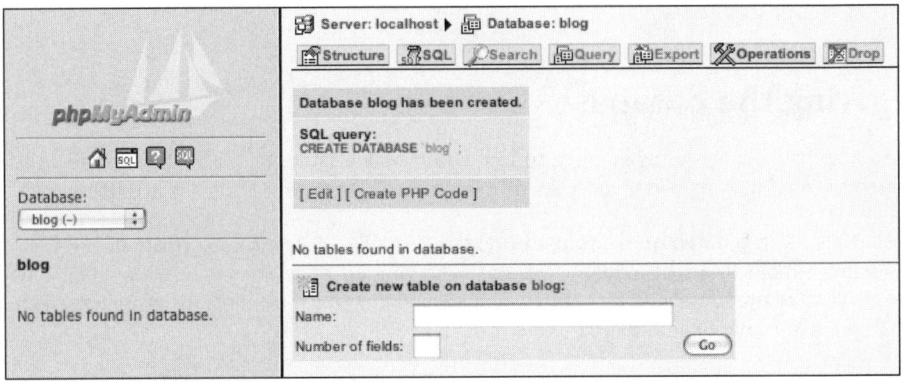

Figure 7-2. Creating the blog database in phpMyAdmin

You are just about ready to create your empty posts table in the database, but there is one final consideration. As well as a name, each field in a table requires a data type that defines—you guessed it—which type of data the column can hold. Data types include numbers, dates, text, and so on. More information can be found on the MySQL website at http://dev.mysql.com/doc/mysql/en/column-types.html. You will be assigning the following data types to your posts table:

Field	Data Type	Explanation
post_id	int	An integer
title	varchar(255)	Text up to 255 characters long
postdate	datetime	A time and date
summary	text	Variable length text
post	text	Variable length text
tstamp	timestamp	An automatically updating timestamp

Now it really is time to create the table in your database. In phpMyAdmin, make sure the database blog is selected in the menu on the left side and then click the Structure tab. In the Create new table on database blog area, type posts into the Name input box and 6 into the Fields input box, and then click Go. On the next screen, input the table definition for each field, as shown in Figure 7-3. Note that for the post_id field you should also select auto_increment in the Extra column and tick the primary column, which will ensure that each new post automatically gets its own unique id number.

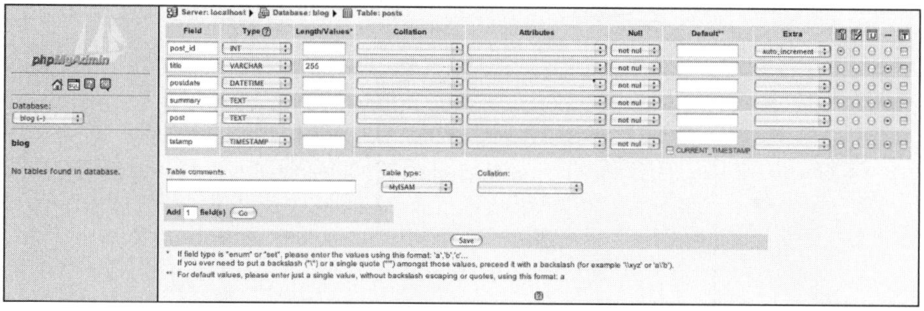

Figure 7-3. Creating the posts table in phpMyAdmin

Now click Save, and the table should be created—you'll see posts added to the left column (see Figure 7-4).

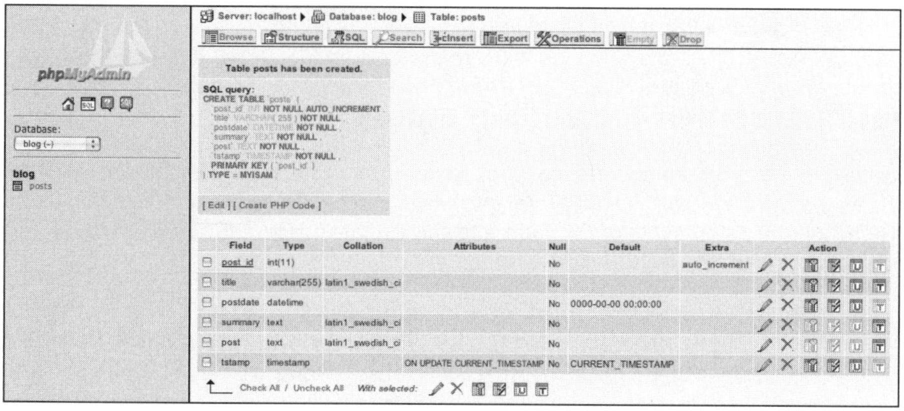

Figure 7-4. Successfully creating the table posts in phpMyAdmin

Building the administration site

You now have a database table in which you can store blog posts. At this point you could just use phpMyAdmin to add new posts to the table. It's not the most convenient of interfaces, however, so now I will show you how to build an administration site for your blog. The administration site will enable you to add and edit blog posts, as well as a few other cool things such as creating a Really Simple Syndication (RSS) feed. Figure 7-5 shows a schematic diagram of how the administration site will fit together. All the pages are available for download on the book's website at http://www.friendsofed.com.

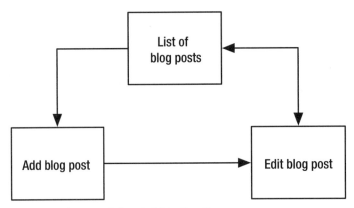

Figure 7-5. Site map of the administration site

Creating a screen for adding a post

Logically, the first screen to create for your administration site should enable the addition of a new post by building an HTML form into which you can type your post and then using PHP to submit the contents of the form into the database. Here's the HTML mark-up for your form:

```
<!DOCTYPE html PUBLIC "-//W3C//DTD XHTML 1.0 Strict//EN"
        "http://www.w3.org/TR/xhtml1/DTD/xhtml1-strict.dtd">
<html xmlns="http://www.w3.org/1999/xhtml" xml:lang="en" lang="en">
<head>
<meta http-equiv="content-type"
  content="text/html; charset=iso-8859-1" />
<title>Add a Post - Blog CMS</title>
</head>
<body>

<h1>Add a post</h1>
<form method="post" action="">
<p>Title: <input type="text" name="title" size="40" /></p>
<p>Date/time: <input type="text" name="postdate" size="40" />
  yyyy-mm-dd hh:mm:ss </p>
```

```
<p>Summary:<br />
<textarea name="summary" rows="5" cols="60"></textarea></p>
<p>Post:<br />
<textarea name="post" rows="20" cols="60"></textarea></p>
<p><input type="Submit" name="submitAdd" value="Add post" /></p>
</form>

</body>
</html>
```

Create a new folder called cms in your website folder and save this HTML document into it, naming the file addpost.php. The extension .php is important because it tells the server that the file contains PHP scripting to process. You can view this page in a browser by going to http://127.0.0.1/cms/addpost.php.

PHP code can be placed anywhere in the HTML document. The beginning and end of each block of PHP code is indicated by <?php . . . ?> delimiters. The PHP code in this document needs to do two jobs: it will collect the post content from the HTML form and insert the post into the database. Your first piece of PHP code will make the form submit to itself. Add the following code to the form:

```
<form method="post" action="<?php echo $_SERVER["PHP_SELF"] ?>">
```

The PHP command echo is a used to write code to the HTML source. $_SERVER is a super-global array containing server information such as headers, paths, and script locations. PHP_SELF is an element within the $_SERVER array and contains the filename of the current script relative to the document root. Using this PHP variable as the form action means you won't have to change anything if the file is moved or renamed. If you now reload the file in your browser and view the source code, you see the form now submits to the current page:

```
<form method="post" action="/cms/addpost.php">
```

> Superglobals are special variables with reserved names; you cannot create your own variable called $_SERVER. They are called superglobals because they are available in all scopes throughout a script, including within functions and methods. All superglobals are prefixed with an underscore (_).

When the form submits with its method set to post, the values typed in by the user are stored in another superglobal array called $_POST. The value of each form control is available as an element in this array. For example, the title of the post as typed in by the user can be extracted using $_POST["title"]. To give PHP access to all the submitted form data, add this code at the very top of your page before the DOCTYPE declaration (note the // prefixing comments and the semicolons required at the end of each line):

```
<?php
// If magic quotes is tuned on then strip slashes
if (get_magic_quotes_gpc()) {
```

```
      foreach ($_POST as $key => $value) {
        $_POST[$key] = stripslashes($value);
      }
    }

    // Extract form submission
    $title = (isset($_POST["title"]))?$_POST["title"]:"";
    $postdate = (isset($_POST["postdate"]))?$_POST["postdate"]:"";
    $summary = (isset($_POST["summary"]))?$_POST["summary"]:"";
    $post = (isset($_POST["post"]))?$_POST["post"]:"";
    $submitAdd = (isset($_POST["submitAdd"]))?$_POST["submitAdd"]:"";

    ?>
```

The first part of this code looks to see whether a PHP setting called magic quotes is turned on (this will vary from installation to installation and may differ from your local machine to the live web server set up by your ISP). If magic quotes is turned on, any single or double quote marks in your form submission will be escaped by a forward slash. For your code to always deal with the same input, this function needs to be reversed, so if magic quotes are turned on, the next few lines in the code step through each element in the $_POST array and remove the slashes so your input is as it was.

The next portion of the script extracts all the form data from the $_POST array and writes it to handy form variables, using a shorthand if statement and the isset function to check whether the value has been set in the $_POST array. For example, the following shorthand code:

```
$title = (isset($_POST["title"]))?$_POST["title"]:"";
```

could also be written as follows:

```
if(isset($_POST["title"])) {
  $title=$_POST["title"];
} else {
  $title="";
}
```

Now that your PHP script has the submitted form data in its grasp, you are ready to insert your post into the database. For PHP to be able to talk to MySQL, it must first open a connection to the database server. The following code does just that:

```
<?php
$db = mysql_connect("localhost", "myUsername", "myPassword") ⇒
or die("Could not connect to database.");
mysql_select_db("blog",$db);
?>
```

Copy these two lines of code into a new document and save them to your root directory as db_connect.php. This script will be reused on every page that needs to connect to the database so it makes sense to save it as an **include**. This way, instead of typing the script into each page, the documents can simply refer to the code in a separate file.

In this script, the mysql_connect() function opens up a connection to the MySQL server using your username and password, so you have to replace myUsername and myPassword with the username and password you used when setting up your development environment in Chapter 2. The mysql_select_db() function then instructs any subsequent SQL queries to be performed against the blog database you set up earlier.

To make your addpost page refer to the db_connect include, and hence enable it to connect to the database, add the following include function to your addpost document (insert just before the closing ?> delimiter):

```
// Open connection to database
include("../db_connect.php");
```

And now to actually insert the submitted blog post into the database. Add the following code to your addpost page, just after the include function:

```
// Prepare data for database
$db_title = addslashes($title);
$db_postdate = addslashes($postdate);
$db_summary = addslashes($summary);
$db_post = addslashes($post);

// If form has been submitted, insert post into database
if ($submitAdd) {
  $sql = "INSERT INTO posts
    (title,postdate,summary,post)
    VALUES ('$db_title', '$db_postdate', '$db_summary', '$db_post')";
  $result = mysql_query($sql);
  if (!$result) {
    $message = "Failed to insert post. MySQL said " . mysql_error();
  } else {
    $message = "Successfully inserted post '$title'.";
  }
}
```

Stepping through the script step by step, the first part prepares the form data for the database:

```
$db_title = addslashes($title);
$db_postdate = addslashes($postdate);
$db_summary = addslashes($summary);
$db_post = addslashes($post);
```

Here I am using the addslashes function to escape any quote marks in the form submission. If this step were omitted, quote marks would cause the SQL query to fail or malfunction.

Next, an if statement checks that the variable $submitAdd has been set:

```
if ($submitAdd) {
```

7

The form's submit button is named submitAdd, so if the form is submitted, the contents of $submitAdd will be the value of the submit button (currently 'Add post'). The next three lines create an SQL query in a variable called $sql:

```
$sql = "INSERT INTO posts
  (title,postdate,summary,post)
  VALUES ('$db_title', '$db_postdate', '$db_summary', '$db_post')";
```

SQL as a language was designed to be human-readable and, for the most part, it is fairly straightforward. The query begins with INSERT INTO posts, which means you will insert a new row in the posts table. The contents of the new row is then defined by the following:

(list of column names) VALUES (list of corresponding values)

The column names are those defined earlier. The associated values were extracted from the form submission into variables at the start of your script. Finally, the mysql_query function is used to send the query to the MySQL server for processing:

```
$result = mysql_query($sql);
if (!$result) {
    $message = "Failed to insert post. MySQL said " . mysql_error();
} else {
    $message = "Successfully inserted post '$title'.";
}
```

If the query works, mysql_query() will return true, otherwise it returns false, so you can check the value of $result to ensure that the insert worked. If the value of $result is false, the $message variable is populated with an error message concatenated with the error text generated by MySQL. Otherwise, we populate $message with a confirmation including the title of the inserted post.

The final step is to write the contents of $message to the screen, so the user can get some feedback. Insert this code after <h1>Add a post</h1>:

```
<?php
if (isset($message)) {
  echo "<p class='message'>$message</p>";
}
?>
```

This code checks that $message exists; if so, it writes the message to a paragraph with a class set to message, so it can be styled later. Now reload the page into your browser and try adding a new post (see Figure 7-6).

After you have a success message, you can go to phpMyAdmin to verify that the insert worked. In phpMyAdmin, click the posts link in the left frame and then click the Browse tab in the right frame. You should see your new post in the posts table. Note that it has been automatically assigned a post_id of 1 (see Figure 7-7).

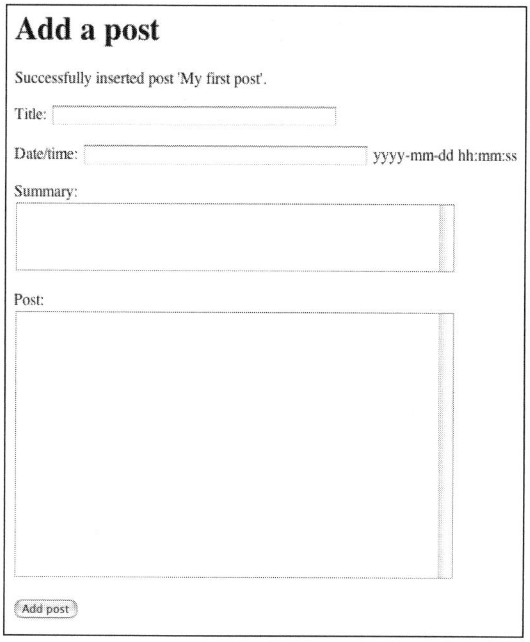

Add a post

Successfully inserted post 'My first post'.

Title: [   ]

Date/time: [   ] yyyy-mm-dd hh:mm:ss

Summary:

[   ]

Post:

[   ]

(Add post)

Figure 7-6. Successfully adding a post in your CMS

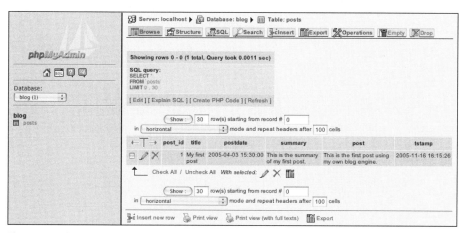

Figure 7-7. The new post as it appears in phpMyAdmin

At this stage, the source code for addpost.php should look like this:

```php
<?php
// If magic quotes is tuned on then strip slashes
if (get_magic_quotes_gpc()) {
  foreach ($_POST as $key => $value) {
    $_POST[$key] = stripslashes($value);
  }
}
```

```php
// Extract form submission
$title = (isset($_POST["title"]))?$_POST["title"]:"";
$postdate = (isset($_POST["postdate"]))?$_POST["postdate"]:"";
$summary = (isset($_POST["summary"]))?$_POST["summary"]:"";
$post = (isset($_POST["post"]))?$_POST["post"]:"";
$submitAdd = (isset($_POST["submitAdd"]))?$_POST["submitAdd"]:"";

// Open connection to database
include("../db_connect.php");

// Prepare data for database
$db_title = addslashes($title);
$db_postdate = addslashes($postdate);
$db_summary = addslashes($summary);
$db_post = addslashes($post);

// If form has been submitted, insert post into database
if ($submitAdd) {
  $sql = "INSERT INTO posts
    (title,postdate,summary,post)
    VALUES ('$db_title', '$db_postdate', '$db_summary', '$db_post')";
  $result = mysql_query($sql);
  if (!$result) {
    $message = "Failed to insert post. MySQL said " . mysql_error();
  } else {
    $message = "Successfully inserted post '$title'.";
  }
}
?>
<!DOCTYPE html PUBLIC "-//W3C//DTD XHTML 1.0 Strict//EN"
        "http://www.w3.org/TR/xhtml1/DTD/xhtml1-strict.dtd">
<html xmlns="http://www.w3.org/1999/xhtml" xml:lang="en" lang="en">
<head>
<meta http-equiv="content-type"
  content="text/html; charset=iso-8859-1" />
<title>Add a Post - Blog CMS</title>
</head>
<body>

<h1>Add a post</h1>

<?php
if (isset($message)) {
  echo "<p class='message'>$message</p>";
}
?>

<form method="post" action="<?php echo $_SERVER["PHP_SELF"] ?>">
<p>Title: <input type="text" name="title" size="40" /></p>
<p>Date/time: <input type="text" name="postdate" size="40" />
```

```
            yyyy-mm-dd hh:mm:ss </p>
            <p>Summary:<br />
            <textarea name="summary" rows="5" cols="60"></textarea></p>
            <p>Post:<br />
            <textarea name="post" rows="20" cols="60"></textarea></p>
            <p><input type="Submit" name="submitAdd" value="Add post" /></p>
            </form>

            </body>
            </html>
```

Creating a screen for updating a post

The user interface for updating a post will be almost identical to that for inserting a new post, so it makes sense to use the same file: addpost.php. The first thing this page needs to know is which post to update. Each post can be uniquely identified by its post_id, and you can use a query string to reference this. A query string is the list of *name=value* pairs in a URL that follow the filename—you have seen them when using search engines and other such sites. Because you now have a post in your database table with a post_id of 1, the URL needed to reference the post is http://127.0.0.1/cms/addpost.php?post_id=1.

As with a form post, the elements of a query string are available to PHP through a super-global variable. This time, you will use the $_REQUEST array, and the id of the post can be obtained by $_REQUEST["post_id"]. With that information in hand, the following code can be added to the end of your script, just before the closing ?> delimiter. This code pulls the post back out of the database:

```
        // Get post_id from query string
        $post_id = (isset($_REQUEST["post_id"]))?$_REQUEST["post_id"]:"";

        // If post_id is a number get post from database
        if (preg_match("/^[0-9]+$/", $post_id)) {
          $editmode = true;

          $sql = "SELECT title, postdate, summary, post FROM posts ➥
        WHERE post_id=$post_id";
          $result = mysql_query($sql);
          $mypost = mysql_fetch_array($result);

          if($mypost) {
            $title = $mypost["title"];
            $postdate = $mypost["postdate"];
            $summary = $mypost["summary"];
            $post = $mypost["post"];
          } else {
            $message = "No post matching that post_id.";
          }
        } else {
          $editmode = false;
        }
```

285

Stepping through the code, the first line extracts the post_id from the query string:

```
$post_id = (isset($_REQUEST["post_id"]))?$_REQUEST["post_id"]:"";
```

Next, the preg_match function uses a **regular expression** to check that the post_id is a number. This is important for two reasons. First, from a practical point of view, the only valid post_ids are numbers, so there is no point dealing with post_ids that are not numbers. Second, from a security point of view, anyone can type anything into a query string, so it's vital to filter out any potentially harmful input. So if a valid-looking post_id has been identified, a flag (by way of the variable editmode) is set so the script knows it is in edit mode (this will be used later):

```
if (preg_match("/^[0-9]+$/", $post_id)) {
    $editmode = true;
```

> Using regular expressions is a way of searching and matching patterns in text. The syntax is complex and seemingly obscure, but they are nonetheless a fast and powerful method of performing extremely specific searches and replacements in text. If you want to learn more about regular expressions, I recommend Nathan A. Good's book Regular Expression Recipes (for more details see www.apress.com/book/bookDisplay.html?bID=396).

Next, an SQL query is used to extract the post from the database. The query is constructed using a SELECT statement of this form:

```
SELECT required fields FROM database table WHERE condition is met
```

This query is then sent to the database using the mysql_query function. On the next line, the mysql_fetch_array function is used to put the first row of SQL query result into an array; because each post_id is unique, there will be only one row returned anyway. This array is stored in the variable $mypost. If the SELECT statement did not return any results, the value of $mypost is null, and a warning is written to $message. If $mypost is not null, the values of the $mypost array are put into individual variables. Note that the elements of the array correspond to the column names in the SELECT statement:

```
$result = mysql_query($sql);
$mypost = mysql_fetch_array($result);

if($mypost) {
    $title = $mypost["title"];
    $postdate = $mypost["postdate"];
    $summary = $mypost["summary"];
    $post = $mypost["post"];
} else {
    $message = "No post matching that post_id.";
}
```

The next step is to repopulate the form with the post pulled out of the database. For each input box, add a value attribute and echo the corresponding PHP variable:

```
<input type="text" name="title" size="40"
  value="<?php if (isset($title)) {echo $title;} ?>" />
```

Similarly for each textarea:

```
<textarea name="summary" rows="5" cols="60">
  <?php if (isset($summary)) {echo $summary;} ?>
  </textarea></p>
```

And this:

```
<textarea name="post" rows="20" cols="60">
  <?php if (isset($post)) {echo $post;} ?>
  </textarea>
```

If you now enter http://127.0.0.1/cms/addpost.php?post_id=1 into your browser, the form should populate with the first post you added. However the submit button will still say Add a post (and if you click it, that's exactly what will happen—you will get a second post identical to the first, but with a post_id of 2). To deal with this, I will introduce **case switching** in PHP. Replace the submit button with this code:

```
<?php
switch ($editmode) {
case true:
  echo "<input type='hidden' name='post_id' value='$post_id' />";
  echo "<input type='Submit' name='submitUpdate'
    value='Update post' />";
  break;
case false:
  echo "<input type='Submit' name='submitAdd' value='Add post' />";
  break;
}
?>
```

The switch statement is similar to a series of if statements on the same expression. On many occasions, you might want to compare the same variable with many different values and execute a different piece of code depending on which value it equals to. This is exactly what the switch statement is for. In this case, you are echoing a different submit button depending on the value of $editmode. You can apply a similar approach to the title and heading of your page. Note that I have also added a hidden form field to the Update post button so the form also submits the post_id of the current post. The script will then know which post to update.

And finally the SQL script to update the post. Insert this code just after where you set $editmode=true:

```
// If form has been submitted, update post
if (isset($_POST["submitUpdate"])) {
  $sql = "UPDATE posts SET
    title='$db_title',
    postdate='$db_postdate',
```

```
        summary='$db_summary',
        post='$db_post'
        WHERE post_id = $post_id";
    $result = mysql_query($sql);
    if (!$result) {
      $message = "Failed to update post. MySQL said " . mysql_error();
    } else {
      $message = "Successfully update post '$title'.";
    }
  }
```

This script is very similar to the insert post code. To start off, the script checks that the Update post button has been clicked. Then an SQL query to update the post is constructed using an UPDATE statement with this syntax:

```
UPDATE table SET column1=value, column2=value WHERE condition is met
```

Note that WHERE clauses in UPDATE statements work in exactly the same way as in SELECT statements.

Now you can add new posts and update existing ones. Reload http://127.0.0.1/cms/addpost.php?post_id=1 in your browser and try updating the text of the post you added earlier. Your result should look something like Figure 7-8.

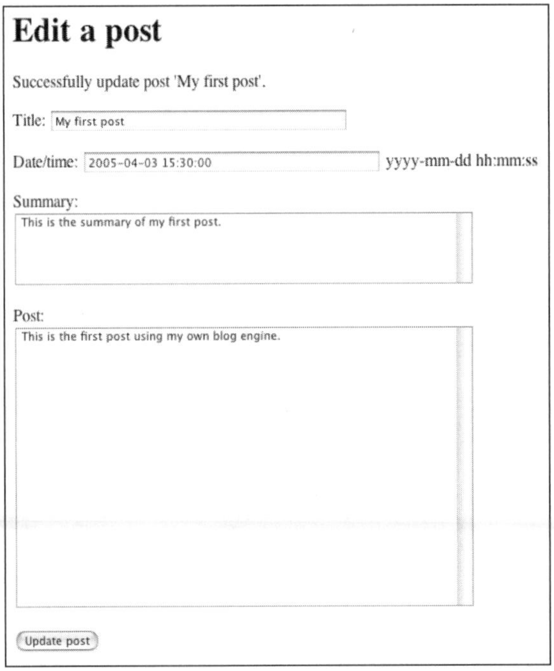

Figure 7-8. Successfully updating a blog post in your CMS

Here is the final code for the addpost.php page:

```php
<?php
// If magic quotes is turned on then strip slashes
if (get_magic_quotes_gpc()) {
  foreach ($_POST as $key => $value) {
    $_POST[$key] = stripslashes($value);
  }
}

// Extract form submission
$title = (isset($_POST["title"]))?$_POST["title"]:"";
$postdate = (isset($_POST["postdate"]))?$_POST["postdate"]:"";
$summary = (isset($_POST["summary"]))?$_POST["summary"]:"";
$post = (isset($_POST["post"]))?$_POST["post"]:"";
$submitAdd = (isset($_POST["submitAdd"]))?$_POST["submitAdd"]:"";

// Open connection to database
include($_SERVER["DOCUMENT_ROOT"] . "/db_connect.php");

// Prepare data for database
  $db_title = addslashes($title);
  $db_postdate = addslashes($postdate);
  $db_summary = addslashes($summary);
  $db_post = addslashes($post);

// If form has been submitted, insert post into database
if ($submitAdd) {
  $sql = "INSERT INTO posts
    (title,postdate,summary,post)
    VALUES ('$db_title', '$db_postdate', '$db_summary', '$db_post')";
  $result = mysql_query($sql);
  if (!$result) {
    $message = "Failed to insert post. MySQL said " . mysql_error();
  } else {
    $message = "Successfully inserted post '$title'.";
  }
}

// Get post_id from query string
$post_id = (isset($_REQUEST["post_id"]))?$_REQUEST["post_id"]:"";

// If post_id is a number, get post from database
if (preg_match("/^[0-9]+$/", $post_id)) {
  $editmode = true;

  // If form has been submitted, update post
  if (isset($_POST["submitUpdate"])) {
    $sql = "UPDATE posts SET
```

```php
          title='$db_title',
          postdate='$db_postdate',
          summary='$db_summary',
          post='$db_post'
    WHERE post_id = $post_id";
    $result = mysql_query($sql);
    if (!$result) {
      $message = "Failed to update post. MySQL said " . mysql_error();
    } else {
      $message = "Successfully update post '$title'.";
    }
  }

  $sql = "SELECT title, postdate, summary, post FROM posts ➥
WHERE post_id=$post_id";
  $result = mysql_query($sql);
  $mypost = mysql_fetch_array($result);

  if($mypost) {
    $title = $mypost["title"];
    $postdate = $mypost["postdate"];
    $summary = $mypost["summary"];
    $post = $mypost["post"];
  } else {
    $message = "No post matching that post_id.";
  }
} else {
  $editmode = false;
}

?>
<!DOCTYPE html PUBLIC "-//W3C//DTD XHTML 1.0 Strict//EN"
       "http://www.w3.org/TR/xhtml1/DTD/xhtml1-strict.dtd">
<html xmlns="http://www.w3.org/1999/xhtml" xml:lang="en" lang="en">
<head>
<meta http-equiv="content-type"
  content="text/html; charset=iso-8859-1" />
<title><?php
switch ($editmode) {
case true:
  echo "Edit a post";
  break;
case false:
  echo "Add a post";
  break;
}
?>
 - Blog CMS</title>
</head>
<body>
```

```php
<h1>
<?php
switch ($editmode) {
case true:
    echo "Edit a post";
    break;
case false:
    echo "Add a post";
    break;
}
?>
</h1>

<?php
if (isset($message)) {
  echo "<p class='message'>$message</p>";
}
?>

<form method="post" action="<?php echo $_SERVER["PHP_SELF"] ?>">
<p>Title: <input type="text" name="title" size="40"
  value="<?php if (isset($title)) {echo $title;} ?>" /></p>
<p>Date/time: <input type="text" name="postdate" size="40"
  value="<?php if (isset($postdate)) {echo $postdate;} ?>" />
  yyyy-mm-dd hh:mm:ss </p>
<p>Summary:<br />
<textarea name="summary" rows="5" cols="60">
  <?php if (isset($summary)) {echo $summary;} ?>
  </textarea></p>
<p>Post:<br />
<textarea name="post" rows="20" cols="60">
  <?php if (isset($post)) {echo $post;} ?>
  </textarea></p>
<p>
<?php
switch ($editmode) {
case true:
  echo "<input type='hidden' name='post_id' value='$post_id' />";
  echo "<input type='Submit' name='submitUpdate' ➥
value='Update post' />";
  break;
case false:
  echo "<input type='Submit' name='submitAdd' value='Add post' />";
  break;
}
?>
</p>
</form>

</body>
</html>
```

7

Creating a screen for listing posts

At this point, you can add and edit blog posts, but when it comes to editing a post you still have to know its post_id and type the number into your browser. Not exactly convenient, I'm sure you'll agree. Far more useful would be a list showing all your blog posts so you can select which post to edit. And that's what I'll show you now.

All that is required is one SELECT statement and a PHP loop. Here's the entire code; save it in your cms directory as index.php (because you'll want it to be the default page in your CMS):

```php
<?php
// Open connection to database
include("../db_connect.php");

// Select all posts in db
$sql = "SELECT post_id, title, DATE_FORMAT(postdate, '%e %b %Y at
%H:%i') AS ➡
dateattime FROM posts ORDER BY postdate DESC";
$result = mysql_query($sql);
$myposts = mysql_fetch_array($result);
?>

<!DOCTYPE html PUBLIC "-//W3C//DTD XHTML 1.0 Strict//EN"
        "http://www.w3.org/TR/xhtml1/DTD/xhtml1-strict.dtd">
<html xmlns="http://www.w3.org/1999/xhtml" xml:lang="en" lang="en">
<head>
<meta http-equiv="content-type" content="text/html; charset= ➡
iso-8859-1" />
<title>All blog posts - Blog CMS</title>
</head>
<body>

<h1>All blog posts</h1>

<?php
if (isset($message)) {echo "<p class='message'>".$message."</p>";}

if($myposts) {
  echo "<ol>\n";
  do {
    $post_id = $myposts["post_id"];
    $title = $myposts["title"];
    $dateattime = $myposts["dateattime"];
    echo "<li value='$post_id'>";
    echo "<a href='addpost.php?post_id=$post_id'>$title</a> ➡
posted $dateattime";
    echo "</li>\n";
  } while ($myposts = mysql_fetch_array($result));
  echo "</ol>";
```

```
    } else {
      echo "<p>There are no blog posts in the database.</p>";
    }
    ?>

    </body>
    </html>
```

Stepping through the code: first a connection to the database is opened as before. Then an SQL statement is constructed to pull all the posts out of the database:

```
SELECT post_id, title, DATE_FORMAT(postdate, '%e %b %Y at %H:%i') ➥
  AS dateattime FROM posts ORDER BY postdate DESC
```

I introduced a couple of new functions here. First, the ORDER BY clause at the end of the query sorts all the posts into date order with the newest first. You can order by more than one field at a time by using a comma-separated list. For example this clause would sort by postdate first and then by title for those posts with the same date:

```
ORDER BY postdate DESC, title ASC
```

The other new function is DATE_FORMAT. Because the postdate field was created with a data type of DATETIME, MySQL can manipulate the date and time data—it couldn't do this if the date were stored as normal text. DATE_FORMAT allows you to output a date and time exactly as you wish. In this case, the postdate, which is currently stored as something like 2005-04-03 15:30:00, is formatted and displayed as 3 Apr 2005 at 15:30. An alias for the formatted date is created using AS dateattime (this is for convenience, as will become apparent later in this section). More information about the date_format function can be found on the MySQL website at http://dev.mysql.com/doc/refman/4.1/en/date-and-time-functions.html.

Moving on to the main body of the HTML document, I have inserted a chunk of PHP after the main heading. This script steps through all the posts retrieved from the database in the afore-mentioned SELECT query and displays them in a list with links through to the edit page. Here's how:

```
<?php
if($myposts) {
  echo "<ol>\n";
```

Firstly the code checks that the $myposts array is not null; in other words, it checks that there are actually some posts to display. If so, it opens an HTML ordered list.

```
do {
  ..
} while ($myposts = mysql_fetch_array($result));
```

Then a do-while loops through all the posts returned by the SELECT query. A do-while loop repeats everything within it until the while expression is no longer true. The key here is that every time the mysql_fetch_array function is executed it advances to the next row in the query result thus populating the $myposts array with the next post pulled from the

7

293

database. $myposts becomes false after there are no more posts to show, and at this point the while expression knows to stop looping.

```
$post_id = $myposts["post_id"];
$title = $myposts["title"];
$dateattime = $myposts["dateattime"];
echo "<li value='$post_id'>";
echo "<a href='addpost.php?post_id=$post_id'>$title</a> ➥
posted $dateattime";
echo "</li>\n";
```

Inside the do-while loop, the blog post information is extracted from the $myposts array and used to display a list item for each post. This list item links through to addpost.php, appending the post_id in the query string as you had to do in your browser earlier. Note that the post date element is accessed using the dateattime alias created in the SELECT statement. If the alias hadn't been created, the formatted date would be accessed using this rather clumsy code:

```
$dateattime = $myposts["DATE_FORMAT(postdate, '%e %b %Y at %H:%i')"];
```

Enter http://127.0.0.1/cms/ in your browser and you should see the list of blog posts currently in your database. The resulting page should look something Figure 7-9.

All blog posts

1. <u>My first post</u> posted 3 Apr 2005 at 15:30

Figure 7-9. Your CMS homepage showing a list of all blog posts in the database

Deleting a post

The final operation required for your CMS is the capability to delete unwanted posts. This functionality will be built into your index.php page by adding a delete button next to the link for each post and adding a delete script. First, insert the delete link into each list item by amending your code as follows:

```
echo "<li value='$post_id'>";
echo "<a href='addpost.php?post_id=$post_id'>$title</a> ➥
 posted $dateattime";
echo " [<a href='".$_SERVER["PHP_SELF"]."?delete=$post_id' ➥
 onclick='return confirm(\"Are you sure?\")'>delete</a>]";
echo "</li>\n";
```

This link sends delete=post_id as the query string so the delete script will know which post to delete. I have also added a JavaScript confirmation to help prevent any unwanted deletions because MySQL has no built-in undo functionality. Here's the delete code; insert it just after the database connection. That way, a deletion will occur before the SELECT query, and hence the post list will be updated correctly:

```
    // If delete has a valid post_id
$delete = (isset($_REQUEST["delete"]))?$_REQUEST["delete"]:"";
if (preg_match("/^[0-9]+$/", $delete)) {

  $sql = "DELETE FROM posts WHERE post_id = $delete LIMIT 1";
  $result = mysql_query($sql);
  if (!$result) {
    $message = "Failed to delete post $delete. MySQL said ➥
" . mysql_error();
  } else {
    $message = "Post $delete deleted.";
  }
}
```

The script is almost identical to that used for updating a post. The only slight difference is the SQL query itself:

```
DELETE FROM table WHERE condition is met
    LIMIT max num of records to act upon
```

The WHERE clause works in an identical way to that used with UPDATE and SELECT. I have added a LIMIT clause as a safety measure to ensure that the DELETE command deletes only a single row. The LIMIT clause can also be used with UPDATE and SELECT statements. As I said earlier, MySQL has no inbuilt undo functionality so the DELETE command is dangerously simple. For example, this command will *delete all the posts* in your table!

```
DELETE FROM table
```

Note that when your post is deleted, the remaining post_ids do not renumber. So if you have three posts and delete post number 2, the remaining posts will still be numbered 1 and 3, and any subsequent new post will be numbered 4. This is a feature of MySQL that ensures database entries remain uniquely identified with the same id. Figure 7-10 shows the result.

All blog posts

1. My first post posted 3 Apr 2005 at 15:30 [delete]

Figure 7-10. Your CMS index page showing the first post and delete link

Finishing touches

To tie together the CMS functionality, you need a way of navigating between the Index page and the Add a Post page, and back. A neat way to achieve this is with another include. The following code simply links between the two CMS pages you have created thus far:

```
<ul id="nav">
  <li><a href="index.php">List of posts</a></li>
  <li><a href="addpost.php">Add a post</a></li>
</ul>
```

Save this code in your cms folder in a file called nav.inc. To include the file in your pages, add this line after the opening <body> tag in index.php and addpost.php:

```php
<?php include("nav.inc") ?>
```

Tart it up

Finally, I'm sure you'll agree that your CMS is looking a little ugly at the moment. What it needs is a little style. Try applying the following stylesheet, or feel free to build your own:

```css
BODY {
  background: white;
  color: #333;
  font-family: "lucida grande", verdana, tahoma, sans-serif;
  font-size: 62.5%;
}

H1 {
  font-weight: normal;
  font-size: 1.8em;
  margin-left:10em;
}

P, UL, OL {
  font-size: 1.2em;
  margin-left: 15em;
}

UL, OL {
  padding-left: 2em;
}

#nav {
  float: left;
  width: 8em;
  margin: 3em 0 0 0;
  padding:1em 2em;
  background: #ddd;
  border: 1px solid #ccc;
}

.message {
  color: red;
}
```

Save this stylesheet in your cms folder as cms.css and import the styles into your pages by adding a style element into the head of index.php and addpost.php:

```html
<style type="text/css"> @import url(cms.css); </style>
```

The resulting index page should look like Figure 7-11.

All blog posts

1. <u>My first post</u> posted 3 Apr 2005 at 15:30 [<u>delete</u>]

- <u>List of posts</u>
- <u>Add a post</u>

Figure 7-11. Your CMS index page with includes and styles in place

Building the blog

Now that you have the administration site up and running, it's time to move on to the fun bit: it's time to build the blog itself. In this section you will learn how to build a homepage showing your post recent posts, how to create an individual page for each post, how to enable comments, how to create an archive of posts, and how to add searching capability to your blog. Figure 7-12 shows a schematic diagram of how your blog will tie together.

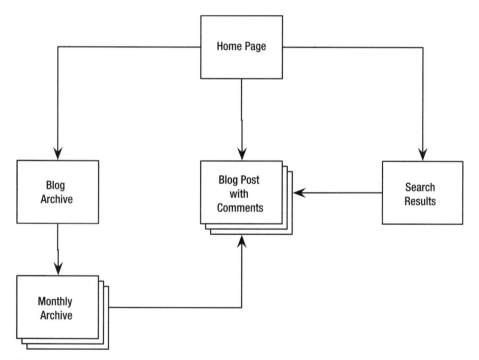

Figure 7-12. Site map of your blog

7

Creating the homepage

For your homepage, I will show you how to display your most recent five posts, provide shortcut links to those posts, and add a search box. With some supporting text, imagery, and styling, your final homepage will look something like Figure 7-13.

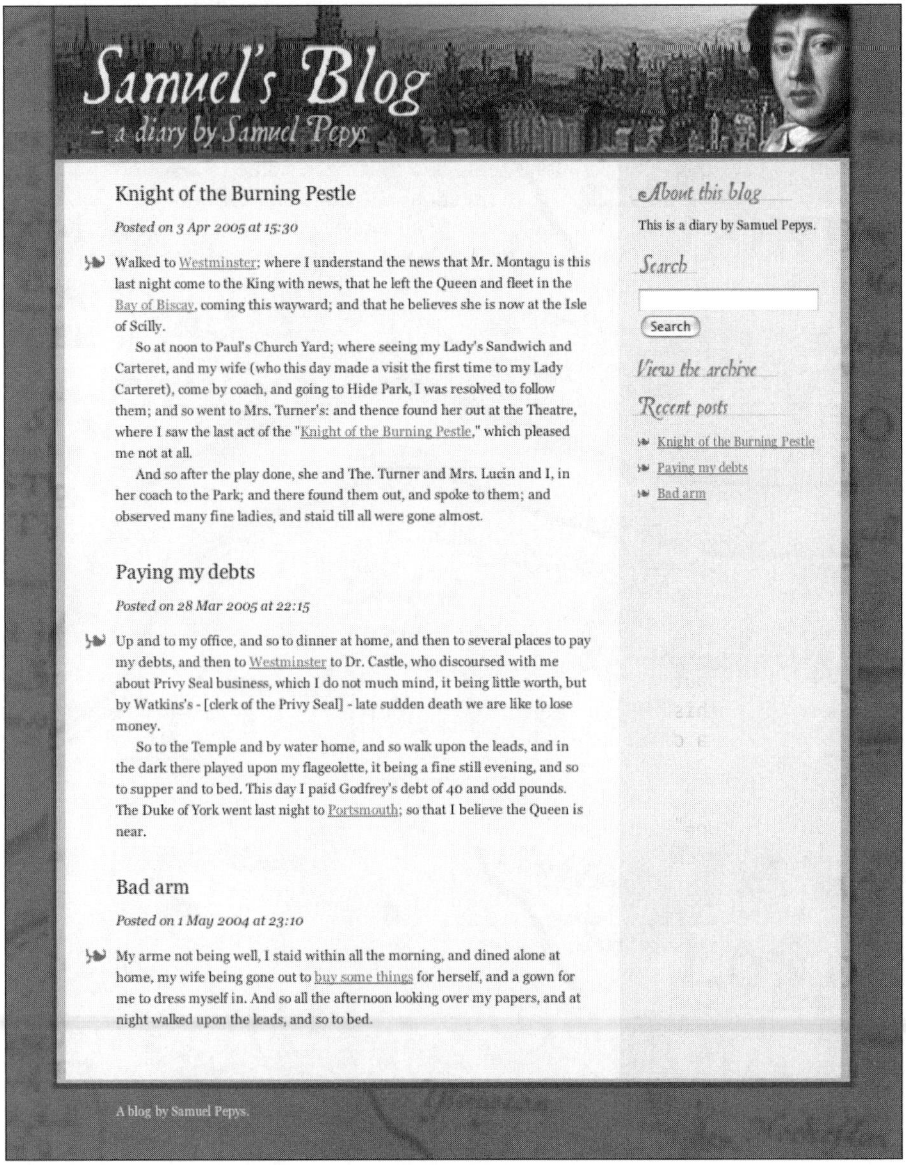

Figure 7-13. Your blog homepage as it will look

Your starting point will be to create this page as an HTML skeleton without any PHP code. Then you'll add PHP to gradually make the page dynamic. Save this HTML in the root of your blog directory as index.php:

```
<!DOCTYPE html PUBLIC "-//W3C//DTD XHTML 1.0 Strict//EN"
        "http://www.w3.org/TR/xhtml1/DTD/xhtml1-strict.dtd">
<html xmlns="http://www.w3.org/1999/xhtml" xml:lang="en" lang="en">
<head>
<meta http-equiv="content-type"
  content="text/html; charset=iso-8859-1" />
<title>Samuel's Blog</title>
<style type="text/css">
@import url(blog.css);
</style>
</head>
<body>

<div id="header">
<h1>Samuel's Blog</h1>
</div>

<!-- this is the main part of the page -->
<div id="maincontent">

<div id="posts">
<!-- the five most recent posts will go here -->
</div>

<div id="sidebar">
<div id="about">
<h3>About this</h3>
<p>This is a diary by Samuel Pepys.</p>
</div>

<form action="search.php" method="get">
<h3 id="search">Search</h3>
<p>
<input type="text" name="q" value="" />
<input type="submit" value="Search" />
</p>
</form>
<h3 id="viewarchive"><a href="archive.php">View the Archive</a></h3>

<div id="recent">
<h3>Recent posts</h3>
<!-- a list of recent post titles will go here -->
</div>

</div>
```

7

```
<!-- sidebar ends -->

</div>
<!-- maincontent ends -->

<div id="footer">
<p>A blog by Samuel Pepys.</p>
</div>

</body>
</html>
```

The stylesheet used for the layout and presentation of this page should be saved in the root of your blog directory as blog.css:

```
/* Layout */

BODY {
  margin: 0;
  padding: 0;
}

#maincontent, #header, #footer {
  width:714px;
  margin: 0 auto;
}

#header {
  height: 142px;
}

#footer {
  padding: 10px 0 3em 0;
}

#maincontent {
  height: 1%;
  overflow: auto;
  padding-bottom: 3em;
}

#posts {
  width: 479px;
  float: left;
}

#sidebar {
  margin-left: 505px;
  padding-right: 25px;
```

```
}

H1 A {
  display: block;
  width: 385px;
  height: 140px;
  text-indent: -1000em;
  margin: 0;
}

/* Typography */

BODY {
  font-family: Georgia, Palatino, serif;
  font-size: 62.5%;
}

HTML>BODY {
  font-size: 10px;
}

H1, H2, H3 {
  margin: 0;
}

H2 {
  font-size: 1.7em;
  font-weight:normal;
  line-height:1em;
  padding-top: 1em;
}

H2 A {
  text-decoration:none;
}

#posts H3 {
  font-weight:normal;
  line-height:1em;
  font-size: 1.4em;
  margin-top: 1em;
}

H4 {
  font-weight:normal;
  font-style:italic;
  line-height:1em;
  font-size: 1.2em;
}
```

7

```css
.post, DL, #posts UL, #comments P, #results P {
  font-size: 1.2em;
  line-height:1.5em;
}

#comments DD P {
  font-size: 1em;
  padding left: 0;
}

DD {
  margin-left: 0;
}

#posts H2, #posts H3, #posts H4, #posts H4, .post, DL,
#posts UL, #comments P, #results P {
  padding-left: 61px;
}

.post P {
  margin-top:0;
}

HTML>BODY .post P {
  margin-bottom: 0;
}

.post P+P {
  text-indent: 1.5em;
}

.post {
  padding-bottom:1em;
}

#sidebar {
  font-size: 1.1em;
  line-height: 1.3636em;
}

#sidebar P, #sidebar UL {
  margin-left: 16px;
  padding-left: 0;
}

#sidebar LI {
  list-style: disc url(/images/ornament_bt.gif);
  margin-left: 16px;
  margin-bottom: 0.682em;
}
```

```
#sidebar H3 {
  margin:1.3636em 0 0.682em 10px;
  text-indent: -1000em;
  overflow: hidden;
}

#sidebar #viewarchive {
  text-indent: 0;
}

#viewarchive A {
  display:block;
  text-indent: -1000em;
}

#footer {
  text-indent: 61px;
  font-size: 1.1em;
}


/* Backgrounds and colours */

BODY {
  background: #583C1D repeat fixed url(/images/map_bg.jpg) center;
  color: #f4f8e4;
}

A {
  color:#6E4720;
}

H2 A {
  color: #000;
}

.post {
  background: no-repeat left 3px url(/images/ornament.gif);
}

#header {
  background: #340301 no-repeat url(/images/header.jpg);
  color: #fff;
}

#footer {
  background: no-repeat url(/images/footer.jpg);
}
```

7

```
#maincontent {
  background: #f4f8e4 repeat-y fixed url(/images/content_bg.jpg) center
98px;
  color: #000;
}

#about H3 {
  background: no repeat url(/images/h_about.gif);
  width: 141px;
  height: 19px;
}

#search {
  background: no-repeat url(/images/h_search.gif);
  width: 57px;
  height: 16px;
}

#recent H3 {
  background: no-repeat url(/images/h_recent.gif);
  width: 135px;
  height: 20px;
}

#viewarchive {
  background: no-repeat url(/images/h_viewarchive.gif);
  width: 128px;
  height: 15px;
}

#addcomment H3 {
  background: no-repeat url(/images/h_addcomment.gif);
  width: 122px;
  height: 16px;
}

/* Forms */
INPUT, TEXTAREA {
  border-width: 1px;
}

INPUT[type=text], TEXTAREA {
  width: 158px;
}

INPUT, TEXTAREA {
  font-size:1em;
}
```

The stylesheet and all the accompanying background images are available for download from the book website at www.friendsofed.com/. I won't explain the stylesheet in this chapter because the previous chapters cover many of the techniques involved. The images should be saved to a new directory called images in your blog directory. All the screenshots from now assume that you have the stylesheet and images in place in your blog directory, so if you are online I suggest you download them now.

Pulling in the posts

You have already been introduced to all the code required to show your recent posts on one page. This was covered when you created the index page for your CMS, so I won't explain much here; instead, you can just insert it straight into your blog homepage: add this code before the DOCTYPE in the index.php file you just created:

```php
<?php
// Open connection to database
include("db_connect.php");

// Select 5 most recent posts
$sql = "SELECT post_id, title, post, DATE_FORMAT(postdate, '%e %b %Y ➥
 at %H:%i') AS dateattime FROM posts ➥
 ORDER BY postdate DESC LIMIT 5";
$result = mysql_query($sql);
$myposts = mysql_fetch_array($result);
?>
```

As before, this code starts by opening a connection to the database. Then this SELECT statement is used to query the database:

```
SELECT post_id, title, post, DATE_FORMAT(postdate, '%e %b %Y ➥
 at %H:%i') AS dateattime FROM posts ➥
 ORDER BY postdate DESC LIMIT 5
```

It is almost the same as before; the only addition is to select the post field and the LIMIT 5 so that only the five most recent blogs are pulled from the database.

Now you need to display the posts in your page. Replace the comment <!-- the five most recent posts will go here --> with this code:

```php
<?php
if($myposts) {
  do {
    $post_id = $myposts["post_id"];
    $title = $myposts["title"];
    $post = format($myposts["post"]);
    $dateattime = $myposts["dateattime"];
    echo "<h2 id='post$post_id'><a href='post.php?post_id=$post_id'
rel='bookmark'> ➥
 $title</a></h2>\n";
    echo "<h4>Posted on $dateattime</h4>\n";
    echo "<div class='post'>$post</div>";
```

7

```
    } while ($myposts = mysql_fetch_array($result));
  } else {
    echo "<p>I haven't posted to my blog yet.</p>";
  }
  ?>
```

This code steps through the MySQL array as in the CMS blog list page, but this time I'm using different HTML to present the post details. The post itself is unformatted so you can (indeed, you should) add all the HTML you require (paragraphs, links, emphasis, and so on) when you enter the post in the CMS. Later on, I will show you how you can automate some of that process so paragraph tags are automatically generated.

Next to insert is code that will enable the posts summary in the sidebar. Replace the comment <!-- a list of recent post titles will go here --> with this code:

```
<?php
mysql_data_seek($result, 0);
$myposts = mysql_fetch_array($result);

if($myposts) {
  echo "<ul>\n";
  do {
    $post_id = $myposts["post_id"];
    $title = $myposts["title"];
  echo "<li><a href='post.php?post_id=$post_id' rel='bookmark'> ➥
$title</a></li>\n";
  } while ($myposts = mysql_fetch_array($result));
  echo "</ul>";
}
?>
```

As you might expect, this code is almost the same, but there is one crucial addition:

```
mysql_data_seek($result, 0);
$myposts = mysql_fetch_array($result);
```

These initial two lines reset the internal row pointer of the MySQL result to the beginning (row 0), so the do-while loop can start at the first post again. This saves the server from unnecessarily querying the database a second time.

Automatically formatting posts

As I said earlier, you will need to add the required HTML to all your blog posts so they are formatted with paragraphs, links, and so on. I'm sure you'd agree that it would be much easier if line breaks and paragraph tags were automatically added to your posts, so now I'll show you a quick function to will do just that:

```
<?php
function format($text) {
  $text = "<p>" . $text . "</p>";
  $search = array("\r", "\n\n", "\n");
```

```
    $replace = array("","</p><p>", "<br />");
    $text = stripslashes($text);
    $text = str_replace($search, $replace, $text);
    return $text;
}
?>
```

The user-defined format function makes use of the PHP str_replace search and replace function to replace line breaks in your posts with <br /> tags, and two line breaks in a row with paragraph tags. Because this function will be useful throughout your blog, save it to your blog root directory in a file called functions.php.

Stepping through the script:

```
function format($text) {
```

The format function accepts an argument called $text, which will be the unformatted post pulled from the database:

```
$text  = "<p>" . $text . "</p>";
$text = stripslashes($text);
```

First, the whole post text is wrapped inside paragraph tags and then any slashes are removed:

```
$search = array("\r", "\n\n", "\n");
$replace = array("","</p><p>", "<br />");
```

$search is an array (think of it as a list) of the text we need to replace in the post. $replace is the corresponding array of text that will take its place. The first substitution performed is to strip out all carriage return characters, as line breaks on Windows machines are represented by two characters: a carriage return (\r) followed by a new line character (\n). Then double-line breaks are replaced with a closing and opening paragraph tag to create a new paragraph. The final substitution is to replace any remaining line breaks with <br /> tags.

```
$text = str_replace($search, $replace, $text);
return $text;
```

Finally, the search and replace arrays are passed along with the text to the str_replace function to perform the actual substitution and the resulting text is returned to wherever the function was called.

Now call the functions.php include in your blog homepage by adding include ("functions.php"); to the PHP script just after the opening <?php delimiter at the very top of your index.php page. Finally, you can call the format function to format your blog post by making this change to your do-while loop:

```
$post = format($myposts["post"]);
```

Headers, footers, and other reusable elements

In the previous section, you created an include file called functions.php that can be reused in any page of your blog. It is useful to put all repeated parts of your code into includes so they can be easily updated if site-wide changes are required further down the line. The header, footer, and search form used in the index.php page will be reused throughout the site, so create the following include files.

First, save this header code as header.php:

```
<div id="header">
<h1>Samuel's Blog</h1>
</div>
```

And replace this code in index.php with `<?php include("header.php"); ?>`. Now do the same with the footer by creating footer.php from this code:

```
<div id="header">
<h1><a href="index.php">Samuel's Blog</a></h1>
</div>
```

And create searchform.php from this code:

```
<form action="search.php" method="get">
<h3 id="search">Search</h3>
<p>
<input type="text" name="q" value="" />
<input type="submit" value="Search" />
</p>
</form>
<h3 id="viewarchive"><a href="archive.php">View the Archive</a></h3>
```

After you replace the footer and search code in your index.php file, you should end up with this complete source listing:

```
<?php
include("functions.php");

// Open connection to database
include("db_connect.php");

// Select 5 most recent posts
$sql = "SELECT post_id, title, post, DATE_FORMAT(postdate, '%e %b %Y ➥
 at %H:%i') AS dateattime FROM posts ➥
 ORDER BY postdate DESC LIMIT 5";
$result = mysql_query($sql);
$myposts = mysql_fetch_array($result);
?>

<!DOCTYPE html PUBLIC "-//W3C//DTD XHTML 1.0 Strict//EN"
        "http://www.w3.org/TR/xhtml1/DTD/xhtml1-strict.dtd">
```

```
<html xmlns="http://www.w3.org/1999/xhtml" xml:lang="en" lang="en">
<head>
<meta http-equiv="content-type"
  content="text/html; charset=iso-8859-1" />
<title>Samuel's Blog</title>
<style type="text/css">
@import url(blog.css);
</style>
</head>
<body>

<?php include("header.php"); ?>

<!-- this is the main part of the page -->
<div id="maincontent">

<div id="posts">
<?php
if($myposts) {
  do {
    $post_id = $myposts["post_id"];
    $title = $myposts["title"];
    $post = format($myposts["post"]);
    $dateattime = $myposts["dateattime"];
    echo "<h2 id='post$post_id'><a href='post.php?post_id=$post_id'
rel='bookmark'> ➥
 $title</a></h2>\n";
    echo "<h4>Posted on $dateattime</h4>\n";
    echo "<div class='post'>$post</div>";
  } while ($myposts = mysql_fetch_array($result));
} else {
  echo "<p>I haven't posted to my blog yet.</p>";
}
?>
</div>

<div id="sidebar">
<div id="about">
<h3>About this</h3>
<p>This is a diary by Samuel Pepys.</p>
</div>

<?php include("searchform.php"); ?>

<div id="recent">
<h3>Recent posts</h3>
<?php
mysql_data_seek($result, 0);
$myposts = mysql_fetch_array($result);
```

```
        if($myposts) {
          echo "<ul>\n";
          do {
            $post_id = $myposts["post_id"];
            $title = $myposts["title"];
          echo "<li><a href='post.php?post_id=$post_id' rel='bookmark'> ➡
        $title</a></li>\n";
          } while ($myposts = mysql_fetch_array($result));
          echo "</ul>";
        }
        ?>
        </div>

        </div>
        <!-- sidebar ends -->

        </div>
        <!-- maincontent ends -->
        <?php include("footer.php"); ?>
        </body>
        </html>
```

Creating a post page

In a blog, every post should have its own page. To enable this you will combine code from the blog homepage (index.php) and the CMS edit post page (addpost.php). Save this code as post.php in the root of your blog directory:

```
<?php
// Open connection to database
include("db_connect.php");

// Get post_id from query string
$post_id = (isset($_REQUEST["post_id"]))?$_REQUEST["post_id"]:"";

// If post_id is a number get post from database
if (preg_match("/^[0-9]+$/", $post_id)) {
  $sql = "SELECT post_id, title, post, DATE_FORMAT(postdate, ➡
  '%e %b %Y at %H:%i') AS dateattime FROM posts
  WHERE post_id=$post_id LIMIT 1";
  $result = mysql_query($sql);
  $myposts = mysql_fetch_array($result);
}

include("functions.php");
?>
```

```
<!DOCTYPE html PUBLIC "-//W3C//DTD XHTML 1.0 Strict//EN"
        "http://www.w3.org/TR/xhtml1/DTD/xhtml1-strict.dtd">
<html xmlns="http://www.w3.org/1999/xhtml" xml:lang="en" lang="en">
<head>
<meta http-equiv="content-type"
  content="text/html; charset=iso-8859-1" />
<title>Samuel's Blog</title>
<style type="text/css">
@import url(blog.css);
</style>
</head>
<body>

<?php include("header.php"); ?>

<!-- this is the main part of the page -->
<div id="maincontent">

<div id="posts">
<?php
if($myposts) {
  do {
    $post_id = $myposts["post_id"];
    $title = $myposts["title"];
    $post = format($myposts["post"]);
    $dateattime = $myposts["dateattime"];
    echo "<h2>$title</h2>\n";
    echo "<h4>Posted on $dateattime</h4>\n";
    echo "<div class='post'>\n $post \n</div>";
  } while ($myposts = mysql_fetch_array($result));
} else {
  echo "<p>There is no post matching a post_id of $post_id.</p>";
}
?>
</div>

<div id="sidebar">

<?php include("searchform.php"); ?>

</div>
<!-- sidebar ends -->

</div>
<!-- maincontent ends -->
<?php include("footer.php"); ?></body>
</html>
```

7

As with the edit post page in your CMS, the blog post page is called with a post_id in the query string so it knows which blog post to display. The blog homepage (index.php) you just created links to the post page like this: post.php?post_id=n where *n* is the post_id of a post. Clicking a link on your homepage should take you to a blog post that looks something like Figure 7-14 (if you haven't already, make sure you have added some blog posts using your CMS).

Figure 7-14. The post page for your first blog post

At this point, you could have a little play by adding a few new posts through your CMS and see how they appear on the homepage and on their individual post pages.

Adding comments

One of the great attractions of blogging is allowing your readers to comment on what you have written. I'll now show you how to add commenting to your blog engine.

Each comment will be stored in the database, so first you need to create a table in which to store the comments. Open up PHPMyAdmin in your browser. Select the database blog in the left side and then click the Structure tab. In the Create new table on database blog area, type comments into the Name input box and 7 into the Number of fields input box, as shown in Figure 7-15, then click Go.

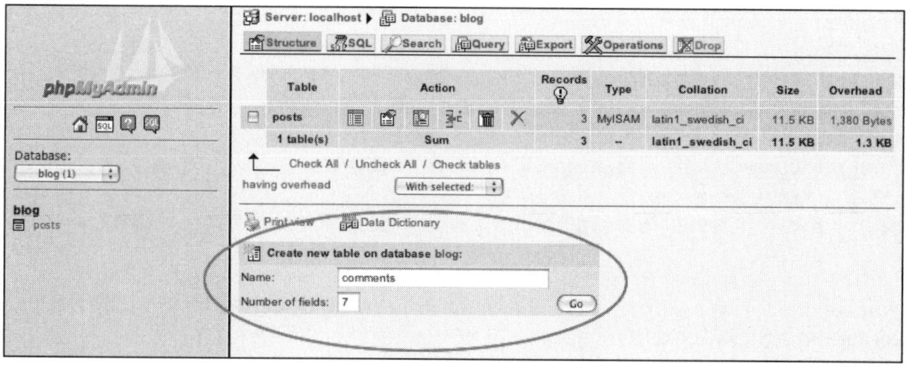

Figure 7-15. Creating a new table

On the next screen, input the table definition for each field, as shown in Figure 7-16. Note that for the comment_id field you should also select auto_increment in the Extra column and click the primary column. This procedure ensures that each new comment automatically gets its own unique id number.

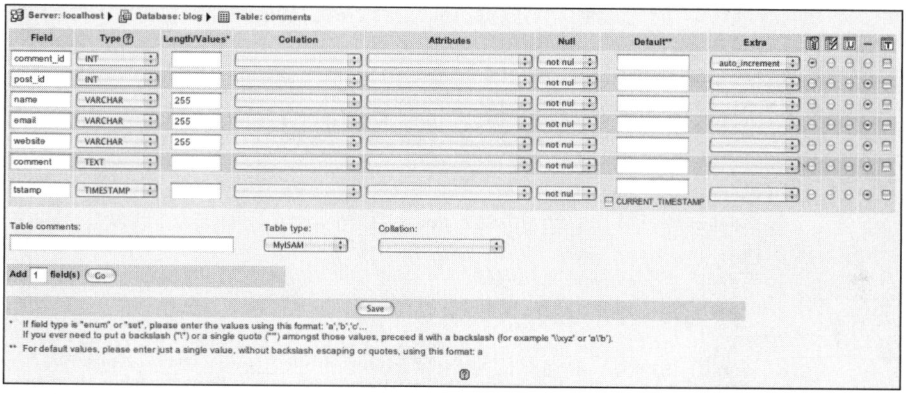

Figure 7-16. Creating the comments table in phpMyAdmin

Click Save and the table should be created—you will see comments added to the left column.

Now that you have a database table in which to store comments, you can add a form to collect comments and a script to insert to those comments into the database. Add this form to the sidebar in post.php, just after the searchform include:

```
<form action="<?=$_SERVER["PHP_SELF"]?>" method="post">
<input type="hidden" name="post_id" value="<?=$post_id ?>" />
<input type="hidden" name="posttitle" value="<?=$title ?>" />
<h3>Add a comment</h3>
<?php
if (isset($message)) {
  echo "<p class='message'>".$_POST["message"]."</p>";
```

313

```
    }
    ?>
    <p>Name: <input name="name" type="text" /></p>
    <p>Email: <input name="email" type="text" /></p>
    <p>Website: <input name="website" type="text" /></p>
    <p>Comment: <textarea name="comment" cols="25" rows="15">
      </textarea></p>
    <p><input type-"submit" name="postcomment" value="Post comment" /></p>
    </form>
```

Now add the following script to the end of the PHP code (just before the closing ?> delimiter) at the top of your document:

```
    // If comment has been submitted and post exists
      then add comment to database
    if (isset($_POST["postcomment"]) != "") {
    $posttitle = addslashes(trim(strip_tags($_POST["posttitle"])));
    $name = addslashes(trim(strip_tags($_POST["name"])));
    $email = addslashes(trim(strip_tags($_POST["email"])));
    $website = addslashes(trim(strip_tags($_POST["website"])));
    $comment = addslashes(trim(strip_tags($_POST["comment"])));

    $sql = "INSERT INTO comments
      (post_id,name,email,website,comment)
      VALUES ('$post_id', '$name', '$email', '$website', '$comment')";
    $result2 = mysql_query($sql);
    if (!$result2) {
      $message = "Failed to insert comment.";
    } else {
      $message = "Comment added.";
      $comment_id = mysql_insert_id();

      // Send yourself an email when a comment is successfully added
      $emailsubject = "Comment added to: ".$posttitle;

      $emailbody = "Comment on '".$posttitle."'"."\r\n"
        ."http://www.your-domain-name.com/post.php?post_id=".$post_id ➥
    ."#c".$comment_id."\r\n\r\n"
        .$comment."\r\n\r\n"
        .$name." (".$website.")\r\n\r\n";
      $emailbody = stripslashes($emailbody);

      $emailheader = "From: ".$name." <".$email.">\r\n"."Reply-To: " ➥
    .$email;

      mail("you@your-domain-name.com", $emailsubject, $emailbody, ➥
    $emailheader);
```

```
        // direct to post page to eliminate repeat posts
        header("Location: post.php?post_id=$post_id&message=$message");
    }
}
```

This code inserts a new comment into the database and e-mails you when a new comment is added. Stepping through the code:

```
if (isset($_POST["postcomment"]) != "") {
```

If the Post comment button has been pressed, the comment can be added to the database.

```
$posttitle = addslashes(trim(strip_tags($_POST["posttitle"])));
$name = addslashes(trim(strip_tags($_POST["name"])));
$email = addslashes(trim(strip_tags($_POST["email"])));
$website = addslashes(trim(strip_tags($_POST["website"])));
$comment = addslashes(trim(strip_tags($_POST["comment"])));
```

The post title (sent as a hidden field), commenter's name, e-mail address, website, and comment are all gathered from the query string and are tidied up by nesting three functions. Firstly strip_tags eliminates any HTML and PHP from the comment input, then trim removes white space (such as spaces and line breaks) from either end of the input, and finally addslashes ensures the text is formatted suitably for database entry.

```
$sql = "INSERT INTO comments
    (post_id,name,email,website,comment)
    VALUES ('$post_id', '$name', '$email', '$website', '$comment')";
$result2 = mysql_query($sql);
if (!$result2) {
    $message = "Failed to insert comment.";
} else {
    $message = "Comment added.";
```

The database insert is performed. Note that the post_id is inserted with the comment so in future the blogging engine will know which comments go with which posts.

```
$comment_id = mysql_insert_id();
```

As when inserting a new post, the comment_id for a new comment is automatically generated by MySQL. The latest id can be retrieved using the mysql_insert_id function.

Now comes part of the script which e-mails yourself the comment so you know as soon as someone comments on your blog. PHP uses the mail function to send e-mail. An e-mail is made up of 4 four parts: the to address, the subject, the body, and the headers (which contain additional information such as the sender's details and cc'd addresses). The mail function works like this:

```
mail(to address, subject, body, headers)
```

7

315

The subject, body, and headers are constructed using the following code:

```
$emailsubject = "Comment added to: ".$posttitle;

$emailbody = "Comment on '".$posttitle."'"."\r\n"
 ."http://www.your-domain-name.com/post.php?post_id=".$post_id Â
 ."#c".$comment_id."\r\n\r\n"
 .$comment."\r\n\r\n"
 .$name." (".$website.")\r\n\r\n";
$emailbody = stripslashes($emailbody);

$emailheader = "From: ".$name." <".$email.">\r\n"."Reply-To: ".$email;

@mail("you@your-domain-name.com", $emailsubject, $emailbody, Â
 $emailheader);
```

Remember to replace www.your-domain-name.com with your website domain, and you@your-domain-name.com with your e-mail address. Note also the @ in front of the mail function. This prevents any errors being written to the screen if for some reason the mail function fails.

And the final line of the comment insert script is as follows:

```
header("Location: post.php?post_id=$post_id&message=$message");
```

The header function creates an HTTP header, which is essentially an instruction to the web server. In this case, the instruction is to go to the post page with a success message appended to the query string. This step prevents readers from submitting their comment twice if they click reload in their browser.

So now readers can add comments to your posts, and you are notified each time that happens. The final step is to show those comments in your blog. Let's look at the script that will pull the comments from the database. Add this script to the end of PHP code at the top of post.php:

```
if ($myposts) {
  $sql = "SELECT comment_id, name, website, comment FROM comments ➡
WHERE post_id = $post_id";
  $result3 = mysql_query($sql);
  $mycomments = mysql_fetch_array($result3);
}
```

If the post exists, the comments for this post are pulled from the database. Next you can display them on the page by inserting this code into the posts div, just after the closing ?> delimiter in your post loop:

```
<div id="comments">
<h2>Comments</h2>
<?php
```

```
if($mycomments) {
  echo "<dl>";
  do {
    $comment_id = $mycomments["comment_id"];
    $name = $mycomments["name"];
    $website = $mycomments["website"];
    $comment = format($mycomments["comment"]);
    if ($website != "") {
      echo "<dt><a href='$website'>$name</a> wrote:</dt>\n";
    } else {
      echo "<dt>$name wrote:</dt>\n";
    }
    echo "<dd>$comment</dd>\n";
  } while ($mycomments = mysql_fetch_array($result3));
  echo "</dl>";
} else {
  echo "<p>There are no comments yet.</p>";
}
?>
</div>
```

This code should be quite familiar to you by now. First, it checks that some comments have been found in the database and then uses a do-while loop to display them on the screen, adding a link to the commenter's name if one was supplied. Notice also that I am using the format function to format the comment.

Figure 7-17 shows what your post page should like after a comment has been added.

Figure 7-17. Post page with a comment added

Creating an archive

For your readers to be able to peruse what you wrote in the past, you will need an archive of blog posts. The archive page I will show you works in two ways. In the first instance, if you pass a valid year and month in the query string (such as archive. php?year=2005&month=2), the archive page will show titles and summaries for the posts you made in that month, as shown in Figure 7-18.

Figure 7-18. An archive page for a single month

Otherwise, the archive page will link to the months in which you have posted, as shown in Figure 7-19.

Figure 7-19. The overall archive page

Here is the entire code for the archive page. Save it as `archive.php` in your root directory:

```php
<?php
// Open connection to database
include("db_connect.php");

$month = (isset($_REQUEST["month"]))?$_REQUEST["month"]:"";
$year = (isset($_REQUEST["year"]))?$_REQUEST["year"]:"";

if (preg_match("/^[0-9][0-9][0-9][0-9]$/", $year) AND ➡
preg_match("/^[0-9]?[0-9]$/", $month)) {
  // Select posts for this month
  $sql = "SELECT post_id, title, summary, DATE_FORMAT(postdate, '%e %b
%Y at %H:%i') ➡
AS dateattime FROM posts ➡
WHERE MONTH(postdate) = $month AND YEAR(postdate) = $year";
  $result = mysql_query($sql);
  $myposts = mysql_fetch_array($result);
  if ($myposts) {
    $showbymonth = true;
    $text = strtotime("$month/1/$year");
    $thismonth = date("F Y", $text);
  }
}

if (!isset($showbymonth)) {
  $showbymonth = false;
// Select posts grouped by month and year
  $sql = "SELECT DATE_FORMAT(postdate, '%M %Y') AS monthyear, ➡
MONTH(postdate) AS month, YEAR(postdate) AS year, count(*) AS count ➡
FROM posts  GROUP BY monthyear ➡
 ORDER BY year, month";
  $result = mysql_query($sql);
  $myposts = mysql_fetch_array($result);
}

include("functions.php");
?>

<!DOCTYPE html PUBLIC "-//W3C//DTD XHTML 1.0 Strict//EN"
        "http://www.w3.org/TR/xhtml1/DTD/xhtml1-strict.dtd">
<html xmlns="http://www.w3.org/1999/xhtml" xml:lang="en" lang="en">
<head>
<meta http-equiv="content-type"
  content="text/html; charset=iso-8859-1" />
<title><?php if(isset($thismonth)) echo $thismonth; ?>
  Archive | Samuel's Blog</title>
<style type="text/css">
@import url(blog.css);
```

7

319

```
        </style>
        </head>
        <body>

        <?php include("header.php"); ?>

        <!-- this is the main part of the page -->
        <div id="maincontent">

        <div id="posts">
        <h2><?php if(isset($thismonth)) echo $thismonth; ?> Archive</h2>

        <?php
        switch ($showbymonth) {


        case true:
        if($myposts) {
          echo "<dl>\n";
          do {
            $post_id = $myposts["post_id"];
            $title = $myposts["title"];
            $summary = $myposts["summary"];
          echo "<dt><a href='post.php?post_id=$post_id' rel='bookmark'> ➡
        $title</a></dt>\n";
          echo "<dd>$summary</dd>\n";
          } while ($myposts = mysql_fetch_array($result));
          echo "</dl>";
        }
        break;

        case false:
        $previousyear = "";
        if($myposts) {
          do {
            $year = $myposts["year"];
            $month = $myposts["month"];
            $monthyear = $myposts["monthyear"];
            $count = $myposts["count"];
            if ($year != $previousyear) {
              if ($previousyear != "") {
                echo "</ul>\n";
              }
              echo "<h3>$year</h3>";
            echo "<ul>\n";
            $previousyear = $year;
            }
            $plural = ($count==1) ? "" : "s";
```

```
      echo "<li><a href='archive.php?year=$year&amp;month=$month'> ➥
    $monthyear</a> ($count post$plural)</li>\n";
      } while ($myposts = mysql_fetch_array($result));
      echo "</ul>";
   }
      break;
   }
   ?>
   </div>

   <div id="sidebar">

   <?php include("searchform.php"); ?>

   </div>
   <!-- sidebar ends -->

   </div>
   <!-- maincontent ends -->
   <?php include("footer.php"); ?>
   </body>
   </html>
```

7

Stepping through the code:

```
<?php
// Open connection to database
include("db_connect.php");

$month = (isset($_REQUEST["month"]))?$_REQUEST["month"]:"";
$year = (isset($_REQUEST["year"]))?$_REQUEST["year"]:"";
```

A database connection is opened as usual, and the query string contents are extracted:

```
if (preg_match("/^[0-9][0-9][0-9][0-9]$/", $year) AND ➥
 preg_match("/^[0-9]?[0-9]$/", $month)) {
```

Here I use two regular expressions to check that the year (exactly four numbers long) and the month (either one or two numbers long) look roughly correct:

```
// Select posts for this month
$sql = "SELECT post_id, title, summary, DATE_FORMAT(postdate, ➥
'%e %b %Y at %H:%i') AS dateattime FROM posts WHERE MONTH ➥
(postdate) = $month
 AND YEAR(postdate) = $year";
  $result = mysql_query($sql);
  $myposts = mysql_fetch_array($result);
```

If the year and month look correct, the posts are retrieved. These posts are identified by using the MONTH and YEAR MySQL functions to match the postdate to the year and month specified in the query string:

```
if ($myposts) {
   $showbymonth = true;
   $text = strtotime("$month/1/$year");
   $thismonth = date("F Y", $text);
 }
}
```

If the database query returns a result (that is, it finds one or more posts for that month), the $showbymonth flag is set to true so the page knows it is showing a month archive. Then the strtotime and date functions are combined to convert the numeric month and year into more readable text such as April 2005. The strtotime function takes a string that looks like a date and tries to turn it into a timestamp that can be processed by PHP. The date function takes a timestamp and formats it into text (much like the MySQL date_format function mentioned earlier in the chapter).

```
if (!isset($showbymonth)) {
   $showbymonth = false;
   // Select posts grouped by month and year
   $sql = "SELECT DATE_FORMAT(postdate, '%M %Y') AS monthyear, ➡
   MONTH(postdate) AS month, YEAR(postdate) AS year, count(*) AS count ➡
   FROM posts  GROUP BY monthyear ➡
   ORDER BY year, month";
   $result = mysql_query($sql);
   $myposts = mysql_fetch_array($result);
}
```

If the $showbymonth flag has not been set (because no posts were found for the specified month, or if no valid month or year were specified), the flag is set to false and the database is queried for all posts. There are a number of new concepts introduced in this SQL query, so I will step through it bit by bit:

```
SELECT DATE_FORMAT(postdate, '%M %Y') AS monthyear,
```

The postdate for each post is formatted as month and year; for example, April 2005.

```
MONTH(postdate) AS month, YEAR(postdate) AS year,
```

The postdate is also formatted as a month and a year separately. These values will be used to construct a link to the archive.

```
count(*) AS count FROM posts  GROUP BY monthyear
```

GROUP BY monthyear is used to combine all the posts that have the same value of monthyear; for example, all the posts made in April 2005. The count(*) function can then be used to output the number of posts that have been grouped together for that value of monthyear; in other words, the number of posts made in April 2005.

```
ORDER BY year, month
```

The results are finally ordered by year and then month.

Skipping through the code to the posts div:

```
<div id="posts">
<h2><?php if(isset($thismonth)) echo $thismonth; ?> Archive</h2>
```

The textual value of the month and year is inserted in the heading.

```
<?php
switch ($showbymonth) {
```

A switch is introduced so different code can be run depending on the value of the showbymonth flag.

```
case true:
if($myposts) {
  echo "<dl>\n";
  do {
    $post_id = $myposts["post_id"];
    $title = $myposts["title"];
    $summary = $myposts["summary"];
  echo "<dt><a href='post.php?post_id=$post_id' rel='bookmark'> ➡
$title</a></dt>\n";
  echo "<dd>$summary</dd>\n";
  } while ($myposts = mysql_fetch_array($result));
  echo "</dl>";
}
break;
```

If showbymonth is true, the familiar do-while loop is executed to display a list of posts for the selected month.

```
case false:
$previousyear = "";
if($myposts) {
  do {
    $year = $myposts["year"];
    $month = $myposts["month"];
    $monthyear = $myposts["monthyear"];
    $count = $myposts["count"];
    if ($year != $previousyear) {
      if ($previousyear != "") {
        echo "</ul>\n";
      }
      echo "<h3>$year</h3>";
    echo "<ul>\n";
    $previousyear = $year;
    }
```

If showbymonth is false, another do-while loop is started. The desired output for the loop is a heading for the year, followed by a list of months in that year:

```
<h3>2004</h3>
<ul>
<li><a href='archive.php?year=2004&amp;month=11'>
  November 2004</a> (1 post)</li>
<li><a href='archive.php?year=2004&amp;month=12'>
  December 2004</a> (4 posts)</li>
</ul>
<h3>2005</h3><ul>
<li><a href='archive.php?year=2005&amp;month=1'>
  January 2005</a> (9 posts)</li>
<li><a href='archive.php?year=2005&amp;month=2'>
  February 2005</a> (12 posts)</li>
</ul>
```

So the headings are not repeated with every row, the normal loop is preceded by some logic that determines whether there has been a change of year; if so, the list is closed, and a new heading is written.

```
    $plural = ($count==1) ? "" : "s";
    echo "<li><a href='archive.php?year=$year&amp;month=$month'> ➡
$monthyear</a> ($count post$plural)</li>\n";
    } while ($myposts = mysql_fetch_array($result));
    echo "</ul>";
}
  break;
}
?>
</div>
```

After the year headings have been checked for, the month is written with a link back to the archive page so that the posts for that month can be viewed on a page. Note the shorthand logic used to determine whether the word *post* should be singular or plural, depending on the number of posts for that month. The following line:

```
$plural = ($count==1) ? "" : "s";
```

could also have been written as follows:

```
if ($count==1) {
  $plural = "";
} else {
  $plural = "s";
}
```

Making your blog searchable

You no doubt have noticed the search form repeated throughout your blog. Thanks to MySQL, adding search capabilities to your blog is easy. All you need to do is add a search index to your posts table. To do this, open up phpMyAdmin in your browser, select the blog database, and click the posts link in the left frame. In the Indexes box (halfway down the screen), type 3 in the Create an index on *n* columns box and click Go (see Figure 7-20).

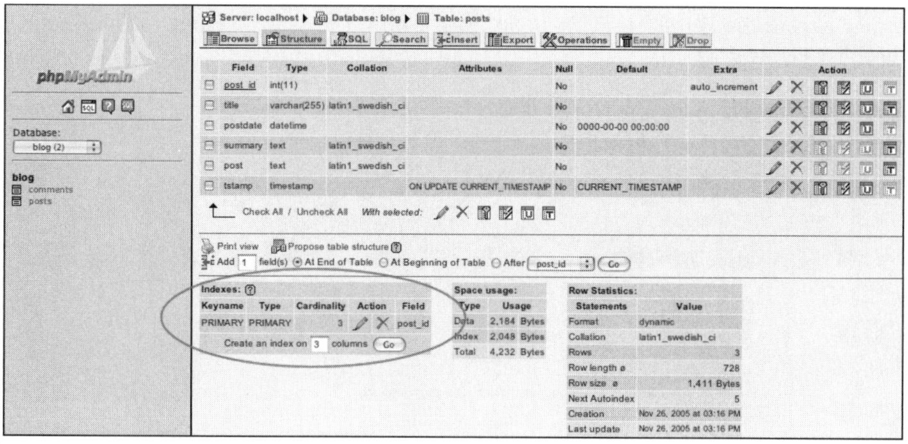

Figure 7-20. Creating an index in PHPMyAdmin

Now fill out the form as shown in Figure 7-21 and click Save.

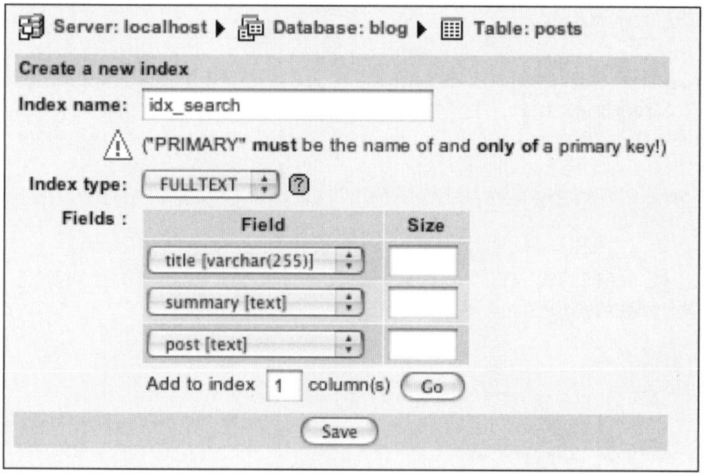

Figure 7-21. Adding a fulltext index to the posts table in phpMyAdmin

What you have just done is added a Fulltext index to the posts table on the title, summary, and post fields. Now when the database text is searched (I'll show you how in the next section), it will search all three fields, giving priority to the title, then the summary, then the post. So if you search for the word "donkey", and one of your posts is titled "Donkey Rides" while another of your posts just has the word "donkey" somewhere in the post, "Donkey Rides" will be returned first in the search results because title is deemed to be more important than the post.

And now to create the search results page, which will show the matching blog posts when someone uses the search form on any of your pages. The search results will look something like Figure 7-22.

Figure 7-22. Search results page

Here is the search results code in its entirety. Copy it into a new document and save it to your root directory as search.php.

```php
<?php
// Open connection to database
include("db_connect.php");

$q = (isset($_REQUEST["q"]))?$_REQUEST["q"]:"";
$q = trim(strip_tags($q));

if ($q != "") {
  // Select posts grouped by month and year
$sql = "SELECT post_id, title, summary, DATE_FORMAT(postdate, ➥
'%e %b %Y at %H:%i') ➥
 AS dateattime FROM posts WHERE ➥
 MATCH (title,summary,post) AGAINST ('$q') LIMIT 50";
  $result = mysql_query($sql);
  $myposts = mysql_fetch_array($result);
}
```

```php
// format search for HTML display
$q = stripslashes(htmlentities($q));

include("functions.php");
?>

<!DOCTYPE html PUBLIC "-//W3C//DTD XHTML 1.0 Strict//EN"
        "http://www.w3.org/TR/xhtml1/DTD/xhtml1-strict.dtd">
<html xmlns="http://www.w3.org/1999/xhtml" xml:lang="en" lang="en">
<head>
<meta http-equiv="content-type"
  content="text/html; charset=iso-8859-1" />
<title>Search | Samuel's Blog</title>
<style type="text/css">
@import url(blog.css);
</style>
</head>
<body>

<?php include("header.php"); ?>

<!-- this is the main part of the page -->
<div id="maincontent">

<div id="posts">
<h2>Search Results</h2>
<div id="results">
<?php
if($myposts) {
  $numresults = mysql_num_rows($result);
  $plural1 = ($numresults==1) ? "is" : "are";
  $plural2 = ($numresults==1) ? "" : "s";
  echo "<p>There $plural1 <em>$numresults</em> post$plural2 ➥
matching your search for <cite>$q</cite>.</p>";
  echo "<dl>\n";
  do {
    $post_id = $myposts["post_id"];
    $title = $myposts["title"];
    $summary = $myposts["summary"];
  echo "<dt><a href='post.php?post_id=$post_id'>$title</a></dt>\n";
  echo "<dd>$summary</dd>\n";
  } while ($myposts = mysql_fetch_array($result));
  echo "</dl>";
} else {
  echo "<p>There were no posts matching your search for ➥
 <cite>$q</cite>.</p>";
}
?>
</div>

</div>
```

```
<div id="sidebar">
<?php include("searchform.php"); ?>
</div>
<!-- sidebar ends -->

</div>
<!-- maincontent ends -->
<?php include("footer.php"); ?>
</body>
</html>
```

The code should be somewhat familiar by now, with a database query first, followed by a do-while loop in the body of your page. However the SELECT statement in the database query warrants further investigation:

```
SELECT post_id, title, summary, DATE_FORMAT(postdate, '%e %b %Y ➡
at %H:%i') ➡
 AS dateattime FROM posts WHERE ➡
MATCH (title,summary,post) AGAINST ('$q') LIMIT 50
```

MySQL text searching is performed by combing the MATCH and AGAINST functions. The arguments passed to the MATCH function should be a comma-separated list of the columns you used to create the fulltext index, and the argument to the AGAINST function should be the search term. MySQL automatically returns the results in order of relevance.

Because you have only a few posts in your database, the fulltext searching can produce some unexpected results, particularly if you search for a word you know to be repeated in all your posts. In this instance, MySQL will deem the word as "common," and you might receive no results for the search. However, as you write more and more, the search results become increasingly accurate.

Indexing your blog database

MySQL fulltext searching is extremely quick because it uses an index. If you were trying to find a topic in a reference book, you would most likely look at the index first, rather than leafing through the book page by page. In essence, this is how database indexes work, too.

Every time you have a WHERE clause in a SELECT query you should ensure that you have an index on each field mentioned in the clause, which can increase speed by an order of magnitude or more (especially for tables with large amounts of data).

When you created the posts table, you set the Primary Key option. When this was done, an index was automatically created for the post_id field. However, some queries are being performed on fields that are not indexed: archive.php also queries the postdate field, and post.php queries the post_id field in the comments table.

To add indexes to these fields, open up phpMyAdmin in your browser, select the blog database, and click the posts link in the left frame. In the Indexes box, type 1 in the Create an index on *n* columns box and click Go. Now name the index as idx_postdate, select Index as the Index type (it is probably already selected) and select postdate as the Fields, then press Save (see Figure 7-23).

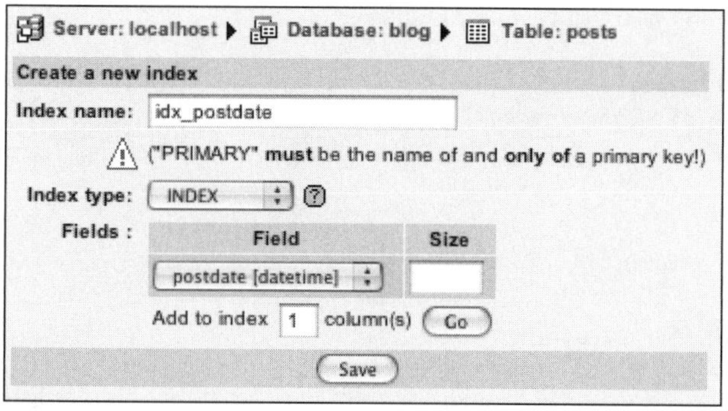

Figure 7-23. Adding an index to the postdate field in phpMyAdmin

Now do the same for the post_id field in the comments table, and your blog database will be fully optimized.

Creating an RSS feed

The final thing every blog should have is an RSS feed, which is a web content syndication format. (RSS stands for Really Simple Syndication.) An RSS feed is an XML file that tells the outside world when you have updated your blog so your readers don't have to keep coming back to your website to find out whether you made any changes. RSS feeds can be read online, through websites such as Bloglines (www.bloglines.com), or by using news reader software. There are many different news readers available for all operating systems.

Your RSS feed might well end up being the most frequently downloaded file on your website. Many robots, indexers, and software will come and grab it so they can keep their users up to date with when your blog has been updated. Assuming that you want your blog to be read (and who doesn't), this is a good thing. However, it also means that your database server could end up fairly stressed if a database query were required every time the RSS file is requested. For this reason, I will show you how to create a static file that is updated only when you make a change to your blog. Because, by definition, static files do not require a database connection, your site will be more easily able to handle lots of nosy RSS software.

Traditionally, the main RSS feed for a site is named index.xml. The first step is to create an empty index.xml file—just create a new document in your text editor and save it to your root directory as index.xml. Because your code will eventually be rewriting this document, it needs to have read-write privileges. On Windows machines that should already be the case, but on Mac OS X machines you need to change the file properties. To do so, locate your index.xml file in Finder and select File ➤ Get Info. Open the Details area of Ownership & Permissions and select Read & Write access for Owner, Group, and Others; then close the Info window (see Figure 7-24).

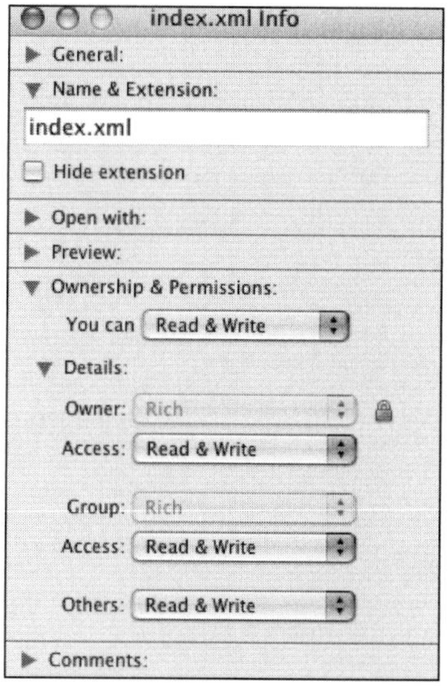

Figure 7-24. Changing file permissions of index.xml on Mac OS X

7

Here is the function that will write your RSS file:

```php
function makerssfeed() {
  // set file to write
  $filename =  $_SERVER["DOCUMENT_ROOT"] . "/index.xml";

  // open file
  $fh = @fopen($filename, "w");

  if($fh) {
    $rssfile = "<rss version=\"2.0\">
<channel>
<title>Samuel's Blog</title>
<link>http://your-domain-name.com</link>
<description>A blog by Samuel Pepys</description>
<language>en-gb</language>";

    // pull blogs from database
    $sql = "SELECT post_id, title, summary, ➥
DATE_FORMAT(postdate, '%a, %d %b %Y %T GMT') as pubdate ➥
FROM posts ORDER BY postdate DESC LIMIT 10";
    $result = mysql_query($sql);

    if ($mypost = mysql_fetch_array($result)) {
      do {
        $post_id = $mypost["post_id"];
        $pubdate = $mypost["pubdate"];
        $summary = format($mypost["summary"]);
        $title = $mypost["title"];
        $title = strip_tags($title);
        $title = htmlentities($title);

        $rssfile .= "    <item>\n";
        $rssfile .= "      <pubDate>$pubdate</pubDate>\n";
        $rssfile .= "      <title>$title</title>\n";
        $rssfile .= "      <link>http://your-domain-name.com/ ➥
post.php?post_id=$post_id</link>\n";
        $rssfile .= "      <description><![CDATA[$summary]]> ➥
</description>\n";
        $rssfile .= "    </item>\n";
      } while ($mypost = mysql_fetch_array($result));
    }

    $rssfile .=" </channel>
</rss>";

    // write to file
    $fw = @fwrite($fh, $rssfile);
```

```
        if (!$fw) {
          $message = "Could not write to the file $filename";
        } else {
          $message = "RSS file updated.";
        }

        // close file
        fclose($fh);
      } else {
        $message = "Could not open file $filename";
      }
      return $message;
    }
```

Your code will be calling the function from more than one place, so the ideal place to add it is in the functions.php include you made earlier. Make sure that the makerssfeed function is placed before the closing ?> delimiter.

I will now step through the function. It is really just a simplified version of your blog home-page: It grabs the ten most recent blog entries from the database and writes them to a file. The main differences will be the RSS file syntax (which is similar to but different from HTML) and some new functions for file handling, which is what we kick off with:

```
    function makerssfeed() {
      // set file to write
      $filename =  $_SERVER["DOCUMENT_ROOT"] . "/index.xml";

      // open file
      $fh = @fopen($filename, "w");

      if($fh) {
```

Here, the full server path of the RSS file is written to the $filename variable. Next, the fopen function is used to open the file for writing (that's what the w means). As mentioned earlier in the chapter, the @ before the function call prevents any ugly errors being written to the screen. I'm writing the fopen function to the $fh variable. If the fopen function failed (perhaps the index.xml file doesn't exist or it is read-only), the value of $fh is false, and there's no point continuing with the function.

```
    $rssfile = "<rss version=\"2.0\">
    <channel>
      <title>Samuel's Blog</title>
      <link>http://your-domain-name.com</link>
      <description>A blog by Samuel Pepys</description>
      <language>en-gb</language>";
```

The script has verified that your RSS file has been opened for writing, so it now starts to piece together the contents of the file. The script will compile the entire file in a variable called $rssfile and then write it to index.xml. Here the script has begun with the opening elements required by RSS (make sure that you change these details to match your

7

331

blog). More information on the RSS 2.0 syntax can be found at feedvalidator. org/docs/rss2.html.

```
// pull blogs from database
    $sql = "SELECT post_id, title, summary, ➥
DATE_FORMAT(postdate, '%a, %d %b %Y %T GMT') as pubdate ➥
FROM posts ORDER BY postdate DESC LIMIT 10";
    $result = mysql_query($sql);
```

The script now performs the familiar SELECT query in which it grabs the latest ten blog post titles and summaries. The postdate is formatted in a special way for RSS feeds and includes the time zone (in this case, GMT), which you may have to change according to where your live website is hosted.

```
if ($mypost = mysql_fetch_array($result)) {
    do {
        $post_id = $mypost["post_id"];
        $pubdate = $mypost["pubdate"];
        $summary = format($mypost["summary"]);
        $title = $mypost["title"];
        $title = strip_tags($title);
        $title = htmlentities($title);

        $rssfile .= "     <item>\n";
        $rssfile .= "       <pubDate>$pubdate</pubDate>\n";
        $rssfile .= "       <title>$title</title>\n";
        $rssfile .= "       <link>http://your-domain-name.com/ ➥
post.php?post_id=$post_id</link>\n";
        $rssfile .= "       <description><![CDATA[$summary]]> ➥
</description>\n";
        $rssfile .= "     </item>\n";
    } while ($mypost = mysql_fetch_array($result));
}
```

This code should again look familiar as the script loops through the posts and writes them to the $rssfile variable. Because you are writing RSS instead of HTML, the mark-up will look different, but it is still structured in a similar manner.

```
$rssfile .="  </channel>
</rss>";
```

Here, the final closing tags are added to the RSS feed. It is now ready for writing to your index.xml file.

```
// write to file
    $fw = @fwrite($fh, $rssfile);
    if (!$fw) {
      $message = "Could not write to the file $filename";
    } else {
```

```
        $message = "RSS file updated.";
    }

    // close file
    fclose($fh);
```

The script uses the fwrite function to write the contents of $rssfile to the $fh file handler created at the beginning of the script. As with fopen, fwrite returns false if the writing process fails. Finally, the fclose function is used to release the index.xml file, and your RSS feed has been updated.

But all you have at the moment is a function that can update your RSS feed. That function is not actually called from anywhere. Your RSS feed will need updating on three occasions: when you add a new blog post, when you update a post, and when you delete a post. The first two instances happen in the addpost.php file. So open that file. Just after the opening <?php delimiter, add this code to bring in the functions.php:

```
    include($_SERVER["DOCUMENT_ROOT"] . "/functions.php");
```

Now find the line that says the following:

```
    $message = "Successfully inserted post '$title'.";
```

Following that line, add this call to the makerssfeed function:

```
    $message .= "<br />" . makerssfeed();
```

Now find this line:

```
    $message = "Successfully update post '$title'.";
```

After that line, add the same call to makerssfeed. The delete blog function is on the index.php page in your CMS, so add the functions.php include to that file in the same way and add the same call to makerssfeed after this line:

```
    $message = "Post $delete deleted.";
```

Now try making a change to one of your blog posts using your CMS, which will force the RSS file to be created. Once you have received the message RSS file updated in your CMS, open up index.xml in your text editor and you should see something like this:

```
    <rss version="2.0">
    <channel>
      <title>Samuel's Blog</title>
      <link>http://your-domain-name.com</link>
      <description>A blog by Samuel Pepys</description>
      <language>en-gb</language>     <item>
          <pubDate>Sun, 03 Apr 2005 15:30:00 GMT</pubDate>
          <title>Knight of the Burning Pestle</title>
          <link>http://your-domain-name.com/post.php?post_id=2</link>
          <description><![CDATA[<p>News of the fleet and an ➥
  afternoon with Mrs. Turner to see a dreadful play.</p>]]> ➥
```

7

```
        </description>
          </item>
          <item>
            <pubDate>Mon, 28 Mar 2005 22:15:00 GMT</pubDate>
            <title>Paying my debts</title>
            <link>http://your-domain-name.com/post.php?post_id=4</link>
            <description><![CDATA[<p>Paying my debts and thence to ➡
    Covent Garden and an Italian puppet play.</p>]]> ➡
        </description>
          </item>
          <item>
            <pubDate>Sat, 01 May 2004 23:10:00 GMT</pubDate>
            <title>Bad arm</title>
            <link>http://your-domain-name.com/post.php?post_id=3</link>
            <description><![CDATA[<p>My arme not being well, ➡
    I staid within all the morning.</p>]]></description>
          </item>
        </channel>
      </rss>
```

Finally, you need to tell the world that you have an RSS feed. Many indexers will automatically look for an index.xml file, but you should also add this line just after the <title> in
your blog homepage to make sure:

```
<link rel="alternate" type="application/rss+xml" ➡
title="RSS 2.0 feed" ➡
 href="http://your-domain-name.com/index.xml" />
```

Once your RSS feed is up and running on your live site, I recommend submitting it to
pingomatic.com, which will automatically notify all the web-based RSS news readers that
your RSS feed exists.

Making it live

And so your blog engine is complete. You now have an administration site to add and edit
blog posts and a blog site with a homepage listing your latest entries, a page for each post
allowing comments, an archive of all past entries, search functionality, and an RSS feed. All
that remains is to move the whole lot onto a live web server.

Migrating your database

I assume that your Internet Service Provider has provided you with FTP access, PHP, and
MySQL. If so, it probably provided you with phpMyAdmin as well. If phpMyAdmin is not
installed, you can use FTP software to copy your phpMyAdmin files to your live server. In
this case, you will probably have to edit the username and password in the
config.inc.php file, as explained in Chapter 2.

Now you're ready to copy your database to your live server. Open up your local installation of phpMyAdmin in your browser and select the blog database. Click the Export tab. Now click the Select All link in the Export box so that the posts and comments tables are both selected. Finally select the Save as file option and click Go (see Figure 7-25). A file called blog.sql should be saved to your default download folder (usually your desktop).

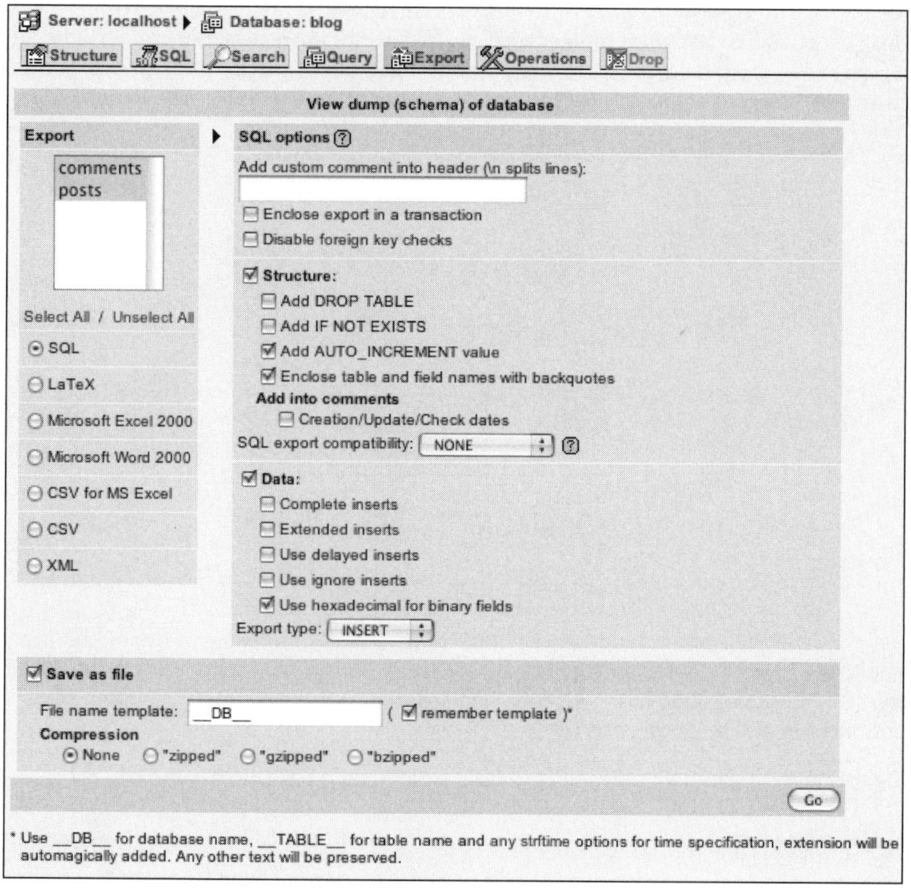

Figure 7-25. Exporting your database in phpMyAdmin

Now you have a complete copy of your database: table structure, indexes, and data. To import this onto your live server, open up the remote installation of phpMyAdmin and create a database called blog. Now click the SQL tab and browse to select your blog.sql file in the Location of the textfile section. Click Go, and your database will be uploaded. Easy as that!

Migrating your files

Next it's time to copy your files across. Edit db_connect.php so it has the correct username and password for your live database. Now open up your FTP software, connect to your web server, and copy the rest of your files and folders into the public_html folder. Check that your index.xml RSS file is read-writeable, as explained earlier.

Finally, you need to password-protect your cms folder. This process will vary from ISP to ISP, but you will usually be provided with an Apache web control panel, which enables you to password-protect directories as well as a whole host of other operations (see Figure 7-26).

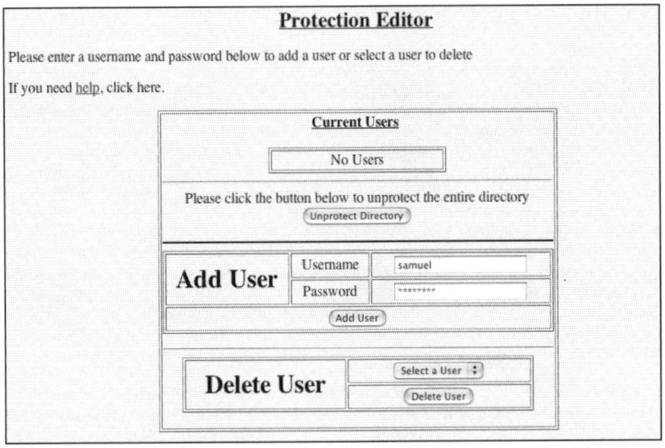

Figure 7-26. Adding password protection using the Apache console

And that's it: you exported and uploaded your entire MySQL blog database, transferred all your files to your public-facing website, and password-protected your CMS. Your blog is now live and awaiting posts and readers.

The future

The great thing about having your own blog engine is that you can keep improving it as you discover more techniques and cool stuff to add. I'll now discuss a few additions you could make to your blog by using the knowledge you have already gained.

Flickr

Flickr (www.flickr.com) is a fantastic photo-sharing site in which you can upload and share photographs, and—what's more—basic registration is free. Flickr provides a number of ways to display your photos on sites other than Flickr, and what better place to show them than your blog? The quickest and easiest way is to use the Flickr badge JavaScript or Flash code. Once you are signed up, you can go to www.flickr.com/badge.gne, follow the instructions, and cut and paste the code into your blog—the ideal place is the sidebar of your homepage.

Post and comment previews

You can provide a preview of a post in your Administration site. To do this, add a Preview button next to Add post or Update post. Use logic, such as case switching, so your script can detect which button has been pressed and then know whether to update the database or display a preview of the form submission on the page.

Adding previews for comments is another good idea because it gives your readers a chance to ensure that their comment will look like they expect. If you force readers to preview their post first by showing the Post button only in preview mode, this can help fend off comment spam (in itself, having your own blog engine goes a long way toward preventing comment spam).

Advanced formatting of posts

As it stands, your posts are only automatically formatted with paragraph and line break tags; any other formatting you require needs to be added as HTML within the post. Luckily, there are some free alternatives available to help speed up your post writing and format your blog more beautifully.

Textile is used within TextPattern (see Chapter 5) and is also available as a separate function from `www.textism.com/tools/textile/license.html`. You can use it to replace the format function in the `functions.php` include file. Textile automatically adds paragraphs and line breaks, automatically links URLs, and has its own simple language for formatting—for example, *this* would place <strong> tags around the word *this*.

Markdown, which is similar to Textile, is available as a PHP function from `www.michelf.com/projects/php-markdown/`. Markdown has some differences from Textile because it converts e-mail–style language into HTML. For more information on Markdown, see `daringfireball.net/projects/markdown/`.

Categorizing your posts

A slightly more advanced addition is to add a categorization system for your blog posts, which would involve creating a categories table with the names of your categories and a category_id for each. Then, in the same way in which you included a post_id field in the comments table so that you knew which post each comment referred to, so you could add a category_id field to the posts table so you know which category each post is in. You would probably also want to add a Categories section to your CMS to help add and edit categories, as well as a post archive page for each category.

Happy blogging

You should now have a fully functioning content management system and blogging engine, complete with comments, search engine, and a whole bunch of ideas for new features. But what your blog really needs is some content, so pick a subject, get writing, and enjoy yourself!

INDEX

friendsofed.com/forums

Join the friends of ED forums to find out more about our books, discover useful technology tips and tricks, or get a helping hand on a challenging project. *Designer to Designer™* is what it's all about—our community sharing ideas and inspiring each other. In the friends of ED forums, you'll find a wide range of topics to discuss, so look around, find a forum, and dive right in!

■ **Books and Information**

Chat about friends of ED books, gossip about the community, or even tell us some bad jokes!

■ **Flash**

Discuss design issues, ActionScript, dynamic content, and video and sound.

■ **Web Design**

From front-end frustrations to back-end blight, share your problems and your knowledge here.

■ **Site Check**

Show off your work or get new ideas.

■ **Digital Imagery**

Create eye candy with Photoshop, Fireworks, Illustrator, and FreeHand.

■ **ArchivED**

Browse through an archive of old questions and answers.

HOW TO PARTICIPATE

Go to the friends of ED forums at **www.friendsofed.com/forums**.

XML for Flash
1-59059-543-2 $39.99 [US]

Actionscript Animation
1-59059-518-1 $49.99 [US]

Flash 8
1-59059-542-4 $36.99 [US]

ASP.NET 2.0 for Flash
1-59059-517-3 $39.99 [US]

DOM Scripting
1-59059-533-5 $34.99 [U]

EXPERIENCE THE DESIGNER TO DESIGNER™ DIFFERENCE

Fireworks MX 2004 ZERO TO HERO
1-59059-306-5 $34.99 [US]

Paint Shop Pro 8 ZERO TO HERO
1-59059-238-7 $24.99 [US]

Windows Movie Maker 2 ZERO TO HERO
1-59059-149-6 $24.99 [U]

PHOTOSHOP MOST WANTED
1-59059-262-X $49.99 [US]

FLASH MX MOST WANTED EFFECTS & MOVIES
1-59059-224-7 $39.99 [US]

FLASH 3D CHEATS MOST WANTED
1-59059-221-2 $39.99 [US]

FLASH MX 2004 GAMES MOST WANTED
1-59059-236-0 $39.99 [US]

ILLUSTRATOR CS MOST WANTED TECHNIQUES AND EFFECTS
1-59059-372-3 $39.99 [U]

Extending Flash MX 2004
1-59059-304-9 $49.99 [US]

Apache Essentials Install, Configure, Maintain
1-59059-355-3 $39.99 [US]

Dreamweaver MX 2004 Design Projects
1-59059-409-6 $39.99 [US]

New Masters of Flash Volume 3
1-59059-314-6 $59.99 [US]

New Masters of Photoshop
1-59059-315-4 $59.99 [U]

Cascading Style Sheets SEPARATING CONTENT FROM PRESENTATION
Second Edition
1-59059-231-X $39.99 [US]

Constructing Usable Shopping Carts
1-59059-408-8 $34.99 [US]

EXTREME PHOTOSHOP CS
1-59059-428-2 $39.99 [US]

WEB STANDARDS SOLUTIONS
1-59059-381-2 $29.99 [US]

PODCAST SOLUTIONS The Complete Guide to Podcasting
1-59059-554-8 $xx.99 [U]